OXFORD CONSTITUTIONAL THEORY

Series Editors:
Martin Loughlin, John P. McCormick, and Neil Walker

Constituting Economic and Social Rights

OXFORD CONSTITUTIONAL THEORY

Series Editors:

Martin Loughlin, John P. McCormick, and Neil Walker

One consequence of the increase in interest in constitutions and constitutional law in recent years is a growing innovative literature in constitutional theory. The aim of *Oxford Constitutional Theory* is to provide a showcase for the best of these theoretical reflections and a forum for further innovation in the field.

The new series will seek to establish itself as the primary point of reference for scholarly work in the subject by commissioning different types of study. The majority of the works published in the series will be monographs that advance new understandings of the subject. Well-conceived edited collections that bring a variety of perspectives and disciplinary approaches to bear on specific themes in constitutional thought will also be included. Further, in recognition of the fact that there is a great deal of pioneering literature originally written in languages other than English and with regard to non-anglophone constitutional traditions, the series will also seek to publish English translations of leading monographs in constitutional theory.

ALSO AVAILABLE IN THE SERIES

The Twilight of Constitutionalism?
Edited by Petra Dobner and Martin Loughlin

Beyond Constitutionalism
The Pluralist Structure of Postnational Law
Nico Krisch

The Constitutional State
N. W. Barber

Sovereignty's Promise
The State as Fiduciary
Evan Fox-Decent

Constitutional Fragments
Societal Constitutionalism and Globalization
Gunther Teubner

Constitutional Referendums
The Theory and Practice of Republican Deliberation
Stephen Tierney

Constituting Economic and Social Rights

Katharine G. Young

OXFORD
UNIVERSITY PRESS

OXFORD
UNIVERSITY PRESS

Great Clarendon Street, Oxford, OX2 6DP,
United Kingdom

Oxford University Press is a department of the University of Oxford.
It furthers the University's objective of excellence in research, scholarship,
and education by publishing worldwide. Oxford is a registered trade mark of
Oxford University Press in the UK and in certain other countries

First published 2012
First published in paperback 2014

Impression: 1

Published in the United States of America by Oxford University Press
198 Madison Avenue, New York, NY 10016, United States of America

British Library Cataloguing in Publication Data
Data available

ISBN 978–0–19–964193–2 (Hbk.)
ISBN 978–0–19–872789–7 (Pbk.)

Printed and bound by
CPI Group (UK) Ltd, Croydon, CR0 4YY

Foreword

MAKING SOCIAL AND ECONOMIC RIGHTS REAL

Hunger, illness, and disadvantage accompany almost every human society. The contest between democracies and collectivist governments for a long time reflects contrasting bets. Some bet that ensuring freedoms of speech and association, voting and belief would best advance human welfare while others bet that collective organization of production of food, medicine and social provision would be better. With the rise of markets replacing communist and socialist governments and the assertion of social and economic rights in liberal democracies, stark ideological fights are displaced by new experiments to meet human needs while advancing free markets—even as economic and social inequality grows across Western democracies, emerging democracies, and newly market-oriented People's Republic of China. Yet just as many doubt whether markets can bloom without robust intellectual freedom, others question whether economic and social rights in market economies are ever more than aspirations on a page.

In this shifting landscape, Katharine Young's *Constituting Economic and Social Rights* enters with a rigorous and thorough analysis of the ethical and practical bases for addressing hunger, homelessness, and illness through constitutional design and political struggle. It is an important effort, integrating theoretical debates, court decisions, and reports of social movements, and embedding a central focus on South Africa's still new constitutional practice within comparisons with efforts in other constitutional systems. The book also provides a thoughtful treatment of the potential and actual influences of international human rights law on national legal strategies, debates, and decisions. With these elements, this book sets the standard for any analysis of social and economic rights, for henceforth proceeding without theory, or without practice, or without comparative or international law resources must be seen as too partial to permit either understanding or assessment of efforts to name rights in addressing basic human needs.

As Young explores, "rights" here are claims that mobilize some and silence others. Sometimes those assisted include corporations and industries which develop their own stakes in struggles over social and economic rights. The traditional view of rights organizing relations between individuals and the state must give way to experiments and pragmatic governance, across public and private sectors, as efforts to redirect food, open access to life-saving medications and housing and other social provisions proceed. Even those who drafted new constitutions must be open to reinterpretation of their own words as they work to put into operation the constitutions of their dreams. Guideposts of minimum standards, openness to local and partial steps, partnership between judges and squatters emerge as people utter the words of constitutions in courts and courts then take up these words to try to forge real practices that judges alone cannot command.

After a court announces a beautiful social or economic right, who can then demand accountability for its actual creation? If markets are to remain fundamental, how does the redistribution implied by social and economic rights take place? If social movements are stakeholders and key players in both motivating constitutional change and testing its legitimacy, how can they marshal cooperation and alliance with market actors? As Young's research and analysis demonstrate, social and economic rights do not exist pre-formed but require a process of engagement and contest. Discussions captured in and accelerated by this rich book can themselves play a real and valuable role in constituting social and economic rights in this new century. Scholars, activists, and students can make a new bet: here's where the action will be as nations struggle with disparate access to protein, water, schooling, speech, courts, power, and hope. Through theories, cases, experiments and struggles, people may make social and economic rights real.

Martha Minow
Dean and Jeremiah Smith Jr. Professor
Harvard Law School

Acknowledgements

I am indebted to my generous teachers, Frank Michelman and Lucie White. I also wish to record my thanks to the spirit of intellectual collaboration shown by my other teachers, colleagues and friends, including Philip Alston, Bill Alford, Raymond Atuguba, Mahama Ayariga, John Braithwaite, Gráinne de Búrca, William Forbath, Hilary Charlesworth, Bina D'Costa, David Kennedy, Duncan Kennedy, Michael Kirby, Sandra Liebenberg, Julieta Lemaitre, Martha Minow, Jeremy Perelman, Kim Rubenstein, Kerry Rittich, Theunis Roux, Amartya Sen, Joanne Scott, Frederick Schauer, William Simon, Henry Steiner, Renuka Thilagaratnam, Louise Trubek, Mark Tushnet and Roberto Unger. I thank the many justices and advocates from South Africa who answered my questions with patience and candor, including former President and Chief Justice Arthur Chaskalson, former Justices Laurie Ackerman, Richard Goldstone, Kate O'Regan, and Albie Sachs, and Justice Zak Yacoob. To Margaret Young and Stanislav Roudavski, I am grateful for encouragements and provocations. Finally, I thank Vlad Perju for his indefatigable partnership.

This project has been supported financially by Harvard University's Project on Justice, Welfare and Economics, the Edmond J. Safra Foundation Center for Ethics, the Weatherhead Center for International Affairs, the Frank Knox Memorial Fellowship, the Harvard Law School Byse Fellowship, the Regulatory Institutions Network of the Australian National University, and the Australian National University College of Law.

Material in the book previously appeared, in a different form, in the following publications and is reprinted with permission of the publishers:

Katharine Young, "The Minimum Core of Economic and Social Rights: A Concept in Search of Content", Reprinted by permission of the Yale Journal of International Law, Volume 33 (2008), pp. 113–175.

Katharine Young, "A Typology of Economic and Social Rights Adjudication: Exploring the Catalytic Function of Judicial Review", International Journal of Constitutional Law, Volume 8 (2010), no. 3, 385–430, by permission of Oxford University Press and New York University School of Law.

Contents

Table of Cases

I. PRIMARY JURISDICTION—SOUTH AFRICA

2. COMPARATIVE JURISDICTIONS

Canada

Germany

United Kingdom

3. INTERNATIONAL CASES

Table of Legislation

1. PRIMARY JURISDICTION—SOUTH AFRICA

2. COMPARATIVE JURISDICTIONS

Australia

Canada

Colombia

France

Germany

Ghana

Hungary

India

Ireland

Namibia

New Zealand

United Kingdom

United States

3. TREATIES AND OTHER INTERNATIONAL INSTRUMENTS

List of Abbreviations

ACHR	American Convention on Human Rights
AfCHR	African [Banjul] Charter on Human and Peoples' Rights
ANC	African National Congress
ARV	antiretroviral
CALS	Centre for Applied Legal Studies (South Africa)
CCC	Constitutional Court of Colombia
CC	Constitutional Court of South Africa
CEDAW	Convention on the Elimination of All Forms of Discrimination Against Women
CRC	Convention on the Rights of the Child
ECHR	European Convention on Human Rights
ECJ	European Court of Justice, or Court of Justice of the European Union
ECOSOC	Economic and Social Council (United Nations)
ECtHR	European Court of Human Rights
EU	European Union
FCC	Federal Constitutional Court of Germany
GDP	Gross Domestic Product
GEAR	Growth, Employment, and Redistribution Policy (South Africa)
HDI	Human Development Index
HRA	Human Rights Act 1998 (UK)
HRC	United Nations Human Rights Committee
ICCPR	International Covenant on Civil and Political Rights
ICESCR	International Covenant on Economic, Social and Cultural Rights
ICJ	International Court of Justice
ICRC	International Committee of the Red Cross
ILO	International Labour Organization
IMF	International Monetary Fund
JCHR	Joint Committee on Human Rights
LRC (Ghana)	Legal Resources Centre (Ghana)
LRC (South Africa)	Legal Resources Centre (South Africa)
NAACP	National Association for the Advancement of Colored People
NGO	nongovernmental organization
OAU	Organization for African Unity

OMC	open method of coordination (EU)
OP	Optional Protocol
PQLI	Physical Quality of Life Index
SCI	Supreme Court of India
TAC	Treatment Action Campaign (South Africa)
TRIPS	Agreement on Trade-Related Aspects of Intellectual Property Rights
UDHR	Universal Declaration of Human Rights
UNCHR	United Nations Commission on Human Rights
UNGA	United Nations General Assembly
UNHCHR	United Nations High Commissioner on Human Rights
UNHRC	United Nations Human Rights Council
UNICEF	United Nations Children's Fund
US	United States
USSC	Supreme Court of the United States
WHO	World Health Organization
WTO	World Trade Organization

1

Introduction: The Path to Transformation

Food, water, health, housing, and education are fundamental to human freedom and dignity. How they are secured within our legal systems affects legal decision-making, public policy-making, and the individual's opportunities for involvement in each. Over the last century, these fundamental material interests have been increasingly cast as human or constitutional rights. The classical liberal paradigm of statist protection of the so-called "negative" rights, and market promotion of welfare, has now been overtaken by the legal protection of economic and social rights and the development of various institutional methods for their interpretation, enforcement, and measurement. Liberal markets and liberal democracies now coexist with economic and social rights.

This new formulation of economic and social rights has evolved out of disparate origins, having shaped—and been shaped by—the tenets of first-world social democracy, second-world Eastern socialism and third world developmentalism. Today, these rights are ratified in human rights treaties, entrenched in new or amended constitutions, enumerated in statute, and/or enunciated in public declarations. These rights include the rights to access food, water, housing, preventive or curative health care, social security, education, labor protections, basic services in sanitation or electricity, and to new forms of property. Sourced heavily in the constitutional changes that took place after the Second World War, economic and social rights enjoy constitutional status in countries in Africa, Asia, Europe, and Latin America, in sub-national units in North America and elsewhere, and in regional and international human rights instruments. They are recognized as explicit textual guarantees, or as implications of other constitutional rights, and are treated as enforceable entitlements or as aspirational guarantees. Against the varied background of common law and civil law traditions, federal and unitary legal systems, and developed and developing economies, economic and social rights accommodate the variety of legal forms that such institutional differences demand.

The fields of comparative law and international law illuminate this variety and difference. International law has expanded beyond the (ever-increasing) developments within the United Nations system to incorporate transnational, local, and regional developments. Comparative constitutional law has created new opportunities for understanding how legal ideas travel and transplant, as well as the distinctive legal concepts internal to different legal systems. Each academic field reflects the growing practical interaction between judges, government officials, monitoring experts, nongovernmental organizations, and social movements.

From these interactions emerge new understandings of the legal forms that fundamental rights take. How these forms endure over the coming decade will impact on the way in which legal systems respond to the series of harms that flow from the fact of economic insecurity in a market-based liberal order: harms that are reflected in the skewing of educational possibilities, in the disparities of health, in the misallocation of goods and services, and in the imbalance of political power. Economic and social rights promise to alleviate the wrongs that a market-oriented world perpetrates on those otherwise unequipped to enjoy its gains. If that promise is delivered, economic and social rights may become part of the law's answer to the indignities and pain caused, at least in part, by law itself.

A. A PROCESS-DRIVEN, VALUE-BASED, AND INTERDEPENDENT CONCEPTION

Defining rights is notoriously difficult. Rights are typically understood as trumps, side constraints, or other anti-utilitarian devices. In the conception undergirding this book, rights are a focal point of interpretive disagreement and agreement, of agitation and contestation, and of monitoring and enforcement, of the fundamental material interests that are reasonably argued to be universal and compelling. Hence, I include both normative consideration of why rights should be treated as important, with a practical understanding of the way in which rights emerge from particular social and cultural practices. By contrast with approaches that divide normative inquiry with empirical evidence, I combine the two in the questions I ask of legal institutions. Rather than seek to ascertain a fixed content of rights for all times and places, I therefore focus on the processes that constitute substantive rights, and how these processes change public law.

This conception of legal rights combines a philosophical inquiry with the comparative study of how rights work in legal systems. It draws attention to the close interrelationship of rights in both senses. First, rights are "pronouncements in social ethics, sustainable by open public reasoning."[1]

[1] *See*, e.g., Amartya Sen, "Elements of a Theory of Human Rights," 32 *Philosophy & Public Affairs* 315 (2004).

Secondly, rights are pronouncements in law, in Bills of Rights, in human rights instruments, or in other constitutional, legislative, or common law forms. This understanding of rights, as products of both morality and of law, relies on the often observed constitutive relationship of morality into law, on the one hand, and the sometime observed constitutive relationship of law into morality, on the other.[2]

From one perspective, the theorization of economic and social rights is grounded in interests that are reasonably argued to be universal, socially significant, and open to social influence.[3] Because all people require access to food and water and housing, medical care when seriously ill, and education when young, the concept of rights allows one to understand such interests in their various cultural instantiations. Moral and political philosophy offers a way to reconstruct the development of economic and social rights—as social-ethical pronouncements—in the institutionalized field of actual constitutional practice. This reconstruction can then help to critically assess ongoing legal-political processes.

But philosophical analysis needs institutional analysis. This book appraises the varied institutional conceptions of constitutional rights, using the tools of comparative law. This variety incorporates the conceptions of constitutional rights as enforceable by a counter-majoritarian institution, such as a court, or alternatively as optimization principles for legislative and administrative decision-making, or as a reference point for interbranch dialogue.[4] What is common to these conceptions is that rights belong to a form of legal entitlement that is, for special reasons, relatively immune to the vagaries of short-term politics or cost-benefit decision-making. This immunity is relative because of background constitutional arrangements. For example, the ability of rights to trump majoritarian decision-making does not automatically equate with the ability of courts to review—and override—legislation.[5] Comparative constitutional law, especially sourced outside of the United States, demonstrates that rights-based immunity from majoritarian or utilitarian decision-making can be institutionally relative.

[2] Ibid., discussing the parent-child relationship of rights first dismissed by Jeremy Bentham, *Anarchical Fallacies; Being an Examination of the Declaration of Rights Issued during the French Revolution* (1792); republished in *The Works of Jeremy Bentham*, vol. II, (J. Bowring, ed., 1843) 501.

[3] Sen, *supra* note 1; *see also* Thomas W. Pogge, *World Poverty and Human Rights: Cosmopolitan Responsibilities and Reforms* (2002); Henry Shue, *Basic Rights: Subsistence, Affluence and U.S. Foreign Policy* (2nd edn., 1996).

[4] Prominent versions of each of these models can be found in Ronald Dworkin, *Taking Rights Seriously* (1977); Robert Alexy, *A Theory of Constitutional Rights* (trans. Julian Rivers, 2002); and Jeremy Waldron, *Law and Disagreement* (1999).

[5] *See*, e.g., Mark Tushnet, *Weak Courts, Strong Rights: Judicial Review and Social Welfare Rights in Comparative Constitutional Law* (2008).

This two-fold conception of rights allows for the ongoing changeability and development of norms. Such a conception, while informed by the fallibility of knowledge and the inevitability of interpretive disagreement, is also democratically defensible.[6] In a pluralist democracy, the meaning given to such rights cannot depend upon the quest for a single and determinate truth, but rather upon the collaborative efforts of an epistemic community who reach only provisional agreement. This provisionality is made clear by the framework of constituting rights, described below. It also supports the interdependence of all sets of fundamental rights.

Reported distinctions between civil, political, and economic, cultural and social rights, have created a discourse around human rights that treats the legalization of economic and social rights as uniquely challenging for our current constitutional democratic systems. In this view, economic and social rights are new to contemporary constitutionalist systems, and should not be shoehorned into current legal constructions. A countering view would celebrate what is old and unexceptional about economic and social rights. My analysis is sympathetic to the second view, and, as such, my process-driven, value-based conception of rights is relevant to all categories.

Hence, this book refutes the overarching attempt to fix categories of rights as settled and distinct. The reported differences are disturbed as soon as values are taken into account. For example, the protection of some rights is justified on the basis of preserving democracy. This argument is usually reserved for civil and political rights, such as the freedom of speech or the right to vote. However, the right to education may be equally important to an informed vote or to the broader fulfillment of the responsibilities of democracy; no less the right to the baseline material security provided by housing to a vote free from patronage, and invested in community. Such rights may therefore be grouped as civil or political rights, as opposed to current terminology.

Equally, what are currently termed civil and political rights, such as the right to speech, and to vote, and to privacy, may themselves be protective of fundamental material interests. Famines, as the argument famously goes, do not occur in democracies.[7] Conversely, atrocities like genocide may occur when traditional economic indicators of development are fulfilled.[8] A due focus on human, rather than economic, development encompasses the full suite of civil, political, economic, social, and cultural rights-based

[6] *See*, e.g., John Dewey, *Liberalism and Social Action* (2000) (1935); Martha Minow, *Making All the Difference* (1990).

[7] Amartya Sen, *Development as Freedom* (1999) 152–3.

[8] Peter Uvin, *Aiding Violence: The Development Enterprise in Rwanda* (1998).

indicators.[9] The "last resort" rights of democratic participation, as "preservative of all rights,"[10] rather than foundational to them, may be necessary to sustain interests in access to food, water, health care, housing, and education.

While economic and social rights were first treated as "subdivisions or extensions of civil and political rights," they were then accepted, in the century preceding the Universal Declaration of Human Rights, as "different in kind," and requiring "differences in implementation."[11] Neither approach should hold today. The separation of rights into categories endures due to the bifurcation of human rights into two foundational international human rights covenants,[12] a bifurcation itself premised on analytical distinctions that have been long criticized. Three characteristics of economic and social rights, in particular, have produced a distinction between them (and with them, cultural rights) and the more privileged category of civil and political rights. First, economic and social rights have been viewed as inappropriate for judicial enforcement. Secondly, they have been viewed as requiring positive action for their enjoyment, as well as significant expenditure. And thirdly, they have been treated as "secondary," in generational terms, to the civil and political rights historically protected in the *Magna Carta* and other foundational (and culturally Western) documents.

In the following chapters I reject the distinctions based on enforceability and of positive action, finding them applicable to both sets of rights, and reject the later chronology of economic and social rights, as it represents a parochial view of the development of our moral concepts. This argument endorses the "indivisibility and interdependence and interrelatedness" of the sets of rights.[13] Indeed, in conceding the central moral and existential connection between the two categories of rights, it becomes inaccurate to exclude a discussion of the civil and political protections that impact so

[9] Sen, *Development as Freedom*, *supra* note 7; *see also* Philip Alston, "Ships Passing in the Night: The Current State of the Human Rights and Development Debate seen through the Lens of the Millennium Development Goals," 27 Hum. Rts. Q. 755 (2005).

[10] *See* Frank Michelman, "Welfare Rights in a Constitutional Democracy," 3 Wash. U. L.Q. 659 (1979) 677.

[11] Jacques Maritain, *The Grounds for an International Declaration of Human Rights* (1947) reproduced in Micheline R. Ishay, *The Human Rights Reader: Major Political Writings, Essays, Speeches, and Documents from the Bible to the Present* (2nd edn., 2007) 5.

[12] Hence, the International Covenant on Civil and Political Rights contains no economic and social rights, which were grouped entirely in the International Covenant on Economic, Social and Cultural Rights. *See* Philip Alston and Gerard Quinn, "The Nature and Scope of States Parties' Obligations under the International Covenant on Economic, Social and Cultural Rights," 9 Hum. Rts. Q. 156 (1987).

[13] Vienna Declaration and Programme of Action, Adopted by the World Conference on Human Rights (25 June 1993), UN Doc. A/CONF.157/23 (12 July 1993). This position was restated by the United Nations General Assembly in its 2006 Resolution creating the Human Rights Council: G.A. Res. 60/251, UN GAOR, 60th Sess., UN Doc. A/RES/60/251 (2006).

significantly on fundamental material interests. Fundamental rights are interdependent, and all are critical to constitutional democracy.

B. "CONSTITUTING" RIGHTS: A THREE-PART FRAMEWORK

It is against the background of the evolving operation of economic and social rights that this book makes its central claim: that a constitutional legal framework protective of rights to food, water, health care, housing, and education is one which establishes processes of value-based, deliberative problem-solving, rather than one which sets out the minimum bundles of commodities or entitlements. It also argues that current constitutional democratic institutions—courts, the legislature, the executive, and agencies—are able to work with collectivities to provide contextualized, participatory, and localized solutions in order to "constitute" such rights.

This book also demonstrates that such deliberative processes must be carefully designed, because conditions of material inequality, severe poverty, and social conflict detract from the advantages that a "soft" process-value approach will bring. Before turning to this claim, the conceptual framework of "constituting" rights is laid out. Such a framework responds to the primary challenges facing the process of "constituting" such rights. These are the challenges of pluralism, of the lawmaking of collectivities, and of the lawmaking of counter-majoritarian courts.

To constitute rights, in the special meaning given to that term within this book, is to make them effective within a legal system. To constitute is not to constitutionalize, although the two processes are related, and assist each other. To constitutionalize commonly refers to the act of entrenching a commitment in constitutional text—the capitalized, written, Constitution: committing to text what no constitutional government can oust.[14] To constitutionalize is often to leave abstract, to maximize present-day consensus and minimize the disruption of future contingencies. The text is critical, and commands the focus of interpretation. To constitute, on the other hand, is to socially institute, so that the commitments are committed to social understanding, and are realized effectively in law. While this approach still concedes the importance of text, it offers a post-interpretive framework in which other processes are also important. Such a study requires attention to the different challenges and outcomes of interpretation, adjudication, and contestation, which are confronted in detail in each Part of this book.

[14] Of course, unwritten (or uncodified) constitutions, such as that which continues to exist in the United Kingdom, dislodge's the purity of this distinction. My own framework looks to a broader set of constituting practices than the statutes, judgments, treaties, constitutional conventions, and royal prerogatives that underlie the unwritten constitution.

(1) *Rights and pluralism*

Economic and social rights are interests held, and claims made, in conditions of pluralism. Modern societies are heterogeneous and legal institutions must contend with openly contested sources of meaning. In such societies, a plurality of competing idioms for articulating justice claims is inevitable. Even rights, themselves just one sub-set of many discursive and conceptual responses to maldistribution, misrecognition, and the claims of injustice, contain a plurality of meanings.

One response to such pluralism is to disavow rights as empty abstractions, and to reject claims of injustice as merely subjective interpretations or intuitive perceptions. A second response is to understand rights as the intersubjective articulations of injustice, to be assessed and interpreted against criteria of reasonableness and consensus. This approach invites, not paralysis (arguably an inevitable attitude of the first response), but engagement with law. Indeed, I argue that a framework for understanding what makes law binding within a community helps us to understand what makes economic and social rights meaningful at all.

The project of "constituting" rights, within social institutions, is one which channels alternative justice claims into a forum in which such claims can be heard by others, and can potentially be recognized by others. For economic and social rights to be "constituted" within social institutions, I suggest that they are grounded on the layered sands of what is right according to reason, what is right according to decision-making authority, and what is right according to experienced social fact. These conceptual foundations provide the support for economic and social rights, as a meaningful challenge to existing (formal or informal) maldistribution. Nonetheless, the three aspects of rights cannot be argued for simultaneously: reason, authority, and social fact may be considered mutually exclusive, or at least mutually disruptive, conceptual standpoints.[15] Instead, participants often shift from one to the other in articulating rights claims.[16]

First, what is right according to reason links the project of constituting economic and social rights with a philosophy of justice. Indeed, it provides such argument with a readily testable institutional form.[17] The guarantee of access to food, health care, housing, water, social security, and

[15] *See*, e.g., the approach of Jeremy Waldron, "Socioeconomic Rights and Theories of Justice," NYU School of Law, Public Law and Legal Theory Research Paper No. 10–79 (2010), arguing that the former may not be relevant to the latter.

[16] I adapt this approach from the treatment of constitutional "bindingness" in Frank I. Michelman, "Constitutional Authorship," in Larry Alexander (ed.), *Constitutionalism: Philosophical Foundations* (2001) 64.

[17] For a suggestion that liberal egalitarianism's institutional commitments "have not kept pace with its theoretical commitments," *see* Will Kymlicka, *Contemporary Political Philosophy* (2nd edn., 2001) 91.

education—whether demarcated as the nonidealized versions of "primary goods" or "private resources" or "fair shares"[18]—is fundamentally important to a range of values that are adduced to justify the ordering of society in terms of the ordering of justice, such as human dignity, equality, and freedom. And because economic and social rights are often instituted in qualified terms—as subject to "available resources" and as limited by "what is reasonable in an open and democratic society"[19]—questions of distributive justice are crucial. What counts as "reasonable" is sensitive to what counts as just.[20]

The first part of this book establishes a framework of reason and economic and social rights. It claims that processes of interpretation, and the adoption of philosophical standpoints of rationalism and consensualism, play the major role in providing meaning and determinacy to fundamental material interests. Rationalism incorporates standpoints that rely on the importance of human dignity, or of the satisfaction of basic material needs, and yet may point in different directions to the ultimate nature and scope of economic and social rights. Nonetheless, the provided answers may overlap with each other, as the epistemic communities of interpreters of economic and social rights do. These interpreters, whether national or international, state-based or non-state, contribute to the legal decision-making important for constituting rights. Part I also describes the institutional pressures of minimalist interpretations, or of invoking the limits of rights as against collective, budgetary, or other utilitarian considerations, and the critical role that the demands of minimalism or limitations, play on economic and social rights.

The existence of reasonable disagreement, and the need for its democratic expression, ensures that what is right according to reason is only a partial answer to the inevitable question of defining the constituted content of economic and social rights. For economic and social rights to be meaningfully operational within our legal systems, the philosophical

[18] The modern prompt for a version of justice alternate to utilitarianism is John Rawls, *A Theory of Justice* (1971) (presenting primary goods as "things which a rational [person] wants whatever else he [or she] wants", at 92), to which we might add, amongst others, the egalitarian quests of Ronald Dworkin, *Sovereign Virtue: The Theory and Practice of Equality* (2000) (presenting a scheme for the distribution of privately owned resources); Michael Walzer, *Spheres of Justice: A Defense of Pluralism and Equality* (1983) (placing emphasis on a communitarian understanding of "fair shares"); Amartya Sen, *The Idea of Justice* (2009) (highlighting the central importance of a person's "capability" to achieve reasonable life goals within a background of nonideal theory).

[19] E.g., South African Constitution ["S. Afr. Const."], 1996 §§ 26(2), 27(2), 36. *See also* International Covenant on Economic, Social and Cultural Rights, 16 December 1966, 993 U.N.T.S. 3, arts. 2(1), 4.

[20] *See*, e.g., Jeremy Waldron, "Socioeconomic Rights and Theories of Justice," *Supra* note 15.

questions of distributive justice must be supplemented by others. This takes us to the next two investigations: of legal authority and social fact.

What is right according to decision-making authority links the project of constituting economic and social rights to the second question of positive law. Traditionally, this has led to a double exclusion. First, lawmakers have been reluctant to institute rights for the poor—the coincidence of lawmaking power with economic power, and the self-interestedness of legislators in furthering that connection, was as obvious to Adam Smith as it was to Karl Marx.[21] The achievements of the modern welfare state have in part corrected this, achievements which were themselves instituted—via landmark statutes as well as constitutional provisions—due to the pressures of class coalitions, mobilizations, and, arguably, the functional requirements of capitalism itself.[22] The second exclusion relates to judges, not legislators: the exclusion of justiciability. For those who align "law" with judicial enforcement, economic and social rights have appeared as "off-the-wall" as the ability of the poor to have their claims against poverty directly actionable in, and remediable by, a court.[23] In positivist legal scholarship, the examination of economic and social rights has therefore been limited in reach. This is doubly the case for US constitutional scholarship, where the US Constitution (despite prominent theories to the contrary[24]) has largely been interpreted as omitting economic and social rights from its rights-protective scope.

Thirdly, what is right according to social fact links the project of constituting economic and social rights with actually existing social understanding. A study of how economic and social rights are constituted in social fact asks not what the law states, but what the people who are governed by the law actually believe to be accepted as law. A study of the empirical, social effect of rights therefore involves an examination of how distributive norms act within social institutions—of the family or the household, of the village or the city, of the

[21] Adam Smith, *The Wealth of Nations*, vol. II (1961) 236, noting "civil government, so far as it is instituted for the security of property, is in reality instituted for the defense of the rich against the poor, or of those who have some property against those who have none at all"; *cf.* Karl Marx, *Capital: A Critique of Political Economy (Volume 1)* (1976).

[22] Of course, this is where Smith and Marx part their temporary company. While the analysis of welfare state emergence is not the focus of this book, parallels between the strong claims of causality in political economy literature (for example, those put forward by Gøsta Esping-Anderson, *The Three Worlds of Welfare Capitalism* (1998)) and my own examination of institutional alignment of certain contributory processes in constituting rights, will become evident.

[23] William E. Forbath, "Constitutional Welfare Rights: A History, Critique and Reconstruction," 69 Fordham L. Rev. 1821 (2001) 1824 (suggesting the heterodoxy of welfare rights within US constitutional scholarship).

[24] *See*, e.g., Frank I. Michelman, "Foreword: On Protecting the Poor through the Fourteenth Amendment," 83 Harv. L. Rev. 7 (1969).

church, of the hospital, of the school, and of the marketplace. These norms act in parallel with formal law, with which they are sometimes in support, but sometimes in conflict.[25] The disjuncture between law and social fact may be greater in Third World developmentalist societies than in First World democracies. The greater strength of informal distributive norms over any formal legal recognition of economic and social rights in developmentalist systems is due not only to the commonly observed paucity of state resources, but to the fact that pre-colonial custom may attract more adherence than postcolonial "law." A fidelity to more than one understanding of normative obligation—often referred to as "legal pluralism"—is therefore greater in postcolonial states, and is now exacerbated by globalization.[26]

Clearly, this multiplicity of foundations—of reason, authority, and social fact—creates complexity and uncertainty for economic and social rights, as for all human rights; all the more so when one cannot choose one or the other foundation, but, I argue, must recognize the importance of all three. Moreover, all three have contained obstacles—or, at least, intellectual brakes—on constituting economic and social rights. In the domain of professional philosophy, some theorists identified recognition, rather than redistribution, as the more pertinent response to material deprivation.[27] Rights were understood to be unsuitable responses to economic and social concerns.[28] This critique joined with the long-standing philosophical rejection of "rights," first on the basis of their individuating and alienating qualities, second on the basis of their opposition to utility, and third for their parochial (namely Western) features.[29] In the domain of legal positivism, the court-sanctioned interpretations of influential constitutions—in particular, of the US Constitution—omitted economic and social rights as mandatory norms for legislative or (particularly) judicial decision-makers to follow.[30] And in empirical fact, liberal, and later, neoliberal economic theory—prescribing

[25] The new institutional economics seek to analyze the "rules of the game" through "informal" norms as well as laws: *see*, e.g., Douglass C. North, *Institutions, Institutional Change and Economic Performance* (1990); *see also* Robert C. Ellickson, *Order Without Law: How Neighbours Settle Disputes* (1991). For a recentering of attention to law's effects *see* Duncan Kennedy, "The Stakes of Law, or Hale and Foucault!" in *Sexy Dressing Etc.* (1993) 83 (foregrounding the work of Robert Hale).

[26] For a description of legal pluralism's origins in colonialism, and resurgence in present-day globalization, *see* Brian Z. Tamanaha, *A General Jurisprudence of Law and Society* (2001).

[27] Nancy Fraser and Axel Honneth, *Recognition or Redistribution? A Political-Philosophical Exchange* (2003).

[28] Maurice Cranston, "Are There Any Human Rights?," 112 *Daedalus* 12 (1983); Charles Fried, *Modern Liberty and the Limits of Government* (2006) (presenting the argument of classical liberalism).

[29] For a discussion of the long-standing critiques of natural rights, from Marx to Bentham to Burke, *see*, e.g., Sen, "Elements of a Theory of Human Rights," *supra* note 1.

[30] *See DeShaney v. Winnebago Cty. Dept. of Soc. Serv.*, 489 U.S. 189 (1989); *Maher v. Roe*, 432 U.S. 464 (1972); *Harris v. McRae*, 448 U.S. 297 (1980); *Lindsey v. Normet*, 405 U.S. 56 (1972); *Dandridge v. Williams*, 397 U.S. 471 (1970).

freedom, efficiency, and growth in order to maximize welfare, and welfare in order to order society—have long dominated the world's most influential and powerful policy-making institutions, and have marginalized the understanding that a baseline of fundamental material interests belong to all, and that the law has a role to play in securing and in enforcing that baseline.

Today, however, all three domains of inquiry have much to offer. For example, a philosophical approach that aligns a "consequentialist system" with "goal rights"—emphasizing the human capability to live a life one has reason to value—allows economic and social rights to be instituted with "versatility and reach," dovetailing with programs for economic development.[31] At the same time, the challenge of examining the legal operation of economic and social rights is met by extending the study of constitutional systems outwards to comparative practice,[32] where economic and social rights are sometimes explicitly entrenched, and often creatively enforced. Positivist legal examination is also assisted by the concept of "constitutive commitments," which reserves a place for economic and social rights in long-standing social beliefs, even in the United States.[33] Third, the dominance of neoliberal economic theory, reaching its peak in the 1990s, was chastened by a greater awareness of market failure and of alternative approaches to development understood by mainstream economists and policy makers. In 2005, the Washington-based institutions of the International Monetary Fund, the World Bank, and the US Treasury Department, formerly associated with the market liberalization policies of the "Washington consensus," began to call for "more humility in their approaches, implying more openness on the range of solutions possible, more empathy with the country's perspectives, and more inquisitiveness in assessing the costs and benefits of different possible solutions."[34] Nonetheless, the global financial crisis of 2008 has triggered opposing responses. On the one hand, early prescriptions were focused on measures to stimulate the

[31] Sen, *Development as Freedom*, *supra* note 7, 212. Sen's contribution adds to the important work of Rawls and Dworkin in answering the question of "equality of what" in distributive justice debates: *see* discussion *supra* note 18.

[32] *See* Constitutions cited at *infra* notes 50–54 (those of India, Ghana, Germany, Colombia, and Canada, as well as human rights statutes in the United Kingdom, Australia and New Zealand). *See*, e.g., the focus on Brazil, Colombia, India, and South Africa, in Roberto Gargarella, Pilar Domingo, and Theunis Roux (eds.), *Courts and Social Transformation in New Democracies: An Institutional Voice for the Poor?* (2006).

[33] Cass R. Sunstein, *The Second Bill of Rights: FDR's Unfinished Revolution and Why We Need It More Than Ever* (2004) 62 (noting rights which have "a special place in the sense that they are widely accepted and cannot be eliminated without a fundamental change in social understanding... A violation would amount to a kind of breach—a violation of a trust"). Sunstein includes certain economic and social rights within this category.

[34] World Bank, *Economic Growth in the 1990s: Learning from a Decade of Reform* (2005) 26; *see further* David M. Trubek and Alvaro Santos (eds.), *The New Law and Economic Development: A Critical Appraisal* (2006).

economy and manage demand by welfare and other public support, following the basic precepts of Keynesian economics. Yet a second response, which has called for austerity and public disinvestment in areas such as health care and education, and has been backed up by negative attitudes towards sovereign debt, hails a return to neoclassical liberal economics.[35] Social protest against austerity measures has in turn intensified the contestations around economic and social rights.

By connecting these approaches, this book also raises to prominence what serial, separate inspections of reason, legal authority and social fact may downplay. This is the role of the "agent" in constituting economic and social rights. For this reason, our attention turns to the participatory processes that slowly, intermittingly and unpredictably influence all three.

(2) *Rights and adjudication*

The phenomenon of the adjudication of economic and social rights is contemporaneous with—and hence similarly youthful to—their express recognition in law. Before the rights entrenchments of the postwar paradigm, the conception of courts as the final arbiters in urgent matters of political or social conflict had been largely restricted to the United States. In that jurisdiction, rights without adjudication and enforcement were no rights at all; a position wholly foreign to the aspirational documents of many other constitutional systems. Yet the developments of the past fifty years have led to an increasing trend towards the judicial enforcement of rights. Consequently, there has been a resulting increase in judicial power, relative to other governmental branches, in matters of public policy affected by rights. This increase has been much criticized, a criticism which has itself been an enduring strand in the reluctance to legalize economic and social rights.

The protections afforded by economic and social rights are now implemented through adjudication and judicial enforcement, in an increasing number of national and international jurisdictions throughout the world. Yet the central questions of legitimacy, and of effectiveness, remain. Part II of this book evaluates the well-studied forms and limits of adjudication against the particular qualities of economic and social rights. In these chapters, I take the traditional debate about judicial review—the hallmark of which is the "counter-majoritarian difficulty" of the judicial branch—and resituate it as a debate concerning the "rights protecting" difficulty of all

[35] *See* "Special Issue: Austerity: Making the Same Mistakes Again—Or Is *This Time* Different?" 31 Camb. J. Econ. 1 (2012); *see also* World Bank, *The World Bank Group's Response to the Global Crisis: Update on an Ongoing IEG Evaluation (Evaluation Brief 8)*, Independent Evaluation Group (2009).

three branches of the judiciary, executive and legislature.[36] In keeping with this approach, I ask how state institutions, including courts, work together (rather than how they achieve their goals in separation), and what uses they make of each other which impact upon economic and social rights. A first step is therefore to abandon the two poles of judicial review—of the judicial power to overturn statutes *or* the legislature's power to render any statute legal—and create a more variegated analysis of the forms that judicial review may take.

In seeking to resolve the role of courts in protecting economic and social rights—the perennial challenge of justiciability mentioned above—one can (somewhat counterintuitively) decenter the judicial branch. The ways in which courts engage in judicial review—the scrutiny they apply, and the remedies they propose—can incorporate a variety of judicial responses to human and constitutional rights. Thus, economic and social rights are meaningful even when they are judicially unenforceable. They can exert pressure as "directive principles of state policy," they can guide statutory interpretation (by judges or other officials), executive policy-making, or other legal actions and actors.[37] Other institutions, such as legislatures, agencies, and independent commissions, also become important. Decentering courts also opens the scene of action to private and/or informal actors, such as the market actors, nongovernmental organizations, and social movements that contest economic and social rights.

(3) *Rights and contestation*

Economic and social rights challenge the assumption that rights are demanded, as they are held: individually. The practice of economic and social rights indicates that they are demanded through collective action, through social movements and nongovernmental organizations acting to mobilize around, and implement, rights. Market actors, who may be contracted to deliver services, or who may be incorporated to sell goods, also participate. What these collectivities demand is itself subject to a reflective interpretation by multiple actors.

If collectivities are currently shaping the terms of economic and social rights, they must contend with the challenge of democratic self-government. That is, those who abide by law may also be understood to be its authors. How can organizations, movements, and associations be the real-time "creators" of economic and social rights, when they are also the

[36] For similarity of approach (but with different conclusions), *see* Jeremy Waldron, "The Core of the Case against Judicial Review," 115 Yale L.J. 1346 (2006).

[37] *See*, e.g., Mark Tushnet, *Weak Courts, Strong Rights*, *supra* note 5; *see also infra*, notes 48–50.

subjects of law? Part III of this book explores the way in which, through the protection afforded by civil and political rights, these collectives are important sources of meaning for economic and social rights. Those who claim economic and social rights can be understood as the "weak publics," the vehicles of public opinion.[38] But while they may have "fluid temporal, social and substantive boundaries," existing, as social movements or stakeholders, quite apart from formal lawmakers, their emphasis on goods—health care, housing, water, food, education, social security—requires them to exist in productive engagement with formal institutions.

If these collectivities shape economic and social rights, they often do so at a disadvantage. As those who map political struggles are quick to point out, there are "social and economic determinants" in the field of political power, even in democracies.[39] People who claim access to fundamental material interests often lack economic resources—the very lack of which impedes the exercise, or the influencing of the exercise, of political power. Political power requires, amongst other things, financial and institutional support, professional knowledge, social capital, and leisure time. As well as these exclusions, the poor are often unable to gain a perspective on the causes of the everyday indignities that they may face—of leaking ceilings, shabby waiting rooms, polluted water, poor sanitation, and, as we will see, un-stocked health clinics.[40] This lack of information results in a skewing of the perspective that will "shape their grievances, establish . . . the measures of their demands, and point to the targets of their anger."[41]

Here, the vehicle of "rights" provides a partial corrective.[42] Inhabiting the space between ethical and legal argument, rights provide a legitimate language of claim-making. While this language may condemn some movements to silence, it will also mobilize others.[43] Their demands are forced to take on terms that identify what is "universal" about their interests, which

[38] Jürgen Habermas, *Between Facts and Norms* (trans. William Rehg, 1996) 307.

[39] From sociology: Pierre Bourdieu, *Language and Symbolic Power* (trans. Gino Raymond and Matthew Adamson, John B Thompson, ed., 1991) 171 (suggesting that "any analysis of the political struggle must be based on the social and economic determinants of the division of political labour"); from political economy, *see* text accompanying note 21.

[40] *See* the case study of *Minister of Health v. Treatment Action Campaign*, 2002 (5) SA 721 (CC), discussed in Chapter 9.

[41] Frances Fox Piven and Richard A. Cloward, *Poor People's Movements: Why They Succeed, How They Fail* (1979) 21.

[42] The emphasis is partial: Lucie White, "Subordination, Rhetorical Survival Skills and Sunday Shoes: Notes on the Hearing of Mrs G," 38 Buffalo L. Rev. 1 (1990).

[43] Alan Hunt, "Rights and Social Movements: Counter-Hegemonic Strategies," 17 J. of L. & Soc. 309 (1990).

help to broaden their collective appeal,[44] and identify a common target of protest in the state. This distinguishes the rights discourse from demands to satisfy "basic needs" or "development goals," through charity, benevolence, or self-interest.[45] Instead, economic and social rights movements reject any passive or supplicant plea for redress: they demand, within their own vocabulary, action by or against the state. The discourse of rights also creates a pressure on collectivities to constrain their own repressive and exclusionary tendencies. This pressure is, of course, an influence rather than a safeguard. Yet the rights discourse calls for collectivities to respect the values that they demand be respected—dignity, for example, or participation.

On the other side, other collectivities contest economic and social rights, outside of social movements and nongovernmental organizations. Other stakeholders, such as the corporations of business and industry, may have much to gain, and much to lose, from particular instantiations of economic and social rights. Their role is also critical. Often, pressure to quantify access to minimum goods and services, such as food, water, housing, health care, and education, leads to a commodification of fundamental interests—a commodification that has conventionally been understood as a main obstacle to the enjoyment of economic and social rights. Part III of this book explores the background legal frames that disturb this assumption.

C. EXPLORING FUNDAMENTAL RIGHTS THROUGH INSTITUTIONS

The three dimensions of constituting rights—of the triple challenge of pluralism in reason, authority, and social fact; of the role of adjudication; and of the collective location of authorship—establish the central framework for this book. The result is a conceptual apparatus that relies on both constitutional theory and on international and comparative law and practice. The book takes as its backdrop one country's constitutional

[44] *See*, e.g., Jennifer Gordon, *Suburban Sweatshops: The Fight For Immigrant Rights* (2005) 162–6 (documenting the quality of rights to "unite" people more effectively than faith traditions or class solidarity). This is not to suggest, however, that all economic and social rights can build the same political power: movements organized around the right to health will have substantively different options from movements organized around the right to housing: *see* Chapters 8 and 9.

[45] Jeremy Waldron, "Rights and Needs: The Myth of Disjunction," in Austin Sarat and Thomas R. Kearns (eds.), *Legal Rights* (1996) 87. *See* United Nations Millennium Declaration, G.A. Res. 55/2, UN GAOR, 55th Sess., UN Doc A/RES/55/2 (2000); *see also* UN Millennium Development Goals, <http://www.un.org/millenniumgoals/> (last visited April 2012) ["MDGs"] (claiming that the eight MDGs—which include the halving of extreme poverty, the halting of the spread of HIV/AIDS, and the provision of universal primary education by 2015—"form a blueprint agreed to by all the world's countries and all the world's leading development institutions"). *See also* Alston, "Ships Passing in the Night," *supra* note 9.

system—South Africa—asking questions of it with a view to providing answers germane to economic and social rights elsewhere. This question links the oldest forms of comparative inquiry, from the ancient Greek historian Herodotus, to Montesquieu, to the present legal–professional settings of constitutional and quasi-constitutional treaty drafting and interpretation.

Drawing general lessons from the particular experience of South Africa relies on the growing maturity of the field of comparative constitutional law. The field's recent resurgence was triggered by the political transitions in Central and Eastern Europe in 1989 as well as in South Africa. These transitions also accompanied economic transformations—viz. the end of the central planning and internal economic integration of the Second World, and of the nonaligned economic independence of the postcolonial Third World.[46] The ensuing pace of globalization brought countless effects. Most pertinently for our purpose is the way in which these events opened up the study of constitutions and constitution-making, just as they displaced the longstanding geopolitical and ideological opposition to economic and social rights.[47]

In examining the transformation of economic and social rights, each chapter draws data from multiple legal settings. We canvas alternative conceptions of economic and social rights—from constitutional law to international human rights law, from the statements of local social movements and transnational social movements, to the statements of courts, and from each to the statements of philosophers. This is not "theory-building through comparison," as one comparative empiricist has praised.[48] Instead, we contend with the recognition that the building blocks of the theory are irreducibly normative, and that a variety of sources must be used to test a set of claims that connect the concerns of distributive justice with empirical reality.

The South African Constitution of 1996, and its pioneering experience with economic and social rights, provides this book's central window on constitutionalism, to which the US Constitution often serves as foil. Other rights-protective constitutions are also included. These comparisons demonstrate that the constitutional recognition of economic and social rights is supported by a variety of institutional models. Therefore, the postcolonial Constitutions of India and Ghana, and in particular their recognition of directive principles of state policy, are included as a critical, if incomplete, answer to the challenge of adjudication.[49] So, too, is the postwar Basic Law

[46] Jeffrey D. Sachs, *The End of Poverty: Economic Possibilities for Our Time* (2005) 46–7.

[47] Heinz Klug, *Constituting Democracy: Law, Globalism and South Africa's Political Reconstruction* (2000) 24–6.

[48] Ran Hirschl, "The Question of Case Selection in Comparative Constitutional Law," 53 Am. J. of Comp. L. 125 (2005).

[49] India Constitution arts. 38, 39, 41–48a; Constitution of the Republic of Ghana, arts. 34–41; for excerpts of these and the constitutions cited *infra*, notes 50–51, *see* Appendix I. *See also* Bunreacht Na hÉireann [Ireland Constitution, 1937] art. 45.

of Germany, and its constitutional "social state" principle and guaranteed existential minimum.[50] The same principle of the social state informs the post-conflict Constitution of Colombia, which guarantees the rule of law based on a social state, as well as a subjective *tutela* action for its enumerated economic and social rights.[51] The innovations of the Colombian Constitutional Court are therefore tested and explored. The passage of the Human Rights Act 1998 in the United Kingdom, a quasi-constitutional instrument which incorporates the European Convention on Human Rights,[52] is also subject to analysis. The Canadian Constitution's notwithstanding mechanism and limitation clause,[53] inserted into the repatriated Charter of Rights of 1992, are also examined as an important source of structural innovation within constitutional text. These comparative jurisdictions complement the book's primary focus on South African constitutionalism.

All of these sources help to inform a set of questions about rights interpretation, adjudication, enforcement, and contestation. These sundry jurisdictions appear in the following chapters, not as comparative legal families, grouped on the basis of their youth or their genealogy, but all of them as broadly constitutionalist systems, with value-based commitments to democracy and the rule of government by law, and with significant institutional commitments to the protection of fundamental material interests. For those taking an originalist view of constitutions, the closeness between the generations of "founders" and the current interpreters of these relatively young constitutions is an important point of difference from older constitutions, challenging the relevance of the operational insights of the new constitutions and new democracies from the more established constitutional systems. Yet for those that view all constitutions as capable of evolution and change, in part independent from the views of the founding framers, such a comparison is timely. The constituted operation of economic and social rights are relevant for new constitutions and old; for countries with "developing" as well as "developed" economies; for countries overcoming colonial control, and for those overcoming their own imperialism.[54]

[50] Grundgesetz für die Bundesrepublik Deutschland (German Basic Law), arts. 1(1), 20(1).

[51] Constitution of Colombia 1991.

[52] Human Rights Act 1998 (UK) (coming into full force 2 October 2000). For other statutory examples, *see*, e.g., Human Rights Act 1993 (NZ), Human Rights (Parliamentary Scrutiny) Act 2011 (Cth) (Australia); Charter of Human Rights and Responsibilities Act 2006 (Vic) and Human Rights Act 2004 (ACT).

[53] Canadian Charter of Rights and Fundamental Freedoms, s. 1, 33.

[54] The approaches of some studies, which compare only "new" constitutions of developing countries, or the constitutions of the Commonwealth (restricting that, again, to those of the developed countries), are not utilized here.

Lastly, the "international bill of rights," and the United Nations committees and tribunals that now accompany these and other international human rights instruments, are important components to the study of economic and social rights. After the Second World War, certain tenets of the ideology of social democracy were entrenched in the United Nations constitutive instruments. The Universal Declaration of Human Rights proclaims that "[e]veryone has the right to a standard of living adequate for the health and well-being of himself and of his family, including food, clothing, housing and medical care and necessary social services, and the right to security in the event of unemployment, sickness, disability, widowhood, old age or other lack of livelihood in circumstances beyond his control," as well as "the right to education," "the right to social security," and "the right to work."[55]

The International Covenant on Economic, Social and Cultural Rights ("ICESCR") updates and extends the Universal Declaration, and commits the rights to treaty form.[56] The Committee on Economic, Social and Cultural Rights—the supervisory body responsible for clarifying the terms and implementation of the ICESCR—has issued important statements about economic and social rights since 1986.[57] Recently, the Committee on Economic, Social and Cultural Rights was granted the authority to receive and consider, subject to receiving ten ratifications, "communications" by individuals claiming a violation of economic and social rights, or by states claiming another State Party is not fulfilling an obligation.[58] These international legal developments are a reference point for judges in interpreting national constitutions, as well as for social movements in making rights-based arguments and endeavoring to attract wider support for those arguments. This book therefore complicates a comparative analysis that would treat national legal systems and international legal systems as separate

[55] Universal Declaration of Human Rights, G.A. Res. 217A, UN GAOR, 3d Sess., 1st plen. mtg., art. 25, UN Doc. A/810 (10 December 1948). *See further* Appendix II; Katharine G. Young, "Freedom, Want and Economic and Social Rights: Frame and Law," 24 Maryland J. Int'l. L. 182 (2009).

[56] International Covenant on Economic, Social and Cultural Rights, 16 December 1966, 993 U.N.T.S. 3; *see further* Appendix II. *See also* Convention on the Elimination of All Forms of Discrimination against Women ("CEDAW"), 3 September 1981, Pt. III; Convention on the Rights of the Child, 20 November 1989, U.N.T.S. 1577.

[57] The Committee, a group of independent experts operating under the mandate of the UN Economic and Social Council, was established in 1986, a decade after the International Covenant on Economic, Social and Cultural Rights entered into force.

[58] Optional Protocol to the International Covenant of Economic, Social and Cultural Rights, G.A. Res. 63/117, UN Doc. A/RES/63/117 (10 December 2008). The Protocol will enter into force after its tenth ratification. *See further* Appendix II. It currently enjoys the support of eight State Parties, including Argentina, Bolivia, Bosnia and Herzogovina, Ecuador, El Salvador, Mongolia, Slovakia, and Spain, and 40 overall signatories (as at June 2012): <http://treaties.un.org/Pages/ViewDetails.aspx?src=TREATY&mtdsg_no=IV-3-a&chapter=4&lang=en>.

entities and domains of analysis. Nonetheless, the institutions underlying the frame of transformative constitutionalism, and of globalism, are introduced in the following two sections.

(1) *Transformative constitutionalism*

South Africa's Constitution provides a rich empirical backdrop for the examination of economic and social rights. Since the entrenchment of economic and social rights in the postapartheid Constitution of 1996 (and the earlier interim Constitution of 1994), South Africa has served as a vanguard of learning about the potentials and challenges of justiciable economic and social rights.[59] This act of entrenchment, which was made after extensive consultation within South Africa, and informed by international and comparative models, accompanied the replacement of a system of racialized and minority-empowered parliamentary sovereignty with parliamentary government and a justiciable Bill of Rights. Thus, the rights to access food, health care, housing, water, social security, and education[60] are entrenched alongside the right to property,[61] and the traditional civil and political rights of voting, association, and expression.[62] All rights are mediated by a limitations clause.[63] The Constitution's ambitions are grand—it pledges to transform South Africa from its apartheid past in a singular direction of democracy and rights.[64]

The constitutional settlement in South Africa was supportive of constitutionalism over other models of limited government, such as consocialism and developmentalism.[65] The favored mode of constitutionalism was one expressly supportive of economic and social rights. The African National Congress ("ANC"), while a resistance movement, had long pledged a Freedom Charter containing various human rights commitments, including

[59] *See,* e.g., David Bilchitz, *Poverty and Fundamental Rights: The Justification and Enforcement of Socio-Economic Rights* (2007); Jeanne M. Woods, "Justiciable Social Rights as a Critique of the Liberal Paradigm," 38 Tex. Int'l. L.J. 763 (2003) 766–7.

[60] S. Afr. Const. 1996 § 7(2), §§ 26 (housing), 27 (health care, food, water, and social security), 29 (education). *See also* § 28 (1)(c) (setting out the rights of children to basic nutrition, shelter, basic health care services, and social services, without qualification by a standard of progressive realization); *see further,* Appendix I.

[61] S. Afr. Const. 1996 § 25.

[62] S. Afr. Const. 1996 §§ 16 (freedom of expression), 17–18 (assembly and association), 19 (campaign and vote).

[63] S. Afr. Const. 1996 § 36 (limitation of rights).

[64] For analysis of South Africa's transformative ambitions, *see* Karl E. Klare, "Legal Culture and Transformative Constitutionalism," 14 S. Afr. J. Hum. Rts. 146 (1998). *See generally* Henk Botha, André van der Walt, and Johan van der Walt (eds.), *Rights and Democracy in a Transformative Constitution* (2003).

[65] Siri Gloppen, *South Africa: The Battle over the Constitution* (1997).

rights in labor, education, food, medical care, and housing.[66] The vision entrenched in the African Charter on Human and Peoples' Rights, consistent with that of many independence movements around the world, had charted a postcolonial economic development with concrete targets for labor, health, and education.[67] In this respect, the formal legal expression of economic and social rights was viewed as an important part of the policy aspirations of good government in Africa, if not the enforceable law of courts.[68] With the end of the Cold War, these aspirations became less politically polarizing than they once had been. Indeed, without the superpower tension of the Cold War, the express anti-communism of the apartheid government became ineffective as a means to win geopolitical support, thus diminishing the power of the white-ruled National Party and changing the dynamics of the internal and external anti-apartheid struggles.

Moreover, the ANC, as the newly elected South African government in 1994, was committed to redressing the legacies of apartheid—redress that demanded more than truth and reconciliation, but also a correction of the maldistributions created by almost half a century of racist property and labor restrictions. For local commentators, economic and social rights were regarded as neither luxuries nor sources of tyranny.[69] Despite the express caution that such rights would distract and disempower in South Africa's new democracy,[70] the majority of the participants in constitution-making saw them as anchors for the postapartheid commitments of transformation in the economic realm.

Yet even with these impressive credentials, the analysis of economic and social rights in South Africa is immensely difficult. For example, although its Constitution contains some of the most far-reaching constitutional provisions with respect to economic and social rights, South Africa has not yet

[66] The Freedom Charter of 26 June 1955 recognized voting and associational and speech rights, as well as rights in labor, education, food, medical care, and housing: reprinted in 21 Columbia Human Rights Law Review 249 (1989). The Freedom Charter was preceded by a 1943 Bill of Rights in the Africans' Claims in South Africa.

[67] African Charter on Human and Peoples' Rights, arts. 15–17, OAU Doc. CAB/LEG/67/3/rev. 5 (27 June 1981), reprinted in 21 International Legal Materials 58 (1981) (entered into force 21 October 1986).

[68] The distinction between the two did not present the difficulties that have absorbed US constitutionalism: *see* Sunstein, *The Second Bill of Rights*, *supra* note 33 (contrasting a US, "pragmatic," focus on a judicially enforceable constitution with an "expressive," aspirational constitutionalism, widespread in Europe and elsewhere).

[69] Etienne Mureinik, "Beyond a Charter of Luxuries: Economic Rights in the Constitution," 8 S. Afr. J. Hum. Rts. 464 (1992); Nicholas Haysom, "Constitutionalism, Majoritarianism, and Socio-Economic Rights," 8 S. Afr. J. Hum. Rts. 451 (1992).

[70] Dennis Davis, "The Case Against Inclusion of Socio-Economic Rights in a Bill of Rights Except as Directive Principles," 8 S. Afr. J. Hum. Rts. 475 (1992).

ratified the ICESCR.[71] The Constitution's famously "transformative" ambitions have sat uneasily against well-publicized reversals in health care, housing, and education policy programs. The ANC's early Reconstruction and Development Programme ("RDP"),[72] which was intended to restructure the economy, and to address the basic needs of the 40 percent of the population (17 million persons) living in absolute poverty, lasted only two years. It had been adopted, by the government led by Nelson Mandela, to directly address the inequalities that were the result of apartheid, by measures such as land reform, wealth redistribution, the promotion of education, and intensive public works programs. After internal and external pressure, RDP was replaced in 1996 by Growth, Employment and Redistribution ("GEAR"), which aimed for sustained growth rather than the redress of injustice, and which adopted the neoliberal economic blueprints of privatization, liberalization, and competition in order to reach its growth targets.

Indeed, two narratives of postapartheid South Africa serve as bookends. In the first narrative, there is a happy story of progress and miracle. This story focuses on the popular conquest of apartheid through remarkably nonviolent means, the entrenchment of economic and social rights in order to guide future distributions in fair terms, and the channeling of seething upsets, frustrations, and violence into the principled forums of the courts. From the successful sequence of the certification of the Constitution by the Constitutional Court,[73] to the first attitude of praise delivered by President Nelson Mandela to a Constitutional Court ruling that was significantly contrary to the executive's interests;[74] from the overthrow of the death penalty,[75] to the prominent court orders to transform rights-infringing housing and health policies,[76] and to the striking down of laws discriminatory to sexual orientation,[77] the constitutionalist aspirations of South Africa's Constitution have met the experienced lives of South Africans with stirring completeness.

[71] As of June 2012.

[72] The African National Congress (ANC), Congress of South African Trade Unions (COSATU), and South African Communist Party (SACP), together released the RDP before the 1994 elections.

[73] *In re Certification of the Constitution of the Republic of South Africa*, 1996 (10) BCLR 1253 (CC).

[74] *Executive Council of the Western Cape Legislature v. President of the Republic of South Africa* 1995 (4) SA 877 (CC) (finding unconstitutional delegation of legislative power to executive).

[75] *S. v. Makwanyane* 1995 (3) SA 391 (CC) (the overturning of the death penalty was the first case heard by the Constitutional Court and the second decided).

[76] *Government of the Republic of South Africa v. Grootboom* 2001 (1) SA 46 (CC) (finding housing policy unconstitutional); *Minister of Health v. Treatment Action Campaign* 2002 (5) SA 721 (CC) (finding health care policy unconstitutional).

[77] *National Coalition for Gay and Lesbian Equality v. Minister of Justice* 1999 (1) SALR 6 (CC) (overturning various laws criminalizing sodomy); *Minister of Home Affairs v. Fourie* 2006 (1) SA 524 (CC) (recognizing same-sex marriage).

In the second story, the miracle is a mirage. The entrenchment of economic and social rights has legitimated the entrenchment of apartheid's property gains, surrendering the new majority's power beyond the cosmetic tinkering of present arrangements.[78] Political (mostly white) elites have masterminded a preservation of power through the courts.[79] Alternatively, power resides in a single party, the ANC, itself immune to the levers of democracy by commanding near universal support. The opening of South Africa onto the international stage has ushered in, not a new culture of universal human rights, but the rigors and blasts of global economic competition.[80] Privatization and deregulation have left the management of economic life to the family, the market, and street crime, where they have long rested. And while delegates argued over the terms of the new Constitution, HIV/AIDS was sweeping, unobstructed, through the most vulnerable communities of South Africa. When finally noticed, the pandemic was met by a policy of denial. In this story, it is injustice, not constitutionalism, that pervades the South African experience.

The truth lies somewhere in both narratives, and in the space between them. Postapartheid South Africa no doubt teeters under the pressure of great expectations and the hardships of its first technical recession since 1992, which it entered in May 2009. The fittingness of each narrative suggests that South Africa may continue to bring to mind "the world in microcosm,"[81] living out the coordinates of global inequality, racism, poverty, and despair as one country. It is a suggestion that makes this comparative study vital, but no less complex.

(2) *Transformative globalism*

Economic and social rights become legally binding within the boundaries of particular political and legal communities, whether internal or as between states. Yet as globalization proceeds, the nation state frame is tested. The key domestic legal and political actors—courts, executives, legislatures—engage so regularly with their foreign counterparts that institutional borrowing, doctrinal migration, and legal convergence become unexceptional.[82] Some

[78] Makau W. Mutua, "Hope and Despair for a New South Africa: The Limits of Rights Discourse," 10 Harv. Hum. Rts. J. 63 (1997) 68–9.

[79] Ran Hirschl, *Towards Juristocracy* (2004) 89–95 (pointing to the rapid transformation of support, from traditional parliamentary supremacy to judicial review, that was effected within South Africa's National Party, as proof of the "hegemonic preservation" that is occurring in the "new constitutionalism").

[80] Allister Sparks, *Beyond the Miracle: Inside the New South Africa* (2003) 170–201.

[81] The microcosm metaphor is suggested by Sparks, ibid., x–xii.

[82] E.g., Anne-Marie Slaughter, *A New World Order* (2004).

constitutions, such as South Africa's, explicitly require interpretation to take place with the consideration of international law, and permit the consideration of comparative law.[83] For others, courts and tribunals develop informal and irregular practices of using international and comparative law to guide the task of interpretation. Those constitutions adopted after the Second World War, whose text is informed by the international bill of rights; or those whose text itself informed those instruments, have various genealogical justifications for this practice.[84] Those constitutions that operate within a regional human rights system have additional pressures to interpret rights compatibly. This is especially the case within Europe, but also in the Americas and Africa.[85] These developments are not restricted to formal national institutions. Those claiming constitutional rights are themselves guided by international and comparative interpretations and practice.

At the same time as the rights provisions of constitutions appear more textually similar, or at least in some kind of dialogue, the question of the obligations of governments beyond their citizens becomes relevant. Globalism forces constitutional law to address the relationship of the government to individuals outside of the formal citizenry. The corpus of international human rights law has already outlined what obligations a state may have to those individuals whose rights are infringed by their government (or by corporations hosted by their government), despite those individuals' exclusion from citizenship or even from their territorial control. Hence, as threats to economic and social protection proceed outside of the nation state, territoriality-bounded rights no longer seem fully plausible.[86] Indeed, the very concept of sovereignty—of a state barring "external interference" in its "internal affairs"[87]—is threatened into irrelevance, as global trade, sanctions, and development policies affect the economic and social rights of individuals in other places.

[83] S. Afr. Const., s. 39. Interpretation of Bill of Rights:

1. When interpreting the Bill of Rights, a court, tribunal or forum—
   a. must promote the values that underlie an open and democratic society based on human dignity, equality and freedom;
   b. must consider international law; and
   c. may consider foreign law.

[84] *See further* Chapter 10. *See also* Katharine G. Young, "The World, through the Judge's Eye," 28 Australian Y.B. Int'l. L. 27 (2009).

[85] E.g., European Convention on Human Rights; American Convention on Human Rights; African Charter of Human and Peoples' Rights.

[86] *See*, e.g., Chimène I. Keitner, "Rights Beyond Borders," 36 Yale J. Int'l L. 55 (2011); Gerald L. Neuman, "Understanding Global Due Process," 23 Geo. Immigr. L.J. 365 (2009) 382–91.

[87] For a classic statement of this arrangement, *see* United Nations Charter, art. 2(7) (suggesting that the Charter does not authorize the United Nations "to intervene in matters which are essentially within the domestic jurisdiction of any state").

In this new global order, the rights and movements of constitutionalism appear to give way to the goals and stakeholders of governance. Governance explores what "governing" can be, without government, or in addition to government. As its adherents suggest, "[t]he language of governance rather than government . . . signals a shift away from the monopoly of traditional politico-legal institutions, and implies either the involvement of actors other than classically governmental actors, or indeed the absence of any traditional framework of government."[88] Governance acknowledges the fluid role of market participants and nongovernmental organizations in influencing the course of law and social life. It explores the opportunity to govern where law appears to be absent or impotent: in world-society, for instance.[89]

The methodological frame of governance is well suited to exploring the ways in which economic and social rights are constituted. Indeed, governance and its intellectual offsprings—"new governance" (which unites democratic theory with the economic sociology of political and market actors) and "global governance" (which extends the study of institutions into transnational and international arenas) share many features of the pragmatist approach taken in this book. Constitutionalism and governance both concentrate on institutions and institutional design, on problems and problem-solving, and on power and its kinetic exercise. Both are oriented towards the possibilities of linking democracy and experiment. Nonetheless, constitutionalism tackles what new governance defers: the need for "anchoring premises beyond the possibility of experimental rejection."[90] It acknowledges, moreover, that law—through creating privileges and immunities—creates the "extralegal" spaces that governance appears to unearth.

This same approach—of mapping "absences" of law through jurisdictional limits—contains the seeds of constitutionalism's answer to globalization. This challenge, for which governance appears to retain its strongest advantage, underlies each aspect of the framework outlined above. It is a challenge that informs the questions raised by each chapter and the provisional development of answers.

The examination of economic and social rights—from food, housing, health care, water, social security, and education—focuses attention on a variety of laws and policies, such as the delivery of goods and services

[88] Grainne de Burca and Joanne Scott, "Introduction: New Governance, Law and Constitutionalism," in Grainne de Burca and Joanne Scott (eds.), *Law and New Governance in the EU and the US* (2006) 1, 2.

[89] Gunther Teubner, "Societal Constitutionalism: Alternatives to State-Centered Constitutional Theory?" in Christian Joerges, Inger-Johanne Sand, and Gunther Teubner, *Transnational Governance and Constitutionalism* (2004) 3.

[90] Neil Walker, "EU Constitutionalism and New Governance," in de Burca and Scott (eds.), *Law and New Governance*, *supra* note 88, 15, at 32.

(whether by public or private actors), the allocative priorities within government policy, and the distributional impact of law. This examination also helps us to interrogate the under-theorized aspects of constitutionalism, democracy, and the tensions that are often thought to underlie them, through standpoints of interpretation, and practices of adjudication, enforcement, and contestation. If we are to understand economic and social rights as law, we must accept the challenges outlined above. Economic and social rights are constituted in conditions of pluralism. They are constituted through social collectivities, as well as through formal institutions such as courts. They are structured as claims against the state, but transcend this dimension by encompassing globally situated actors and by addressing threats to interests occurring outside of the state. It is to these challenges that later chapters turn.

PART I

CONSTITUTING RIGHTS BY INTERPRETATION

An obligation to protect fundamental material interests, through aid or remuneration, has long been established in the codes and declarations of both secular and monotheistic traditions.[1] Over two centuries ago, economic and social rights came to be argued as just as fundamental to human beings, as the civil and political rights that were being specified and proclaimed in various bills of rights. The recognition that one could not be free if one was impoverished was made possible and practicable by advances in science and industry, which promised that the means of livelihood could be accessible to everyone.[2] During the eighteenth century, economic and social rights were associated with the right to property, such that property protections, then considered so basic to liberty and the pursuit of happiness as to be a human right, could be relied on to secure other material interests. Later, when concern about the relationship between the ownership of property and its use, and about private rights and public responsibility, disturbed the primacy of property rights, interests in education, work and health were defined in separate terms. In the nineteenth century, public systems of education were instituted, bargaining and arbitration systems for the workplace were established, various food and drugs legislation was enacted (often under the constitutional authority of the police power[3]),

[1] *See* statements collected in Micheline R. Ishay (ed.), *The Human Rights Reader: Major Political Essays, Speeches, and Documents From Ancient Times to the Present* (2nd edn.,2007); *see also* Samuel Moyn, *The Last Utopia: Human Rights in History* (2010) 17–18, 63–5, 222 (countering the "myth of deep origins" for civil and political rights while granting the pertinence of such sources for economic and social rights and the values they incorporate).

[2] Jacques Maritain, "The Grounds for an International Declaration of Human Rights" (1947), in Ishay, ibid., 5.

[3] For the US history, *see* Wendy Parmet, "From Slaughterhouse to Lochner: The Rise and Fall of the Constitutionalization of Public Health," 40 *J. of Am. Hist.* 476 (1996).

and medical and nutritional services were established in many states. In the twentieth century, social security was designed to protect individuals from the hazards of incapacity or unemployment. By the time of the Universal Declaration, in 1948, these rights were all accepted as worthy of inclusion in an international instrument designed to proclaim the "common standard of achievement for all peoples and all nations."[4]

While the commitment to economic and social rights was unassailable, at least by the delegates at the Universal Declaration's drafting,[5] their accepted and intended legal meaning was not as firm. Despite somewhat specified provisions in respect to the right to work (equal pay for equal work, for instance, access to trade unions, and remuneration allowing for an existence worthy of human dignity),[6] and the right to education (free and compulsory for elementary years, and directed to the full development of the human personality),[7] other protections—such as of food, clothing, housing, and medical care—were equated with the much more approximate "adequate standard of living."[8] Pronouncements of these rights remained deliberately abstract. It is worth recalling the complete divergence of political economies then present within the UN membership of fifty-six states.[9] The eighteen-member delegation to the United Nations Commission on Human Rights included Western and Communist viewpoints, as well as those from China, Chile, India, Lebanon, and the Philippines.[10]

Within the Universal Declaration, "everyone, as a member of society"[11] is entitled to economic and social rights, and everyone bears responsibility, whether towards one another, or through work, family, or community relationships, through every "organ of society,"[12] or through the greater "social and international order."[13] The state is not enumerated as a duty-holder. Its importance is nowhere expressed but everywhere assumed, given that it was governments who were the final arbiters of the text. Nonetheless,

[4] Universal Declaration of Human Rights, G.A. Res. 217A, U.N. GAOR, 3rd Sess., 1st plen. mtg., art. 25, UN Doc. A/810 (10 December 1948) ["Universal Declaration"].

[5] For a description of the normatively charged moment of global politics at the adoption of the Universal Declaration of Human Rights, and the way in which its drafters understood themselves to be striving for universal acceptance, *see* Katharine G. Young, "Freedom, Want, and Economic and Social Rights: Frame and Law," 24 Maryland J. of Int'l. L. 182 (2009) 182–4, 186.

[6] Universal Declaration, art. 23. *See further*, Appendix II.

[7] Universal Declaration, art. 26.

[8] Universal Declaration, art. 25.

[9] Compare with present 192 UN member states.

[10] Young, "Freedom, Want and Economic and Social Rights," *supra* note 5.

[11] Universal Declaration, art. 22.

[12] Universal Declaration, Preamble.

[13] Universal Declaration, art. 28.

even within the state-centric paradigm of 1948, Article 22 of the Universal Declaration proclaims that both "national effort and international cooperation" would lead to the realization of the economic and social rights of all persons.

In the later human rights instrument dedicated to economic and social rights, certain rights are made more determinate. The right to food protected in the International Covenant on Economic, Social and Cultural Rights ("ICESCR") (drafted by 1966 and entered into force by 1976), includes freedom from hunger, to be met with specific programs of production, conservation, and distribution.[14] The right to health requires the control of epidemics and occupational diseases, environmental hygiene, and attention to the stillbirth rate and infant mortality.[15] The right to education requires states without compulsory, free primary education to adopt a detailed plan within two years.[16] Despite these specifications, all obligations are made relative by the state party's overarching commitment to them: to undertake "to take steps, individually and through international assistance and co-operation, especially economic and technical, to the maximum of its available resources, with a view to achieving progressively the full realization of the rights."[17]

The drafters of national constitutions (and of the amendments to constitutions) adopt similar strategies of abstraction, flexibility, and lowest-common-denominator consensus. These strategies are also applied to economic and social rights. No longer given only implied protection through the police power, public health, equality, and/or due process provisions, express constitutional economic and social rights have begun to articulate the interests to be protected: usually medical care (not, unlike the ICESCR, health *per se*), housing, and education. These are given their own qualifications and limitations. This leeway provides a revisability and flexibility that is justified on the democratic, as well as fiscal, grounds that are discussed later in this book.

There are a number of ways that such flexibility is expressed in text. Constitutional rights often guarantee access to the goods and services that protect fundamental interests, rather than the goods and services *per se*, and the provision of access is made subject to available resources. Thus, for example, South Africa's Constitution protects the right of everyone "to have access to adequate housing," and "to have access to health care services," "sufficient food and water," and social security.[18] These are all to be "progressively realized" through "reasonable legislative and other measures,

[14] ICESCR, art. 11. *See further*, Appendix II. [15] ICESCR, art. 12. [16] ICESCR, arts. 13, 14.

[17] ICESCR, art. 2(1). [18] S. Afr. Const., arts. 26(1), 27(1).

within . . . available resources."[19] Other provisions are more concrete and less relative. Everyone has the right "to a basic education, including adult basic education."[20] The right of every child to "basic nutrition, shelter, basic health care services and social services" is stated without qualification.[21] Such provisions now demand a determinacy to equate with their significance. Yet determinacy is not easily grasped.

Of course, the problem of indeterminacy is not unique to economic and social rights. All rights are dependent upon language, and are therefore open to multiple interpretations. To say that civil and political rights, for example, simply mean what the words mean is to leave them unacceptably ambiguous. The right to a fair trial, for example, requires value judgments and an understanding of the practicalities of the judicial system. The right to free expression requires an interpretation of why such a right is valuable to a human being—for their dignity, the development of their personality, or their proper political representation, for example—and why other values or interests may be more or equally important. This task is achieved through a theory of interpretation. No less is true for economic and social rights.

Part I of the book explains the interpretive standpoints and processes that constitute economic and social rights. Of course, interpretation drives the other aspects of rights discussed in other Parts—the opportunities for enforcement, and the contours of contestation. But the interpretive possibilities of language and text create their own, standalone, testable, opportunities for rights to food, health care, housing, and education to become enforced in law or otherwise binding on legal decision-makers. By working out the principles and structures of reasoning that are now available with respect to constitutional and international human rights, we can understand the parameters within which such rights are constituted against varied legal and political backgrounds. First, I describe interpretive standpoints that prioritize the rational processes that align with basic needs or human dignity, or the consensus-based processes that approximate agreement on rights. Second, I illustrate the minimalist pressures to interpret rights, through the doctrinal setting of minimum core characteristics (or interests) that are internal to rights, or through other forms of institutional detachment. Third, I explore the varied ways in which rights are limited, through doctrinal escape clauses, amendment provisions, default decision rules, or through the form of quasi-utilitarian reasoning known as balancing. What I describe, in these three illustrations, is not an abstracted formula for the interpretation of economic and social rights. Rather, these three chapters

[19] S. Afr. Const., arts. 26(2), 27(2). [20] S. Afr. Const., art. 29(1).
[21] S. Afr. Const., art. 28(1)(c).

attempt to expand our understanding of the full scale of interpretive possibilities that accompany such rights, by applying current lessons from constitutional and international human rights law. Understanding the resources and pressures of interpretation helps to contain the indeterminacy of economic and social rights, and provides them with a more certain existence in politics and law.

attempt to expand our understanding of the full scale of interpretive possibilities that accompany such rights, by applying current lessons from constitutional and international human rights law. Understanding the resources and pressures of interpretation helps to contain the indeterminacy of economic and social rights, and provides them with a more certain existence in politics and law.

2

Interpretive Standpoints

Education enhances innovation. Health enhances pleasure. Food enhances culture. Housing enhances personality. Is this why we protect these goods as human or constitutional rights? Despite the evident importance of innovation, pleasure, culture, and personality—some of which are also understood, on their own terms, as fundamental human rights—economic and social rights are dependent on a range of other important values that deem them worthy of special moral and legal protection. What those values are is revealed in a philosophical examination of human values, and in a study of the interpretive positions taken by decision-makers. These standpoints supply meaning and content to economic and social rights, for claimants, advocates, judges, legislators, and officials to contest and/or to follow.

There is a technical legal answer to the question of why education, health, food, and housing are protected as rights. Education has been deemed important for livelihood and democracy, food is important for survival and dignity, health is important for dignity and equality, and housing is important for livelihood and the exercise of an independent vote. So much is clear from an examination of comparative case law and the pronouncements of international human rights bodies discussed below. Indeed, such legal resources indicate that the boundaries cannot be tightly drawn, with an inevitable overlap of distinct rights and of their justifications. This chapter advances two interpretive theories that give meaning to economic and social rights: those of rationalism and consensualism. Under rationalism, some have suggested that human dignity is common to all economic and social rights; others have suggested that the more pertinent consideration is human survival. Under consensualism, some have suggested that the agreement reached by a majority of states, or constituents, supplies a more ready and predictable answer. As I will discuss in detail, these positions are important steps towards understanding the importance of economic and social rights, and towards giving them meaning in our legal and social institutions. I end with suggesting that the two standpoints are, perhaps unexpectedly, neither rivals in the processes which constitute economic and social rights, nor are they irreconcilable.

A. RATIONALISM

The first standpoint, which I label "rationalist," connects the process of giving meaning to economic and social rights with the process of justification. This justificatory approach is common to those who interpret the law in order to apply it: judges. What is less acknowledged is the relevance of the task to other legal decision-makers as well, such as those who implement, supervise, or monitor legal obligations. Justification is also relevant to the task of advocates and claimants. This is because justification, based on the rational principles of why such rights are important, is necessary for persuasion. Hence, our framework of constituting economic and social rights is connected, at all levels, to rationalism.

Rationalism locates the meaning of economic and social rights within speculative reason. This interpretive approach reaches for an ethical standard, perhaps extrinsic from the legal text in which the rights are located, for prescribing the most promising legal content to rights. For example, rationalism may seek to discover how the liberal values of human dignity, equality, and freedom, or the more technical measure of basic needs, may be sustained within a formulation of economic and social rights. Indeed, although the values of human dignity, or of basic needs, may be in tension, they invite a serious exploration of the reasons for protecting economic and social rights.

This posture of rationalism can be introduced with an example taken from the right to adequate housing. Henry Shue, for example, justifies this right on the basis of the importance of the right to shelter, which flows from a right to be protected from exposure to the elements, which in turn finds its basis in one's ability to survive.[1] Jeremy Waldron, on the other hand, emphasizes the justification of freedom which underlies the right to access a place for activities like sleeping, excreting, and washing, when such activities are prohibited in public places and are prohibited elsewhere by the organization of private property.[2] Others rely on the importance of the right to housing to render authentic the exercise of civil and political rights, such as voting. We can also reason that the absence of housing impairs the exercise of individual freedom of choice and private autonomy more generally, a freedom which is necessary for the legitimacy of positive

[1] Henry Shue, *Basic Rights: Subsistence, Affluence and U.S. Foreign Policy* (2nd edn., 1996), *see also* David Bilchitz, *Poverty and Fundamental Rights: The Justification and Enforcement of Socio-Economic Rights* (2007), at 187.

[2] Jeremy Waldron, "Homelessness and the Issue of Freedom," 39 UCLA L. Rev. 295 (1991).

law.[3] All of these theories rely on a chain of justificatory reasoning that commonly accompanies rights arguments. They also incorporate a justification as to why the foundational norms—such as survival, or freedom—are superior or fundamentally important.

Taken as a class of reasons, however, the different bases presented for the right to housing demonstrates the possibility of diverging rationalist justifications. In the following section, I compare two rival approaches within rationalism, which mirror the steps taken by commentators on the right to have access to housing. The first sets out the most compelling and cogent requirements for physical survival, relying on the "basic needs" of rights holders as a sufficiently determinable standard for economic and social rights. The second elaborates the most compelling requirements for human flourishing, drawing from philosophical accounts of foundational values for ascertaining the meaning of economic and social rights.

(1) Protecting basic needs

In the first rationalist formulation, the meaning given to economic and social rights reflects the aspects of the right that satisfy the "basic needs" of the rights holder, rather than any supplementary, elective, or more ambitious level of interests. This type of inquiry orients the interpretation of the economic and social right to the minimally tolerable levels of food, water, health, housing, and education. Yet this formula provides little guidance in substantiating the right without answering a second question—that is, what are the "basic needs" needed for? Claims of needs have a relational structure, taking the form "[a] needs x in order to y."[4] This question may be answered instrumentally—for example, "basic needs" are the material interests or resources required for basic functioning, or conversely for human flourishing (which are two very different normative goals, the latter of which relates directly to our second basis of a rationalist interpretation of economic and social rights). Or we may answer this question categorically—if we accept that categorical reasoning can be distinguished from instrumental reasoning[5]—and find that "basic needs" are those required for "a minimum condition for a bearable life,"[6] or for "a decent chance at a reasonably healthy and active life of more or less normal length."[7]

[3] Jürgen Habermas, *Between Facts and Norms: Contributions to a Discourse Theory of Law and Democracy* (trans. William Rehg, 1996).

[4] E.g., Nancy Fraser, *Unruly Practices: Power, Discourse and Gender in Contemporary Social Theory* (1989) 163.

[5] Brian Barry, *Political Argument* (1965) 48–9.

[6] Jeremy Waldron, "Rights and Needs: The Myth of Disjunction," in Austin Sarat and Thomas R. Kearns (eds.), *Legal Rights* (1996) 87, 92–3.

[7] Shue, *Basic Rights*, *supra* note 1.

The emphasis on survival has guided the interpretation of the economic and social rights present in the International Covenant on Economic, Social and Cultural Rights ("ICESCR"). The "international experts" who devised the early principles of implementation, first in 1987 and then in 1998, adopted a survivalist orientation. In seeking to determine the legal content of economic and social rights under the ICESCR, they emphasized minimum subsistence rights and hence the connection between economic and social rights and survival.[8] Similarly, the Committee on Economic, Social and Cultural Rights ("the Committee"), in providing General Comments as an authorized commentary of the ICESCR, emphasized the "minimum essential levels of each of the rights."[9] This position, which stressed the satisfaction "of essential foodstuffs, of essential primary health care, of basic shelter and housing, or of the most basic forms of education"[10]—was suggestive of the more categorical (or more flatly instrumental) formula of "basic needs" amounting to survival and life. The Inter-American Commission on Human Rights, interpreting the supranational human rights relevant to consenting American states,[11] also affirmed the connection between the rights of survival and basic needs, linking both instrumentally to personal security. They noted that:

> The essence of the legal obligation incurred by any government in this area is to strive to attain the economic and social aspirations of its people, by following an order that assigns priority to the basic needs of health, nutrition and education. The priority of the "rights of survival" and "basic needs" is a natural consequence of the right to personal security.[12]

Under the rationalist standpoint, survival links logically to life. Interpreters of both international human rights and constitutional provisions have made

[8] The Limburg Principles on the Implementation of the International Covenant on Economic, Social and Cultural Rights, UN Doc. E/CN.4/1987/17, Annex, *reprinted in* (1987) 9 Hum. Rts. Q. 122, 126; *see also* The Maastricht Guidelines on Violations of Economic, Social and Cultural Rights, ¶ 9–10, UN Doc. E/C.12/2000/13, *reprinted in* (1998) 20 Hum. Rts. Q. 694.

[9] UN Economic and Social Council [ECOSOC], Committee on Economic, Social and Cultural Rights, *Report on the Fifth Session, Supp. No. 3, Annex III*, UN Doc. E/1991/23 (1991) ["*General Comment No. 3*"], ¶ 10.

[10] *General Comment No. 3*, ibid., ¶ 10.

[11] The Inter-American Commission on Human Rights is an organ of the Organization of American States Charter, and interprets the human rights, including economic and social rights, recognized in the American Declaration of the Rights and Duties of Man and the American Convention on Human Rights: *see* American Declaration of the Rights and Duties of Man, OAS Res. XXX, International Conference of American States, 9th Conf., OA5 Doc. OEA/ser.L./V/1.4 rev. (April 1948) *and* American Convention on Human Rights ("Pact of San Jose, Costa Rica"), Organization of American States (22 November 1969), *available at* <http://www.unhcr.org/refworld/docid/3ae6b36510.html>.

[12] *Annual Report (1979–1980)*, Inter-Am. C.H.R., OEA/Ser.L/V/II.50, doc. 13 rev. 1, at 2 (1980), *available at* <http://www.iachr.org/annualrep/79.80eng/chap.6.htm>.

this connection, drawing on the intuitive relation between the material protections necessary for the right to life on the one hand, and the rights to food, water, health, and housing on the other. For example, the United Nations Human Rights Committee—the body of independent experts that monitors the implementation of the International Covenant on Civil and Political Rights—extended the application of the right to life to the contexts of preventive health and food programs, by requiring the adoption of positive measures to protect life through the elimination of threats to health and nutrition. The Human Rights Committee extended its mandate to a survivalist interpretation of economic and social rights, by stating:

> The Committee has noted that the right to life has been too often narrowly interpreted. The expression "inherent right to life" cannot properly be understood in a restrictive manner, and the protection of this right requires that States adopt positive measures. In this connection, the Committee considers that it would be desirable for States parties to take all possible measures to reduce infant mortality and to increase life expectancy, especially in adopting measures to eliminate malnutrition and epidemics.[13]

More recently, human rights advocates involved in the inter-American context have suggested that the right to life should form the orienting framework for economic and social rights litigation.[14] Those who propose an expansive construction of the right to life, which is indirectly protective of economic and social rights, favor an interpretation of economic and social rights, which make these rights worthy of legal protection only when threats to life are also connected to them.

Courts in domestic systems have also referenced the right to life in cases involving economic and social rights protection, such as in the context of emergency health care in India,[15] access to shelter in India,[16] and minimum welfare in Canada.[17] Even early participants in the American welfare rights

[13] International Covenant on Civil and Political Rights, adopted 19 December 1966, S. Exec. Doc. E, 95–2 (1978), 999 U.N.T.S. 171 (entered into force 23 March 1976), art. 6, which was cited by the Compilation of General Comments and General Recommendations Adopted by Human Rights Treaty Bodies, at 127, UN Doc. HRI/GEN/1/Rev.6 (2003) ¶ 5.

[14] James L. Cavallaro and Emily Schaffer, "Less As More: Rethinking *Supra*national Litigation of Economic and Social Rights in the Americas," 56 Hast. L.J. 217 (2004).

[15] *Samity v. State of W.B.* (1996) 4 S.C.C. 37 (Sup. Ct. India) (deriving the right to emergency health care from the constitutional right to life).

[16] *Ahmedabad Mun. Corp. v. Nawab Khan Gulab Khan* (1996) Supp. 7 S.C.R. 548 (Sup. Ct. India) (right to life incorporated right to shelter and requirement of alternative housing for evictees); *Olga Tellis v. Bombay Mun. Corp.* (1985) 3 S.C.C. 545 (Sup. Ct. India) (right to dwell on pavements accepted as part of the right to life and the right to livelihood).

[17] *Gosselin v. Quebec (Attorney General)* [2002] S.C.R. 84, 429, 641 (Can.) (Justice Arbour, dissenting, arguing that the right to life is infringed by a large decrease of social security to recipients under 30).

movement pointed to the right to life—and the right to live—as the foundation of the constitutional protection of citizens' welfare entitlements.[18]

Of course, these examples are attributable to the legal persuasiveness of the right to life, which is protected in the foundational texts of both constitutions and human rights instruments in a form sometimes substituting for, and sometimes surpassing, the protections of other material interests. In this sense, it is strategically sound, and jurisdictionally contingent, to invoke the connections between the right to life and to a certain quality of life, thus justifying other economic and social rights.[19] For example, emergency health care is expanded to a right to health, or livelihood concerns justify a right to education. Nonetheless, an expansion of the right to life as the primary—if indirect—norm for protecting economic and social rights may result in a diluted scope of the right to life for other interests, as well as an uneven coverage of material interests. Such pragmatic assessments have been characterized as introducing the problems of "norm dilution" and "underbreadth," in inadequately protecting either interest.[20]

There are, however, other reasons to emphasize life. A connection between economic and social rights and the basic needs required for life and survival is useful because it focuses attention on the most urgent steps necessary for the satisfaction of those rights, which precondition the exercise of all rights—what Henry Shue has termed "basic rights."[21] This focus on life and survival can transcend the prioritization of civil and political rights over economic and social rights by drawing attention to the moral equivalence of subsistence rights and security rights because of their mutual relation to survival. The interest in life thus cuts against the so-called "first" and "second" generation of human rights.

Indeed, Shue suggests not only a moral equivalence, but a greater moral duty to prevent deprivations of the material essentials of survival, because of the utter helplessness that the latter can engender.[22] Putting to one side the question of who the relevant duty holders are and what the correlative duties consist of,[23] the focus on life, survival, and basic needs has the additional advantage of pointing to the requirements for rights protections that are apparently self-evident, rather than requiring a more controversial

[18] Martha F. Davis, *Brutal Need: Lawyers and the Welfare Rights Movement, 1960–1973* (1993), 37. *See also* Edward V. Sparer, "The Right to Welfare," in Norman Dorsen (ed.), *The Rights of Americans* (1971) 82.

[19] Cavallaro and Schaffer, "Less As More," *supra* note 14.

[20] Tara Melish, "Rethinking the 'Less as More' Thesis," 39 N.Y.U. J. of Int'l. L. & Pol. 171 (2006).

[21] Shue, *Basic Rights*, *supra* note 1.

[22] Ibid., 25.

[23] Cecile Fabre, *Social Rights under the Constitution: Government and the Decent Life* (2000) 53–4 (suggesting that Shue's argument sacrifices important features of rights).

examination of what is needed for the satisfaction of more elaborate aims, and a "thicker" understanding of the good life.[24] For proponents of the survival-based view, the boundaries drawn around economic and social rights are neater, and more cognizable, than those around more ambitious formulations. Thus, a fixed set of entitlements may emerge, helped by less open-ended criteria such as triage or urgency.[25]

Despite the influence of Shue's survivalist frame, significant problems remain with the rationalist interpretation that focuses on "basic needs." Most significant is the objection that the minimalist focus on survival and life misses the important connections between dignity and human flourishing that are intrinsic to many interpretations of the right to life. These expansive interpretations, issued by both international human rights tribunals and national courts, allow the protection of "life" to serve as a vehicle for other norms, without prioritizing scientific survival. Advocates of a survival-based "basic needs" inquiry dismiss these more elevated conceptions of life as both too encompassing and too unlimited, likening them to "a free-for-all provision, implicated by default in all human rights abuses that affect a person's 'dignity' or 'life prospects.'"[26] Yet what these detractors miss is that the focus on biological survival can set the interpretation of economic and social rights on the wrong ground. A focus on needs may disclose little about what (or "whose") basic functioning deserves priority. We need additional principles over simple survival, for example, those we would find when we ask whether the right to health should support the requirements of the elderly population—a group with a potentially endless list of medical needs,[27] or of the medical requirements of the terminally ill.[28]

Moreover, the emphasis on minimalism becomes suggestive, when attached to life, of a more scientific assessment of the commodities necessary for biological survival. This assessment reveals its own controversies and indeterminacies. As Amartya Sen pointed out long ago, the requirements of survival are not as straightforward as they might appear.

> People have been known to survive with incredibly little nutrition, and there seems to be a cumulative improvement of life expectation as the dietary limits are raised... There is difficulty in drawing a line somewhere, and the

[24] E.g., Bilchitz, *Poverty and Fundamental Rights*, *supra* note 1, at 179–80.

[25] Bilchitz, *Poverty and Fundamental Rights*, *supra* note 1, at 187.

[26] Melish, "Rethinking the 'Less as More' Thesis," *supra* note 20, at 326.

[27] *See generally* Norman Daniels, "Justice between the Young and the Old: Rationing from an International Prospective," in James W. Walters (ed.), *Choosing Who's to Live: Ethics and Aging* (1996) 24, at 25 (referring to fears of the elderly population's "'bottomless pit' of needs").

[28] *See, e.g.*, *Soobramoney v. Minister of Health, Kwazulu-Natal* 1998 (1) SA 765 (CC) at 771–2 (S. Afr.).

> so-called "minimum nutritional requirements" have an inherent arbitrariness that goes well beyond variations between groups and regions.[29]

The determinations of "normal" life expectancy and mortality patterns, the adequate caloric and nutritional food packages, and the minimum room for habitable space, all fail as determinate universal content of the rights to food, health, or housing. Even the lower-scale norm of "freedom from hunger" gives rise to many interpretations, even when limited to nutrition.[30] Such determinations of normal life cannot ascertain, for all cases and all times, the minimum volume of clean water required for survival.[31] Of course, the existence of a range of disagreement around the line drawn can still deliver a nominate standard which may allow for a context-sensitive adjustment in particular cases with little precedential importance. This concession takes us outside of the rule-like features of economic and social rights, understood as the outcome demanded by a legal right, and into the more flexible arena of setting standards and devising benchmarks.[32]

The survivalist mode of investigation recalls the discourse of "basic needs," ascendant in the development literature and World Bank policies of the 1970s.[33] This discourse, which indicated a turn away from pure economic growth strategies towards social indicators and anti-poverty strategies, was an earlier rendering, and perhaps forecaster, of the focus on "human" development and the millennium development goals.[34] One effect of the attention to "basic needs" was to make explicit the instrumental benefits of basic needs satisfaction for a national economy, rather than regarding such a focus as anathema to economic growth.[35] Another more directly pertinent effect was to sponsor research into the "inner limit" of human needs in areas of nutrition, housing, health, literacy, and employment. For example, the United Nations Environment Programme encouraged research on an "inner limit" of minimum human needs, which, along

[29] Amartya Sen, *Poverty and Famines: An Essay on Entitlement and Deprivation* (1982) 12.

[30] Jean Drèze, "Democracy and the Right to Food," in Philip Alston and Mary Robinson (eds.), *Human Rights and Development: Towards Mutual Reinforcement* (2005) 45, at 55.

[31] *See*, e.g., *Mazibuko v. The City of Johannesburg* 2010 (4) SA 1 (CC).

[32] *See infra* Chapters 3 and 4.

[33] Robert S. McNamara, President of the World Bank, To the Board of Governors: Washington D.C., 25 September 1972, in *The McNamara Years at the World Bank: Major Policy Addresses of Robert S. McNamara 1968–1981* (1981), at 228 (advocating the paradigm to reconcile the "growth imperative" with social justice by giving "greater priority to establishing growth targets in terms of essential human needs").

[34] Philip Alston, "Ships Passing in the Night: The Current State of the Human Rights and Development Debate Seen through the Lens of the Millennium Development Goals," 27 Hum. Rts. Q. 755 (2005).

[35] E.g., International Labour Organization, *Employment, Growth and Basic Needs: A One-World Problem* (1976).

with an "outer limit" of ecological requirements, would act as constraints on development policy.

The World Bank dispensed with the basic needs strategy in the 1980s, in favor of the more interventionist approach of "structural adjustment," which it believed would better respond to the globally dependent development challenges for developing countries. Citing the debt crisis, the rise in oil prices, and the slow growth in aggregate demand in developed countries, the World Bank sought greater control of national development policies than ex post remedial support of basic needs.[36] Yet the failure of the basic needs strategy can be attributed to its own rationalist shortcomings as well as to global trends. Even advocates of the approach warned that it could collapse into a technical exercise of finding the conditions in which the abstract human animal could survive. Johan Galtung suggested problems of theoretical abstraction, as well as "cultural biases and historical specificities" in the concept of needs.[37] Detractors of the approach warned of the irrelevance of prescribing "inner limits" for actual populations. As critic Gilbert Rist remarked, its usefulness was restricted to "anti-societies" or "non-societies."[38] And finally, as Philip Alston noted in his early survey of the connections between human rights and basic needs, the development hierarchy promoted by the latter approach (with its opposition to non-material indicators of development and its limited approximation of what civil and political rights might entail) did not match the normative goals of human rights.[39]

It is a stretch, but not a great stretch, to suggest that the criticisms of the basic needs strategy also apply to the survival-based interpretation of economic and social rights. Although the basic needs strategy was developed in the development field, without reference to economic and social rights, there is an important analogy between them. Both the basic needs strategy and the survival-based interpretation of economic and social rights attempt to bracket other dimensions of human values by prescribing the "inner limits" of survival. Yet such values are bracketed at great cost. Not only does bracketing these values limit the usefulness of survival-based interpretations for rights-holders (because the prioritized targets may not reflect their actual needs), the approach has the potential to actively harm their interests, by

36 *See*, e.g., James M. Cypher and James L. Dietz, *The Process of Economic Development* (2nd edn., 2004), at 516.

37 Johan Galtung, *Goals, Processes, and Indicators of Development: A Project Description* (1978) 13.

38 Gilbert Rist, *The History of Development: From Western Origins to Global Faith* (new rev. edn., 2002) 163, 167–8.

39 Philip Alston, "Human Rights and Basic Needs: A Critical Assessment," 12 Hum. Rts. J./Revue des droits de l'homme 19 (1979), at 55–6.

reducing them to "passive . . . recipients of predefined services rather than as agents involved in interpreting their needs and shaping their life conditions."[40] There are empirical links between material deprivation and a lack of democratic voice, because of the lack of accountability when things go wrong.[41] The "last resort" rights of democratic participation (which is "preservative of all rights,"[42] whereas life is "foundational to all rights") are important in guiding the definition of economic and social rights. This demands consideration of a competing rationalist standpoint, which engages more explicitly with the values behind rights.

(2) *Protecting human dignity*

A value-based interpretation goes further than the "basic needs" inquiry by emphasizing not what is strictly required for life, but rather a more holistic approach as to what it means to be human. There is, of course, a connection between these teleological theories and those related to "life," especially the most expansive conceptions of life, which seek to imbue human life with a special meaning and give substance to the right to live as a human being. As the South African Constitutional Court has noted:

> It is not life as mere organic matter that the Constitution cherishes, but the right to human life: the right to live as a human being, to be part of a broader community, to share in the experience of humanity . . . The right to life is more than existence—it is a right to be treated as a human being with dignity.[43]

I distinguish the value-based interpretation of economic and social rights by its primary emphasis on human dignity. This section examines how human dignity, a value that arguably represents the reigning ideology of both human rights and liberal constitutionalism, substantiates economic and social rights.[44]

The value of dignity evokes the individual's claim to be treated with respect and to have one's intrinsic worth recognized, and has origins in Christian natural law, Kantian philosophy, and more existential theories of personal autonomy and self-determination. Dignitarian interpretations of

[40] Fraser, *Unruly Practices*, *supra* note 4, 174. For an application of Fraser's terminology to South Africa's economic and social rights, *see* Sandra Liebenberg, "Needs, Rights and Transformations: Adjudicating Social Rights," 17 Stellenbosch L. Rev. 5 (2006) 26.

[41] Sen, *Poverty and Famines*, *supra* note 29.

[42] *See* Frank Michelman, "Welfare Rights in a Constitutional Democracy," 3 Washington U. L.Q. 659 (1979) 677.

[43] E.g., *S v. Makwanyane* 1995 (3) SA 391 (CC) ¶ 326–7 (S. Afr.) (Referring to the Interim Constitution).

[44] Louis Henkin, *The Age of Rights* (1990) 6–10.

rights inform much of the canon of international human rights, from the Universal Declaration of Human Rights onwards.[45] The preamble of the ICESCR, like the International Covenant on Civil and Political Rights ("ICCPR"), acknowledges that the rights enunciated within them "derive from the inherent dignity of the human person."[46] One school of international legal scholarship views human dignity as central to an inventory of values, applicable to the world order. Thus, the founders of the New Haven School of international law sought to both contain and stimulate a policy-oriented jurisprudence founded on dignity, using anthropological and historical sources.[47]

Like the international human rights treaties, most of the constitutions entrenched after the Second World War give particular emphasis to human dignity.[48] In such constitutions, jurists have relied almost inevitably on human dignity when peeling back the justifications for rights.[49] In US constitutional law, dignity has played an important, albeit more covert, role, partly hampered by the predominantly negative character attributed to US constitutional rights.[50]

There are other juridical examples of how the norm of dignity guides the interpretation of economic and social rights, or supplementary protections. The German Constitutional Court has used it to give meaning to the "existential minimum" of social welfare in the German Basic Law, by which society is obliged to provide everyone with the socio-economic conditions adequate for a dignified existence.[51] As Robert Alexy argues,

[45] Universal Declaration of Human Rights, pmbl., G.A. Res. 217A, at 71, UN GAOR, 3rd Sess., 1st plen. mtg., UN Doc. A/810 (12 December 1948); *c.f.*, American Declaration of the Rights and Duties of Man, OAS Res. XXX, International Conference of American States, 9th Conf., OA5 Doc. OEA/ser.L./V/1.4 rev. (April 1948) (beginning with: "The American peoples have acknowledged the dignity of the individual . . . "; followed by preamble, beginning: "All men are born free and equal, in dignity and in rights . . . "); African Charter on Human and Peoples' Rights, art. 5, OAU Doc. CAB/LEG/67/3/rev. 5 (27 June 1981), *reprinted in* 21 I.L.M. 58 (1981) (entered into force 21 October 1986) ("Every individual shall have the right to the respect of the dignity inherent in a human being . . . ").

[46] ICESCR, 16 December 1966, 993 U.N.T.S. 3 at pmbl.; ICCPR, *supra* note 13, at pmbl., *see also* UN Charter, pmbl. (expressing belief in "the dignity and worth of the human person").

[47] Myres S. McDougal, Harold D. Lasswell, and Lung-chu Chen, *Human Rights and World Public Order: The Basic Policies of an International Law of Human Dignity* (1980).

[48] E.g., Mary Ann Glendon, *A World Made New: Eleanor Roosevelt and the Universal Declaration of Human Rights* (2001) 175, 263; *see* e.g., Grundgesetz für die Bundesrepublik Deutschland (German Basic Law), art. 1, § 1 (making human dignity "inviolable").

[49] *See*, e.g., Lorraine E. Weinrib, "Constitutional Conceptions and Constitutional Comparativism," in Vicki C. Jackson and Mark Tushnet (eds.), *Defining the Field of Comparative Constitutional Law* (2002) 3, 15, and 26.

[50] E.g., Gerald L. Neuman, "Human Dignity in United States Constitutional Law," in Dieter Simon and Manfred Weiss (eds.), *Zur Autonomie des Individuums [For Individual Autonomy]* (2000) 249.

[51] BVerfG 1, 97 (104.f) (*Welfare Judgment* of 1951); BVerfGE 40, 121 (133) (*Orphans Pension II* of 1975); BVerfGE 43, 291 *(Numerus Clausus II Judgment)*; *see now* Social Welfare Minimum, BVerfG, 1 BvL 1/09 vom

the value of dignity has helped the Constitutional Court to derive enforceable subjective rights in welfare and education, when teamed with other values such as liberty and life.[52] The South African Constitutional Court has also affirmed the important relationship between dignity and social assistance.[53] During his tenure as President of the Constitutional Court, Arthur Chaskalson asked rhetorically "how can there be dignity in a life lived without access to housing, health care, food, water or in the case of persons unable to support themselves, without appropriate assistance?"[54] The question has continued to guide subsequent cases dealing with economic and social rights under the South African Constitution. At the regional level, the African Commission on Human and Peoples' Rights has held that the right to food "is inseparably linked to the dignity of human beings and is therefore essential for the enjoyment and fulfillment of such other rights as health, education, work and political participation."[55]

Advocates of the value of human dignity contend that it enriches socio-economic jurisprudence, first by justifying claims for social services when groups lack the material conditions necessary for a life of dignity, and secondly by focusing on the actual needs and circumstances of each individual.[56] Interpretations of dignity consistent with the protection of economic and social rights affirm "that people who are denied access to the basic social and economic rights are denied the opportunity to live their lives with a semblance of human dignity,"[57] and that "a social failure to value human dignity is at stake when individuals and groups experience deprivations of subsistence needs."[58] Such a value goes beyond mere survival needs, by attending to the effect on dignity of various redistributive interventions or omissions.

9.2.2010, Absatz-Nr. (1-220) ("the Hartz IV Case") (FCC) (holding that provisions in federal social assistance legislation did not comply with arts. 1.1. and 20.1 of the Basic Law, as insufficient to guarantee a subsistence minimum that is consistent with human dignity).

[52] Robert Alexy, *A Theory of Constitutional Rights* (trans. Julian Rivers, 2002) 290–3.

[53] *See, e.g.*, *Khosa v. Minister of Social Development* 2004 (6) SA 505 (CC) ¶¶ 41, 52 (S. Afr.); *Mashavha v. President of the RSA* 2004 (12) BCLR 1243 (CC) ¶ 51 (S. Afr.).

[54] Arthur Chaskalson, "Human Dignity as a Foundational Value for Our Constitutional Order," 16 S. Afr. J. Hum. Rts. 193 (2000) 204 ("[T]he social and economic rights . . . are rooted in respect for human dignity").

[55] *Soc. And Econ. Rights Action Ctr. v. Nigeria*, Communication No 155/96, ¶ 68 (African Commission on Human and Peoples' Rights) (2001), *available at* <http://www1.umn.edu/humanrts/africa/comcases/155-96b.html> (declaring obligation not to destroy or contaminate food sources).

[56] Sandra Liebenberg, "The Value of Human Dignity in Interpreting Socio-Economic Rights," 21 S. Afr. J. Hum. Rts. 1 (2005) 18.

[57] Pierre de Vos, "Substantive Equality after *Grootboom*: The Emergence of Social and Economic Context as a Guiding Value in Equality Jurisprudence," Acta Juridica 52 (2001) 64.

[58] Liebenberg, "The Value of Human Dignity in Interpreting Socio-Economic Rights," *supra* note 56, at 23.

Nonetheless, the value of dignity creates its own challenges for substantiating the content of economic and social rights. As recognized by commentators in both international human rights law and constitutional law, "dignity" can be measured subjectively or objectively, or in particularist or universalist guises.[59] In its subjective sense, dignity (and its correlative—the harm of injury to dignity) refers to the subjective effect of treatment on a claimant's feelings of self-worth and self-respect.[60] The subjective measure of dignity allows context and individual circumstances to be taken into account, yet it also has two disadvantages. First, it is precisely this sensitivity to context that prevents its usefulness as a more general guide to determining economic and social rights, if we understand those rights to require a fixed and universal (or even society-wide) measure. Secondly, the subjective measure of harm to dignity pulls the interpretation of rights in a conservative direction, by keeping the status quo of unequal material entitlements in place. It is not implausible that in the area of economic and social rights, subjective dignity might be harmed by redistribution away from the wealthy and might also fail to disturb the low expectations of poor people about their entitlements. Such expectations are often formed through habit—the observed tendency of those "subject to deprivation to lower their standards regarding what they need, want, and deserve."[61] An interpretation that is guided by an assessment of subjective dignity may do little to challenge the current set of distributions in society and may, in fact, obstruct redistributive efforts.

An objective notion of dignity addresses these difficulties. In the past, objective protections of dignity for economic and social rights tended to revert to the formulaic conceptions of basic needs.[62] Nonetheless, the objective notion may satisfy broader aims. A comparative approach, for example, may help us examine the broad and constitutionally mediated notion of objective dignity.[63] For example, South Africa's constitutional protection of equality prohibits harm to dignity, but such harm must be experienced in a measure not inconsistent with a society-wide standard. This standard acknowledges South Africa's "transformative" ambitions.[64] Thus, if a class of people adversely affected by particular social programs which vigorously reallocate material

[59] E.g., Oscar Schachter, Editorial Comment, "Human Dignity as a Normative Concept," 77 Am. J. of Int'l. L. 848 (1983); *cf.* Weinrib, "Constitutional Conceptions and Constitutional Comparativism," *supra* note 49, at 15–16.

[60] John Rawls, *A Theory of Justice* (1971), at 225, 386–9.

[61] Varun Gauri, "Social Rights and Economics: Claims to Health Care and Education in Developing Countries," in Alston and Robinson (eds.), *Human Rights and Development*, *supra* note 30, at 78, 80.

[62] *See* Schachter, Editorial Comment, *supra* note 59 at 851.

[63] Frank I. Michelman, "Reasonable Umbrage: Race and Constitutional Antidiscrimination Law in the United States and South Africa," 117 Harv. L. Rev. 1378 (2004).

[64] For a discussion of transformative constitutionalism, *see* Chapter 1.

resources—by way of a steeply progressive income tax, inheritance tax, land redistribution, land title reform, reorganization of public education, or public health funding—feels subjective indignation at the burden of such resource allocation, the constitutional protection of dignity is probably not engaged.[65] This is because such allocations may be objectively justified in their local context: the "umbrage" felt is not "reasonable" within the circumstances, so constitutional rights have not been negatively affected. The concept of "reasonable umbrage" helps to divide objective (reasonable) and subjective considerations of dignity. The harm to a person's dignity—the "umbrage" that they feel at an action by government—may be considered "reasonable" only if it is consistent with the expressed and understood aims of the state within its constitutional culture.[66] Thus, while the concept of reasonable umbrage may apply to other rights-respecting constitutional systems, its triggers will be constitutionally contingent.

If we reverse this application of "reasonable umbrage" to regulate not only the application of overly redistributive policies, but also those which are insufficiently redistributive, we may imagine that the rationalist definition of the rights to food, water, health, housing, and education are infringed when current allocations or proposed reallocations of material resources cause "reasonable umbrage" in the population at large. Because of its link to dignity, reasonable umbrage at the content of socio-economic policies or programs would be something less than an outrage to the conscience of humanity—a standard relevant to international criminal law[67]—and something more than an annoyance. This objective standard should, of course, pay particular attention to the habitual acceptance of conditions of poverty as tolerable or even inoffensive to dignity—for those who do not experience it, just as for those who do.[68]

[65] Michelman, "Reasonable Umbrage," *supra* note 63, at 1412–14 n. 169 (citing *Pretoria v. Walker* 1998 (2) SA 363 (CC) ¶ 118, 118 (S. Afr.); *see also Law v. Canada (Minister of Employment and Immigration)* [1999] S.C. R. 497 (SCC), ¶ 53 (Can.).

[66] Michelman, "Reasonable Umbrage," *supra* note 63.

[67] Rome Statute of the International Criminal Court, 17 July 1998, UN Doc. A/CONF.183/9 (1998), reprinted in 37 I.L.M. 999 (1998), corrected through 8 May 2000, by UN Doc. CN.177.2000.TREATIES-5, *available at* <http://www.un.org/icc>, Preamble ("Mindful that during this century millions of children, women and men have been victims of unimaginable atrocities that deeply shock the conscience of humanity"); *see also* David Marcus, "Famine Crimes in International Law," 97 Am. J. of Int'l. L. 245 (2003) (arguing for the formal criminalization—as crimes against humanity—of intentional or reckless government policies which result in mass starvation); Press Release, United Nations, Subcommission on the Promotion and Protection of Human Rights, "Subcommission Continues Debate on Realization of Economic, Social and Cultural Rights," UN Doc. HR/SC/99/11 (12 August 1999) (then-Expert Asbjørn Eide declaring that "[t]he scope of hunger [is] appalling in its magnitude . . . and an outrage to the conscience of mankind").

[68] Contrast text accompanying Gauri, "Social Rights and Economics," *supra* note 61, with statement of the Committee to the Vienna World Conference, UN Doc. E/1993/22.Annex III, paras. 5 and 7 (declaring

The redistributions (and lack of redistributions) that impact on dignity in post-apartheid South Africa, or even in our other constitutions under study, may be very different from what is considered "reasonable" in the more laissez-faire constitutional culture of the United States.[69] The ambitions of universality in interpreting economic and social rights based on an objectively defined notion of dignity are, in reality, very difficult to satisfy. Rationalism requires a context. The "relative" scale of the dignitarian experience, matching different levels of commodities, is explained well by Amartya Sen's overt recognition of how the baseline of goods required for "appearing in public without shame" varies between different societies. Sen traces this conception to Adam Smith's idea of "necessary goods,"[70] and suggests that "[i]n a country that is generally rich, more income may be needed to buy enough commodities to achieve the *same social functioning*."[71] The interpretation of economic and social rights will be similarly inconsistent, not only because of varied resources, but because of the different cultural expectations that may run parallel to this influence.

(3) *Reasonable disagreement*

Rationalism sets up a normative investigation into why we value economic and social rights and which aspects of the related (and claimed-for) material interests should be deemed most cogent and compelling. This approach is helpful in ensuring that advocates are able to articulate the legal content of economic and social rights through vocabularies that draw attention to the important ethical justifications for economic and social rights (as for all human rights). This approach is consistent with the insight that rights belong to a privileged category of legal entitlement that is, for special reasons, immune to the vagaries of short-term politics or cost-benefit decision-making.

Yet, as I have shown, as between the "basic needs" and "human dignity" inquiries, there are no axioms that can deliver an uncontested interpretation of economic and social rights. Rationalism must contend with disagreement. Because normative foundations are open to disagreement, economic and social rights will look different to an advocate of human flourishing in comparison with an advocate of basic survival; just as they will appear differently in various instantiations of both survival and dignity.

that the "magnitude, severity and constancy of... deprivation have provoked attitudes of resignation, feelings of helplessness and compassion fatigue").

[69] Michelman, "Reasonable Umbrage," *supra* note 63, at 1418.

[70] Ibid., *citing* Adam Smith, *An Inquiry into the Nature and Causes of The Wealth of Nations* (1975) (1776) 351–2.

[71] Amartya Sen, *Inequality Reexamined* (1992) 115.

Such accounts lead in different directions, thwarting efforts at providing a certain, determinate content to economic and social rights. It follows that the rationalist meaning attributed to economic and social rights, defined according to other political theories—from egalitarian liberalism to communitarianism to market socialism[72]—proliferates in content and scope. For example, a rationalist interpretation of economic and social rights might emphasize the material basis that is necessary for an independent citizenry, or at least to avoid extreme disparities in wealth, education and power, as civic republicanism would prescribe.[73] Or an interpretation following communitarianism may reflect a community's own model of sharing out welfare goods.[74]

Other attempts at providing the rationalist contours and boundaries of the norms of distributive justice similarly demur at delivering abstractions and reference-ready lists. If we consider the normative project of articulating the necessary baselines of "human capability" across differently situated societies and groups, we find a deliberate refusal to settle on a fixed interpretation, due to the social variation present in attempts to describe poverty.[75] This approach—proposed by Amartya Sen and Martha Nussbaum—emphasizes human capability—that is, the ability to pursue a life that one has reason to value—over other indications of human flourishing, such as freedom from illegitimate government intervention (from civil and political rights proponents) or to a basic income (from welfarists).

Yet the question of drawing up a list of the basic features of human capability, even provisionally, divides the positions of its central advocates. Martha Nussbaum's universalist project "isolates those human capabilities that can be convincingly argued to be of central importance in any human life, whatever else the person pursues or chooses,"[76] as the appropriate and minimalist underpinning of basic constitutional principles.[77] Her current,

[72] *Compare* Rawls, *A Theory of Justice*, *supra* note 60 (liberal egalitarianism) with Michael Walzer, *Spheres of Justice: A Defense of Pluralism and Equality* (1983) (communitarianism), and Roberto Mangabeira Unger, *False Necessity: Anti-Necessitarian Social Theory in the Service of Radical Democracy* (rev. sub. edn., 2004) (market socialism).

[73] Jon D. Michaels, "Note: To Promote The General Welfare: The Republican Imperative To Enhance Citizenship Welfare Rights," 111 Yale L.J. 1457 (2002) (invoking civic republican as the appropriate theoretical foundation for US welfare rights); William H. Simon, "Social-Republican Property," 38 UCLA L. Rev. 1335 (1990) (combining market socialism with republicanism).

[74] Michele Estrin Gilman, "Poverty and Communitarianism: Toward a Community-Based Welfare System," (2005) 66 U. of Pitts. L. Rev. 721 (2005) 735–6, 800–1 (adapting the communitarian theories of Michael Walzer, Michael Sandel, and Amitai Etzioni); Goodwin Liu, "Rethinking Constitutional Welfare Rights," 61 Stanford L. Rev. 203 (2008) (deploying Walzer's conception of welfare goods for justiciable welfare rights).

[75] Sen, *Inequality Reexamined*, *supra* note 71, at 108–9.

[76] Martha C. Nussbaum, *Women and Human Development* (2000) 74.

[77] Ibid., 5, drawing parallels with John Rawls, *Political Liberalism* (1996).

ten-point version sets out the importance of the following principles: life; bodily health; bodily integrity; the use of the senses, imagination, and thought; the development of emotions; practical reason; forms of social affiliation; concern for other species; opportunity for play; and the political and material control over one's environment.[78] (We can contrast this with the inventory of eight values devised by the New Haven School of international law, which included power, enlightenment, wealth, well-being, skill, affection, respect and rectitude as belonging to all legal systems).[79]

Nussbaum's attempt to list the basic human values is criticized by feminist and democracy theorists for being insufficiently concerned with human difference and particularity.[80] Amartya Sen's two objections to the list—namely its possible inattentiveness to context and its possible displacement of public reasoning[81]—are pertinent in evaluating other minimalist attempts to give meaning to economic and social rights in a theory of distributive justice.

Disagreement is not merely a feature of philosophical debate, but is also quickly revealed by constitutional comparison.[82] The values of equality and liberty, for example, are more appropriate, for some, in formulating a normative minimum for economic and social rights, and may produce both more concrete and interventionist measures.[83] In German constitutional law, for example, the value of equality rivals dignity as a guide to the Basic Law's protection of an "existential minimum." Some German commentators argue that, in measuring the standard of living of rights claimants in relation to that of others, an equality norm is more reliable than investigations into dignity.[84]

Thus, from survival, life, dignity, equality, and freedom, we can find that different rationalist interpretations deliver different content for each economic and social right. The problem with competing values is endemic, even before parsing out the different weight given to particular values for each right. An interpretation of the right to education, for example, may draw more heavily on freedom, while an interpretation of the right to health

[78] Ibid., 77–80.

[79] W. Michael Reisman, Siegfried Wiessner, and Andrew R. Willard, "The New Haven School: A Brief Introduction," 32 Yale J. Int'l. L. 575 (2007).

[80] E.g., Karin Van Marle, "'The Capabilities Approach,' 'The Imaginary Domain,' and 'Asymmetrical Reciprocity': Feminist Perspectives on Equality and Justice," 11 Feminist Legal Studies 255 (2003) 256, 272–3.

[81] Amartya Sen, "Elements of a Theory of Human Rights," 32 *Philosophy and Public Affairs* 315 (2004) 333 n. 31.

[82] E.g., Mark Tushnet, *Weak Courts, Strong Rights: Judicial Review and Social Welfare Rights in Comparative Constitutional Law* (2008).

[83] *See*, e.g., Frank I. Michelman, "Foreword: On Protecting the Poor Through the Fourteenth Amendment," 83 Harv. L. Rev. 7 (1969) 35 (developing a theory of a constitutional right to "minimum protection").

[84] Alexy, *A Theory of Constitutional Rights*, *supra* note 52, 284 (emphasizing the assessment of "factual" equality).

may rely more on the value of dignity. The emphasis on institutions forces the analysis to engage with such descriptions.

The problem is also present before we recognize the highly contingent resonance of each value in different constitutional systems.[85] There is no escape from disagreement, which I argue suggests that the rationalist enterprise is to be approached with caution for the purposes of legal analysis. While the normative compulsion behind economic and social rights should be the subject of dialogue and contestation, the resulting legal standard should retain a more open, contestable, or fluid formulation. Disagreement is a part of law.

Of course, the concept of an "overlapping consensus," forged on the basis of what all reasonable conceptions might be,[86] provides some assistance. John Rawls advanced such a resolution to the problem of reasonable disagreement, by appeal to what each person (or state) *ought to* agree on. Yet such a formula leads to the thinnest and most abstract formulation of economic and social rights—a formula more suited to a lexical ordering rather than a definitive entitlement in discrete areas of health, education, food, or shelter. Moreover, the formula for a reasonable overlap fails to invite the voice necessary for an inquiry into the evolving moral language of rights. Relying on a "thought experiment" to generate an idealized overlapping consensus, while useful, may flout the norms of self-government and participation that are important to law.[87]

Advocates often disagree over what is basic to rights, even as they agree with the general attempt to deliberate. In order to respond to this disagreement, many endorse an "ethic of fallibility," which requires all who engage in the deliberation to recognize the possibility that they are mistaken.[88] Such an ethic requires any interpretation of rights to be institutionally revisable. Moreover, this ethic leads to efforts to create *actual* consensus within the interpretation of economic and social rights. It is to this project that we now turn.

B. CONSENSUALISM

A second interpretive standpoint privileges the societal consensus surrounding economic and social rights. Under consensualism, economic and social rights gain their legal meaning by tying their fortunes to the basic—and not hypothetical—consensus reached within the communities constituting each

[85] E.g., Edward J. Eberle, *Dignity and Liberty: Constitutional Visions in Germany and the United States* (2002).

[86] Rawls, *Political Liberalism*, *supra* note 77, 133–4.

[87] Frank I. Michelman, "Law's Republic," 97 Yale L.J. 1493 (1988) 1511 (condoning Rawls's experiment while drawing attention to its problems for the norm of self-government).

[88] E.g., Jeremy Waldron, *Law and Disagreement* (1999).

field. Such an approach unites the themes of legitimacy and democratic self-determination common to both international and constitutional law. This approach asks not what rationalist value should be given priority in each right, but rather whether, and where, consensus has been reached on the content of each economic and social right. From the standpoint of consensualism, the content of each economic and social right is the agreement that is reached about it.

Applying the consensual test to economic and social rights has advantages in ascertaining the settled meaning of each right, while allowing for pluralist disagreement to occupy its fringes. In this way, it is akin to H. L. A. Hart's famous distinction between "a core of certainty and a penumbra of doubt,"[89] which accompanies the application of general legal rules to particular situations. This approach has much in common with rationalism, in that it tends to prefer the most persuasive rational articulations of economic and social rights.[90]

While sharing features of rationalism, consensualism also explicitly addresses two of its central challenges: first, that resolving disagreement by reference to an abstract, overlapping consensus of reasonable political theories does not resolve the demands for representation and voice; and second, that even broad ethical agreements may not resonate enough with social understanding to constitute law.[91] Consensualism is able to address these challenges by focusing on an observed empirical agreement. Such consensus is always retrospective, so to speak, as well as reconstructed and selective, as we will see below. Yet a consensus on some characteristics of economic and social rights—or at least, some approximation thereof—may serve the normative goals of sovereign equality in international law and self-government in constitutional law, or following an alternative normative register, the translation of reason through the "modern *ius gentium*."[92] Consensualism thus aspires to render politically legitimate—and legally valid—the application of economic and social rights as law.

(1) *Generating consensus*

Consensualism is used by those seeking to establish economic and social rights at the international level. Consensus flows from "the application of legal norms to concrete cases and situations by international treaty monitoring bodies as well as by domestic courts [which] have contributed to the

[89] H. L. A. Hart, *The Concept of Law* (2nd edn., 1994), at 123.

[90] *See infra* Chapter 2, section C.

[91] Hart, *The Concept of Law*, *supra* note 89.

[92] Jeremy Waldron, "Foreign Law and the Modern *Ius Gentium*," 119 Harv. L. Rev. 128 (2006).

development of universal minimum standards and the common understanding of the scope, nature and limitation of economic, social and cultural rights."[93] This approach is also adopted by the detractors of economic and social rights, when they claim that an absence of consensus is the reason to delay the elaboration of economic and social rights. For example, Michael Dennis and David Stewart have emphasized the importance of present-day, rather than generative, consensus, and have decried the "'build it and they will come' attitude."[94] In their own work, they find present-day consensus on economic and social rights to be lacking due to "widespread differences in domestic approaches to the treatment of [such] rights."[95]

As an orienting theory in international law, the search for consensus on economic and social rights is supported by the general sources of international law: international custom, itself heavily reliant on a general consensus, as well as consented-to conventions, general principles, and the writings of eminent publicists.[96] The first formal source, customary international law, is undergirded by the widespread support of declarations and other resolutions on human rights, widely-ratified treaties with overlapping content, or more specific obligations with respect to economic and social rights, such as widely ratified human rights treaties or regional agreements. Consensus here measures state consent, and the international opinions that are issued from their supervisory committees and tribunals are also relevant, both to developing customary international law, and to clarifying the content of treaty obligations.

In recent years, such sources have increased in the area of economic and social rights. The ICESCR itself now has 160 States Parties, who have not only registered their support for the broad provisions of the ICESCR, but have submitted to the procedures of supervision that were established by the Committee in 1986.[97] This rivals the 167 States Parties enjoyed by the ICCPR.[98] The Universal Periodic Review process, established by the United Nations in 2006 as part of the work of the new Human Rights Council, creates a state-driven mechanism to potentially examine economic and

[93] The Maastricht Guidelines on Violations of Economic, Social and Cultural Rights, reprinted in 20 Hum. Rts. Q. 691 (1998) 694.

[94] Ibid.

[95] E.g., Michael J. Dennis and David P. Stewart, "Justiciability of Economic, Social, and Cultural Rights: Should There Be an International Complaints Mechanism to Adjudicate the Rights to Food, Water, Housing, and Health?," 98 Am. J. of Int'l. L. 462 (2004) 475.

[96] For the sources of international law, *see* Statute of the International Court of Justice, art. 38(1)(b) 26 June 1945, 59 Stat. 1055, 33 U.N.T.S. 993.

[97] For status of ratifications, *see* United Nations Treaty Collection, *available at* <http://treaties.un.org> (follow "databases" hyperlink; then follow "Status of Treaties" hyperlink) (accessed June 2012).

[98] Ibid.

social rights, particularly those of the UDHR, within 193 Member States.[99] Regional human rights treaties also recognize economic and social rights.[100] Increased adjudication of economic and social rights in international and supranational bodies, such as the European Court of Human Rights and the Inter-American Commission on Human Rights, leads to a greater source of consensus, or, as one scholar has called it, "normative development."[101] Other international bodies, such as the European Committee on Social Rights supervising the European Social Charter, and the United Nations resolutions and legal texts addressing economic and social rights, are also relevant. Moreover, the protection of economic and social rights in other treaties, which have attracted the ratification of more States Parties, such as the Convention on the Rights of the Child (with 193 States Parties) and International Labour Organization ("ILO") Convention No. 182, concerning the worst forms of child labour, become relevant in measuring the consensus on economic and social rights.[102]

Also significant is the substantive commitment and implementation behind ratification, aside from the numbers of ratifications.[103] Thus, consensualism also references the national measures for protecting economic and social rights, such as federal and state constitutional texts, stable and long-lasting legislative regimes protective of economic and social rights, and judicial precedent. This is one way in which we see international human rights law and domestic law converging.

Consensualism is consistent with the practice-bound determinations of the Committee on Economic, Social and Cultural Rights, which originally relied largely on the accretion of content from state reports to formulate a consensus-based standard of meaning. Consensualism is akin to the positivist approach of the Committee, which has relied explicitly on the reports of States Parties to elucidate the developing content of economic and social

[99] United Nations General Assembly Resolution 60/251. *See*, e.g., *Report of the United States of America Submitted to the Office of the UN High Commissioner for Human Rights for the Universal Periodic Review*, August 2010 (including current protections and initiatives of economic and social rights).

[100] African Charter on Human and Peoples' Rights, art. 5, OAU Doc. CAB/LEG/67/3/rev. 5 (27 June 1981), reprinted in 21 I.L.M. 58 (1981) (entered into force 21 October 1986); American Declaration of the Rights and Duties of Man, OAS Res. XXX, International Conference of American States, 9th Conf., OA5 Doc. OEA/ser.L./V/1.4 rev. (April 1948); Convention for the Protection of Human Rights and Fundamental Freedoms, 4 November 1950, Europ.T.S. No. 5; 213 U.N.T.S. 221. *See* <http://conventions.coe.int/Treaty/en/Treaties/Html/005.htm>; European Social Charter, 18 October 1961, 529 U.N.T. S. 89, E.T.S. No. 35, *See* <http://www.coe.int/T/DGHL/Monitoring/SocialCharter/>.

[101] David Marcus, "The Normative Development of Socioeconomic Rights through Supranational Adjudication," 42 Stan. J. Int'l. L. 53 (2006) 63.

[102] Convention on the Rights of the Child, New York, 20 November 1989, U.N.T.S. 1577 (entered into force 2 September 1990) ILO, Convention No. 182, Geneva, 16 June 1999, (entered into force 19 November 2000), *See* <http://www.ilo.org/ilolex/english/convdisp1.htm>.

[103] Ryan Goodman and Derek Jinks, "Measuring the Effects of Human Rights Treaties," 14 Euro. J. Int'l. L. 171 (2003).

rights. For example, in 1991, the Committee's Chairperson Philip Alston suggested that "clarification" of the normative content of the rights to food, health, housing and education, should "be achieved through the examination of States parties' reports . . . [T]he approaches adopted by States themselves in their internal arrangements (and explained in their reports to the Committee) will shed light upon the norms, while the dialogue between the State and the Committee will contribute further to deepening the understanding."[104] It is worth recalling the significant integration of national economies that was occurring at the time of this statement—with the end of the economic separation of Central and Eastern Europe, and with it the viability of the model of central economic planning,[105] consensus was apparently more accessible.

The Committee's heavy focus on state practice has arguably resulted from the absence of an enforceability mechanism under the ICESCR. Unlike the ICCPR, the ICESCR does not give its Committee the jurisdiction to hear complaints.[106] The development of an informal jurisdiction to interpret the meaning of States Parties' obligations, by a close reading and distillation of the content of state reports therefore allowed the Committee to compensate for its lack of formal authority to hear individual complaints and issue binding interpretations.

Instead, the Committee worked to build a general consensus, and to register non-compliance with it, with two tools: the "Concluding Observations" that it issues on individual States Parties reports, and the "General Comments" that it issues to provide an overview and framework for evolving doctrine.[107] In this understanding, practice builds consensus and vice versa. The Concluding Observations process is now strengthened by the country analyses that the Committee is prepared to undertake in the absence of States Parties' own reports. The Committee also produces Concluding Observations on the basis of information presented by specialized agencies and nongovernmental organizations ("NGOs").[108]

[104] Philip Alston, "The Committee on Economic, Social and Cultural Rights," in Philip Alston (ed.), *The United Nations and Human Rights: A Critical Appraisal* (1992) 473, at 491; *see also General Comment No. 3*, *supra* note 9, ¶ 10.

[105] Jeffrey D. Sachs, *The End of Poverty: Economic Possibilities for Our Time* (2005) 46–7.

[106] *See* First Optional Protocol to the International Covenant on Civil and Political Rights, 16 December 1966, 999 U.N.T.S. 302 (establishing Human Rights Committee); International Covenant on Civil and Political Rights, 16 December 1966, 999 U.N.T.S. 171 (entered into force 23 March 1976). *But see* Optional Protocol to the International Covenant of Economic, Social and Cultural Rights, G.A. Res. 63/117, U.N. UN Doc. A/RES/63/117 (10 December 2008), text accompanying *infra* note 112.

[107] Matthew Craven, *The International Covenant on Economic, Social, and Cultural Rights: A Perspective on it Development* (1995) 87–9.

[108] Eibe Riedel, "New Bearings to the State Reporting Procedure: Practical Ways to Operationalize Economic, Social and Cultural Rights—The Example of the Right to Health," in Sabine von Schorlemer

The legal status of the General Comments is ambiguous; however, their status is bolstered by the fact that the Committee began publishing them after an invitation by the Economic and Social Council.[109] According to some observers, the General Comments which have been published from these efforts have developed an authoritativeness usually reserved for advisory opinions, are more meaningful than those issued by the Human Rights Committee,[110] and enjoy "considerable legal weight."[111] Hence, if its methodology deviates too far from consensus, the Committee (and the General Comments it issues) likewise loses legal authority.

This tangential creation of legal authority may change once the Committee hears formal complaints. The long-standing efforts, by the Committee and others, to establish a more formal complaints jurisdiction, were significantly promoted by the newly established Human Rights Council (formerly the United Nations Commission for Human Rights).[112] These efforts were rewarded in December 2008 by the adoption of the Optional Protocol to the ICESCR. The Optional Protocol will authorize the Committee to begin hearing "communications" against States Parties, by individuals, groups of individuals, or other States Parties. This system will enter into force once the Optional Protocol is ratified by ten States Parties.[113] It is expected that such communications will generate more consensus under the ICESCR.

The search for consensus is a major feature in the growing field of comparative constitutional law.[114] Consensus serves the function of signaling universal principles, on the one hand, or mere functional convergence, on the other.[115] Evidence of consensus is therefore helped by comparison. Let us consider the United States, which signed the ICESCR in 1978, but has

(ed.), *Praxishandbuch UNO: Die Vereinten Nationen im Lichte globaler Herausforderungen* (author's trans.: *UN Manual, The United Nations in the Light of Global Challenges*) (2003) 345, 347.

[109] ECOSOC Resn. 1987/5 (26 May 1987) in UN Doc. E/C.12/1989/4, at 27, para 9 (1988)). The Resolution was endorsed by the General Assembly: United Nations General Assembly, *Indivisibility and interdependence of economic, social, cultural, civil and political rights* A/RES/42/102, 93rd plenary meeting (7 December 1987), ¶ 5.

[110] M. Magdalena Sepúlveda, *The Nature of the Obligations under the International Covenant on Economic, Social and Cultural Rights* (2003) 42.

[111] Craven, *The International Covenant on Economic, Social, and Cultural Rights, supra* note 107, 91.

[112] *See* Catarina de Albuquerque (Chairperson-Rapporteur of the Optional Protocol Working Group), *Report of the Open-Ended Working Group to Consider Options Regarding the Elaboration of an Optional Protocol to the International Covenant on Economic, Social and Cultural Rights on its third session,* UN Doc. E/CN.4/2006/47 (14 March 2006). For summary, *see* <http://www2.ohchr.org/english/issues/escr/intro.htm>; But *cf.* Dennis and Stewart, "Justiciability of Economic, Social, and Cultural Rights," *supra* note 95 (criticizing attempts to establish a complaints mechanism).

[113] Optional Protocol to the International Covenant of Economic, Social and Cultural Rights, G.A. Res. 63/117, UN Doc. A/RES/63/117 (10 December 2008). For current ratifications, *see* Chapter 1, *supra* note 58.

[114] E.g., Vicki Jackson and Mark Tushnet, *Comparative Constitutional Law* (2nd edn., 2006).

[115] Mark Tushnet, "The Possibilities of Comparative Constitutional Law," 108 Yale L.J. 1225 (1999).

not ratified it.[116] To explore aspects of consensus from the United States, this approach would draw attention to the explicitly protected rights provided for in some state constitutions, which are surprisingly protective of welfare, and sometimes education and public health.[117] It would also note the judicial pronouncements that uphold a set of minimum constitutional entitlements with respect to public education and welfare in the United States Supreme Court, albeit indirectly.[118] Finally, consensualism would find relevant the body of legislative protections that have existed in the United States since the New Deal. In fact, the historical efforts of Franklin D. Roosevelt have arguably served to engender several cultural commitments in the United States, including at least support for the right to a minimum degree of education, the right to a minimum amount of social security, the right to be free from monopoly, and perhaps even the right to a job.[119] Such commitments continue to be endorsed.[120] Through comparative analysis of socio-legal equivalents, a converging set of principles regarding socioeconomic protection is empirically "uncovered" rather than deductively constructed.

(2) Consensus as a normative concept

I argue that consensualism is no less normative than rationalism, differing only because it reaches for "consent"—itself a norm—over speculative elaboration of the values of human dignity or basic needs. In the sense that consent is valued as a norm for its own sake (rather than valued instrumentally, for its ability to guide what will satisfy some norms that resist direct articulation or clarification), its importance lies in its ability to deliver legitimacy to the operation of both international and constitutional law. In this sense, consensus bears a relation to—and may be a proxy for—the more stringent requirement of state consent, itself the basic creed of international law,[121] and to the ideal of democratic self-rule in

[116] *See generally* Barbara Stark, "Economic Rights in the United States and International Human Rights Law: Toward an 'Entirely New Strategy,'" 44 Hast. L.J. 79 (1992).

[117] E.g., Constitution of the State of New York, art XI, § 1, art XVII, §§ 1,3; Helen Hershkoff, "Positive Rights and State Constitutions: The Limits of Federal Rationality Review," 112 Harv L. Rev. 1131 (1999).

[118] Lawrence G. Sager, *Justice in Plain Clothes: A Theory of American Constitutional Practice* (2004) 95–102.

[119] Cass Sunstein, *The Second Bill of Rights: FDR's Unfinished Revolution and Why We Need It More Than Ever* (2004).

[120] President Barack Obama, Remarks by the President at the Acceptance of the Nobel Peace Prize, Oslo, 10 December 2009 (*available at* <http://www.whitehouse.gov/the-press-office/remarks-president-acceptance-nobel-peace-prize>) (noting freedom from want and freedom from fear ground the links between civil and political rights and economic security and opportunity).

[121] *See* Ian Brownlie, *Principles of Public International Law* (6th edn., 2003) 4.

constitutional law.[122] Consensus renders the coercion implicit in law legitimate, by helping ensure the sovereign equality of all states (in international law), or the equal participation of all citizens (in constitutional law), in the agreement to be bound by laws. In this way, the norm of consensus unifies the two fields.[123]

The importance of consensus in international law is evidenced in the voluntarist structure of both treaties and customary international law. For general treaty regimes, consent precedes ratification and the acceptance of obligation.[124] The importance of consent helps to explain the practice of allowing (certain) treaty reservations. It also explains the "margin of appreciation" which is granted to constrain the application of international law in domestic legal systems, and which is also justified on democracy and value pluralism grounds.[125] For customary international law, consensus is also a foundational feature. The positive sources of customary international law—*opinio juris* and state practice—are important proxies for consent, even if expressed tacitly.[126] In permitting exceptions, custom again gives priority to consent, precluding customary law's application to persistently objecting states.

Nonetheless, the centrality of consensus shifts with respect to human rights. For both treaty-based and customary human rights norms, the norm of consensus is secondary to the higher moral goals suggested by these conventions. For the obligations which flow from these moral goals, consent may be both constitutive and destructive.[127] For example, while states' ratifications are required in order to establish obligations, the principal human rights treaties are purportedly universal in scope, and there are limits to the reservations that countries may make in becoming parties.[128] Under one conception of consent, the invalidity of certain reservations may maximize, rather than obstruct, its operation.[129] On another view, however, the norm of consensus is overridden by others: particularly in the case of

[122] *See* Stephen Holmes, "Precommitment and the Paradox of Democracy," in Jon Elster and Rune Slagstad (eds.), *Constitutionalism and Democracy: Studies in Rationality and Social Change* (1988) 195, 195–7.

[123] *See also* Gerald L. Neuman, "Human Rights and Constitutional Rights: Harmony and Dissonance," 55 Stanford L. Rev. 1863 (2003) 1864–5.

[124] Vienna Convention on the Law of Treaties, 23 May 1969, 1155 U.N.T.S. 331.

[125] Eyal Benvenisti, "Margin of Appreciation, Consensus, and Universal Standards," 31 N.Y.U. J. Int'l. L. & Pol. 843 (1999) 845–946.

[126] Statute of the International Court of Justice, art. 38(1)(b) 26 June 1945, 59 Stat. 1055, 33 U.N.T.S. 993.

[127] Martti Koskenniemi, "The Fate of Public International Law: Between Technique and Politics," 70 Modern L. Rev. 1 (2007) 4–5 (citing *Belilos v. Switzerland*, Eur. Ct. H.R., 132 Eur. Ct. H.R. 28, 60 (1988)).

[128] E.g., Reservations to the Convention on the Prevention and Punishment of the Crime of Genocide, Advisory Opinion, 1951 ICJ 15 (May 28) 24.

[129] Ryan Goodman, "Human Rights Treaties, Invalid Reservations, and State Consent," 96 Am. J. of Int'l. L. 531 (2002).

human rights obligations. This is because human rights treaties have been established to protect minorities.[130] Similarly, the peremptory norms of custom, which rely on a normative rather than consensus-based hierarchy, are supposed to counteract the expressions of sovereignty in international law that conflict with particularly important norms of behavior.[131]

Some commentators seek to dissolve the conflict between consensus and ethical normativity by "universalizing"[132] the norms themselves. Political strategies, diplomatic initiatives, agreement on certain explicit principles, and the conclusion of international accords, are all strategies to generate consensus around international human rights. Abdullahi An-Na'im, for example, suggests that "human rights are much more credible . . . if they are perceived to be legitimate within the various cultural traditions of the world."[133] The argument that the Universal Declaration of Human Rights constitutes customary international law follows in this vein. Its supporters usually evoke, not its superior moral persuasiveness (as one might expect), but rather the latent consensus present at its adoption by the General Assembly in 1948, or alternatively to be found in its later invocation by many of the world's courts and decision-makers.[134] Individual consent may be in tension with higher valued norms, but a broader consensus may nevertheless be generated and promoted to alter this fact. Thus, by grounding the interpretation of economic and social rights in a developing consensus, its validity across the varied regimes is better assured.

The norm of consensus operates in a similar way in constitutional law, by helping to secure the legitimacy and validity of constitutional norms. In constitutional theory, consensus operates to register the necessary degree of self-government of citizens of a constitutional polity. Alexander Bickel famously claimed that "coherent, stable—and *morally supportable*—government is possible only on the basis of consent."[135] More recent scholarship in constitutional theory points to the versions of wider cultural agreement that shift over time, but are always indirectly informing the interpretation of rights in constitutional adjudication.[136]

[130] *See*, e.g., Benvenisti, "Margin of Appreciation, Consensus, and Universal Standards," *supra* note 125, 850–3.

[131] Vienna Convention on the Law of Treaties art. 53, 23 May 1969, 1155 U.N.T.S. 331, 344; *see also* Restatement (Third) of the Foreign Relations Law of the United States § 102 cmt. k (1986). For these implications for arguments about a minimum core, *see* Chapter 3.

[132] Susan Waltz, "Universalizing Human Rights: The Role of Small States in the Construction of the *Universal Declaration of Human Rights*," 23 Hum. Rts. Q. 43 (2001) 45.

[133] Abdullahi Ahmed An-Na'im (ed.), *Human Rights in Cross-Cultural Perspectives: A Quest for Consensus* (1991), 3.

[134] Christian Tomuschat, *Human Rights: Between Idealism and Realism* (2nd edn., 2008) 63.

[135] Alexander M. Bickel, *The Least Dangerous Branch: The Supreme Court at the Bar of Politics* (2nd edn., 1986) 20.

[136] Robert C. Post, "Foreword: Fashioning the Legal Constitution: Culture, Courts and Law," 117 Harvard L. Rev. 4 (2003).

Consensualism also serves as an operational guide for other norms, rather than a norm for its own sake. In this view, the importance of consensus is due, not to its connection to the self-representation of the units expressing agreement, but rather to its ability to assist in the determination of normative principle. Here, consensus (and particularly international consensus) is important because it reveals the normative standards that evolve with reason. It is this use that Jeremy Waldron advocates in extolling the US Supreme Court's use of international and foreign law in interpreting the US Bill of Rights.[137] In (re)joining late an enterprise which many other national courts have long followed,[138] (and, indeed, which the Supreme Court itself had originally pursued[139]), the majority of the Court noted that trends in other countries could shed light on the constitutionality of the practice of capital punishment for juvenile offenders. It was significant to the question of constitutionality that the United States was an outlier in this practice.

Consensus here points to "a set of enduring intermediate principles that one might use as touchstones for real-world legal systems."[140] Such an approach harkens to the early aim, within international law, to represent the "common law of mankind." These principles—captured by the traditional concept of the law of nations, or *ius gentium*—reflect the common agreement on principles of (domestic) law which are demonstrated by the work of judges, jurists, and lawmakers from different parts of the world.[141] Because the relevant consensus remains incomplete and must be supplemented by a sense of justice to guide newer norms (a sense itself informed by the character of the consensus), the approach depends upon a reflective equilibrium between natural and positive law.[142] This equilibrium differs from the "overlapping consensus" of moral principles discussed in relation to the rationalist approach, precisely because of its connection to positive law.

(3) The limits of consensus

Whether necessary for sovereignty and self-government on the one hand, or for well-informed legality on the other, the consensualist approach to the interpretation of economic and social rights is beset by several limitations. In brief, the approach fails because it makes legitimate only the lowest

[137] *See* Waldron, "Foreign Law and the Modern *Ius Gentium*," *supra* note 92.

[138] *See*, e.g., Bangalore Principles, *infra*, discussed in Chapter 10.

[139] *See*, e.g., Sarah Cleveland, "Our International Constitution," Yale J. Int'l. L. 1 (2006).

[140] Waldron, "Foreign Law and the Modern *Ius Gentium*," *supra* note 92, 134 (citing St. Thomas Aquinas, *Summa Theologica* Pts. I–II, Q. 95, Art. 4, Reply I, 298 (R.J. Henle trans., 1993).

[141] Waldron, "Foreign Law and the Modern *Ius Gentium*," *supra* note 92, 132, 133, 137.

[142] Ibid., 136 (citing Rawls, *A Theory of Justice*, *supra* note 60, 48–51).

common denominator of international protection; a problem exacerbated by the relative dearth of explicit pronouncements on what the agreed formulations of economic and social rights are and what they should be. Moreover, consensualism founders on its inability to give appropriate guidance on the decision as to whose consensus is to count. Should be it judicial consensus as a special place for unfolding reason, or governmental and intergovernmental declarations as a more appropriate test for legitimate law (captured at a particular, normatively-charged moment or subject to ongoing development); or alternatively the consensus established between special experts in policy areas influencing economic and social rights (such as those drawn from public health, trade unions, businesses, education, housing, water resources, or land reform areas), who are more familiar with the institutions and organizations that constitute the concrete efforts to deliver on the material requirements behind rights?

The "lowest common denominator" implication is particularly problematic for approaching the content of economic and social rights. The dearth of agreement is due in part to the late secularization of the protection of material interests in human rights history compared with other categories (or "generations") of rights. Thus, although moral and humanist duties of material assistance were present within different religious expressions, their later secularization was delayed, partly by their purported incompatibility with the "rights" formulation.[143] The lack of consensus is also a feature of the ideological disagreements of the Cold War period, when Western governments worked actively to demote the importance of economic and social rights,[144] although it should be noted that this aspect of the historical record is contested.[145] The human rights NGOs headquartered in the West, including Human Rights Watch and Amnesty International, followed the lead of the Western governments in avoiding claims of economic and social rights in their human rights advocacy.[146]

Even with the end of the polarization of the Cold War, consensus continues to lead to conservative, general, and abstract expressions of the

[143] *See*, e.g., Micheline R. Ishay, *The Human Rights Reader: Major Political Writings, Essays, Speeches, and Documents From the Bible to the Present* (2nd edn., 2007).

[144] Philip Alston and Gerard Quinn, "The Nature and Scope of States Parties' Obligations under the International Covenant on Economic, Social and Cultural Rights," 9 Hum. Rts. Q. 156 (1987); Glendon, *A World Made New*, *supra* note 48, 115–17.

[145] Daniel J. Whelan and Jack Donnelly, "The West, Economic and Social Rights, and the Global Human Rights Regime: Setting the Record Straight," 29 Hum. Rts. Q. 908 (2007).

[146] Aryeh Neier, *Taking Liberties: Four Decades in the Struggle for Rights* (2005), p. xxx (founder of Human Rights Watch opposing the concept of economic and social rights as "profoundly undemocratic"); *see also* Kenneth Roth, "Defending Economic, Social and Cultural Rights: Practical Issues Faced by an International Human Rights Organization," 26 Hum. Rts. Q. 63 (2004) 65–72.

content of economic and social rights. Especially in the case of the justification for self-government, the most comprehensive version of agreement represents the thinnest or broadest (as well as lowest) common denominator. As a long-standing criticism of the treaty system makes clear, the requirement for consensus across different legal systems impedes a norm's progress and development. The abstraction and conservatism deemed necessary to encourage widespread ratification, for example, may diminish the entire exercise.[147] Practically, this leads to a bias towards the status quo, as well as to deliberately vague, uncontroversial, and unimaginative expressions. As one observer notes, the choices for international organizations, in normative development across widely variant legal, cultural, and economic reference points, are either to do nothing, or to do very little.[148] While there is promising potential for translating economic and social rights across fresh elaborations of non-Western traditions, such as within Confucian and Islamic thought,[149] the present pressure of consensus may distort the duties embodied in those traditions. This translation relies on the pluralism internal to—as well as external to—each ethical tradition. As postmodern and postcolonial scholars have long described, non-Western traditions have competing versions of the more accurate, or more compelling formulation, of their ethical requirements. Yet the resulting consensus may also be more "declared" than "lived,"[150] and move too far from traditional or current practices to be plausible within it.

Moreover, a requirement for consensus fails to meet its own standards for self-government and equality by leading to the paradox (in the case of unanimous requirements) that if 1 percent of the community does not subscribe to a consensus, it fails to succeed, in which case the opinion of 99 percent is violated.[151] Replacing unanimity requirements with majority consensus presents its own paradox because of the inevitable tendency to prejudice the minority articulation of rights. As we have seen, the claims of minorities, which may be overborne by majority interests in majoritarian

[147] *See* Bruno Simma, "Consent: Strains in the Treaty System," in R. St. J. Macdonald and Douglas M. Johnston (eds.), *The Structure and Process of International Law* (1983) 485, 494.

[148] Andrew Byrnes, "Toward More Effective Enforcement of Women's Human Rights through the Use of International Human Rights Law and Procedures," in Rebecca J. Cook (ed.), *Human Rights of Women: National and International Perspectives* (1994) 189, 202.

[149] Joshua Cohen, "Minimalism about Human Rights: The Most We Can Hope For?," 12 *J. Pol. Phil.* 190 (2004) 192 at 205, 208 and sources cited therein; *see generally* Micheline Ishay, *The Human Rights Reader*, *supra* note 143, xv–xix, 1–72.

[150] Kirsten Hastrup, "Representing the Common Good: The Limits of Legal Language," in Richard Ashby Wilson and Jon P. Mitchell (eds.), *Human Rights in Global Perspective: Anthropological Studies of Rights, Claims and Entitlements* (2003) 16, 16–17.

[151] *See also* Martti Koskenniemi, *From Apology to Utopia: the Structure of International Legal Argument* (rev. edn., 2005) 310.

democratic systems, are a main reason for the existence of rights.[152] This returns us to the argument that the very design of the international system of human rights is to counter the shortcomings of a consent-based system, rather than support consensus at all costs.

If the limits of consensualism are different for national systems of law, it is a difference in degree and not in kind. It is the pluralism which exists across different national (and sub-national) systems that leads to abstract and broad versions of consensus in international law. The same pluralism is a feature of modern constitutional politics, although in a less exaggerated form (since the diversity of the world's cultural traditions is not represented in any single nation). For the constitutional legitimacy which is linked to self-government, we rely on broad and capacious expressions of consensus rather than narrow determinants. There are evident contradictions in distilling a concrete content for economic and social rights consistent with these trends towards breadth and abstraction.

If we take a more realist view of how and where consensus is achieved in international and national policy debates, we may become even more uneasy. Official agreements are heavily influenced by compromise rather than genuine participation (let alone reason). Sometimes, the compromise tends towards coercion. This criticism applies to the field of constitutional law-making, where the shortcomings of legislative, administrative, and judicial expressions of "consensus" have been long-standing objects of empirical study.[153] In the same way, this criticism applies to the burgeoning and less studied field of international law-making, including the work of international organizations, supranational tribunals, and the more informal transnational conferences and expertise-sharing, which constitute the global consensus.[154]

Indeed, the influence of economists' theories of liberalization and deregulation, ubiquitous in the restructuring and structural adjustment environment of the 1990s, are more visible, and yet less legitimate instantiations of consensus in the international environment. During this period, the macroeconomic strategies of the "Washington consensus" converged on the desirability of growth strategies that would remove economic and social entitlements and thus harm the poor—at least in the short term.[155] The

[152] Benvenisti, "Margin of Appreciation, Consensus, and Universal Standards," *supra* note 125, 850.

[153] *See* Henry M. Hart Jr. and Albert M. Sacks, *The Legal Process: Basic Problems in the Making and Application of Law* (1958) (William N. Eskridge, Jr and Philip P. Frickey, eds., 1994).

[154] Abram Chayes et al., *International Legal Process* (2 vols., 1968); Harold Hongju Koh, "Review Essay: Why Do Nations Obey International Law?," 106 Yale L.J. 2599 (1997).

[155] Joseph E. Stiglitz, *Globalization and Its Discontents* (2002), at 11–16, 73–4, 134–42; *see also* David P. Forsythe and Eric A. Heinze, "On the Margins of the Human Rights Discourse: Foreign Policy and

neoliberal blueprints were influential in informing regime change in the transitioning post-communist states. They were also a key component of the structural reforms and poverty-reduction strategies in development projects, which were prerequisites for the award of loans or debt relief.[156] More recent disturbances of the global financial system have led to the adoption of austerity measures that immediately restrict the economic security of the poor.[157] The "consensus" on structural reforms is empirically apt, even if it hides the real motivations behind the adoption of such policies.

It is perhaps no coincidence that the overtly state-oriented commentary of the Committee drifted away from state practice during the 1990s, or at least looked for broader instantiations of consensus than those offered by evidence of states' convergence on neoliberal economic policies. Counter-examples from state practice were available—sometimes expressed by national courts defending their constitutional regimes against the reforms promoted by the executive at the instigation of the international financial institutions. For example, Kim Lane Scheppele has described the Hungarian Constitutional Court's rejection of internationally prescribed market reforms, based on constitutional economic and social rights, and has analyzed why such a result was not forthcoming in Russia.[158] And the "chastening" of the economic prescriptions in light of empirical evidence[159] suggests that the driving ideas of this period were not in fact expressions of consensus, but rather deviations from longer-term and truer instantiations. Lawrence Sager, writing about American constitutional law, promotes a similar critique with respect to the retrogression in US welfare policy in recent years.[160] He argues that a long-term view can "blunt the force of contemporary political currents,"[161] while still paying heed to an underlying constitutional consensus.

Recourse to the long-term view leaves consensus on uncertain ground. When is a consensus "truly" given, and when is it a deviation? Are there

International Welfare Rights," in Rhoda E. Howard-Hassman and Claude E. Welch Jr. (eds.), *Economic Rights in Canada and the United States* (2006) 55, 63.

[156] E.g., Peter Uvin, *Human Rights and Development* (2004); Frances Stewart and Michael Wang, "Poverty Reduction Strategy Papers within the Human Rights Perspective," in Alston and Robinson (eds.), *Human Rights and Development*, *supra* note 30, 447, 462–70.

[157] World Bank, *The World Bank Group's Response to the Global Crisis: Update on an Ongoing IEG Evaluation (Evaluation Brief 8)*, Independent Evaluation Group (2009).

[158] E.g., Kim Lane Scheppele, "A Realpolitik Defense of Social Rights," 82 Texas L. Rev. 1921 (2004).

[159] *See* David M. Trubek and Alvaro Santos (eds.), *The New Law and Economic Development: A Critical Appraisal* (2006); *see also* Dani Rodrik, *One Economics, Many Recipes: Globalization, Institutions, and Economic Growth* (2007).

[160] Sager, *Justice in Plain Clothes*, *supra* note 118, 158–9.

[161] Ibid., 158.

other norms more relevant to the interpretation of the right, such as the quality of reasoning (as we saw was featured in the rationalist approach), in place of the quantity of belief?[162] In the end, these features suggest an important insight: namely, that focusing on consensus alone thwarts the definition of economic and social rights. There is good reason to explore other rationales, both because consensus pulls the content too broadly and thinly, and because both of its theoretical promises—of self-governing pluralism in both international and constitutional law, and of epistemic power in the clarification of correct applications of principles—prove elusive. Perhaps consensus merely popularizes the inquiry.

C. BLURRING THE DISTINCTION

Our discussion of rationalism and consensualism has highlighted rival views of the nature of economic and social rights and how those responsible for interpretation—judges, legislators, policy-makers, advocates—should approach the challenge of interpreting them. On the surface, these positions make different assumptions about the criteria that an interpretation of each right ought to satisfy. Rationalism appears to identify the substantive values that economic and social rights ought to advance, such as freedom or dignity or life. Consensualism appears to value less substantive considerations, such as the completeness of the participation of the relevant community, in agreeing upon the meaning of economic and social rights. In rating participation so highly, this interpretive standpoint itself upholds a substantive value—of participation.

Clear examples of the rationalist and consensualist standpoints are distinguishable. Nonetheless, I do not claim that exercises of interpretation fall on one or the other side of a categorical divide. The rationalist standpoint cannot depart entirely from consensus, and the consensualist standpoint gives latent support for rational argument.

Rational ethical argument must acknowledge the importance of consensus. For a rational argument to be made, it must rely on generally accepted linguistic practice; and for a rational argument to produce law, it must rely on the agreement of those that accord it that status. Indeed, what is rational may actually take its shape from the need to persuade, over time,[163] thus collapsing any sharp distinction between reason and consensus. Moreover, what is rational may also be molded on the need for effectiveness and stability, in law.[164]

[162] *Cf.* Shue, *Basic Rights*, *supra* note 1, 73. *See also* Thomas M. Franck, *Fairness in International Law and Institutions* (1995).

[163] Michael Walzer, *Interpretation and Social Criticism* (1987) 47–8.

[164] John Rawls, *A Theory of Justice*, *supra* note 60, 455.

Similarly, even the most consensus-based standpoints must acknowledge the importance of reason. Interpretations that conflict grossly with rationalism are unlikely to be accepted as consensus. For example, certain reservations for human rights treaties are simply unable to be made; certain viewpoints of constitutional rights are simply unacceptable.

In view of this area of overlap, the division between rationalism and consensualism may define not polar opposites of economic and social rights interpretation, but rather regions of interpretive guidance that are given priority. Moreover, in revealing these areas of common overlap, the similarities between rationalism and consensus also reveal an important flaw. Neither approach conceives of how the interpreter is situated in relation to the act of interpretation—the position and values of judges, for example, or of United Nations Committee members, or of claimants with a certain experience of material deprivation. I suggest that the anticipated meaning of economic and social rights depends not only upon a general interpretive standpoint, such as rationalism or consensualism, but upon who the interpreters are likely to be. Both rationalism and consensualism may lead to abstract interpretations that fail to resonate with rights-claimants, or to provide an indication of how priorities should connect with programs, or to give a reliable measure for effective enforcement or supervision in positive law.

This demand is partly answered by taking an institutional perspective, and acknowledging the constraints that operate differently on courts, committee members, legislators, officials, and advocates. Indeed, this is an important area of distinction between international human rights law, and constitutional law, which, up until now, have been treated as complementary.[165] It becomes significant as to whether those activities are taking place within or outside a single nation-state frame.

The rationalist link between people's material interests and important values may be the same, despite the institution in which they choose to lodge their claim. The need for consensus over the interpretation given may also be the same, whether the hearing is made in court, or before a Parliament, Congress or Assembly, or at an international Committee. What is different may be the institutional constraints of interpreters. There may be a pressure to adopt minimalist interpretations of the legal obligations that flow from economic and social rights; there may also be pressure to allow for limits. These are pressing in the constitutional context. It is to these interpretive activities that we now turn.

[165] Neuman, "Human Rights and Constitutional Rights," *supra* note 123, 1868–69. *See further* Chapter 10.

3

Interpreting the Minimum

The pressure that legal institutions face in interpreting economic and social rights is often expressed as the pressure to determine the minimum content of each right. A minimalist focus applied to rights asks: what is "the least that every person can demand and the least that every person, every government, and every corporation must be made to do,"[1] given present-day constraints? Hence, the interpretation of minima is not addressed to the great aspirations of an ideal system of justice, but rather to the most basic interests common to the experience of being human, and how they might be expressed as rights.[2] By paying attention to such constraints, a "minimalist" rights strategy implies that maximum gain to rights is sometimes achieved by minimizing goals.

Interpreting the minimum of economic and social rights is compatible with ethical pluralism. It is an outlook capable of accommodating the fact that "people from different cultures may continue to disagree about what is good, but nevertheless agree about what is insufferably, unarguably wrong."[3] In this sense, the minimalist standpoint connects with the consensualist position discussed in Chapter 2. A universal assent amongst the many religious, philosophical, ethical, and political traditions may be possible: yet only "if the universalism implied is self-consciously minimalist."[4] Nonetheless, a high degree of consensus may not necessarily correlate to a minimum definition. One human rights commentator argues that only suffering which is unmerited and caused by gross physical cruelty is within a minimalist interpretation of rights. In this narrow view, the suffering that is caused by material deprivation does not represent minimalism.[5] Others disagree, suggesting that economic and social rights are wholly

[1] Henry Shue, *Basic Rights: Subsistence, Affluence and U.S. Foreign Policy* (2nd edn., 1996), xi.

[2] Ibid.

[3] Michael Ignatieff, "Human Rights as Ideology," in Amy Gutmann (ed.), *Human Rights as Politics and Idolatry* (2001) 53, 56.

[4] Michael Ignatieff, "Dignity and Aging," in Gutman, ibid., 101, 173.

[5] Ignatieff, "Human Rights as Ideology," *supra* note 3.

within minimalist rights interpretations, and that the presence or absence of active cruelty is beside the point.[6]

Propelling these substantive debates are more pragmatic demands. Those who favor a downward pressure on rights interpretation suggest that more expansive interpretations may be too costly to be realized, may threaten to overburden the resources required to monitor and enforce rights, or may set in train an undesirable substitution of narrow legal principles for looser political judgments, such as the unfocused claims of "rights talk."[7]

Interpreting minima thus fits within the institutional constraints that occur in the diverse sites in which economic and social rights are claimed and decided. First, international legal decision-makers can accommodate their limited institutional authority by appearing to make only the most minimal interpretation available. Second, judges, whether domestic or international, can accommodate the pressure for their rulings to be narrow and be meant only for the circumstances of a particular case. Third, administrative decision-makers are able to discharge their official discretion which is limited in scope for democratic reasons, especially at the lower levels of a bureaucracy. It is no wonder that a doctrinal counterpoint to a minimalist standpoint was articulated relatively early in the field of application of economic and social rights. This was the introduction of the doctrine of the "minimum core" by the United Nations Committee on Economic and Social Rights ("the Committee"), more than two decades ago.

A. THE MINIMUM CORE IN INTERNATIONAL HUMAN RIGHTS LAW

The "minimum core" seeks to establish a minimum legal substance for the economic and social rights under the International Covenant on Economic, Social and Cultural Rights ("ICESCR").[8] By focusing on the "minimum essential levels" of food, health, housing, and education,[9] the concept seeks to avoid deontological excess. The focus on a minimum core trades rights inflation for rights ambition, channeling the attention of advocates towards the severest cases of material deprivation and treating these as violations by states towards their own citizens or even to those individuals

[6] Shue, *Basic Rights*, *supra* note 1; Joshua Cohen, "Minimalism about Human Rights: The Most We Can Hope For?," 12 *J. Pol. Phil.* 190 (2004) 192.

[7] For a discussion of "rights talk," *see* Chapter 8.

[8] *See* UN Economic and Social Council (ECOSOC), Committee on Economic, Social and Cultural Rights, *Report on the Fifth Session, Supp. No. 3*, Annex III ¶ 10, UN Doc. E/1991/23 (1991) ["*General Comment No. 3*"].

[9] Ibid.

outside their territorial reach. Since 1990, the Committee has used the "minimum core" to give substance to the ICESCR's enumerated rights to food, health, and education,[10] and the emerging right to water.[11]

Commentators have also proposed the minimum core as the doctrine to guide the interpretation of the economic and social rights protected in other international human rights instruments, such as children's rights and the rights guaranteed within the Inter-American human rights system.[12] The Committee itself has applied the minimum core to numerous fields of legal relations, not only to its supervision of national systems of political–economic organization, but also to its supervision of States Parties' individual (and collective) activities in development[13] and security regimes.[14] For example, the Committee has required "national and international developmental policies including anti-poverty strategies" to respect a minimum core or risk noncompliance with the ICESCR.[15] In sanctions policy, too, punitive measures must be designed to protect the minimum core of the economic and social rights of vulnerable populations, in areas such as food, pharmaceuticals, and sanitation supplies. Otherwise, parties to the sanctions are liable in international law, making them noncompliant with human rights, which is usually the same charge as the one they are making against the governing elite to which they are applying political and economic pressure.[16]

[10] *See*, e.g., ECOSOC, Committee on Economic, Social and Cultural Rights, *General Comment No. 14: The Right to the Highest Attainable Standard of Health (art. 12 of the ICESCR)*, UN Doc. E/C.12/2004 (11 August 2000), ¶ 43 ["*General Comment No. 14*"]; ECOSOC, Committee on Economic, Social and Cultural Rights, *General Comment No. 13: The Right to Education (art. 13)*, ¶ 57, UN Doc. E/C.12/1999/10 (8 December 1999) ["*General Comment No. 13*"]; ECOSOC, Committee on Economic, Social and Cultural Rights, *General Comment No. 12: The Right to Adequate Food (art. 11)*, ¶ 8, UN Doc. E/C.12/1999/5 (12 May 1999) ["*General Comment No. 12*"].

[11] ECOSOC, Committee on Economic, Social and Cultural Rights, *General Comment No. 15: The Right to Water (arts. 11, 12)*, UN Doc. E/C.12/2002/11 (20 January 2003), ¶ 37 ["*General Comment No. 15*"].

[12] *See*, e.g., Thomas Hammarberg, *Children, in Economic, Social and Cultural Rights*, in Asbjørn Eide, Catarina Krause, and Allen Rosas (eds.), *Economic, Social and Cultural Rights: A Textbook* (2nd edn., 2001) 353, 366–7 (Convention on the Rights of the Child); Tara Melish, *Protecting Economic, Social and Cultural Rights in the Inter-American Human Rights System: A Manual on Presenting Claims* (Inter-American Commission on Human Rights 2002) 170–1.

[13] *General Comment No. 15*, *supra* note 11, ¶ 38; *General Comment No. 14*, *supra* note 10, ¶¶ 39–40, 45; ECOSOC, Committee on Economic, Social and Cultural Rights., *Substantive Issues Arising in the Implementation of the International Covenant on Economic, Social and Cultural Rights: Poverty and the International Covenant on Economic, Social and Cultural Rights*, UN Doc. No. E/C.12/2001/10 (10 May 2001), ¶ 17 ["*Statement: Poverty and the Covenant*"].

[14] ECOSOC, Committee on Economic, Social and Cultural Rights, *General Comment No. 8: The Relationship Between Economic Sanctions and Respect for Economic, Social and Cultural Rights*, ¶ 7, UN Doc. E/C.12/1997/8 (12 December 1997) ["*General Comment No. 8*"].

[15] *Statement: Poverty and the Covenant*, *supra* note 13, ¶ 17.

[16] *General Comment No. 8*, *supra* note 14.

(1) *Early criticisms*

The minimum core doctrine seeks to achieve rights protection through rights minimalism. Yet, rights ambition is a difficult stance, and even minimalist ambitions can be misplaced. Critics of the doctrine of the "minimum core" have suggested that paring down such rights to an essential core threatens the broader goals of economic and social rights, or pretends a determinacy that does not exist.[17] A long-standing criticism faults the minimum core approach for directing our attention only to the performance of developing states, leaving the legal discourse of economic and social rights beyond the reach of those facing material deprivation in middle or high income countries and diminishing the reputation of even-handedness within the Committee.[18] A more recent criticism points to the doctrine's tendency to rank different claimants of rights, while ignoring the more salient assessment of rights versus macroeconomic growth or defense policies.[19]

Preliminary conceptual questions remain unanswered. Is the minimum core in Mali the same as the minimum core in Canada?[20] This question divides those who advocate for a distinction between a relative (state-specific) minimum core for richer countries and an "absolute" universal one to be respected by all states, and those who suggest that such a distinction undermines the universality of human rights.[21] If country-specific, is it otherwise context-sensitive or context-blind?[22] Is it a more general or more precise instantiation of the parent right?[23] Again, there is a

[17] E.g., Brigit Toebes, "The Right to Health," in Eide, Krause, and Rosas, *Economic, Social and Cultural* Rights, *supra* note 12, 169, 176.

[18] *See* Matthew Craven, *The International Covenant on Economic, Social, and Cultural Rights: A Perspective on its Development* (1995) 143–4, 152.

[19] Karin Lehmann, "In Defense of the Constitutional Court: Litigating Economic and Social Rights and the Myth of the Minimum Core," 22 Am. U. Int'l L. Rev. 163 (2006).

[20] *Compare* Asbjørn Eide, "Economic, Social and Cultural Rights as Human Rights," in Eide, Krause, and Rosas, *Economic, Social and Cultural Rights*, *supra* note 12, 9, 27 with Craig Scott and Philip Alston, "Adjudicating Constitutional Priorities in a Transnational Context: A Comment on Soobramoney's Legacy and *Grootboom's* Promise," 16 S. Afr. J. Hum. Rts. 206 (2000) 250.

[21] Fons Coomans, "In Search of the Core Content of the Right to Education," in Danie Brand and Sage Russell (eds.), *Exploring the Core Content of Economic and Social Rights: South African and International Perspectives* (2002) 159, 167; Geraldine Van Bueren, "Of Floors and Ceilings: Minimum Core Obligations and Children," in *Exploring the Core Content*, ibid., 183, 184.

[22] *Compare* Coomans, *supra* note 21, 180 with Danie Brand, "The Minimum Core Content of the Right to Food in Context: A Response to Rolf Künneman," in *Exploring the Core Content*, ibid., 99, 106.

[23] *Compare* David Bilchitz, *Poverty and Fundamental Rights: The Justification and Enforcement of Socio-Economic Rights* (2007) 198 with Scott and Alston, "Adjudicating Constitutional Priorities in a Transnational Context," *supra* note 20, 250.

division of opinion on the validity of the claims of universality within the concept, and how such claims may obstruct its application.

As applied, the doctrine is no less problematic. The Committee has, since 1990, variously equated the minimum core with a presumptive legal entitlement, a non-derogable obligation, and the foundation of extraterritorial liability. In the first category, it follows that states are held responsible for infringing a determined minimum, unless "every effort has been made to use all resources that are at its disposal to satisfy, as a matter of priority, those minimum obligations."[24] In the second, "a State party cannot, under any circumstances whatsoever, justify its non-compliance with . . . core obligations . . . which are non-derogable"[25] and which "continue to exist in situations of conflict, emergency and natural disaster."[26] And in the third, the obligations flowing from the minimum core make it "particularly incumbent on all those in a position to assist, to provide 'international assistance and cooperation, especially economic and technical' to enable developing countries to fulfil" their minimum core.[27] Under this understanding, the burden raised by the minimum core may require the state to prove, in order to escape liability, that it has unsuccessfully sought international support to ensure the realization of the right.[28] The three categorizations are, of course, incompatible.

One response to these conceptual and doctrinal criticisms is to jettison the concept of the minimum core. Some commentators have urged this course of action. In some cases, these critics take positions of skepticism, which would apply to both a "minimum core" and to rights in general—first, that "universality" in the claims of differentially situated people is an impossible goal, and, second, that contextualized claims, advanced locally, are too complex to be addressed by the discourse and institutions of rights. In other cases, critics are quick to express support for the relative latitude of the economic and social rights framework, but criticism of the doctrinal constraint of a minimum core.[29] Such a concept, they suggest, contributes

[24] *General Comment No. 3, supra* note 8, ¶ 10. *See* Chapter 4 for discussion of limitations.

[25] *General Comment No. 14, supra* note 10 ¶ 47.

[26] *Statement: Poverty and Covenant, supra* note 13, ¶ 18; *General Comment No. 14, supra* note 10, ¶ 45. *See*, e.g., Report of the Special Rapporteur of the UN Commission on Human Rights on the situation of human rights in Kuwait under Iraqi occupation, UN Doc. E/CN.4/1992/26, para 52 (endorsing minimum core obligations as non-derogable).

[27] *Statement: Poverty and Covenant, supra* note 13, ¶¶ 16, 18. The Covenant refers to "international assistance and cooperation," or similar formulations, in arts. 2.1, 11.2, 15.4, 22, and 23.

[28] E.g., *General Comment No. 12, supra* note 10, ¶ 17; *see also* Eide, "Economic, Social and Cultural Rights," *supra* note 20, at 27; *see also Statement: Poverty and the Covenant, supra* note 13, ¶ 16.

[29] *See*, e.g., Erika de Wet, *The Constitutional Enforceability of Economic and Social Rights* (1996) 96; Lehmann, "In Defense of the Constitutional Court," *supra* note 19.

to juridical confusion in international human rights law and will create similar problems in national legal systems.[30]

(2) *Three accomplishments*

The conceptual criticisms provoke more than conceptual interest. Nonetheless, it is important to contextualize them in light of the doctrine's intended and actual roles. In international human rights law, the concept anticipates three accomplishments. For those attempting to give legal bite to the standard of obligation established by the ICESCR, the minimum core initiates a common legal standard that can control the inherent relativism of the programmatic standard of "progressive realization" set out in the text of the ICESCR.[31] The obligation to "progressively realize" economic and social rights, which distinguishes the ICESCR from other human rights instruments, gives States Parties the latitude to implement rights over time depending upon the availability of necessary resources, rather than requiring them to guarantee rights immediately.[32] Nevertheless, the Committee has insisted that the "progressive realization" of the ICESCR rights requires the taking of "deliberate, concrete and targeted" steps.[33] The minimum core aims to provide an understanding of the direction that the steps should follow and indicate when they become retrogressive.[34] The Committee has linked retrogression to moves away from full realization, rather than moves below any minimum. However, there are unexplored parallels between the ratcheting effect of the standard of retrogression and a state-specific minimum core. The minimum core would offer some conceptual assistance in imposing accountability for deliberately retrogressive measures.[35] This connects with the goal of proposing a more rigorous signal for noncompliance in incidences of failure to fulfil the minimum core, which has been suggested as one of "violations" under the ICESCR.[36]

[30] Tara Melish, "Rethinking the 'Less as More' Thesis: Supranational Litigation of the Economic, Social, and Cultural Rights in the Americas," 39 N.Y.U. J. Int'l. L. & Pol. 171 (2006) 178 n. 13.

[31] *See* Philip Alston, "Out of the Abyss? The Challenges Confronting the New U.N. Committee on Economic, Social and Cultural Rights," 9 Hum. Rts. Q. 332 (1987) 359–60.

[32] *See* International Covenant on Economic, Social and Cultural Rights, 16 December 1966, 993 U.N.T.S. 3 (entered into force 3 January 1976), art. 2(1); *cf.* International Covenant on Civil and Political Rights, art. 2, adopted 19 December 1966, S. Exec. Doc. E, 95–2 (1978), 999 U.N.T.S. 171 (entered into force 23 March 1976), *available at* <http://www2.ohchr.org/english/law/ccpr.htm> ["ICCPR"]. For the adoption of "progressive realization" in national formulations, *see*, e.g., S. Afr. Const., §§ 26(2), 27(2).

[33] *General Comment No. 3*, ¶ 9.

[34] Ibid.

[35] Craven, *The International Covenant*, *supra* note 18, 131–2.

[36] Audrey R. Chapman, "A 'Violations Approach' for Monitoring the International Covenant on Economic, Social and Cultural Rights," 18 Hum. Rts. Q. 23 (1996).

Secondly, for those hoping to provide an objective standard across different state systems of political economy, the minimum core concept purports to advance a baseline of socioeconomic protection across varied economic policies and vastly different levels of available resources.[37] The 160 States Parties to the ICESCR represent much of the present-day diversity in choices of political and socioeconomic ordering. For advocates worried about commandeering sovereign macroeconomic choice, a minimum content for economic and social rights would seem to limit (if not eliminate) this risk by increasing the scope for states to pursue their own "particular form of government,"[38] through setting minimum standards within the human rights framework.[39]

Thirdly, for commentators wishing to introduce a manageable legal impetus into global redistributive debates, the minimalist connotations of the minimum core concept signal an acceptable moderation. Advocates from the development field suggested in the 1980s that minimum standards would provide the basis for a more progressive, if restrained, redistribution of resources rather than more extensive efforts, placating the self-interest of developed states.[40] These commentators also sought to delimit economic and social entitlements to their barest forms in order to avoid the disruption of production incentives, which could work against their practical success. In employing now ubiquitous economic forecasting, they warned that "[a]brupt, overambitious attempts at large scale redistribution might produce disincentives to production and attendant dislocations to the point where the position of the least advantaged might in fact be lowered."[41]

While the logic of these three arguments continues to hold, the first and the second are accompanied by traces of anachronism. When advocates today claim "retrogression" in debates about economic and social rights, they are more concerned with establishing the deliberateness of the state policy or its causal effect, rather than whether it has impacted some essential minimum.[42] Thus, a more compelling debate is focused on whether

[37] *See*, e.g., The Limburg Principles on the Implementation of the International Covenant on Economic, Social and Cultural Rights, UN Doc. E/CN.4/1987/17, Annex, *reprinted in* (1987) 9 Hum. Rts. Q. 122, 126; *see also* The Maastricht Guidelines on Violations of Economic, Social and Cultural Rights, ¶ 9–10, UN Doc. E/C.12/2000/13, *reprinted in* (1998) 20 Hum. Rts. Q. 694.

[38] *General Comment No. 3, supra* note 8, ¶ 8.

[39] Matthew Craven, "The Protection of Economic, Social and Cultural Rights under the Inter-American System of Human Rights," in David J. Harris and Stephen Livingstone (eds.), *The Inter-American System of Human Rights* (1998) 289, 316.

[40] Bård-Anders Andreassen, Tor Skålnes, Alan G. Smith, and Hugo Stokke, "Assessing Human Rights Performance in Developing Countries: The Case for a Minimal Threshold Approach to the Economic and Social Rights," in *Human Rights in Developing Countries 1987/1988: A Yearbook on Human Rights in Countries Receiving Narcotic Aid* (1988) 333, 342.

[41] Ibid., 341–2.

[42] *General Comment No. 3 supra* note 8, ¶ 9.

deliberateness necessarily connotes an intention to reduce the enjoyment of economic and social rights,[43] or is instanced by official disrespect and other state behaviour.[44] Similarly, when advocates of the minimum core today assert its modesty in relation to States Parties' sovereign political–economic choices, they are usually aware that many policies have been conditioned by international financial institutions rather than states themselves and that "sovereignty" is often more respected in the breach. Such international institutions have self-professed missions to "guide the economic trajectory of entire nations."[45] Moreover, the pressures of global exports and trade, as well as transnational production, have produced universal (if uneven) influences on national social and economic policy.[46] The global impact of the crisis in financial markets of 2008 exposed the extent of this reach.

I suggest that the third argument, along global redistributive lines, holds the most relevance for contemporary debates. Although the legal support for the Committee's recent assertion that the minimum core gives rise to "national responsibilities for all States, and international responsibilities for developed States, as well as others that are "in a position to assist" [47] requires more analysis, one can see why a minimum legal standard would be a prerequisite. The Committee's system of liability makes states that are in a position to assist in the protection of the minimum core liable for not doing so, based on the cogency of a legal minimum. States that are unable to deliver the minimum core to their citizens may resist sanction if they sought international support that was not forthcoming.[48]

Legal support for this inquiry rests on the obligation to provide "international assistance and cooperation"[49] in the collective realization of economic

[43] *Office of the UN High Comm'r for Human Rights, Economic, Social and Cultural Rights: Handbook for National Human Rights Institutions,* at 28, UN Doc. HR/P/PT/12 UN Sales No. E.04.XIV.8 (2005).

[44] Thomas Pogge, *World Poverty and Human Rights: Cosmopolitan Responsibilities and Reforms* (2nd edn., 2008). For a variety of government positions, from intransigence, incompetence to inattentiveness, *see* Chapter 6.

[45] James M. Cypher and James L. Dietz, *The Process of Economic Development* (2nd edn., 2004) 516; *see also* Joseph E. Stiglitz, *Globalization and Its Discontents* (2002).

[46] David Held and Anthony McGrew (eds.), *Governing Globalization: Power, Authority and Global Governance* (2002); World Bank, *The World Bank Group's Response to the Global Crisis: Update on an Ongoing IEG Evaluation (Evaluation Brief 8)*, Independent Evaluation Group (2009).

[47] *Statement: Poverty and the Covenant, supra* note 13, ¶ 16.

[48] E.g., *General Comment No. 12, supra* note 10, ¶ 17.

[49] ICESCR, art. 2(1), *supra* note 32. *See also* the reference to international cooperation in art. 11 (the right to adequate standard of living and, in particular, the right to food and to be free from hunger); art. 15(4) (cooperation in the scientific and cultural fields); and arts. 22–23 (the role of the specialized agencies and other forms of international action). *See also* UN Charter arts. 55, 56; Sigrun I. Skogly, *Beyond National Borders: States' Human Rights Obligations in International Cooperation* (2006) 83–98.

and social rights under the ICESCR. A minimalist definition of economic and social rights is needed to mediate the legal, as well as political and philosophical,[50] challenges of holding states accountable for the socio-economic deprivations experienced by citizens of or individuals in other states. Alternatively, legality stems from the core's status (which is itself highly contestable) as customary international law, and even as treaty-overriding *jus cogens*. Indeed, the ideal of peremptory norms, which are given a higher value than other norms in international law, is an important piece of the puzzle of the minimum core's origins. Like the peremptory norms against genocide or crimes against humanity, the minimum core of economic and social rights is suggested by some to be non-derogable in character. That is, no law or policy can override it. This urge to rank norms, against the trend of consensus,[51] evokes the tensions discussed in Chapter 2.

(3) Core obligations

In an effort to delineate between rights and duties, and focus attention upon its supervisory competence for the latter, the Committee has begun to formulate the "core obligations" rather than the "minimum core content" of economic and social rights. This approach investigates whether a minimum obligation of performance (not outcome), or a minimum set of obligations of performance, can correlate to the minimum core. The shift to obligations reflects two constructive points in the economic and social rights canon. The first is that a focus on the duties required to implement rights, rather than the outcomes envisaged by the rights, enables the analysis of realistic and institutionally informed strategies for rights protection. That is, a focus on obligations points the way to the solutions for "what it actually takes to enable people to be secure against the standard, predictable threats to their rights."[52] The second reason for the shift to obligations is that analysis of the duties that correlate to each right confronts the erroneous dichotomy of "positive" and "negative" rights, making clear how all rights—civil, political, economic, social, and cultural—contain correlative duties to both ("negatively") refrain from, as well as ("positively") perform, certain acts in certain circumstances. This analysis illuminates the equally significant point that the "negative" nonintervention duties are not, a priori, more

[50] *See* Joshua Cohen and Charles Sabel, "*Extra Rempublicam Nulla Justitia?*," 34 *Phil. & Pub. Aff.* 147 (2006) (replying to the statism of Thomas Nagel, "The Problem of Global Justice," 33 *Phil. & Pub. Aff.* 113 (2005)).

[51] For a seminal expression, *see* Prosper Weil, "Towards Relative Normativity in International Law?," 77 Am. J. Int'l L. 413 (1983).

[52] Shue, *Basic Rights*, *supra* note 1, 160.

important than the "positive."[53] Thus, "core obligations" are both negative and positive and are actively addressed to both judicial and other legal institutional settings.

This insight can explain the Committee's departure from its earlier project to identify the minimum core obligation via a gradualist and consensus-informed starting point, to its present efforts to produce a template of "core obligations" that straddle different rights, duties of positive provision, and wider institutional strategies. The Committee now uses the "core obligations" list to outline the necessary steps of "operationalizing" rights, which attempts to circumvent the difficult questions of the outcome-oriented content of legal entitlement. In some ways, this has introduced a more technical vocabulary around "core obligations" which seeks both to guide state action and to signal "violations" under the ICESCR.[54]

The Committee's first attempt to enumerate the basic "core" obligations of economic and social rights leaned heavily on the "organizing principles" that would be necessary to substantiate the content of each right in more concrete terms. These principles focused on the availability, accessibility, and quality of the material good relating to each right. Those who have utilized these operational principles make a distinction between their operation in policy, and their operation in law, suggesting that their impact is greatest in directing the former, and less useful for directing law.[55] In later Comments, the Committee continues to reference the operational principles of availability, accessibility and quality, although no longer in reference to "core obligations."[56]

In the case of the right to health, for example, the Committee's General Comment prioritizes the declarations of international experts in health, population, and development, and refers to the mutually supporting rights of access to food, shelter, housing, sanitation, and potable water.[57] One "core obligation" is to provide essential drugs defined under the World Health Organization ("WHO") Action Programme on Essential Drugs;[58]

[53] For further discussion, *see infra* Chapter 6, section C(1). This is nevertheless contentious. *See* Cecile Fabre, *Social Rights under the Constitution: Government and the Decent Life* (2000), at 47–9 (suggesting the doctrine of acts and omissions intuits that, in most cases, negative duties are more important).

[54] Chapman, *supra* note 36, (proposing the "violations approach" as a more rigorous signal of non-compliance for the failure to fulfill minimum core obligations).

[55] ECOSOC, Comm. on Human Rights, Economic, Social and Cultural Rights: The Right of Everyone to the Enjoyment of the Highest Attainable Standard of Physical and Mental Health, ¶¶ 33–40, UN Doc. (ek) E/CN.4/2004/Add.1 (1 March 2004) (*prepared by* Special Rapporteur Paul Hunt) ["ECOSOC, Right to Health"]

[56] *General Comment No. 15, supra* note 11, ¶ 12; *General Comment No. 14, supra* note 10, ¶ 12. *See also* ECOSOC, Committee on Economic, Social and Cultural Rights, *General Comment No. 18: The Right to work (art. 6)*, ¶ 12.

[57] *General Comment No. 14, supra* note 8, ¶ 43.

[58] Ibid., ¶ 43(d).

another is to implement a national public health strategy, "on the basis of epidemiological evidence, addressing the health concerns of the whole population."[59] It is difficult to determine whether the Committee designated these obligations as "core" on philosophical or strategic grounds. That is, it is unclear whether it was their greater moral salience or their immediate practicability that led to certain obligations' inclusion in the list. On both grounds, the core obligations in respect to the right to health are subject to criticism. For example, one commentator recommended that domestic health care priorities not be set by the Committee's approach, because of its overlooking of the HIV/AIDS pandemic.[60] Another suggested that the essential drugs goal was impossible to meet by all but a few rich States.[61] The Committee's response to the practicability of the core obligations (and by implication, their affordability) is to posit a duty of assistance and cooperation on both States Parties and non-state actors who are "in a position to assist."[62]

The right to health care may seem an unfair example. Of all economic and social rights, the right to health (and, with it, the right to health care) is perhaps most notorious for vagueness and indeterminacy. The value of health is multiple and variable: it relates in critical ways to the celebrated human values of dignity, life, capability, liberty, bodily integrity, and equality of opportunity, values which all point to different interpretive results.[63] Similarly, at the level of tangible goods, the right to health raises the following boundary problem. In order to deliver on its promise to meet everyone's "highest attainable level of health"[64] (or similar standard), the right raises an endless chain of duties across the multiple social determinants that underlie individual health.[65] This book refers to both the right to health and health care: the former encompasses measures to be protected from, for example, environmental pollution or contaminated water, while the right to health care refers to medical scenarios for preventing and curing health. Overlap is, of

[59] Ibid., ¶ 43(f).

[60] Karrisha Pillay, "South Africa's Commitment to Health Rights in the Spotlight: Do We Meet the International Standard?," in Brand and Russell, *Exploring the Core Content*, *supra* note 21, 61, 66–8.

[61] Benjamin Mason Meier, "Employing Health Rights for Global Justice: The Promise of Public Health in Response to the Insalubrious Ramifications of Globalization" 39 Cornell Int'l. L.J. 711 (2006) 735–6.

[62] *General Comment No. 15*, *supra* note 11, ¶ 38 ("particularly incumbent on States parties . . . and other actors in a position to assist"); *General Comment No. 14*, *supra* note 10, ¶ 45.

[63] E.g., Norman Daniels, *Just Health* (2008) (founding it on equality of opportunity); *c.f.*, e.g., Eugene Volokh, "Medical Self-Defense, Prohibited Experimental Therapies, and Payment for Organs," 120 Harv. L. Rev. 1814 (2007) (providing libertarian justification to health care). For contestations around these definitions, see *infra* Chapters 8 and 9 (presenting case studies on the right to health in Ghana and South Africa).

[64] ICESCR, art. 12.

[65] E.g., Mary Anne Bobinski, "Health Disparities and the Law: Wrongs in Search of a Rights" 29 Am. J. L. & Med. 363 (2003).

course, inevitable. Even when confined to the medical context alone, as is South Africa's right "to access health care services,"[66] a minimalist definition of the right to health care is burdened by the ever-expanding promise of science and technology. People's needs in health care are not entirely independent of supply. That is, the more that technology in health care develops, the greater the right's potential scope. (This is doubly challenging in a country such as South Africa, where some of the world's first heart transplants were performed at the same time as a high percentage of the urban South Africans who were classified as black lived in squatter settlements.)[67] From a differently edged concern, the problem of moral hazard suggests that a fixed definition of core obligations in health care might encourage people to take unnecessary health risks.[68] One way of resolving this complexity is to see the right to health as reliant on an incompletely theorized agreement,[69] something that the core obligations approach appears to deflect.

In later General Comments, the core obligations identified by the Committee are more general. A General Comment published in 2005 on the right to work suggests that "core obligations" relate mainly to duties of nondiscrimination.[70] The substance of these "core obligations" contains little overlap with the normatively prioritized principles of the right to work in other, specialized, treaties. For example, the core obligations of the right to work, as determined by the Committee, share little with the "core labor rights"—against child labor and forced labor—which figure in the conventions and declarations of the International Labour Organization.[71] This suggests a pragmatic, turf-defining interpretation of core obligations, rather than a normative prioritization or consensualist approach to any strictly minimum core.

(4) The link with justiciability

The accomplishments of the minimum core, particular to the international system, allowed the Committee to, firstly, answer the relativism of

[66] S. Afr. Const., § 27(1).

[67] Gaps in health care are thus cited as a central dimension of inequality: *see*, e.g., Amy Chua, "Markets, Democracy, and Ethnicity: Toward A New Paradigm for Law and Development," 108 Yale L.J. 1 (1998), 66–7 (noting that "apartheid essentially created two economies").

[68] E.g., Mark Kelman, "Health Care Rights: Distinct Claims, Distinct Justifications," 3 Stan. L. & Pol'y. Rev. 97 (1991).

[69] Jennifer Prah Ruger, "Toward a Theory of a Right to Health: Capability and Incompletely Theorized Agreements," 18 Yale J. of L. & Human. 273, 306–11 (2006).

[70] *General Comment No. 18*, *supra* note 56, ¶ 31.

[71] *See* ILO, 1998 Declaration on Fundamental Principles and Rights at Work; *see also* ILO, Convention No. 182, Geneva, 16 June 1999 (entered into force 19 November 2000), *available at* <http://www.ilo.org/ilolex/english/convdisp1.htm>.

progressive realization, secondly, create a minimum baseline across diverse sovereign systems, and thirdly, carve out a minimum sphere for extraterritorial obligations. A fourth, relatively recent role, connects the doctrine more explicitly with adjudicatory or quasi-adjudicatory practices in both international and domestic law. This is the connection of the minimum core with justiciability. Supporters of this approach contend that the "inherently justiciable" elements of economic and social rights make "a very sound starting point for any discussion about the 'core content,'" pointing to "the interrelated and mutually enforcing" aspects of justiciability and minimalism.[72]

This connection draws justiciability into a substantive minimum. The substantive dimensions of economic and social rights are nevertheless still contested. Some commentators suggest that the minimum core concept relates only to obligations of result, because it is able to signal only the extent to which individuals are enjoying or will enjoy their rights, rather than assess the policies and procedures that bring about that result. Thus, for example, Tara Melish presents a helpful four-dimensional quadrant of the duties flowing from economic and social rights—utilizing both the result-conduct and individual-collective distinction—and places the minimum core obligation in the result-based and individual-based category of duties.[73] This, Melish suggests, is relevant to the work of supranational adjudicatory bodies, like the Inter-American Court of Human Rights.[74] As the Committee itself moves closer to hearing individual complaints,[75] this aspect of the minimum core may become ever more relevant.

These aims towards justiciability are consistent with the Committee's own endorsement of the minimum core as a guide for the domestic adjudication and enforcement of the ICESCR.[76] In this way, the minimum core helps it to confront the perception of lack of content, and of nonjusticiability, which have been described as two parts of a negative feedback mechanism that sidelines economic and social rights in international human rights law.[77] The Committee perceives justiciability as a relatively minor part of its work, preferring to ease the way for other, less juridical promotions of rights. However, the trend towards justiciability is increasing

[72] *See*, e.g., Pierre de Vos, "The Essential Components of the Human Right to Adequate Housing—A South African Perspective," in Brand and Russell, *Exploring the Core Content*, *supra* note 21, 23, 23–4, 26.

[73] Melish, "Rethinking the 'Less as More' Thesis," *supra* note 30, 248.

[74] Ibid.

[75] Optional Protocol to the ICESCR, G.A. Res. 63/117, UN Doc. A/RES/63/117 (10 December 2008).

[76] *See*, e.g., *General Comment No. 18*, ¶ 49; *General Comment No. 15*, ¶ 57; *General Comment No. 14*, ¶ 60; *General Comment No. 12*, ¶ 33.

[77] E.g., David Marcus, "The Normative Development of Socioeconomic Rights Through Supranational Adjudication," 42 Stan. J. Int'l L. 53 (2006), at 55 (describing the perception of a lack of content and of non-justiciability as two parts of a negative feedback mechanism).

in domestic and international domains,[78] and there is some interest in using the minimum core as the appropriate vehicle for courts. For example, in endorsing the ratification and incorporation of the ICESCR, the Committee has suggested that incorporation "enables courts to adjudicate violations of the right [to health, to water etc.], or at least its core obligations, by direct reference to the Covenant."[79] This takes us to the prospects of the minimum core in constitutional law.

B. PROSPECTS FOR CONSTITUTIONAL LAW

The ability of the minimum core to migrate from international human rights law to constitutional law is furthered by the textual similarities between rights protected in different constitutions (and the international human rights covenants), and by the transnational judicial dialogue that complements and expands upon those similarities.[80] We might expect the minimum core to travel between different constitutional systems in one of two ways: as a concept with a substantively defined content, borrowing its substance from the interpretations of economic and social rights issued in the General Comments and other statements of the Committee, or alternatively as the latent structure of minimum legal content to be given substance via developments in domestic jurisprudence (and selective international and comparative jurisprudence) on economic and social rights. The choice of incorporation—of substance or of form—might reflect the monist or dualist nature of the domestic legal system, or the general perspective towards international and comparative law taken by its courts and other branches.[81]

For those concerned with international doctrine, these possibilities also reflect the divergence of approach between universal and country-specific cores. It is unclear, however, whether the substantive content would be filled in by judges, other branches of the state, or outside of the positive legal domain altogether—via the growing influence of claims of social movements and advocacy networks, which are also linked transnationally.[82] So far, the domestic operation of the doctrine has been debated only in juridical terms—as the orienting tests for justiciability, for justification of rights-limitations, or for progressive realization, as will be seen below.

[78] *See* generally, Part II of this book.

[79] *General Comment No. 14*, *supra* note 10, ¶ 60; *see also General Comment No. 15*, *supra* note 11, ¶ 57 (encouraging incorporation of instruments recognizing the right to water).

[80] *See*, e.g., Sujit Choudhry, "Migration as a New Metaphor in Comparative Constitutional Law," in Sujit Choudhry (ed.), *The Migration of Constitutional Ideas* (2006).

[81] For a broader discussion of binding and persuasive norm migration, *see* Chapter 10.

[82] *See* generally, Part III.

Indeed, in contrast to international human rights law, the concept of the minimum core does not yet have the same purchase in efforts to interpret economic and social rights in national constitutional law. Of national courts, the South African Constitutional Court ranks among those most carefully engaged with arguments for and against a minimum core of economic and social rights. The ability of the concept to set out a minimum sphere of legal protection in the many other constitutional democracies with economic and social rights guarantees is suggested as one fruitful exercise of constitutional cross-fertilization in the legal systems of Colombia,[83] where the Constitutional Court has explicitly adopted the minimum core in relation to the right to health, as well as the disparate constitutional systems of India, Argentina, Hungary, and Spain.[84]

The unevenness of the migration of the minimum core doctrine obscures its deeper connection with constitutional law. A little digging reveals that the concept inherits its structure from the German Basic Law (and the now redundant Turkish Constitution of 1961),[85] where the "core," or "essential content" of certain constitutional rights lie beyond the reach of permissible limitation.[86] The same conceptual rights structure is a product of the fact that, in both constitutional and international human rights law, there are categorical or peremptory norms that permit no derogation or limitation, and presumptive norms, that may be limited under strictly justifiable terms.[87] The delineation of core and noncore rights purports to specify this distinction.

Despite the fact that the "essential content" provision in the German Basic Law gives rise to a "remarkable variety of views as to what it means,"[88] the protection of an essential component of rights that remains secure against limitation is a common structural feature of constitutions, either articulated as part of the right itself, or within a constitutional limitation clause.[89] The Interim South African Constitution borrowed directly from the German Basic Law in its entrenchment of the "essential

[83] Alicia Ely Yamin and Oscar Parra-Vera, "How Do Courts Set Health Policy? The Case of the Colombian Constitutional Court," 6(2) *PLoS Med* (2009).

[84] Fons Coomans, "Some Introductory Remarks on the Justiciability of Economic and Social Rights in a Comparative Constitutional Context," in Fons Coomans (ed.), *Justiciability of Economic and Social Rights: Experiences from Domestic Systems* (2006) 1, 9–13.

[85] Esin Örücü, "The Core of Rights and Freedoms: The Limits of Limits," in Tom Campbell et al. (eds.), *Human Rights: From Rhetoric to Reality* (1986) 37.

[86] Grundgesetz für die Bundesrepublik Deutschland (German Basic Law) (F.R.G.) art. 19(2).

[87] Stephen Gardbaum, "Human Rights as International Constitutional Rights," 19 Euro. J. Int'l L. 749 (2008) 751. *See further* Chapter 4.

[88] David P. Currie, *The Constitution of the Federal Republic of Germany* (1994) 178 n. 15.

[89] For further discussion of limitations, *see* Chapter 4.

content" provision, a formulation which was also included in the Namibian and Hungarian Constitutions.[90] However, the South African Constitutional Court expressed difficulty in the provision's interpretation, which it suggested arose "from the uncertainty as to what the 'essential content' of a right is, and how it is to be determined."[91] The final South African Constitution adopted a different formulation, dispensing with the prohibition on negating the "essential content" of rights within the limitations clause and establishing a different test.[92]

This genealogy signals the first constitutional operation of the minimum core—as a concept which mediates the necessary "limitations" on rights by requiring a particular level of justification if the minimum of the right is not satisfied, which the state, rather than the claimant, must prove. Similarly, because the minimum core concept confronts the degree to which rights can be "progressively realized" (that is, justifiably delayed), as well as formally limited, it can borrow from international law to target retrogressive policies, and also indicate when the state's negative obligations to respect rights are violated. Finally, proponents of the concept suggest that it can assist in the development of a justiciable minimum for economic and social rights.[93] It is this third operation, which also implicates the others, that is given the greatest attention in national debates.

(1) *Underscoring justiciability*

The conceptual and institutional roles of the minimum core are linked. The ability of courts to hear complaints about economic and social rights, and to provide remedies for successful complaints, is constrained by the limits of the judicial role against the policy-making and law-making powers of the elected branches. A focus on minima helps to ensure that the content of justiciable economic and social rights is so institutionally limited that their enforcement by courts may have a negligible effect on the separation of powers, curtailing judicial action except in cases of extreme social and economic deprivation, or when only negative violations of economic and social rights are perpetrated.[94] Some have suggested that the minimum core doctrine helps to determine this constraint.[95]

[90] Interim S. Afr. Const., § 33 (1) (b). Constitution of the Republic of Namibia, 1990, § 22(a); The Fundamental Law of Hungary, April 2011, art. 1(3); *see also* The Constitution of the Republic of Hungary, 1949, rev. and restated 1989, §§ 8(2), 57(4) (as at January 2011) (succeeded).

[91] *S. v. Makwanyane* 1995 (3) SA 391 (CC) ¶ 132 (S. Afr.).

[92] S. Afr. Const., § 36.

[93] *See*, e.g., de Vos, "Essential Components," *supra* note 72, 24, 26.

[94] For an example of such proposals, *see infra*, notes 128–29.

[95] For an explicit incorporation of urgency and protection of survival into the core, *see* Bilchitz, *Poverty and Fundamental Rights*, *supra* note 23, 187–91.

How does the doctrine of the minimum core resolve the justiciability challenges of economic and social rights? The South African Constitution is one model.[96] In the earliest economic and social rights claims heard by the Constitutional Court, the plaintiffs and amicus curiae argued vigorously for the minimum core to advance their claims of housing and health care rights. One advocacy group asserted that, without the judicial incorporation of the minimum core, the new Constitution's economic and social rights might become "empty rights and false promises."[97]

Proponents of the minimum core in South Africa pointed to its compatibility with the three accompanying doctrinal tests applied to economic and social rights. The minimum core assists in the judicial determination of, first, the obligation to negatively respect such rights, second, the obligation to "progressively realize" such rights in their protection and fulfillment, and third, the obligation to justify any limitations on particular grounds. Importantly, the core would not necessarily correlate only with "negative" obligations. Hence, the minimum core might present the stand-alone protected content from which a negative obligation would immediately flow, without inquiry into progressive realization.[98] And in relation to the more positive obligations, the minimum core would provide a standalone content of such rights. Unlike other core formulations, a limitation justification would be available. Nonetheless, it would take a very restricted form. Thus, if the state did not deliver on this content, it would be required to justify its failure under the limitations clause of section 36. If it satisfied the minimum core, yet had failed to expand upon it, on the other hand, it might be called upon to justify this failure under the more open progressive realization tests of section 26(2) and section 27(2).[99] In relation to these tests of the "limits" of positive obligations, which are discussed further in Chapter 4, the debates in

[96] *See*, e.g., Bilchitz, ibid., 179–83; Scott and Alston, "Adjudicating Constitutional Priorities in a Transnational Context," *supra* note 20.

[97] *See*, e.g., Press Release, Community Law Centre on its Amicus Intervention, Statement on Constitutional Court Case: *Treatment Action Campaign* v. *Minister of Health* (30 April 2002) (on file with author) (calling for the recognition of a "basic core right to the necessities of life"); *see also* Heads of Argument on Behalf of the Amici Curiae in *Grootboom* (*S. Afr. v. Grootboom* 2001 (1) SA 46 (CC) 66 (S. Afr.)) ¶¶ 26–9, 34–6, 2001 (1) SA 46 ¶ 33 (CC) (S. Afr.) (Human Rights Commission of South Africa and Community Law Centre, represented by Geoff Budlender) (relying on the minimum core to substantiate the right of access to housing).

[98] E.g., *Jaftha v. Schoeman* 2005 (1) BCLR 78 (CC), 91 (S. Afr.); Sandra Liebenberg, "Needs, Rights and Transformations," 17 Stellenbosch L. Rev. 5 (2006), 22–4. *See also Maphango v. Aengus Lifestyle Properties (Pty Ltd)* Case CCT 57/11 [2012] ZACC 2 (March 13, 2012) (CC).

[99] *See* Kevin Iles, "Limiting Socio-Economic Rights: Beyond the Internal Limitations Clause," 20 S. Afr. J. Hum. Rts. 448 (2004), 448, 452, 455–63.

relation to the South African Constitution reflect those in international human rights law.[100]

In South Africa, the Constitution provides for a right of access to courts, and requires all of the organs of the state to ensure their accessibility.[101] Rights advocates argued that incorporating the minimum core doctrine would have an important role in this respect. In particular, the minimum core would become important for its potential to reverse the onus of proof in socioeconomic claims. Once claimants were able to prove that their minimum core was not protected, the suggestion went, it would be for the state, rather than the applicant, to prove that it has taken the required "reasonable legislative and other measures, within its available resources, to achieve the progressive realization"[102] of the right,[103] or to show that any limitation "is reasonable and justifiable."[104] In reversing this very large onus onto the government, the minimum core could help to ensure a "practical justiciability," turning a "paper right" of access to court into a practical reality.[105] Domestic justiciability makes this reversal of proof considerably more meaningful than its present (plausible, and yet contested[106]) operation in international law, given the current supervisory procedures and lack of a complaints jurisdiction.[107]

This possibility is, of course, controversial. Many opponents of the concept suggest that the minimum core cannot resolve the justiciability challenges posed by economic and social rights, but instead only amplifies them. A justiciable minimum core may do all the things its advocates want—reverse onuses, provide baselines for progressive realization, and trigger obligations for the government to justify any limitations—and yet may also drastically alter the separation of powers between courts, the legislature, and the executive. This objection rests in the long-articulated concern that if judges are allowed to adjudicate on the meaning and content of economic and social rights, they will assume greater power over setting

[100] Amrei Müller, "Limitations to and Derogations from Economic, Social and Cultural Rights," 9 Hum. Rts. L. Rev. 557 (2009).

[101] S. Afr. Const. 1996 § 34, *see also* § 165(4).

[102] S. Afr. Const. 1996 §§. 26(2), 27(2).

[103] Sandra Liebenberg, "The Value of Human Dignity in Interpreting Socio-Economic Rights," 21 S. Afr. J. Hum. Rts. 1 (2005), at 22–6.

[104] S. Afr. Const. 1996 §. 36; ibid., 26–9 (emphasizing a heightened proportionality analysis).

[105] Liebenberg, ibid., 23 nn. 93–94 (referring to the arguments of the amicus curiae in *TAC* represented by Wim Trengove SC, found in ¶ 30.2).

[106] Craven, *The International Covenant*, *supra* note 18, 142–4.

[107] For a discussion of the current status of the communications procedure, *see* Chapter 2, text accompanying notes 112–13.

socioeconomic policy, which they are neither competent to decide nor accountable to administer.[108]

Within this debate, the minimum core coincides with a strong model of judicial review and represents a proxy for a substantive justiciable minimum. Mark Tushnet, for example, suggests that the minimum core doctrine inevitably requires a large measure of scrutiny and a high level of justification in reviewing the acts of government that result in deprivation of rights.[109] Indeed, as a model of review which accords with strong—or, as I have labeled it, supremacist courts—the minimum core's incorporation has, in fact, coincided with a heightened degree of judicial scrutiny and a less flexible remedy.[110] Later, when this book turns to a more explicit comparison of courts, we will see how the Colombian Constitutional Court's incorporation of the minimum core, from international human rights law, has reflected, and in turn affected, its "supremacist" role conception.

The institutional objection that Tushnet articulates, which rests on democratic grounds, accords with the official responses to the minimum core issued by both the government and the judiciary in South Africa. First, the government has opposed the incorporation of the minimum core—on a rationale that is unsurprising. In interviews, government officials expressed caution at the latitude that the concept presents for the judiciary and the constraint that it presents for government action. In argument before the Court, the government has advanced the more flexible measure of "reasonableness" in judicial review.[111]

The Constitutional Court has agreed. Rejecting the arguments of advocates, the Constitutional Court has chosen to place the minimum core under the more general purview of reasonableness. As will be detailed in Chapter 4, it has preferred to weigh an argued-for substantive minimum as one factor within an overarching test of reasonableness. For example, in *Grootboom*,[112] the Constitutional Court refused to rule on what the minimum core of the right to housing should be, citing its lack of sufficient information to make such a determination. Instead, it chose the more flexible route of assessing the reasonableness of the government's housing policy. In this respect, the Court relied on the values of the Constitution to

108 *See further* Part II of this book.

109 Mark Tushnet, "Social Welfare Rights and the Forms of Judicial Review," 82 Tex. L. Rev. 1895 (2004) 1903–5.

110 *See* Chapter 7.

111 *See* interviews in Aarthi Belani, "The South African Constitutional Court's Decision in *TAC*: A 'Reasonable' Choice?" (Ctr. for Human Rights & Global Justice Working Paper, No. 7, 2004) 36–7 n. 169, *available at* <http://www.chrgj.org/publications/wp.html> (find link under 2004 working papers).

112 *S. v. Grootboom* 2001 (1) SA 46 (CC) 66 (S. Afr.).

provide a normatively charged account of reasonableness, so that the government's failure to cater to all groups was held to have failed to meet the Constitution's requirements. Similarly, in ruling on the government's refusal to distribute antiretroviral drugs in *TAC*,[113] the Court refused to articulate a minimum core of the right to health, instead holding that the government's obstruction of efforts to prevent mother-to-child transmission of HIV/AIDS with antiretrovirals was unreasonable in light of the Constitution's protection of the right of access to health care.

The most recent rejection of the minimum core in South Africa concerned the determination of complaints addressed to the constitutional right to access water in the *Mazibuko* decision. Given the ready commodification of water into units, it would appear that this economic and social right would be appropriately regulated by the minimum core doctrine. The lower courts were all sympathetic to the notion that a minimum liter limit per day could usefully guide the interpretation of this right and its minimum core. The lower courts did disagree, however, on what the quantified minimum should be—the High Court judge finding fifty liters to be appropriate, while the Supreme Court ordered that the City of Johannesburg was required to supply a minimum of forty-two liters.[114] The fifty-liter minimum was based on the advice of an international expert, whose methodology was consistent with the basic needs approach, discussed in Chapter 2.[115] The Supreme Court consulted the Committee's General Comment No. 15 on the right to water, and also referred to the principles of availability and accessibility as well as the minimum core.

Yet on appeal, the Constitutional Court refused to engage in any statement of a minimum,[116] holding that a court-adopted quantified standard would be inconsistent with the constitutional duty of "progressive realization" and with the proper role of courts in a constitutional democracy. This may not be so much a matter of doctrine, as an overarching approach of judicial deference.[117] Nevertheless, the minimum core was perceived to require too high a degree of scrutiny of government evidence and too

[113] *Minister of Health v. Treatment Action Campaign* 2002 (5) SA 721 (CC), 272 (S. Afr.).

[114] Compare *Mazibuko v. City of Johannesburg* [2008] 4 All SA 471 (W); [2009] ZAGPHC 106 (18 April 2008); Case No. 06/13865 (ordering the city to supply 50l of free water per person per day); with *City of Johannesburg v. Mazibuko* 2009 (3) SA 592 (SCA); 2009 (8) BCLR 791 (SCA); Case No. 489/08 [2009] (ordering 42l per person per day). The lower court also utilized *General Comment No. 15*.

[115] P. H. Gleick, "Basic Water Requirements for Human Activities: Meeting Basic Needs," 21(2) *Water International* 83–92 (1996).

[116] *Mazibuko v. The City of Johannesburg* 2010 (4) SA 1 (CC).

[117] *See further* Chapter 5. See also Lucy Williams, "The Role of Courts in the Quantitative-Implementation of Social and Economic Rights: A Comparative Study," 3 Constitutional Court Review 13 (2010).

demanding a pressure of remedy. Since *Mazibuko*, the prospects of a justiciable minimum core are now at their dimmest in the South African context.

The criticisms of the minimum core as a juridical guide to economic and social rights are partly resolved by considering the appropriate role of judicial review. This theme is taken up in Part II of this book. The challenges of the minimum core are also resolved by a brief reflection on the distinction between legal rules and standards. The institutional and doctrinal implications of this distinction are fruitfully analyzed in constitutional scholarship, albeit not in relation to economic and social rights (but certainly in relation to other constitutional rights with social and economic implications).[118] Rules provide certainty and predictability in legal decision-making but are fallible in the sense that they can lead to individual injustice. Standards, on the other hand, can provide the discretion needed to address context and individual circumstance. However, they create their own problems of uncertainty and distance from the legal decision-maker's ideals of neutrality and nonarbitrariness. While the minimum core has implicitly been considered a rule in the debates for and against its incorporation in constitutional law, its operation as a standard has not been assessed. The minimum core is open to operate as a rule or a standard, just as the broader economic and social right, in which it rests, may operate in both ways. This theme is taken up further in the discussion of proportionality in Chapter 4.

Hence the minimum core, as rule, provides for predictability in its application, yet presents the same problems of an inability to address particularity and difference and an almost inevitable expansion of the role of courts. If defined to accord with a claimant's survival or dignity interests, it may become institutionally difficult for the courts to enforce. And if defined as a rule to accommodate these institutional questions—reduced in effect by the doctrines of standing, ripeness, mootness, and political questions, for example,[119] and by the limited availability of rights-respecting remedies—it may become too distant from the aims of the right. The minimum core, as standard, allows for attention to context, and yet creates a movable, changeable, core, which is dependent upon the circumstances of the case. Whether this standard creates an expansion of the judicial role is contingent on its application.

This tension between rules and standards can be presented as an issue of form. Yet this tension also raises larger substantive issues about the nature of economic and social rights and their ability to deliver protection against the

[118] E.g., Kathleen Sullivan, "The Justices of Rules and Standards," Harv. L. Rev. 11–123 (1992). *See also* Frederick Schauer, "The Convergence of Rules and Standards," N.Z. L. Rev. 303 (2003).

[119] *See* US Const. art. III, § 2; *see*, e.g., Abram Chayes, "The Supreme Court 1981 Term, Foreword: Public Law Litigation and the Burger Court," 96 Harv. L. Rev. 4 (1982) 59.

myriad forms of powerlessness and deprivation that are experienced within systems of law. The difficulty of establishing a hard line rule in such cases has led many to favor more standard-based assessments, with a different qualitative character, such as an assessment of the "reasonableness" of the government's action in any particular case.[120] Standards can be both general and situationally sensitive, thus overcoming a conceptual difficulty in the variety of operations of the minimum core. Standards can resolve the preference for a court-established minimum core as the "general standard" of obligation on the state,[121] along with the advice to courts "to exercise best judgment in the national and local context . . . balanc[ing] reaction to deprivation on a 'calling it as we see it' case-by-case basis with a pragmatic sense of what remedies are desirable and likely to prove effective."[122] The ability of such standards to resolve the problems of judicial discretion are further discussed below in Chapter 4. The main point is, however, that if the minimum core is retained in constitutional law, it can be treated as a standard rather than a rule, or, alternatively, as an important ingredient within a broader standard, such as the standard of reasonableness, as is now applied in South African constitutional law.[123]

(2) Other minimalist approaches

The minimum core doctrine is not the only minimalist approach. Other approaches avoid the doctrine altogether. One such alternative is to observe the limits of institutional competence and to understand the minimum of rights in light of these limits. This approach would settle different minimum content for the two institutional contexts most problematic in enforcing the appropriate constraints on rights in accordance with democracy—courts and administrators. Indeed, this institutionally focused approach is consistent with well-known strategies of decision-making in all government branches. It leaves open the possibility that rights claimants conceive of, and argue for, their own conceptions of the minimum of rights. Yet judicial and administrative notions of minimalism can differ from these, set against the background problem of judicial and administrative overreach.

For courts, achieving minimalism in rights interpretation may be accomplished by what Cass Sunstein has termed "judicial minimalism." Under this

[120] *See infra*, Chapter 4.

[121] Bilchitz, *Poverty and Fundamental Rights*, *supra* note 23, 198 ("the role of the court in this respect would be to set the general standard that constitutes the minimum core obligation of the state").

[122] Ibid., *see also* Scott and Alston, "Adjudicating Constitutional Priorities in a Transnational Context," *supra* note 20, 250.

[123] *Mazibuko v. The City of Johannesburg* 2010 (4) SA 1 (CC) [52]–[68].

pragmatic principle, minimalism correlates with narrow rulings, which govern only the circumstances of a particular case, and shallow rulings, which avoid providing a deep theory of the legal provision at issue.[124] The minimum obligation of any economic and social right that would be enforced by a court would therefore be case-specific and under-theorized. Nonetheless, such decisions create their own problems, as Sunstein acknowledges. Narrow rulings create problems for lower courts, for other branches of government, and for ordinary people, who may be left without much guidance on what the law is. Sunstein suggests that such uncertainty may nevertheless be the price of stability, especially for controversial issues of social policy.[125] Yet he notes that the usefulness of judicial minimalism may be contingent on tradition and timing. For "the most glorious periods of democratic life," he suggests that "national decisions reflect a high degree of theoretical depth, and they are wide rather than narrow."[126] For countries experiencing this period (and he includes South Africa in this assessment[127]), a departure from minimalism is a good thing.

Others theories of minimalism in judicial interpretation are established more substantively. In advancing the protection of economic and social rights in the context of the equal protection clause of the 14th Amendment of the US Constitution, Robin West has advocated a limited judicial role in protecting citizens against "abject subjection to the whims of others occasioned by extreme states of poverty."[128] Rodolfo Arango, writing against the backdrop of both the South African and Colombian constitutional systems, argues for a judicial role in the correction of extreme deprivations of economic and social rights, in a compensatory mode.[129] Again, these minimalist positions point to a limited judicial role when a particular set of arrangements are established, which may be too complex to be summarized as a minimum core. We will pursue this role, in greater depth, in Part II of this book.

A second type of institutionally cogent minimalism is that reserved for the executive branch of government. For administrative decision-makers, minimalism can help to contain the problems of unregulated discretion. The

[124] Cass R. Sunstein, *One Case at a Time: Judicial Minimalism on the Supreme Court* (1999).

[125] Cass R. Sunstein, *Radicals in Robes: Why Extreme Right-wing Courts Are Wrong for America* (2006), 29.

[126] Cass R. Sunstein, "Beyond Judicial Minimalism," 43 Tulsa L. Rev. 825 (2008). *See further* Part III for an analysis of adjudication.

[127] Ibid.

[128] Robin West, "Toward an Abolitionist Interpretation of the Fourteenth Amendment," 94 W. Va. L. Rev. 111 (1991) 144–8, 153.

[129] E.g., Rodolfo Arango, "Basic Social Rights, Constitutional Justice, and Democracy," 16 *Ratio Juris* 141 (2003).

tension between rules and standards is familiar to administrative debates and economic and social rights. Indeed, welfare reformers in the late 1960s and 1970s in the United States implemented a set of rules in order to ascertain welfare eligibility, thus replacing a professional social work vision in which caseworkers had the authority to make situationally sensitive judgments about credibility. One way through this was to ensure that officials responsible for administering the law would be given minimal discretion. Official discretion, especially at the lower-levels, is thereby much valued, but is also restricted in scope. A minimalist standpoint reflects disillusionment with the expansive regulatory programs of the welfare state that delegate authority to expert bureaucratic agencies, often entrusting such decision-makers with a vague and vast discretion.[130] In an early study, Jerry Mashaw analyzed the ways in which a minimalist orientation within administrative decision-making can further democratic and efficiency-related goals.[131] As administrative structures increase in scope, often encapsulating global decision-making processes, such minimalism is ever more valued.[132]

Yet the problem with all these institutionally focused answers is that minimalism may limit institutional innovation and possibility.[133] Such limits may themselves be inconsistent with democracy, in so far as this concept supports both the realization of self-determination and individual freedom, as well as material progress.[134] Minimalism may fragment different approaches to economic and social rights, eschewing the indivisibility of rights that is an essential component of their enjoyment. For example, a minimalism of setting food stamp, or social security support, or water quotas, without regard to the broader array of programs that provide benefits and solutions to the deprivation of health, housing, education, or water, is bound to produce only minimal results. A more "complex customization" and coordination of services might be required.[135]

The observance of institutional competence must be teamed with an additional step—a reflective questioning of what has been suppressed or otherwise unrealized within our current institutions of courts, legislators,

[130] *See* the characterization offered by Charles F. Sabel and William H. Simon, "Minimalism and Experimentalism in the Administrative State," 100 Geo. L.J. 53 (2011).

[131] Jerry L. Mashaw, "The Economics of Politics and the Understanding of Public Law," 65 Chi.-Kent L. Rev. 123 (1989).

[132] *See, e.g.*, Benedict Kingsbury, Nico Krisch, and Richard Stewart, "The Emergence of Global Administrative Law," 68 Law & Contemp. Probs. 15 (2005).

[133] Sabel and Simon, "Minimalism and Experimentalism," *supra* note 130.

[134] For an approach which emphasizes individual emancipation and material progress, as the twin goals of democracy, *see* Roberto Mangabeira Unger, *Democracy Realized: The Progressive Alternative* (1998).

[135] Sabel and Simon, "Minimalism and Experimentalism," *supra* note 130.

and executives. Otherwise, minimalism fails to recognize the defects and contingencies of our inherited political (and economic) institutions. And it fails to acknowledge the reinvention that is produced when legal systems include economic and social rights in their constitutionalist projects.

(3) Minimalist measurements

The challenge of minimalism is also implicated in how the enjoyment of economic and social rights is measured—and how indeed a right can be properly perceived to be secured, realized, or fulfilled. We have seen how this is resolved with reasonableness standards, or minimum core arguments. Yet standards rely on criteria of their own. Often, the measures of legal obligations are process-based: the tripartite duties to respect, protect, and fulfill rights incorporate a recognition that the conduct of States Parties is more important than the results they happen to reach.[136] Yet conduct impacts on results, and vice versa.[137] It thus becomes necessary to incorporate measures that appreciate this iterative quality of secured rights. While process-based measures may be easier to track, their uncritical usage can distract from the substantive goals of economic and social rights. For example, an important US welfare reform of 1996 (the Personal Responsibility and Work Opportunity Act) heralded new result-oriented performance indicators, that measured welfare-roll reduction, rather than client-centered fairness, personal needs, or overall human welfare. Poverty measurements were thus highly skewed, because individuals were removed from the welfare rolls for reasons other than the lack of need.[138] A highly distorted measure of success was then created. Measurements therefore require baselines or minimums of both substance and process.

The measurement of minimums underlies many of the approaches that rely on "extreme poverty" or other "minimum thresholds" for establishing obligations under economic and social rights. Indeed, such a measure—of minimum essential thresholds—was initially incorporated within the minimum core doctrine at international human rights law.[139] Of course, the most basic of such measures may satisfy only duties of humanitarianism rather than of justice, since redress for extreme poverty may do little to disturb fundamental injustices.[140] Or they may lack the obligatory structure

[136] *See*, e.g., *General Comment No. 14*, *supra* note 10, ¶ 33.

[137] Craven, *The International Covenant*, *supra* note 18.

[138] Tara J. Melish, "Maximum Feasible Participation of the Poor: New Governance, New Accountability, and a 21st Century War on the Sources of Poverty" 13 Yale Hum. Rts. & Dev't. L.J. 1 (2010) 39.

[139] *General Comment No. 3*, *supra* note 8, ¶ 10.

[140] Nagel, "The Problem of Global Justice," *supra* note 50.

suitable for rights, which divides the Millennium Development Goals from economic and social rights.[141] Nonetheless, an exploration of minimalist measurement is illuminating.

With this caveat in mind, one can draw lessons from the measurement of poverty, a condition which is often—although not invariably—experienced by those whose economic and social rights are not protected. In this endeavor, it is worth noting that there are many choices and little consensus.[142] In his early study of poverty in England, B. S. Rowntree asked his investigators to consider whether people were "living in obvious want and squalor" and relied on their subjective assessments to provide an overall measurement.[143] This subjective researchers' approach was complemented by a "primary poverty line," which was based on the amount of income needed to purchase an austere basket of goods—the "minimum necessaries for the maintenance of merely physical efficiency."[144]

Tracking the problems attached to a moving minimum core, measures of poverty have since developed to incorporate relative income measures, real income measures, participation standards (items necessary for participation in normal activities and consumption), consensual deprivation measures (which sample the population as to what they regard as "necessities"), or a combination of these classifications. Each of these approaches has limitations—particularly in obscuring gendered experiences, or other adaptive expectations of those living in poverty.[145] Many suggest a combination of indicators is the only way to avoid the gaps and inaccuracies of measurement, such as incorporating a "US-style" poverty line, an "Irish-style" measure that ascertains income measures at the bottom when the rest are rising rapidly, and a "European-style" measure of relative income.[146] It is clear that the measurement of poverty can be neither one-dimensional nor infallible. With the incorporation of economic and social rights, this multidimensionality and fallibility increasingly becomes a legal concern.

[141] E.g., Philip Alston, "Ships Passing in the Night: The Current State of the Human Rights and Development Debate Seen through the Lens of the Millennium Development Goals," 27 Hum. Rts. Q. 755 (2005); Thomas Pogge, *Politics as Usual: What Lies behind the Pro-Poor Rhetoric* (2010). *Compare* with LaDawn Haglund and Rimjhim Aggarwal, "Test of Our Progress: The Translation of Economic and Social Rights Norms into Practice," 10 J. of Hum. Rts. 494 (2011).

[142] John Hills, *Inequality and the State* (2004) 39.

[143] B. S. Rowntree, *Poverty: A Study of Town Life* (1901) cited in Hills, ibid., 39.

[144] Hills, ibid.

[145] Pogge, *Politics as Usual, supra* note 141; *see also* Varun Gauri, "Social Rights and Economics: Claims to Health Care and Education in Developing Countries," in Philip Alston and Mary Robinson (eds.), *Human Rights and Development: Towards Mutual Reinforcement* (2005).

[146] Hills, *supra* note 142, at 47.

Indicators and benchmarks have both been used to measure the enjoyment of economic and social rights. Indicators usually refer to a set of statistics that "indicate" phenomena that are not directly measurable, and may be based on either quantitative or qualitative information, as long as it can be consistently measured over time.[147] Indicators may invite cross-national comparisons, but may also take a deliberately self-referential character when applied to economic and social rights.[148] Benchmarks are goals or targets set according to the differing situations of each country, and are sometimes referred to as "minimum thresholds."[149] Thus, in an important respect, they do not "rank" rights, so much as prioritize different temporal targets for an evolving rights protection to meet.

Both indicators and benchmarks have been prominent within the Committee's practice under the ICESCR. For example, through a practice of "scoping"—which involves both the relevant state and the Committee—the Committee designates adjustable targets for each State Party to achieve by the next reporting period.[150] The targets provide a focal point on what the State Party intends to achieve, and what the Committee deems appropriate. A range of factors are taken into account in setting this target—these go behind what is realizable according to the "maximum of available resources,"[151] as the ICESCR requires, but includes a range of other factors. This is important to make visible the mechanisms available to a state in addressing poverty, mechanisms that do not rely simply on resources.[152]

Broader efforts of measurement are thus able to encompass a more expansive goal, such as realizing human capabilities,[153] rather than providing for bundles of commodities or a basket of goods. Like the parallel measures taken for the Human Development Index ("HDI") of the

[147] Maria Green, "What We Talk About When We Talk About Indicators: Current Approaches to Human Rights Measurement," 23 Hum. Rts. Q. 1062 (2001) 1076–7.

[148] Katarina Tomaševski, "Indicators," in Eide, Krause, and Rosas, *Economic, Social and Cultural* Rights, *supra* note 12, 531, 542.

[149] Green, *supra* note 147, 1080.

[150] E.g., *General Comment No. 15, supra* note 11, ¶ 54; *General Comment No. 14, supra* note 10, ¶ 58; Eibe Riedel, "New Bearings to the State Reporting Procedure: Practical Ways to Operationalize Economic, Social and Cultural Rights—The Example of the Right to Health," in Sabine von Schorlemer (ed.), *Praxishandbuch UNO: Die Vereinten Nationen Im Lichte Globaler Herausforderungen* (author's trans: *UN Manual, The United Nations in the Light of Global Challenges*) (2003) 345, at 356. Eibe Riedel has been a long-standing member of the Committee.

[151] ICESCR, art. 2(1).

[152] Alicia Ely Yamin, "Reflections on Defining, Understanding and Measuring Poverty in Terms of Violations of Economic and Social Rights Under International Law, 4 *Geo. J. on Fighting Poverty* 273 (1997) 300; *cf.* Robert Robertson, "Measuring State Compliance with the Obligation to Devote 'Maximum Available Resources' to Realizing Economic, Social and Cultural Rights," 16 Hum. Rts. Q. 693 (1994).

[153] E.g., Yamin, ibid., 300. For the delineation of such goals, *see supra* Chapter 2.

Human Development Reports,[154] indicators that are more nuanced than income measures are relevant. The HDI measures life expectancy, literacy rates, gross enrolment ratios, and per capita GDP, combining these to produce a number on a 0 to 100 scale. Another aggregate measure is the Physical Quality of Life Index ("PQLI"), which also measures infant mortality, and is considered to be a closer measure of subsistence rights.[155] These can be produced with the data provided by government statistical agencies and intergovernmental organizations, to indicate the fulfillment of economic and social rights or the success of rights-based approaches in different sectors, such as health, education, and welfare.[156] Like poverty measures, however, these development indicators are aggregate and misrepresent the gender, ethnicity, religion, and other social categories traditionally associated with exclusion, and traditionally associated with an increased deprivation of rights.

The iterative quality of this enterprise is evident, as targets set metrics and metrics set out the interpretive possibilities within economic and social rights. As early as 1990, the Special Rapporteur on Economic, Social and Cultural Rights called for "indicators [to] . . . assist in the development of the 'core contents' of some of the less developed rights in this domain, and [to] provide a basis from which a 'minimum threshold approach' can be developed."[157] A special meeting of experts in 1993 concluded that the task of setting indicators relied first on a clarified content of the rights and obligations: "[o]nly then would it be possible to identify the most appropriate way to assess progressive achievement, which may or may not involve the use of statistical indicators."[158] Yet there is a certain chicken-and-egg aspect to this argument. While there is, of course, an important relationship between the underlying norms that guide the formulation of indicators and their adherence to rights, what is needed to guide this assessment may be a more open formulation of rights, rather than the fixed and narrow parameters—of a substantive minimum core or other minimalist doctrine.

[154] *See* Mahbub ul Haq, "The Birth of the Human Development Index," in Sakiko Fukuda-Parr and A. K. Shiva Kumar (eds.), *Readings in Human Development: Concepts, Measures and Policies for a Development Paradigm* (2003) 103.

[155] Todd Landman, "Measuring Human Rights," in Michael Goodhart (ed.), *Human Rights: Politics and Practice* (2009) 45, 55.

[156] Landman, ibid., 55; *see also* Sakiko Fukuda-Parr, "Human Rights and Politics in Development," in Goodhart, ibid., 164, for critiques of MDGs.

[157] Special Rapporteur Danilo Türk, *Realization of Economic, Social and Cultural Rights*, ¶ 7, *delivered to the U.N. Economic and Social Council [ECOSOC]*, UN Doc. E/CN.4/Sub.2/1990/19 (6 July 1990).

[158] *See* The Secretariat of the World Conference on Human Rights, *Report on Other Meetings and Activities*, ¶ 153, *delivered to the General Assembly*, UN Doc. A/CONF.157/PC/73, 33 (20 April 1993).

Measurement—and hence accountability for compliance—would proceed more effectively.

There are challenges in the use of indicators and benchmarks. By presenting a veneer of objectivity and by allowing measures to become the ends rather than the means of rights fulfillment, indicators and benchmarks—or, at least, their fixed or uncritical usage—can flout the substantive promise of human rights.[159] They are most effective at confronting this possibility when they are set within a participatory process and when they articulate clear connections with rights, expressed as "dynamic and constantly changing"[160] standards rather than absolute concepts. This approach demands "an open accounting of where judgment lies, why it has been located there, and upon what evidence it is based."[161] It is furthered by openness—and revisability—in the interpretation of rights.

Of course, completely open-ended norms perpetuate the image of economic and social rights as vague and imprecise. Nonetheless, once it is acknowledged that all rights are open to contestation, such a criticism should not distract from the efforts to set indicators and benchmarks. While these technical measures inescapably require norms in the first place (a point made clear by the differences between rights-based and development indicators), there is reason to doubt that a rule-like minimum is the best expression of what those rights are. The articulation of the right that admits of its own openness is more able to ground a meaningful—and hence a more trustworthy, responsive, or accountable—indicator for local and international monitoring.

Just as indicators and benchmarks are important for the international legal field, so too do they play a role in the constitutional field. In domestic law, indicators can be useful, and yet also iteratively misleading. For example, in the United States, after legislative reforms in 1996,[162] easy-to-measure performance indicators were used to measure welfare-roll reduction as a proxy for decreasing poverty. This approach ignored client-centered fairness, personal needs, or overall human welfare,[163] and led to skewed incentives and highly ineffective welfare strategies. Thus, indicators

[159] Annjanette Rosga and Margaret Satterthwaite, "The Trust in Indicators: Measuring Human Rights," 27 Berk. J. Int'l. L. 253 (2009).

[160] Ramon C. Casiple, Emerging Framework and Approaches in Determining ESC Rights' Standards and Indicators: Philippine Grassroots Experience, Montreux (2000), at 4, *available at* <http://www.portal-stat.admin.ch/iaos2000/casiple_final_paper.doc> (last accessed April 2012); *see also* Rosga and Satterthwaite, ibid., 314.

[161] Rosga and Sattherthwaite, *supra* note 159.

[162] Personal Responsibility and work Opportunity Act 1996 ("PRWORA") (U.S.).

[163] Melish, "Maximum Feasible Participation of the Poor," *supra* note 138, 39 (discussing the PRWORA).

must be used with care and openness. This approach may suggest different standards for different subunits (for example, city or rural areas). Standards that rely on open normative criteria can then be ratcheted up or bootstrapped in a wider national effort of coordination.[164] Here, benchmarking singles out an approach to regulation which is oriented to information gathering and learning, and which is more compatible with the flexibility and tailoring required for a social provision. A fuller exploration of this "experimentalist" program is developed in Chapter 9, after we consider the limiting techniques of economic and social rights in the remainder of this Part, and their enforcement in Part II.

There are other modeling approaches, as well as direct measurement, that can indicate when laws and policies will impact most adversely on the most vulnerable. All economic systems generate winners and losers (often termed the "haves" and the "have-nots")—those who gain, and those who lose, as a result of present economic arrangements. The market mechanism also offers a useful way of measuring (as well as creating) winners and losers. Law and economic analysis, especially that scholarship that loosens the grip of efficiency analysis, may also offer important tools in response. For example, law and economics scholarship can help to measure the distributive effects of law.[165] By substituting the predictive goal of economic analysis as distribution, rather than efficiency, the often counterintuitive effects of law and regulation may be discerned. This, like all modeling, requires follow-up empirical assessment, and a careful and reflective use of the chosen measures.

C. COUNTERING A MINIMALIST DISCOURSE

We have seen that the minimum core may be effective as a standard for exerting downward pressure on institutionally problematic protections of economic and social rights. We can understand, from a system perspective, the different ways in which the role of courts, legislatures, policy-makers, and administrators should be constrained. We have also seen more substantive articulations of minimalism that are arguably more focused on the reasons for entrenching economic and social rights in the first place. It is

[164] *See* Michael C. Dorf and Charles F. Sabel, "A Constitution of Democratic Experimentalism," 98 Colum. L. Rev. 267 (1998). For a review of this widespread movement in Europe, *see*, e.g., Tony Atkinson, Bea Cantillon, Eric Marlier, and Brian Nolan, *Social Indicators: The EU and Social Inclusion* (2002) (describing the setting of common objectives and the design of national policies and reporting procedures within the open method of coordination).

[165] *See*, e.g., Christine Jolls, "Accommodation Mandates," 53 Stan. L. Rev. 223 (2000) 230–72.

also important to consider the effect of minimalism on the claimants themselves.

These remarks on language follow the intuition that there is much to be gained from a concept that directs attention and priority in the area of economic and social rights to those groups most marginalized, vulnerable, and subject to the greatest level of material disadvantage. This applies to both international and national planes of legal decision-making. And yet this intuition requires a different intellectual strategy than that raised by the other activities. Rather than attempting to reconcile the minimum core concept with settled foundations or institutional constraints, we may assess its potential both instrumentally and critically. In one sense, this appraisal is in keeping with the wider project of instrumentalizing the vocabularies of social justice, with all of its attendant dangers and opportunities.[166] In other, more aesthetic, terms, this strategy departs from the search for the "rhetoric of order" behind the claims of the minimum—especially the "minimum core"—of economic and social rights, but instead seeks to assess the concept as an "energy source," one that might inspire or motivate change or reform.[167] We are no longer within the "rigorously charted moral space of the analytical philosophers"[168] that the rationalist approach most fully recalls, nor do we rely on the positivist toolkit of consensualism or the empirical focus of measurement. Instead, we must adopt instrumental, motion-oriented metaphors to investigate this claim.

Such analysis may invite a different prospect and a different politics in the minimum core concept or other minimalist agendas. It is not one that can prescribe a more determinate formula for the Committee, for supranational tribunals and constitutional courts, or socioeconomic policy-makers. Instead, it assesses whether, for example, a minimum core concept might catalyze claims and broach new alliances, by drawing attention to the expressive and symbolic features of a "minimum" sphere of legal protection. It recognizes that the language deployed in claims of material distribution or redistribution—discourses involving poverty, material need and the statistics of available GDP—has profound political consequences. In other words, even if a concept has an admirable legal pedigree or a recognizable institutional operation, it is still meaningful to investigate how it structures the political and cultural discourse around the redistributions in question.

[166] E.g., Nancy Fraser and Axel Honneth, *Recognition or Redistribution? A Political-Philosophical Exchange* (2003); *see also* Kerry Rittich, "The Future of Law and Development: Second Generation Reforms and the Incorporation of the Social," 26 Mich. J. Int'l. L. 199 (2004) 241.

[167] Pierre Schlag, *Rights in the Postmodern Condition*, in Austin Sarat and Thomas R. Kearns (eds.), *Legal Rights* (1996) 263, 264.

[168] Ibid., 264.

Theorists of the welfare state, in the United States and elsewhere, have long sought to expose the damaging moral and political work done by the words used to describe the condition of "the poor." Key words like "dependency,"[169] especially in the United States, have focused attention on a perceived lack of self-reliance and self-control on behalf of certain groups. Labels like "pauper" have sought to separate able-bodied people from the disabled, sick, and elderly. Indeed, in every needs-based program, advocates and detractors alike have drawn distinctions between the "deserving" and the "undeserving" poor.[170] Such distinctions stigmatize claimants by introducing classifications that are at odds with the notion of rights. This stigma contributes to a failure to shore up political support for economic and social rights and, indeed, is at the base of political backlash against them.[171]

It is thus necessary to investigate whether the core and noncore distinctions of economic and social rights simply repeat these categorizations. The fact that the concept seeks to set universal entitlements for every individual based on the theory of rights apparently distinguishes it from merits-based classifications by adopting "targeting within universalism" and "helping the poor by not talking about them"[172] as long-term and politically-nuanced policy strategies. But I believe that it is necessary to further investigate whether the minimum core language also manages to smuggle the desert-based classifications back in. It becomes necessary to examine, for example, the ideological consequences flowing, respectively, from the survival-based or dignity-based investigations in rationalism, described in Chapter 2 above.[173]

Secondly, this attention to language must examine how the concept may confront the dominant discourses of material redistribution in particular contexts. Does the minimum core, for example, run counter to the privatization, deregulation, and liberalization discourses, which work both to undermine and to depoliticize the guarantee of a minimally protected

[169] *See* Nancy Fraser and Linda Gordon, *A Genealogy of Dependency: Tracing a Keyword of the U.S. Welfare State*, *19 Signs* (1994) 309.

[170] Michael B. Katz, *The Undeserving Poor: From the War on Poverty to the War on Welfare* (1989) 8 (describing how American political discourse on poverty "slipped easily, unreflectively, into a language of family, race, and culture rather than inequality, power, and exploitation"); Thomas Ross, "The Rhetoric of Poverty: Their Immorality, Our Helplessness," 79 Geo. L.J. 1499 (1991).

[171] Fraser and Honneth, *Recognition or Redistribution*, *supra* note 166.

[172] E.g., Theda Skocpol, "Targeting with Universalism: Politically Viable Policies to Combat Poverty in the United States," in Christopher Jencks and Paul E. Peterson (eds.), *The Urban Underclass* (1991) 411, 427 (proposing targeting within universalism).

[173] Liebenberg, *Needs, Rights and Transformation*, *supra* note 98, 35 (celebrating "the manner in which Mokgoro J in *Khosa* subverts the normal discourse around social assistance creating dependency on the State by highlighting its role in relieving the burden on poor communities and fostering the dignity of permanent residents").

economic and social right? By setting up an explicit incommensurability with economic vocabularies, the minimum core concept has the most potential to confront the assumptions of neoliberalism.[174] However, its operation may produce, in some contexts, entirely the opposite effect. This is because the minimalist focus within the core may well legitimate neoliberalism, especially if the claim for the minimum core is made in order to increase the bundles of commodities or consumption share of the disadvantaged, while failing to challenge the underlying economic institutions that have produced the disadvantage in the first place. For example, as Nancy Fraser argues, in a form which parallels the distributive questions raised at the margins of present-day law and economics,[175] the effect of a minimum-wage guarantee in a neoliberal regime might be to subsidize (if indirectly) the employers of low-wage, temporary labor, and possibly act to depress all wages. In a social democratic regime, in contrast, the guaranteed minimum might alter the balance of power between capital and labor, and also provide a long-term resistance to the commodification of labor power.[176] This type of analysis is needed before we simply align our intuitive support for the language of minimalism with our support for those suffering the greatest material deprivation.

The language of rights-claiming matters—it requires critical analysis, rather than mere acceptance, especially when misrecognition and stigma are so quick to accompany the claims of the poor. This analysis is a contextual, rather than abstract one. For this reason, Part III of this book delves more closely into the language of claim making, and the broader cultural and institutional resources attached to that language. Yet other discourses—the discourse of limits, and the discourse of enforcement—are first examined in the rest of Part I and in Part II.

174 Philip Harvey, "Aspirational Law," 52 Buff. L. Rev. 701 (2004) (suggesting that economic and social rights can directly challenge neoclassical economics).

175 *See*, e.g., Duncan Kennedy, "Law and Economics from the Perspective of Critical Legal Studies," in *The New Palgrave Dictionary of the Economics of Law* (1998) 465.

176 *See* Fraser and Honneth, *Recognition or Redistribution*, *supra* note 166, 78.

4

Interpreting Limits

The interpretation of economic and social rights exerts a constant pressure on their legal application. This pressure is indeterminate. The form that it takes may be due to the values underlying the interpretive standpoint adopted, presented in Chapter 2, or to the institutional conception of minimalism required of positive law, described in Chapter 3. Yet there are even greater pressures on rights. In this chapter, we consider how the application of economic and social rights may be limited according to the same legal apparatus that establishes them. Indeed, the limits placed on the protection of rights, and the justifications given for those limits that make their lack of protection legitimate in law, can be of greater practical import than either interpretive theories or minimalist doctrine. A brief presentation of the varying modes of limiting rights is provided below, before a more targeted discussion of the modes of reasonableness review and proportionality analysis that have become influential legal instruments in the limitation of economic and social rights.

The permissibility of limitations on economic and social rights follows the truism that no constitutional rights are absolute. Constitutions may be suspended or amended; their guarantees may be flexible, merely directive, or otherwise under-enforced. Constitutional law itself ensures that such constraints on rights are subject to their own constraints. Constitutions endure through compromise, and the compromise (according to the principles of constitutionalism) may be disciplined by institutional design. In this way, distinct from the fundamental moral rights of liberal philosophy, constitutional rights may be subject to a set of principles that lead to their weaker, more relative, institutional protection. I canvas these principles below, in a grouping that may, at first, seem unusual. Nonetheless, I argue that they all belong to a category of laws that allows for the legitimate curtailment of the obligations which correlate with rights. These principles are thus all integral to the practical interpretation, implementation, and enforcement of economic and social rights.

It will be seen that the justifiable limits to the enjoyment of economic and social rights are closely aligned with unjustifiable limits—of what aspects cannot be abridged, in any circumstance. Herein lies the connection between the limits of rights and their unlimitable cores. Indeed, the doctrine of the minimum core seeks to establish a content of economic and social rights that precludes the operation of such limits, by presenting "the limits of limits."[1] Yet, as Chapter 3 made clear, even minimum cores are exposed to limitations, and their absoluteness has been substituted for standard-based, albeit heightened, forms of protection of rights. In this chapter, we will see how the developed procedures of limitation puts to one side the conceptual challenges represented by an absolute and substantive minimum, and focuses instead on the contexts in which duties to respect rights guarantees are mediated.

Before categorizing the ways in which economic and social rights are legitimately limited in and by law, it is worth returning to the distinction between negative and positive obligations. Such distinctions are well-described by the conceptual separation of duties to respect, protect, promote and fulfill economic and social rights, familiar in international human rights law and in constitutional law.[2] The first duty formulates a negative obligation, and the others set out the area in which the state has a positive obligation to act. Importantly, these provisions apply to civil, political, economic, social, and cultural rights.

Hence, the protection of rights may be limited by an act that results in a failure of the duty to respect the right in question, or by an omission, which leads to a failure of the duty to protect, promote, and fulfill. Because economic and social rights often (but not always) correlate to positive obligations on the part of the state, the limits on rights often occur through omissions. When the state is not providing adequate services in health care, for example, it is limiting the rights through omission and failures of protection, promotion, and fulfillment. Yet when it actively deprives individuals of their health, through, for example, selectively polluting in certain areas, the state is limiting individual rights through actions and by failing duly to respect the right. Whether these limits are legitimate is established through law.

One analysis argues that all economic and social rights count as "positive," as do civil and political rights, because government action is

[1] Esin Örücü, "The Core of Rights and Freedoms: The Limits of Limits," in Tom Campbell et al. (eds), *Human Rights: From Rhetoric to Reality* (1986) 37.

[2] From international law, *see*, e.g., *General Comment No. 12 on the Right to Food* (1999), ¶ 15; Asbjørn Eide, *The Right to Food as a Human Right*, UN Doc. E/CN.4/Sub.2/1987/23. From constitutional law: *see*, e.g., S. Afr. Const., § 7(2).

implicated at every step.[3] Others suggest that some distinction between acts and omissions of the state can be very useful in appraising the intentions and deliberateness of certain actions.[4] This is especially pronounced in the assessment of justifiable limitations, as will be seen below. The distinction between duties to respect, protect, promote, and fulfill delineate the distinction between negative and positive obligations more fully. Yet if the distinction between negative and positive obligations is to remain, as a shorthand categorization, it is important in the area of economic and social rights to establish that "negative" nonintervention duties are not, a priori, more important than positive.[5] All are subject to constraints, and to the question of whether those constraints are legitimate. Six modes of permissible limitation are sketched below.

A. LIMITS BY DESIGN: SIX MODES

It is common to understand the limitations on rights in terms of the strictly outlined "limitation clauses" of modern constitutions and of international human rights instruments.[6] Indeed, the constitutional trend towards recognizing economic and social rights has, in many instances, been matched by the trend of designing the appropriate "escape clauses" or "claw-back" clauses for failure to protect rights in certain instances.[7] These limitation clauses are surely the most obvious aspect of defining the formal limit on economic and social rights. Nonetheless, there are institutional features of the exercise of "limiting" economic and social rights that exist outside this single clause. Their conceptual and doctrinal implications are introduced briefly below.

(1) *Progressive realization*

First, expressly protected economic and social rights are commonly limited by the obligation of "progressive realization," which introduces a relative standard for the discharging of duties owed by the state. This relativity extends to obligations to respect, protect, promote, and fulfill rights. In international human rights law, for instance, the treaty commitment that is made by each

[3] Stephen Holmes and Cass R. Sunstein, *The Cost of Rights: Why Liberty Depends on Taxes* (1999); *see also* Sandra Fredman, *Human Rights Transformed: Positive Rights and Positive Duties* (2008).

[4] Cecile Fabre, *Social Rights under the Constitution: Government and the Decent Life* (2000) 47–9.

[5] Henry Shue, *Basic Rights: Subsistence, Affluence and U.S. Foreign Policy* (2nd edn., 1996) 52.

[6] E.g., ICESCR, art. 4; *see also* S. Afr. Const., § 7(3) ("The rights in the Bill of Rights are subject to the limitations contained or referred to in section 36, or elsewhere in the Bill"); *see also* § 36.

[7] Lorraine E. Weinrib, "The Postwar Paradigm and American Exceptionalism," in S. Choudhry (ed.), *The Migration of Constitutional Ideas* (2006) 84.

State Party with respect to economic and social rights is one of taking steps "to the maximum of its available resources, with a view to achieving progressively the full realization of the rights . . . by all appropriate means, including particularly the adoption of legislative measures."[8] This formulation is now reflected in national legal systems. South Africa's Constitution entrenches an obligation upon the state to "take reasonable legislative and other measures, within its available resources, to achieve the progressive realisation of each of these rights" (including rights to have access to housing, health care, food, water, and social security).[9] Locally, this is referred to as an "internal limitation" on such rights, because of its entrenchment within the rights-protection provisions.[10] Progressive realization thus sits apart from, and in an uncertain relationship to, South Africa's general limitation clause.[11]

The "progressive realization" standard is not applied to civil and political rights, neither in the international bill of rights,[12] nor in national constitutions such as South Africa's. Nonetheless, "internal" limits on civil and political rights continue to apply. In South Africa, the protection of freedom of expression, for example, is expressly limited so as not to extend to incitements to imminent violence or hate speech,[13] as has been understood jurisprudentially elsewhere.[14] Moreover, some economic and social rights, such as the right to emergency medical treatment,[15] or the right of children to basic nutrition, shelter, basic health care services, and social services,[16] are not "internally" limited by the standard of progressive realization. Other regional human rights treaties disregard it altogether. The African Charter on Human and Peoples' Rights, for instance, does not qualify economic and social rights with respect to their progressive realization, nor with respect to resource constraints.[17] Thus, despite the fact that the language

[8] ICESCR, art. 2(1).

[9] S. Afr. Const., §§ 26(2), 27(2).

[10] Kevin Iles, "Limiting Socio-Economic Rights: Beyond the Internal Limitations Clause," 20 S. Afr. J. Hum. Rts. 448 (2004).

[11] *See* Iles, ibid.

[12] E.g., ICCPR, art. 2(1) (requiring states to take immediate steps to respect rights). The Universal Declaration of Human Rights refers to "Progressive Measures" of securing the recognition and observance of rights: *see* Preamble.

[13] E.g., S. Afr. Const., § 16(2).

[14] E.g., *R v. Keegstra* [1990] 3 S.C.R. 697 (SCC); *Virginia v. Black*, 538 U.S. 343 (2003) (USSC); *Coleman v. Power* (2004) 220 CLR 1 (HCA) (Canadian, US, and Australian courts curtailing the constitutional support for certain speech).

[15] S. Afr. Const., § 27(3).

[16] S. Afr. Const., § 28(1)(c); *see also* Convention on the Rights of the Child, 20 November 1989, U.N.T.S. 1577.

[17] African Charter on Human and Peoples' Rights (adopted 27 June 1981, OAU Doc. CAB/LEG/67/3 rev. 5, *reprinted* in 21 I.L.M. 58 (1982), entered into force 21 October 1986), arts. 15, 16; *compare* with ICESCR, art. 2(1).

of "progressive realization" has not been applied to civil and political rights, it is incorrect to suggest that the use of this formulation supports the traditional dichotomies of civil and political, and economic and social, rights.

How should the obligation of "progressive realization" be understood? Taken literally, the duty appears untenable—entrenching too high a standard, which assumes an ever-expanding economic growth in order to realize economic and social rights; or too linear an obligation, when the choice of direction of realization is so open-ended. Moreover, progressive realization would seem unhelpful in delineating the negative obligations to respect economic and social rights,[18] since the respect of rights does not readily admit an ever-escalating aspect.

Despite these problems, the obligation of "progressive realization" has been utilized, in Committee comments and the arguments of States Parties, in international human rights law. As a standard, it helps to clarify the requirements of "non-retrogression," which requires laws and policies that remove (or retrogress) particular economic and social rights to be justified. The Committee on Economic, Social and Cultural Rights has developed criteria in order to evaluate whether any "retrogressive measures" taken by States Parties under the International Covenant on Economic, Social and Cultural Rights ("ICESCR") are justified,[19] particularly in light of the resources available to states. This criteria has been linked to the obligation of progressive realization. Nonetheless, the standard has been less useful to the legal decision-makers in national systems. Unlike the Committee on Economic, Social and Cultural Rights, the South African Constitutional Court has not dwelled on the meaning of "progressive realization," preferring instead to assess actions against their reasonableness, rather than against the consistency of their trajectory with any forward-moving trend. This approach is described in section B, below.

The application of the "progressive realization" form of relativity is therefore more pertinent to the doctrinal developments under the ICESCR. In particular, "progressive realization" may work to alleviate one criticism of non-retrogression standards. Some observers criticize non-retrogression standards as retaining an inherent bias towards the status quo. Because presently protected economic and social rights are usually enjoyed

[18] Sandra Liebenberg, *Socio-economic Rights: Adjudication under a Transformative Constitution* (2010).

[19] *See*, e.g., UN Economic and Social Council (ECOSOC), Committee on Economic, Social and Cultural Rights, *General Comment No. 14: The Right to the Highest Attainable Standard of Health (Article 12 of the International Covenant on Economic, Social and Cultural Rights)*, ¶¶ 32 and 38, UN Doc. E/C.12/2004 (11 August 2000) ["*General Comment No. 14*"]; *General Comment No. 13: The Right to Education (art. 13)*, ¶ 45, UN Doc. E/C.12/1999/10 (8 December 1999); *General Comment No. 15: The Right to Water (arts. 11, 12)*, ¶¶ 19 and 42, UN Doc. E/C.12/2002/11 (20 January 2003) ["*General Comment No. 15*"]; *General Comment No. 19: The Right to Social Security (art. 9)*, ¶¶ 42 and 64, UN Doc. E/C.12/GC/19 (4 February 2008) ["*General Comment No. 19*"]; *Comment No. 18: the Right to Work (art. 6)*, ¶¶ 21 and 34, UN Doc. E/C.12/GC/18 (6 February 2006) ["*General Comment No. 18*"].

by the middle (and above middle) classes, a prohibition against retrogressive measures may leave the non-enjoyment of economic and social rights by the poor undisturbed and indeed entrench that non-enjoyment.[20] The test of progressive realization presents a legal reminder that non-retrogression principles must be applied against the consideration of individuals and groups presently without economic and social rights, and hence that a particular limitation of economic and social rights may be justified through some form of balancing. In this respect, it forms a very similar function to other limitation inquiries.

(2) *Reasonable limitation*

The progressive realization standard can be contrasted with a standalone limitation clause, which allows the state to justify a departure from particular constitutional rights: the general limitations clause. In many constitutional bills of rights and regional human rights systems (and expressly in those developed after the Second World War), constitutional rights may be limited, by law, where their limitation is defended on reasonable and justifiable grounds.[21] In South Africa, for example, this clause is referred to locally as the "external limitation" clause. Hence, the Constitution establishes that the recognized rights may be limited, although:

> ... only in terms of law of general application to the extent that the limitation is reasonable and justifiable in an open and democratic society based on human dignity, equality and freedom, taking into account all relevant factors, including—
>
> 1. the nature of the right;
> 2. the importance of the purpose of the limitation;
> 3. the nature and extent of the limitation;
> 4. the relation between the limitation and its purpose; and
> 5. less restrictive means to achieve the purpose.[22]

In this respect, South Africa's Bill of Rights is the most recent instantiation of the constitutional acknowledgment that the limitation of rights, when prescribed by law, is warranted and manageable. In perhaps the most prominent example, Canada's Charter of Rights and Fundamental Freedoms contains a limitation clause, which allows its constitutional rights to be restricted "by law as can be demonstrably justified in a free and

[20] David Landau, "The Reality of Social Rights Enforcement," 53 Harv. Int'l. L.J. 189 (2012). For political features which exacerbate this tendency, *see* discussion in Chapter 5, *infra*.

[21] Stephen Gardbaum, "Limiting Constitutional Rights," 54 UCLA L. Rev. 789–854 (2007); Weinrib, *Postwar Paradigm*, *supra* note 7.

[22] S. Afr. Const., § 36.

democratic society."[23] The German Basic Law allows for certain restrictions on its basic rights, so long as the "essence" of the right is not affected (again indicating an explicit connection with the minimum core arguments foreshadowed in Chapter 3).[24]

These constitutional instruments are matched in international human rights law by provisions that set out procedures for the legitimate limitation of economic and social rights under defined conditions. The ICESCR, for example, allows States Parties to subject rights to those limitations that "are determined by law only in so far as this may be compatible with the nature of these rights and solely for the purpose of promoting the general welfare in a democratic society."[25] This choice of text may justify a narrower set of limitations than other human rights treaties, since limitations must be "solely" for the purpose of promoting general welfare.[26]

The ability to impose limitations, and the conditions on their imposition, are also set out in other international instruments,[27] including the Universal Declaration of Human Rights.[28] The ability of such clauses to resolve conflicts between rights (such as between freedom of expression and respect for privacy), as well as conflicts between rights and general welfare (such as between the freedom of movement and public health), has led to a greater study of their applicability to civil and political rights.[29]

[23] Canadian Charter of Rights and Fundamental Freedoms, § 1; *see also R v. Oakes* [1986] 1 S.C.R. 103 (SCC).

[24] Basic Law of Germany [1949], art. 19. The Interim Constitution borrowed from this clause protecting the "essential content" in Interim S. Afr. Const., § 33 (1) (b); yet the final Constitution omitted this requirement. For other comparative formulations, see *supra* Chapter 3, text accompanying note 90.

[25] ICESCR, art. 4. Note also art. 8, which establishes a different clause for the limitation of the right to strike and to join trade unions.

[26] *Compare* with Council of Europe, European Social Charter, 18 October 1961, ETS 35, art. 31(1), and Article G of the Council of Europe, Revised European Social Charter, 3 May 1996, ETS 163, which permits limitations that are "prescribed by law and are necessary in a democratic society for the protection of the rights and freedoms of others or for the protection of public interest, national security, public health or morals."

[27] Other treaties which contain limitations include ICCPR, arts. 12, 18, 19, 21, 22; Council of Europe, European Convention on Human Rights ("ECHR"), 4 November 1950, ETS 5, art. 8; Organization of American States, American Convention on Human Rights ("ACHR"), "Pact of San Jose," Costa Rica, 22 November 1969, art. 32(2); African Charter on Human and Peoples' Rights, OAU Doc. CAB/LEG/67/3/ rev. 5 (27 June 1981), *reprinted* in 21 I.L.M. 58 (1981) (entered into force 21 October 1986), art. 14.

[28] UN General Assembly, Universal Declaration of Human Rights, G.A. Res. 217A, UN GAOR, 3rd Sess., 1st plen. mtg., UN Doc. A/810 (12 December 1948), art. 29(2), allowing limitations "for the purpose of securing due recognition and respect for the rights and freedoms of others and of meeting the just requirements of morality [and] public order" in addition to the purpose of promoting general welfare. This provision applies to all rights.

[29] *See*, e.g., UN Commission on Human Rights, Siracusa Principles on the Limitation and Derogation of Provisions in the ICCPR, E/CN.4/1985/4 (28 September 1985) ¶ 35; *see also* UN Human Rights Committee (HRC), *CCPR General Comment No. 29: Derogations during a State of Emergency (article 4)*, CCPR/C/21/Rev.1/Add. 11 (31 August 2001).

Conceptualizing appropriate limits on economic and social rights through a general limitations clause is perhaps not as straightforward as with some other rights. The clause has itself rarely been invoked in state practice. Yet there are some exceptions. At the time of drafting of the ICESCR, for example, French and US representatives argued that the right to education should be open to limitation in accordance with "the just requirements of morality."[30] While this argument was rejected by the majority of delegates, these rationales have foreshadowed present curtailments on access to education in Europe.[31] Moreover, the Committee on Economic, Social and Cultural Rights's own consideration of the ICESCR's general limitations clause may increase now that it has been introduced in the reporting guidelines of the Committee on Economic, Social and Cultural Rights, which states follow in submitting their periodic reports on the implementation of the ICESCR.[32]

Some argue that the general limitations clause provides a more useful measure for evaluation than the "progressive realization" standard of obligation.[33] Despite the atypical use of the limitation clause as a defense for nonrealization, this argument points to the greater control of the reasons for which economic and social rights may be limited, and on the way in which limits can be effected.[34] This foreshadows the shift from interpretation to justification that is opened up by the use of such clauses.[35]

Under the ICESCR, the limitations clause allows only reasons of general welfare to justifiably limit rights and requires the form of general laws to do so. At the time of drafting, a representative warned that the clause should not allow states to delay the "implementation of such rights as those to education, health and social security in order to concentrate all its resources on economic development, thus sacrificing the interests of the present

[30] Summary Record of the 306th meeting of the UN Commission on Human Rights, 6 June 1952, E/CN.4/SR.306 at 8 (Mrs Roosevelt, USA); discussed in Amrei Müller, "Limitations to and Derogations from Economic, Social and Cultural Rights," 9 Hum. Rts. L. Rev. 557 (2009) 572.

[31] The European Court of Human Rights, under the ECHR, has affirmed certain restrictions in educational contexts (although complaints were brought on grounds of freedom of choice and conscience and religion). E.g., *Sahin v. Turkey; Dogru v. France* (application no. 27058/05) and *Kervanci v. France* (application no. 31645/04).

[32] *See*, e.g., ECOSOC, Committee on Economic, Social and Cultural Rights, *The Guidelines on Treaty Specific Documents to be Submitted by State Parties under articles 16 and 17 of the International Covenant on Economic, Social and Cultural Right*, ¶ 14, UN Doc. E/C.12/2008/2 (24 March 2009), read in conjunction with the *Compilation of Guidelines on the Form and Content of Reports to be Submitted by States Parties to the International Human Rights Treaties*, UN Doc. HR/GEN/2/Rev.5 (29 May 2008) at ¶ 40(c); *see also* Müller, *supra* note 30, 566.

[33] Müller, *supra* note 30.

[34] Ibid., 569.

[35] Mattias Kumm, "The Idea of Socratic Contestation and the Right to Justification: The Point of Rights based Proportionality Review," 4(2) Law and Ethics of Human Rights (2010).

generation to those of the next."[36] Thus, unlike the standard of "progressive realization," which may justify nonfulfillment of rights on the basis of insufficient available resources, the general limitations clause is understood to foreclose justifications of scarce resources. Instead, "general welfare" is said to refer to the dignity and wellbeing of the community, without attention to economic arguments.[37] Those seeking a greater role for the general limitations clause also point to the fact that limitations must be "compatible with the nature of these rights,"[38] a formulation unique to the ICESCR amongst human rights treaties, but shared in comparative constitutional law, such as in the German Basic Law and the South African Bill of Rights.[39] Nonetheless, this formulation relies on a determinate and final content for economic and social rights, which faces the shortcomings of the minimum core described in Chapter 3. I suggest below that the proportionality and balancing tests established under the general limitations clause are more significant to its operation.

(3) *Suspension or derogation*

A third method for limiting economic and social rights arises through their formal suspension and derogation. In consequence, if not in form, a suspension or derogation allows for the legal—and justified—limit on the enjoyment of rights in a way similar to the progressive realization and general limitation clauses discussed above. When severe military, economic, or political disturbances occur, constitutions may provide for the suspension of, or derogation from, particular rights in order to reestablish stability. Thus, in cases of military emergency, rights such as freedom of movement, assembly rights and private property rights may be curtailed. Crises that are not military in nature, such as natural or environmental disasters, economic collapses, or life-threatening disease epidemics, may also warrant a temporary suspension of rights. There is a disagreement as to how constitutions should respond to states of emergencies. Some suggest that explicit constitutional limitations are more likely to control the government actions taken within emergencies, and deter abuses, while others suggest that

[36] Summary Record of the 235th meeting of the UN Commission on Human Rights, 2 July 1951, E/CN.4/SR.235 at 13 (Mr. Santa Cruz, Chile). *See also* Philip Alston and Gerard Quinn, "The Nature and Scope of States Parties' Obligations under the International Covenant on Economic, Social and Cultural Rights," 9 Hum. Rts. Q. 156 (1987).

[37] Müller, *supra* note 30, 573–4, 593; Alston and Quinn, ibid.; *see also* the debates of the 234–236th and 306–308th meetings of the UN Commission on Human Rights in 1951 and 1952.

[38] ICESCR, art. 4. For example, Müller, ibid., 579.

[39] *See* Basic Law of Germany [1949], art. 19; S. Afr. Const., § 36(1)

constitutional regulation may cast a veneer of legitimacy on the abuse of these powers.[40]

Our example of the South African Constitution outlines a comprehensive set of controls. Declared states of emergency in South Africa must be temporary, and must be renewed periodically by super majorities in the legislature.[41] Some rights are non-derogable and may not be suspended—the rights to life and to dignity included. According to the Constitution's terms, economic and social rights may be derogated from during declared states of emergencies. Rights that may fall within an expanded understanding of economic and social rights may not be derogated from, such as children's right to be protected from exploitative labor practices, the right not to be subjected to medical or scientific experiments without informed consent, and rights against slavery and servitude.[42] The Constitution also expressly requires that derogation be consistent with international law.[43]

Under international law, temporary derogations of most human rights may be permitted in times of emergency that "threatens the life of the nation."[44] The events that may justify derogation must be grave and catastrophic, such as "a war, a terrorist emergency, or a severe natural disaster, such as a major flood or earthquake."[45] These events must amount to an "exceptional situation of crisis or emergency which affects the whole population and constitutes a threat to the organized life of the community of which the State is composed."[46] Once imposed, derogations continue to be regulated by international law, which continues to be minimally protective of economic and social rights. If the derogations occur during armed conflict, whether international or non-international, rules of international humanitarian law become applicable.[47] For example, humanitarian law

[40] For a summary of arguments, *see* N. Dorsen, M. Rosenfield, A. Sajo, and Susanne Baer (eds.), *Comparative Constitutionalism* (2002).

[41] *See* S. Afr. Const., § 37. For the derogation provisions of human rights legislation, *see* Human Rights Act 1998 (UK), § 42, which complies with the ECHR. Its purpose has been suggested as "simply to enable it to be made clear that the inconsistency was deliberate and not inadvertent, and thereby to constitute an aid to the courts in construing the statutory provision": Lord Scott, *A v. Secretary of State of the Home Department* [2005] 2 AC 68, 147. Note that this exists under a statute that does not allow courts to invalidate rights-incompatible legislation, as judicial declarations of incompatibility are unenforceable. *See further* Chapter 6.

[42] S. Afr. Const., § 28(1)(e); § 12(2)(c), § 13 (slavery).

[43] S. Afr. Const., § 37(4)(i).

[44] ICCPR, art. 4(1). *See also* ECHR, art. 15; also ACHR, art. 27. For interpretation, *CCPR General Comment No. 29*, *supra* note 29, art. 4.

[45] *CCPR General Comment No. 29*, ibid.

[46] European Court of Human Rights (ECHR), *Case of Lawless v. Ireland (No. 3) Judgment (Merits)* (1 July 1961) (Series A, No. 3).

[47] *CCPR General Comment No. 29*, *supra* note 29, ¶ 3.

codified in the Geneva Conventions,[48] and their Protocols,[49] provides additional protections to the right to food and medical supplies for a population caught in the midst of war. States have an affirmative "duty of ensuring the food and medical supplies of the population" during armed conflict, and must allow humanitarian aid organizations to pursue their activities,[50] thereby indicating continuing (if limited) duties to respect and protect economic and social rights even in emergency scenarios.

Under the ICCPR, certain rights are expressly non-derogable.[51] The Human Rights Committee has expanded the list of non-derogable rights beyond those expressed in the ICCPR.[52] It has given three justifications for holding certain rights to be non-derogable: first, certain rights may not be suspended if "their suspension is irrelevant to the legitimate control of the state of national emergency"; secondly if derogation is impossible; and thirdly if "without [some protections] there would be no rule of law."[53] The first limb would protect certain economic and social rights from derogation, such as food or health, where derogation would worsen, rather than resolve, a conflict situation.[54] Moreover, the non-derogability of economic and social rights might be implied on the broader theory that the rights that are non-derogable are those most likely to be violated in emergencies, those particularly important to protect the dignity of individuals and to guaranteeing their survival in situations of emergency.[55]

[48] International Committee of the Red Cross ("ICRC"), The (Fourth) Geneva Convention Relative to the Protection of Civilian Persons in Time of War, 12 August 1949, 75 U.N.T.S. 487.

[49] International Committee of the Red Cross (ICRC), Protocol Additional to the Geneva Conventions of 12 August 1949, and relating to the Protection of Victims of International Armed Conflicts (Protocol I) (8 June 1977, 1125 U.N.T.S. 609, *available at* <http://www.unhcr.org/refworld/docid/3ae6b37f40.html>) and ICRC, Protocol Additional to the Geneva Conventions of 12 August 1949, and relating to the Protection of Victims of Non-International Armed Conflicts (Protocol II) (8 June 1977, 1125 U.N.T.S. 609, *available at* <http://www.unhcr.org/refworld/docid/3ae6b37f40.html>) have been ratified by the vast majority of states. Provisions guaranteeing access to humanitarian aid are considered part of customary international law and therefore binding on all states regardless of ratification.

[50] *See* Resolution 4(g)(2) of the 26th International Conference of the Red Cross and Red Crescent (*available at* <http://www.icrc.org/eng/resources/documents/misc/57jmvm.htm>). *See also* UN General Assembly, *Humanitarian Assistance to victims of natural disasters and similar emergency situations*, G.A. Res. 43/131, UN GAOR, 75th Sess., UN Doc. A/RES/43/131 (8 December 1988).

[51] ICCPR, arts. 6, 7, 8(1), 8(2), 11, 15, 16, and 18.

[52] *CCPR General Comment No. 29*, *supra* note 29.

[53] *See* UN Human Rights Committee (HRC), *CCPR General Comment No 24: Issues Relating to Reservations Made Upon Ratification or Accession to the Covenant or the Optional Protocols thereto, or in Relation to Declarations under Article 41 of the Covenant* ¶ 10, CCPR/C/21/Rev.1/Add.6 (4 November 1994).

[54] *See* M. Magdalena Sepulveda, *The Nature of the Obligations under the International Covenant on Economic, Social and Cultural Rights* (2003) Ch. 6, § 3.4.

[55] The ECHR adopts this; the ACHR, on the other hand, lists all rights, the suspension of which cannot conceivably be necessary during emergencies: *see* Joan Fitzpatrick, *Human Rights in Crisis* (1994), at 64; *see also* Müller, *supra* note 30, 562–3.

Similarly, the indivisibility of economic and social and civil and political rights is heightened with respect to non-derogable rights. For example, a non-derogable aspect of the right to health is implicated in the non-derogable right to be free from torture. A non-derogable aspect of the right to work is implicated in the non-derogable right to be free from slavery and servitude.[56] A non-derogable aspect of the right to health and food, in so far as it relates to the right to be protected from epidemics and malnutrition, is implicated in the non-derogable right to life.[57]

The ICESCR does not expressly provide for derogation in the same way that the ICCPR does (itself lacking a general limitations clause);[58] and many suggest that certain rights (such as subsistence rights) continue to apply in states of emergency.[59] One can assume, as commentators have in relation to the limitations clause, that the availability of a progressive realization standard precluded the need for an alternative "escape clause."[60] Moreover, general international law principles (outside of humanitarian laws) apply, subject to certain modifications. It follows from the doctrines of necessity and *force majeure* at international law that treaties may be terminated or suspended or otherwise not followed in certain circumstances.[61] These provisions have been applied to human rights treaties without derogation clauses.[62]

As with limitation clauses, the principle of proportionality governs the availability of derogations from rights, additional to the requirement of an express declaration of a state of emergency. Hence, derogations from rights

[56] These are explicitly non-derogable: *see CCPR General Comment No. 29, supra* note 29, ¶¶ 13–16; *see also* UN Commission on Human Rights, Siracusa Principles on the Limitation and Derogation of Provisions in the ICCPR, E/CN.4/1985/4 (28 September 1985).

[57] UN Human Rights Committee (HRC), *CCPR General Comment 6: Article 6 (Right to Life)* (30 April 1982).

[58] ICCPR, art. 4.

[59] Consider the differences in opinion in the International Court of Justice on the applicability of the ICESCR to a military occupation in Legal Consequences of the Construction of a Wall in the Occupied Palestinian Territory, Opinion of 9 July 2004 [2004] ICJ Rep 131 (considering the impact of the right to work, to health, to education, and to an adequate standard of living under the ICESCR and CRC). *Compare* with the Report of the Special Rapporteur of the UN Commission on Human Rights in the situation of human rights in Kuwait under Iraqi occupation, UN Doc. E/CN.4/1992/26, para 52 (endorsing minimum core obligations as non-derogable). *See further* Chapter 3, section A(1).

[60] Müller, *supra* note 30, 591.

[61] Vienna Convention on the Law of Treaties, 23 May 1969, 1155 U.N.T.S. 331, arts. 54–64. *See also* the International Court of Justice in the *Gabcikovo-Nagymaros Project* (Hungary/Slovakia), Judgement of 25 September [1997] ICJ Rep 7, 7 §§ 49–59; Ian Brownlie, *Principles of Public International Law* (6th edn., 2003) 448.

[62] International Labour Conference, International Labour Office, *Report of the Commission instituted under article 26 of the Constitution of the International Labour Organisation to examine the complaint on the observance by Poland of the Freedom of Association and Protection of the Right to Organise Convention, 1948 (No. 87) and the Right to Organise and Collective Bargaining Convention, 1949 (No. 98) presented by delegates at the 68th Session of the International Labour Conference*, GB227/3/6 (June 1984) (*available at* <http://www.ilo.org/public/libdoc/ilo/GB/227/GB.227_3_6_engl.pdf>).

must be strictly connected with, and proportionate to, the goal of overcoming the emergency scenario.[63] Moreover, the principle of nondiscrimination applies. Hence, every measure taken must bear a reasonable relationship to the threat. At times, derogations may resemble limitations—when limitations are based on "national security," for example, similar assessments of proportionality apply. Nonetheless, the two are distinct, since limitations may occur during everyday settings when rights conflict, may take place over longer periods of time, and must be determined by law.

(4) Override or reservation

A fourth mode of limiting economic and social rights exists through the technique of override, or the arguably parallel technique of reservation. The Canadian Charter offers a prototype for an override provision, which allows the Parliament to override certain rights in the Charter (including court-based interpretations of the right), if it does so explicitly.[64] Under the Charter, the override power does not apply to certain rights, such as democratic rights, mobility rights, and language rights.[65] The non-applicability of the override power to these provisions equates with non-derogability under international human rights law, and the override is often understood as a form of suspension. Indeed, it is telling that the South African Bill of Rights preferred an express derogation clause rather than an override clause.[66] Nonetheless, the power of override is broader than the power of suspension or derogation because it may be grounded on reasons unrelated to exceptional states of emergency.

The override clause in Canada was designed to preserve parliamentary sovereignty, and thus temper the judiciary's ability to invalidate legislation. The legislature therefore retains the power to re-enact legislation that has been invalidated by the judiciary according to the latter's assessment of rights incompatibility. Indeed, adoption of the override was a critical political compromise needed to ensure the enactment of the Canadian Charter,

[63] ICCPR art. 4(1), only "to the extent strictly required by the exigencies of the situation"; *see also CCPR General Comment* 29, *supra* note 29, ¶ 9. *See also* Construction of a Wall in the Occupied Palestinian Territory, Opinion of 9 July 2004 [2004] ICJ Rep 131, [34].

[64] Canadian Charter of Rights and Fundamental Freedoms, § 33.

[65] Canadian Charter, §§ 2–5, § 6, § 16–23.

[66] This is significant, when many of its rights are closely modeled on Canada's Charter of Rights and Fundamental Freedoms. *See*, e.g., Iain Currie and Johan de Waal, *The Bill of Rights Handbook* (5th edn., 2005) at 165 ("The principal model for the *South African Bill of Rights* is the *Canadian Charter of Rights and Freedoms* which contains a list of rights and a general limitation clause governing the limitation of those rights").

which overcame "the impasse on entrenchment by tempering judicial review of rights claims with a legislative escape."[67]

For this reason, it is incorrect to suggest derogation provisions mirror the override provision.[68] The latter supports the value of an institutional dialogue between courts and legislatures.[69] When there is irresolvable disagreement over the reasonableness of the legislative objectives behind rights-limiting legislation, "section 33 provides a carefully structured outlet for the extraordinary dialogue,"[70] allowing legislation to operate "notwithstanding" an incompatible judicial declaration. The override power in Canada is not limited to situations of emergency or other content-based justifications; nonetheless the procedural conditions for invoking it are argued to restrict its misuse or abuse.[71] While the legislature is given the final word, the override expires after five years, which fosters a continuing dialogue between the legislature and the court. This is intended to further a dialogue between the legislature and the people.[72] The constituency is "clearly warned about what is being done in its name,"[73] and may choose to respond through the ballot box, with elections necessarily taking place within a period of five years. Similar clauses have been utilized in other domestic human rights instruments,[74] although some put greater conditions on the use of the override, making its resemblance with derogation clauses greater.[75]

I suggest the structure of the override is more akin to the use of reservations at international human rights law, rather than emergency procedures. Both devices seek to contain reasonable disagreement between institutions

[67] Lorraine Weinrib, "Learning to Live with the Override," 35 McGill L. J, 541 (1990) 563.

[68] *Compare* with Julie Debeljak, "Balancing Rights in Democracy: The Problems with Limitations and Overrides of Rights under the Victorian Charter of Human Rights and Responsibilities Act 2006," 32 Melburne U.L.R. 455 (2008).

[69] P. Hogg, A. Bushell, and W. Wright, "Charter Dialogue Revisited—Or 'Much Ado About Metaphors'," 45 Osgoode Hall L.J. 1 (2007).

[70] Kent Roach, *The Supreme Court on Trial: Judicial Activism and Democratic Dialogue* (2001) 264–5.

[71] Hogg, Bushell, and Wright, *supra* note 69.

[72] Christine Bateup, "The Dialogic Promise: Assessing the Normative Potential of Theories of Constitutional Dialogue," 71 Brook. L. Rev. 1109 (2006); Christine Bateup, "Reassessing the Dialogic Possibilities of Weak-Form Bills of Rights," 32 Hastings Int'l. & Comp. L. Rev. 529 (2009).

[73] Roach, *supra* note 70, 265.

[74] Human rights legislation from Saskatchewan, Quebec, and Alberta also contains devices like the notwithstanding clause: *Human Rights Code*, S 1979, *Charter of Human Rights and Freedoms*, Q 1977, *Bill of Rights*, A 1972. In 1992, Israel added a device similar to the "notwithstanding clause" to its Basic Law. This power, however, could be used only in respect to "freedom of occupation."

[75] E.g., Charter of Human Rights and Responsibilities Act 2006 (Vic)—"exceptional circumstances" must exist to justify the use of the override provision, including "threats to national security or a state of emergency which threatens the safety, security and welfare of the people of Victoria": *see* Debeljak, *supra* note 68, 441.

(between legislatures and judiciaries at the domestic level, and between states and international oversight institutions at the international level).[76] In the case of human rights treaties, reservations may be made by States Parties wishing to express disagreement with a particular treaty provision and restrict its application. By declaration, the state may seek "to exclude or to modify the legal effect of certain provisions."[77] This can be done unless the reservation is "prohibited by the treaty" or is "incompatible with the object and purpose of the treaty."[78] When applied against the special "humanitarian and civilizing purpose" of human rights treaties, reservations have been held to require a higher standard to be legitimate.[79]

Like the override, the availability of reservations is based on a compromise necessary for the legal effectiveness of the underlying norms: allowing states to make reservations assists the goals of universal membership to these treaties,[80] provides greater flexibility in international practice, and assures apprehensive states of the protection of their interests after ratification.[81] Nevertheless, the Human Rights Committee has held that reservations that offend customary international law, and especially those that offend peremptory norms of international law, are not compatible with the object and purpose of the ICCPR;[82] nor are they permitted under international law. Hence, reservations may not attempt to restrict rights that are non-derogable: a state may not reserve its right to engage in slavery, torture, or arbitrarily deprive of life, for example.[83] The Human Rights Committee has confirmed that reservations cannot be made for non-derogable obligations.[84] An unacceptable reservation may be severable.[85]

[76] The analogy cannot be taken too far. For example, the Human Rights Committee has suggested that reservations which seek to reject the Committee's competence to interpret the requirements of any provisions of the Covenant would be impermissible: *see CCPR General Comment No. 24*, *supra* note 53, ¶ 11. For more on the relationship between constitutional rights and international human rights, *see infra*, Chapter 10.

[77] Vienna Convention on the Law of Treaties, 23 May 1969, 1155 U.N.T.S. 331, art. 2(1)(d).

[78] Vienna Convention on the Law of Treaties, 23 May 1969, 1155 U.N.T.S. 331, art. 19. *See also Restatement (Third) of Foreign Relations Law of the United States* (1987), § 313.

[79] International Court of Justice, *Reservations to the Convention on the Prevention and Punishment of the Crime of Genocide (Advisory Opinion)* [1951] ICJ Rep 15.

[80] Ibid.

[81] Rebecca Cook, *Reservations to the Convention on the Elimination of All Forms of Discrimination against Women*, 30 Va. J. Int'l. L. 643 (1990) 650.

[82] *CCPR General Comment No. 24*, *supra* note 53, ¶ 8.

[83] Ibid.

[84] Ibid. ¶ 10.

[85] Ibid. ¶ 18. *See also* Ryan Goodman, "Human Rights Treaties, Invalid Reservations and State Consent," 96 Am. J. Int'l. L. 531 (2002).

So far as the ICESCR is concerned, there have been over forty reservations made by States Parties.[86] Many of these have related to rights to self-determination, labor rights, and rights to education, as well as to the duty of equal treatment of foreigners. India, for example, has declared a restricted application of the right to self-determination—a formulation shared by some States Parties[87] and objected to by many others.[88] India has also given precedence to its Constitution over many provisions of the ICESCR. Ireland, for example, has recognized the inalienable right and duty of parents to provide for the education of children, thus in part curtailing children's direct rights against the state.[89] Many States Parties formulate their reservations to allow for the postponement of certain obligations.[90] This, too, leads to the inevitable limitation on economic and social rights.

(5) Ease of amendment

A fifth way of understanding the susceptibility of economic and social rights to legal curtailment relates to their ease of amendment at the constitutional or treaty level. Like other restrictions, amendments take place under predefined conditions (which of course vary across constitutions). For constitutions, the greater the ease of constitutional amendment, the smaller is the division between constitutional and ordinary law, and constitutional and ordinary politics.[91] As a crude description, "[a]mendability suggests . . . that basic rights are ultimately at the mercy of interest-group politics," as Holmes and Sunstein note.[92] Unlike the other forms of limitations discussed above (with the exception, perhaps, of the override and reservation), the legitimacy of the amendment depends on the percentage of votes in favor of it, rather than its reasoned justification, although the two requirements bear a relation to each other.[93]

86 United Nations Treaty Collection, *Status of Treaties—Depository Notifications* (3 October 2011) <http://treaties.un.org/Pages/ViewDetails.aspx?src=TREATY&mtdsg_no=IV-3&chapter=4&lang=en>.

87 For example, Indonesia: ibid.

88 For example, France, Germany, Netherlands: ibid.

89 Ibid.

90 E.g., Madagascar and Zambia (on the basis of present non-implementation of primary education on the basis of financial considerations), Barbados (1973), UK (equal pay for men and women) (upon signature in 1968) ibid. On 5 September 2003, the Government of New Zealand withdrew its reservation postponing paid maternity leave or leave with adequate social security benefits, which it had reserved against art. 10(2) "in the economic circumstances foreseeable at the present time"): ibid.

91 For application, *see* Stephen Holmes and Cass R. Sunstein, "The Politics of Constitutional Revision in Eastern Europe," in Sanford Levinson (ed.), *Responding to Imperfection: The Theory and Practice of Constitutional Amendment* (1995) 275.

92 Holmes and Sunstein, "The Politics of Constitutional Revision," ibid., 275.

93 *See supra*, discussion of this relation in Chapter 2.

The US Constitution is among the most difficult of constitutions to amend—requiring passage by a two-thirds majority in each chamber of the federal Congress, followed by ratification by three-quarters of the fifty state legislatures.[94] In South Africa, the Constitution may be amended by two-thirds of the members of the National Assembly (that is, at least 267 of the 400 members).[95] If the amendment affects the Bill of Rights, including its economic and social rights, at least six of the nine provinces in the National Council of Provinces must also approve.[96] Some constitutions, although generally amendable, reserve certain provisions from alteration. The German Basic Law, for example, forbids amendment that would be counter to the inviolability of human dignity, constitutionalized in article 1, and the general principles of the state, constitutionalized in article 20, which guarantee democracy, republicanism, social responsibility, and federalism.[97] Despite these expressly designed amendment techniques, it is worth pointing out the delicate political and recognition-based questions that underlie amendment processes. Formal amendments that are adopted in contravention of a constitution's prescriptions may nevertheless be valid.[98]

An obdurate constitution puts pressure on the courts to mitigate its intractability by expansive judicial interpretation.[99] Nonetheless, the power of change is, in that case, restricted to the judiciary. Due to this imbalance, several countries have decided to entrench rights through lesser protections, such as the override and limitations clauses discussed above. A model popular in many countries with inherited models of parliamentary sovereignty allows for the protection of rights through ordinary legislation, which may be amended either by normal or somewhat heightened parliamentary procedures.[100] Hence, if economic and social rights were to be

[94] United States Constitution, art. V; *see also* Australian Constitution, § 128; *see also* Dorsen, et al., *supra* note 40, 131. Note also that referendum is required in Ghana: Constitution of the Republic of Ghana, §§ 289–91.

[95] S. Afr. Const., § 74 (1)

[96] S. Afr. Const., § 74 (2). There have been sixteen amendments since 1996, none affecting the Bill of Rights.

[97] Basic Law of Germany, art. 79(3). *See also Privacy of Communications Case*, BVerfGE 30, 1 (1970) ("*the Klass Case*") (FCC).

[98] E.g., De Gaulle's 1962 amendment to *La Constitution du 4 octobre 1958* [French Constitution of 4 October 1958].

[99] Donald Lutz, "Towards a Theory of Constitutional Amendment," in Levinson (ed.), *Responding to Imperfection, supra* note 91, 237, 266.

[100] *See*, e.g., Human Rights Act 1998 (UK); Human Rights Act 1993 (NZ); Human Rights (Parliamentary Scrutiny) Act 2011 (Cth) (Australia); Charter of Human Rights and Responsibilities Act 2006 (Vic); and Human Rights Act 2004 (ACT). *See infra*, Chapter 7, section E(2).

legislated in such systems,[101] they would be more amendable, and hence subject to that form of limitation. These models are also relevant to the question of enforcement, the last of our modes of limits by design.

(6) Directive principles or qualified enforcement

Finally, economic and social rights may be subject to qualified enforcement. One institutional design for qualified enforcement is that of enumerating economic and social rights as "Directive Principles," which are protected constitutionally, but not (without further legislation) judicially. In India, the legislature and executive are encouraged by the Constitution's Directive Principles to pursue social and economic welfare measures, which are not by themselves judicially enforceable.[102] Modeled on the Irish Constitution, these positive obligations extend to a variety of areas of economic and social policy. The expansive list, entrenched alongside fundamental rights, includes "the right to an adequate means of livelihood."[103] While directed to the elected branches, commentators have also suggested that Directive Principles are intended to curb any propensity of the judiciary to interpret fundamental rights with an economically conservative agenda.[104] The judiciary may also interpret legislation, and develop the common law, in line with those rights modeled as Directive Principles, which has led to the indirect enforcement of economic and social rights, via an inclusive interpretation of the constitutional fundamental rights, such as the right to life. Hence, to categorize Directive Principles as nonjusticiable is a fraught exercise.[105] So too are the unenforceable declarations that may be issued by statutory bills of rights.[106]

While Directive Principles represent formal and express models of qualified enforcement, any constitution may contain qualified enforcement. Because the scope of a constitutional right need not be coterminous with the scope of its judicial enforcement, most constitutions have a form of qualified enforcement. This may be understood as a form of restricting the absoluteness of rights. In his study of the US Constitution, Lawrence Sager proposes that a series of fundamental rights are protected through

[101] These statutory bills of rights largely omit economic and social rights. For a proposal for inclusion in one such statute, *see* Hilary Charlesworth, Andrew Byrnes, Renuka Thilagaratnam, and Katharine Young, *Report of the Australian Capital Territory Economic, Social and Cultural Rights Research Project* (2010).

[102] Constitution of India, art. 37.

[103] Ibid., art. 39.

[104] Carl Baar, "Social Action Litigation in India: The Operation and Limits of the World's Most Active Judiciary," in Donald Jackson and C. Neal Tate (eds.), *Comparative Judicial Review and Public Policy* (1992).

[105] *See* discussion of the Indian Supreme Court's approach to enforcement in Chapter 7, section C.

[106] *See further* Chapter 7, sections D and E, discussing this feature of the Human Rights Act 1998 (UK).

"underenforcement."[107] These include fundamental economic and social rights, which Sager suggests (against mainstream constitutional opinion) form part of the US Constitution. In arguing that "unenforced margins of under-enforced norms should have the full status of positive law . . . save only that the federal judiciary will not enforce these margins,"[108] Sager presents a coherent model of Directive Principles, without the classifications learned by comparison.

A second way in which qualified enforcement occurs is through the margin of appreciation doctrine, which was established under the European human rights system. This doctrine gives states a certain measure of discretion in the implementation of the European Convention on Human Rights (including in limitations and derogations scenarios), subject to review by the European Court of Human Rights. The nonintrusive standard of review prescribed by the "margin of appreciation" is argued to be compatible with the subsidiary nature of international law.[109] It has been deployed, to an increasing and yet uneven extent, by other international courts and tribunals.[110] While the margin of appreciation may equally be portrayed as a matter of interpretation, rather than enforcement, its institutional justification makes it similar to other forms of qualified enforcement.

Because economic and social rights are legally uncertain, and because they may be conceived as result-oriented in nature,[111] some have argued the margin of appreciation is a useful and applicable doctrine for the field. Result-oriented norms are indifferent to the way in which a desired object is attained, and provide for a broad discretion as regards the choice of means and manner of implementation. Hence, it is arguable that economic and social rights contain a *de facto* margin of appreciation doctrine in relation to application.[112]

[107] Lawrence G. Sager, *Justice in Plain Clothes: A Theory of American Constitutional Practice* (2004) 86–90.

[108] Ibid., 88.

[109] Yuval Shany, "Toward a General Margin of Appreciation Doctrine in International Law?" 16 Euro. J. Int'l. L. 907 (2005) 912. *See also Certain Aspects of the Laws on the Use of Languages in Education in Belgium (the Belgian Linguistics Case No. 2)* (1968) 1 EHRR 252, at 281–2.

[110] *Case Concerning Oil Platforms (Islamic Republic of Iran v. US)* [2003] ICJ Rep 90; *Avena and Other Mexican Nationals (Mexico v. US)* [2004] ICJ Rep 128; Legal Consequences of the Construction of a Wall in the Occupied Palestinian Territory, Opinion of 9 July 2004 [2004] ICJ Rep 131.

[111] Shany, "Toward a General Margin of Appreciation Doctrine in International Law?" *supra* note 109; *see also* Matthew Craven, *The International Covenant on Economic, Social and Cultural Rights: A Perspective on its Development* (1995).

[112] Shany, ibid., 917.

B. THE JUSTIFICATION OF LIMITS

What is common to these six legal modes of limitation is the process of justification that is established. That is, governments must establish reasons for limiting rights, and be prepared to publish and to defend those reasons. Whether it be through an internal or external limitations clause, or through formal suspension, override, amendment, or underenforcement, reasons must be given to justify the non-absoluteness of economic and social rights protection. Justifying limitations is therefore intertwined with interpreting rights, yet the steps are nevertheless distinct. Justification provides a focus on the duty-holder and establishes rights through a "culture of justification."[113] Justifying limitations may also reverse the burden of proof, making the state, rather than the party, demonstrate that the limitation does not vitiate a right.[114]

This focus on justification is key to conceiving of economic and social rights as legally, as well as morally, equivalent to civil and political rights, and as therefore subject to equivalent processes of interpretation, application, and enforcement. As an early proponent of economic and social rights for the South African Constitution, Etienne Mureinik, posed the question:

> What difficulty inhibits a court from asking, as it might in respect of a first-generation right: given the constitutional commitment to eradicate starvation, is this statute, or this administrative programme, or even the annual Budget, justified? In answering that question, the court would of course be conscious that there are many theories about how to eradicate starvation, and that it is the government's prerogative to choose among them, just because it is politically accountable and it commands the necessary expertise. A court would never be entitled to interfere with a government's honest and rational programme for eradicating starvation simply because it disapproved of the underlying political or economic theory... But the court would be entitled to ask the government to explain how it envisaged eradicating starvation. That in itself would improve the quality of government, because any decision-maker who is aware in advance of the risk of being required to

[113] Etienne Mureinik, "A Bridge to Where? Introducing the Interim Bill of Rights," 10 S. Afr. J. Hum. Rts. 31 (1994). In application to South Africa, Mureinik described the "culture of justification" as marking the change from the old apartheid style "culture of authority." *See further* Johan van der Walt and Henk Botha, "Democracy and Rights in South Africa: Beyond a Constitutional Culture of Justification," 7(3) *Constellations* 341 (2000) 342.

[114] *General Comment No. 14, supra* note 19, ¶ 28. *See also* Müller, *supra* note 30, 585. For a similar operation for the test of progressive realization, *see* the criteria for evaluating retrogressive measures taken due to resource scarcities: ECOSOC, Committee on Economic, Social and Cultural Rights, *Statement by the Committee: An Evaluation of the Obligation to Take Steps to the "Maximum of Available Resources" under an Optional Protocol to the ICESCR*, ¶ 11, E/C.12/2007/1 (10 May 2007); ECOSOC, Committee on Economic, Social and Cultural Rights, *General Comment No. 12: The Right to Adequate Food (art. 11)*, UN Doc. E/C.12/1999/5 (12 May 1999) ¶ 25; *General Comment No. 14, supra* note 19, ¶32; *General Comment No. 15, supra* note 19, ¶ 19; *General Comment No. 19, supra* note 19, ¶ 42.

justify a decision will always consider it more closely than if there were no risk.[115]

Legitimate limitations occur when a proper justification is given for the abridgement of the right. The exercise of "balancing" conflicting rights, or conflicting rights and interests, or the assessment of the "proportionality" of the restriction of the right, are prominent modes for deciding whether limitations are acceptable curtailments, or are rather infringements of constitutional rights.

Balancing is not uncontroversial. On one view, the balancing of rights is an oxymoron. The very purpose of rights is to install a deliberate incommensurability between what belongs to the heightened protection, and what may be assailed by cost-benefit decision-making or majoritarian preferences. Ronald Dworkin's well-known view of "rights as trumps" has been taken to mean that such principles precede other considerations except in catastrophic instances; policies on the other hand, remain susceptible to limitation by other considerations of policy.[116] An incommensurability of values provides protection against efficiency or welfarist arguments, which are not accorded the same moral importance. Such incommensurability also provides protection against the interests of the majority.[117] It follows from incommensurability that "different values or goods cannot be measured by the same metric." Yet trumping may not be entirely incompatible with balancing. If rights are understood to trump "excluded reasons," rather than "key interests,"[118] then their heightened protection may exist properly alongside the protection of other interests. Hence, only laws adopted for certain illegitimate reasons are those that threaten values—such as liberty—supportive of rights.[119]

Proponents of constitutional balancing suggest that it may ensure a greater degree of rights protection than absolute formulations. Economic and social rights are taken more seriously, not by introducing a paper barrier of incommensurability, but—conversely—by emphasizing the cost considerations that go into all rights.[120] On this view, rights do not lose their strength if they

[115] Etienne Mureinik, "Beyond a Charter of Luxuries: Economic Rights in the Constitution," 8 S. Afr. J. Hum. Rts. 464 (1992) 464–71.

[116] Ronald Dworkin, *Taking Rights Seriously* (1977), 82–4, 297–9; now *see* Ronald Dworkin, *Justice for Hedgehogs* (2011); Richard H. Pildes and Elizabeth S. Anderson, "Slinging Arrows at Democracy: Social Choice Theory, Value Pluralism, and Democratic Politics, " 90 Colum. L. Rev. 2121 (1990) 2148–50 (presenting a hierarchy behind incommensurability and pointing to criticisms).

[117] Frederick Schauer, "Commensurability and its Constitutional Consequences," 45 Hastings L.J. 785 (1994) 792.

[118] *See* Jeremy Waldron, "Pildes on Dworkin's Theory of Rights," 19 J. L. Stud. 301 (2000) 304. *See* Frank Michelman, "Foxy Freedom?," 90 Boston U. L. Rev. 949 (2010) 954.

[119] Dworkin, *Justice for Hedgehogs*, *supra* note 116; Michelman, ibid., 954.

[120] Holmes and Sunstein, *The Cost of Rights*, *supra* note 3. For a criticism, *see* Jonathan M. Barnett, "Rights, Costs, and the Incommensurability Problem," 86 Va. L. Rev. 1303 (2000) 1323–7.

include social and economic considerations in their very definition, but become manageable tools of balancing different, and oftentimes differently weighted, considerations. The move from rules to standards, discussed in Chapter 3 above, also provides a contextual device for measuring the progressive realization, reasonable limitation, or other structural qualification of economic and social rights. The metric of benchmarking is relevant to standards based decision-making by political institutions. Balancing, too can be seen as consistent with standards, and is suited to the reasoned judicial role (and is primarily, although not exclusively, conducted there). This occurs through the modalities of the "reasonableness review" of apparent infringements of rights, and the more general operation of proportionality analysis.

C. THE TEST OF REASONABLENESS

As we noted in Chapter 3, the South African Constitutional Court prefers the formula of "reasonableness" in interpreting and applying the obligations that fall to the state by the constitutional rights of everyone to access health care, food, water, housing and social security, and education.[121] The Constitutional Court also accepts a process of balancing and proportionality, in order to justify the limitations on rights. In doing so, the Constitutional Court has rejected a stand-alone doctrine of the minimum core, as rule. This rejection accords with the view that, despite the superficial potential of the minimum core to inform the exercise of balancing, the concept itself is arguably redundant when considered alongside the protection of economic and social interests as rights. That is, the language of rights already heightens the normative protection that the interest is due, which is then, at a second and separate stage, subject to balancing.

It will be recalled that, in South Africa, economic and social rights, which are deliberately open-textured, are made subject to obligations on the state to take "reasonable measures" to "progressively realize" the rights.[122] Reasonableness was substituted for the thinner administrative law concept of rationality.[123] Indeed, the standard of reasonableness was relied on in disciplining many of the Constitution's ambitious or otherwise vague provisions. Limitations on rights must be justified on reasonable grounds.[124]

121 S. Afr. Const. 1996 § 7(2). Also *see* §§ 26 (housing), 27 (health care, food, water, and social security), 29 (education). *See also* § 28 (1)(c) (setting out the rights of children to basic nutrition, shelter, basic health care services and social services, without qualification by a standard of progressive realization).

122 S. Afr. Const. 1996 §§ 26(2), 27(2).

123 Sandra Liebenberg, "Socio-Economic Rights: Revisiting the Reasonableness Review / Minimum Core Debate," in Stuart Woolman and Michael Bishop (eds.), *Constitutional Conversations* (2008) 305.

124 S. Afr. Const. 1996 § 36.

Even the clause governing the administrative duties upon the state calls for reasonableness and accountability in administration.[125] It is not yet clear how these standards of reasonableness differ in application.[126]

It was by no means a foregone conclusion that the textual emphasis on reasonableness would be translated as integral to judicial practice. Yet the use of reasonableness has become a key feature for adjudicating economic and social rights in a series of landmark cases (as it has for other constitutional provisions).

Hence, in finding a public hospital's decision to ration dialysis machines away from chronically ill patients to be fully compliant with the right to access health care, the Constitutional Court relied on the reasonableness of the decision of the hospital's ethics committee and of the provincial government's budget.[127] This case is the classic of the "tragic choices," one that presents no easy solution for the state.[128] Because people's needs in health care are often articulated in relation to supply (due to medical advancements, or marketized drugs), or treatment is self-evidently life saving, the state cannot satisfy everyone's legitimate health needs. Due to the cost of medicine, the possibility of medical treatment cannot automatically grant the right: since other social programs, including preventive programs, would be crippled as a result. The Court acknowledged these difficulties, and relied on the test of reasonableness in order to refuse the claim. Again, in its second decision on the right to health care, the South African Constitutional Court relied on a test of reasonableness. In finding a health department's refusal to roll out an antiretroviral drug which would prevent mother-to-child-transmission of HIV at birth to be an infringement of the right to access health care, the Constitutional Court held that the government policy on obstructing the use of privately available medicines was unreasonable.[129] The fact that antiretrovirals could convert HIV/AIDS from a death sentence to a chronic disease, and in the immediate case could prevent transmission at all, was morally significant to this assessment, which drew a critical light on many of the state's justifications for its refusal.

[125] S. Afr. Const. 1996 § 33. *See also* Promotion of Administrative Justice Act 2000 (South Africa) ("PAJA").

[126] *Khosa v. Minister of Social Development* 2004 (6) SA 505 (CC) (Mokgoro J); *see also* Iles, *supra* note 10.

[127] *Soobramoney v. Minister of Health, Kwazulu-Natal* 1998 (1) SA 765 (CC). This case was argued as one that raised the right to life, as well as the prohibition on the denial of emergency treatment, rather than the right to health care. This had clear doctrinal advantages for the claimant, in that these provisions do not allow for the more calibrated obligation of "progressive realization." The Court chose, instead, to consider the right to health care, denying that this should be considered a life protecting or an emergency procedure.

[128] Guido Calabresi and Philip Bobbitt, *Tragic Choices* (1978).

[129] *Minister of Health v. Treatment Action Campaign* 2002 (5) SA 721 (CC). For a fuller discussion, *see infra* Chapter 9.

Similarly, the test of reasonableness has been used in other economic and social rights decisions. In finding a housing department's omission of vulnerable people in emergency need of housing from its national housing policy to be an infringement of the right to access housing, the Constitutional Court held that the government had acted unreasonably.[130] In finding a legislative restriction on welfare benefits for non-citizen permanent residents to be an infringement of the right to access social security and the right to equality, the Constitutional Court held that the legislative distinction between citizens and permanent residents was unreasonable.[131] In finding an eviction of residents from uninhabitable buildings to be an infringement of the right to access housing, the Constitutional Court held that a meaningful consultation was required between the municipality and potential evictees before an eviction could be reasonable. And in finding a relocation of a massive inner-city housing settlement to be compatible with the right to access housing, the Constitutional Court held that the long-term planning of a city could reasonably take place at the cost of some short-term challenges.[132]

The Constitutional Court has suggested that the doctrinal test of reasonableness allows it to assess "the nature of the duty, the social and economic context in which it arises, the range of factors that are relevant to the performance of the duty, the extent to which the duty is closely related to the core activities of the duty bearer . . . and the extent of any threat to fundamental rights should the duty not be met as well as the intensity of any harm that may result."[133] The principle of proportionality common in other rights-protective constitutional systems reflects the idea that "[t]he more grave is the threat to fundamental rights, the greater is the responsibility on the duty-bearer."[134] While it considers resource capacity within this equation, the Court's application of proportionality makes it alert to the problems of blank utilitarianism. Resource constraints are relevant to what may "hamper the organ of state in meeting its obligation."[135] Yet these must be proven, not assumed. Hence, "[d]etails of the precise character of the resource constraints, whether human or financial, in the context of the overall resourcing of the organ of the state will need to be provided."[136]

[130] *Government of the Republic of South Africa v. Grootboom* 2001 (1) SA 46 (CC).

[131] *Khosa v. Minister of Social Development* 2004 (6) SA 505 (CC).

[132] *Residents of Joe Slovo Community Western Cape v. Thubelisha Homes*, 2010 (3) SA 454 (CC).

[133] *Rail Commuters Action Group v. Transnet Ltd t/a Metrorail* 2005 (2) SA 359 (CC); *Bato Star Fishing (Pty) Ltd v. Minister of Environmental Affairs* 2004 (4) SA 490 (CC).

[134] Robert Alexy, *A Theory of Constitutional Rights* (1986) (Julian Rivers trans., 2002).

[135] *Bato Star Fishing (Pty) Ltd v. Minister of Environmental Affairs* 2004 (4) SA 490 (CC).

[136] Ibid.

The Court uses the "[r]easons given for the decision" in making its assessment.[137] So understood, the Court suggests that "[t]he standard of reasonableness . . . conforms to the constitutional principles of accountability . . . and of effectiveness, for it does not unduly hamper the decision-makers' authority to determine what are reasonable and appropriate measures in the overall context of their activities."[138] This is a difficult line to draw: on the one hand, the Constitutional Court is attempting to independently scrutinize the government's decisions, and on the other, it is seeking not to interfere in the government decision-maker's own assessment of rationality and reasonableness. In noting the importance of deference to administrative decision-makers, the Constitutional Court seeks to provide such review at the same time as respecting the "multiplicity of routes to follow to achieve the goal."[139]

The test of reasonableness brings constitutional rights review and administrative review in closer operation: finding a middle ground of scrutiny between the two.[140] Of course, this bridging comes with its own virtues and vices—economic and social rights appear more manageable and familiar to the procedures of a functioning administrative system; and yet undoubtedly their specially protected status is loosened by bringing constitutional protection and ordinary administrative procedures into closer alignment.

Nonetheless, the justificatory test of reasonableness has many supporters. The use of reasonableness is said to avoid the risk of over- or under-inclusivity in defining economic and social rights.[141] More specifically, the posture is consistent with two institutional rules for limiting the judicial role. First, reasonableness is consistent with the Constitutional Court's early-expressed institutional rule "never to anticipate a question of constitutional law in advance of the necessity of deciding it" and "never to formulate a rule of constitutional law broader than is required by the precise facts to which it is to be applied."[142] Moreover, it is consistent with the evolving South African doctrine of "subsidiarity," which provides that where there is a statute that has been enacted to give effect to a right, a litigant must apply for relief in terms of the legislation rather than in terms

137 Ibid., [45].

138 *Rail Commuters Action Group v. Transnet Ltd t/a Metrorail* 2005 (2) SA 359, [88] (CC); *Bato Star Fishing (Pty) Ltd v. Minister of Environmental Affairs* 2004 (4) SA 490, [45] (CC).

139 *Rail Commuters Action Group v. Transnet Ltd t/a Metrorail* 2005 (2) SA 359, [60] & [86] (CC).

140 Geo Quinot and Sandra Liebenberg, "Narrowing the Band: Reasonableness Review in Administrative Justice and Socio-Economic Rights Jurisprudence in South Africa" 22 Stell L. Rev. 639 (2011).

141 Carol Steinberg, "Can Reasonableness Protect the Poor? A Review of South Africa's Socio-Economic Rights Jurisprudence" 123 S. Afr. L.J. 264 (2006) 273.

142 *Zantsi v. Council of State, Ciskei* 1995 (4) SA 615 (CC).

of the Constitution, or alternatively challenge the legislation as inconsistent with the Constitution.[143]

Reasonableness also provides a vehicle for the court to consider expert, professional, and local opinion. This position can be characterized as an insistent inquiry into, rather than a permissive acceptance of, the opinions of experts, professionals, and claimants in relation to economic and social rights. In the *TAC* case, for example, the Constitutional Court considered the prior approval of the antiretroviral Nevirapine by the South African Medical Review Board and the World Health Organization to be a crucial indicator of the unreasonableness of the government's prevention of the roll-out of the drug to expecting mothers.[144] It considered the experiential evidence of doctors and nurses who were prevented from administering the drug: their testimony, which described the compromise of their professional ethics that was caused by the public prohibition of the drug, was influential in the assessment of reasonableness. Using prominent analysis from health care ethics, we might suggest that reasonableness review requires an assessment of the most important reasons for particular health care allocation decisions—such as helping those who are worst off, helping those who would benefit most from medical intervention, assisting the largest possible number of people, or ensuring people have fair chances of receiving assistance, regardless of urgency.[145] Of course, the weight given to moral reasons is balanced, in the non-ideal situation, by other factors.[146] In the *TAC* decision, the Court was able to marshal an inclusive approach to its reasoning, due in part to the litigants' own efforts at coordinating the evidence of doctors, nurses, and scientists in making the assessment.[147] The evidence, drawn from the social sciences, proved critical.[148]

[143] *Nokotyana* v. *Ekurhuleni Metropolitan Municipality* 2010 (4) BCLR 312 (CC); *see also* Lourens du Plessis, "Interpretation," in Stuart Woolman, Michael Bishop, and Theunis Roux (eds), *Constitutional law of South Africa* (2nd edn., 2006) 142–58. This application of subsidiarity is combined with a noted difference in the judicial stance with respect to the review of pro-poor legislation: Jackie Dugard and Theunis Roux, "The Record of the South African Constitutional Court in Providing an Institutional Voice for the Poor: 1995–2004," in Roberto Gargarella, Pilar Domingo and Theunis Roux (eds.), *Courts and Social Transformation in New Democracies: An Institutional Voice for the Poor?* (2006) 107, 116. This is discussed in greater detail in Chapters 5–6, *infra*.

[144] *Minister of Health v. Treatment Action Campaign* 2002 (5) SA 721 (CC).

[145] Norman Daniels, *Just Health: Meeting Health Needs Fairly* (2008). For a critical analysis of the "rescue" principle in health care rationing, *see* Ronald Dworkin, *Sovereign Virtue: The Theory and Practice of Equality* (2000) 307.

[146] For a treatment of the different paradigms of health care analysis, including moral and market paradigms, *see* Einer Elhauge, "Allocating Health Care Morally," 82 Cal. L. Rev. 1449 (1994) 1452.

[147] *See* discussion in Chapter 9, *infra*.

[148] For an early intervention in noting the importance of such evidence, in a right to health analysis, *see* Martha Minow, "Defining the Right to Adequate Health," in Jonathan Mann and Henry Steiner (eds.),

In other cases, the local knowledge rendered by claimants has been influential and claimant expectations have influenced the assessment of reasonableness. In *Grootboom*, the failure of the municipality responsible for housing to engage with the community was evidence of the lack of reasonableness in the government's policy.[149] In a later evictions case, the Constitutional Court joined the procedural and substantive aspects of reasonableness, noting that "sustainable reconciliations" of different interests could be achieved through a "proactive and honest engagement" between the parties. Through "respectful face-to-face engagement or mediation through a third party," "mutually acceptable solutions" could be found.[150] In this way, the Court constructed the standard of "meaningful engagement" as factoring into its test of reasonableness. Hence, if an evictor does not engage meaningfully with occupiers, the constitutional obligation of reasonableness is unlikely to have been discharged.[151] In *Olivia Road*, the purported eviction of residents on habitability grounds was subject to a staged inquiry into reasonableness.[152] The Court noted the importance that both sides act reasonably in good faith, and that they must adopt openness in engagement. This brought the standard of review into the ordering of a remedy, which is described further in Chapters 5 and 6.

The constitutional doctrine of reasonableness therefore uses a form of proportionality reasoning, standards rather than rules, and an informed deference to administration, or to the evidence of experts or local opinion.[153] Whether it can continue to provide a contextual and inclusive reasoning process remains to be seen: If it leads to more deference to government, and more contextualization on each fact, it may not provide either protection or certainty. Yet we can understand reasonableness as a localized expression of the proportionality test. As stated early by the Court, "[t]he limitation of constitutional rights for a purpose that is reasonable and necessary in a democratic society involves the weighing up of competing values, and ultimately an assessment based on proportionality."[154] The Constitutional Court of South Africa's efforts with respect to its limitations clause have been commended as leading to "the best expression of the connection

Social Rights and the Right to Health: An Interdisciplinary Discussion Held at Harvard Law School in September, 1993 (1995) 17, 30.

149 *Government of the Republic of South Africa v. Grootboom* 2001 (1) SA 46, [87] (CC).

150 *Port Elizabeth Municipality v. Various Occupiers* 2005 (1) SA 217, [39] (CC).

151 *See Occupiers of 51 Olivia Road v. City of Johannesburg*, 2008 (3) SA 208 (CC).

152 Ibid., [14].

153 *See, e.g., Bato Star Fishing (Pty) Ltd v. Minister of Environmental Affairs* 2004 (4) SA 490, [45] (CC).

154 *S. v. Makwanyane* 1995 (3) SA 391, [104] (CC) (per Chaskalson P).

between [the] three categories [of] proportionality, reasonableness and necessity" available.[155] It is to the test of proportionality that we now turn.

D. PROPORTIONALITY IN LIMITS

The Constitutional Court of South Africa has focused on the reasonableness of the government's actions in a series of decisions shaping the review of economic and social rights. Reasonableness review aligns with the textual protection of economic and social rights, the reason-centeredness of the Constitution, and the culture of justification it demands. Yet other constitutional systems practice a more general form of proportionality. Outside of the leading example of Germany, the European human rights system, as well as the constitutional systems of Canada, India, and Israel, apply rights and their limitations by assessing the latter against their proportionate aims and means.[156] Hence, proportionality has now become an adequate descriptor of global constitutional practice, particularly for the rights recognized in constitutions or human rights treaties post-World War II.[157] Even US constitutional law, by providing escalating tiers of scrutiny for particular constitutional rights, exercises a form of balancing analysis.[158]

Proportionality follows a two-stage analysis that replicates many of the steps of the modes described in section A of this chapter. The first step consists in determining whether an act infringes the scope of the right, as that meaning has been interpreted. If it does, a *prima facie* violation of a right has occurred. The second step consists in determining whether that infringement is justified under the limitations clause, or other limiting provision. There is debate as to the number of steps, or "stages," in this approach, and the ways in which analysis can be divided. Nonetheless, it is only by passing through different steps of analysis that, if the infringement is found to be unjustified, there is a definitive violation of the right.[159] The standards of limitation may themselves be subject to disagreement. Moreover, while courts have taken the lead in assessing the proportionality of law or policies that may override rights, there is nothing about the test that prevents

[155] Wojciech Sadurski, "Reasonableness and Value Pluralism in Law and Politics," in Giorgio Bongiovanni, Giovanni Sartor, and Chiara Valentini (eds), *Reasonableness in Law* (2009) 129, 135.

[156] *See* generally David Beatty, *The Ultimate Rule of Law* (2004).

[157] Weinrib, *Postwar Paradigm*, *supra* note 7.

[158] T. Alexander Aleinikoff, "Constitutional Law in the Age of Balancing," 96 Yale L.J. 943 (1987); regarding particular judges: Kathleen Sullivan, "Post-Liberal Judging: The Roles of Categorization and Balancing," 63 U. Colo. L. Rev. 293 (1992).

[159] Mattias Kumm, "Political Liberalism and the Structures of Rights: On the Place and Limits of the Proportionality Requirement," in S. Paulson, G. Pavlakos (eds.), *Law, Rights, Discourse: Themes of the Work of Robert Alexy* (2007); *see also R v. Oakes* [1986] 1 S.C.R. 103 (SCC).

legislatures from engaging in a proportionality inquiry—and a lot that is complementary.[160]

This global practice of proportionality is described, and extended, by Robert Alexy, who has provided a formula of proportionality from reconstructing German constitutional jurisprudence. Alexy argues that balancing is not arbitrary and is subject to its own discipline. Under Alexy's formula, proportionality provides rights protection by requiring a reason of sufficient strength and priority before rights can be limited. Like the social and economic resources that they purport to guarantee, rights are also subject to the law of diminishing marginal utility: "The greater the degree of non-satisfaction of, or detriment to, one principle, the greater must be the importance of satisfying the other."[161] Constitutional rights may be treated structurally as principles, and, to be legitimate, any conflicting principles must be suitable, necessary (using the least restrictive means), and proportionate. The principles of suitability and necessity refer to what is factually possible, whereas the principle of proportionality refers to what is legally possible.

Alexy's schema is highly technical, and its intricacy is worth demonstrating with an example. Let us take the conflict presented by protecting the right to property and the right to access housing in a legal system of available land and housing. Under the proportionality framework, both rights to provide property and housing must be optimized to the greatest extent possible. First, the principle of suitability means that interference with one principle must contribute to the realization of the other. We might consider whether a particular interference with the protection of property will contribute to the realization of the principle of a right to housing. This is an empirical question, but one can forecast that its satisfaction would not be difficult.[162] For example, a government which disregards certain planning procedures, protective of private property, in order to provide for the temporary housing of flood victims, may satisfy the question of suitability without undue effort.[163] Secondly, the principle of necessity requires that there be no other less restrictive means available by which to achieve the same result. This, too, depends upon the empirical facts at hand—and satisfaction is more difficult. If, for example, by provision of alternative shelter on land that does not disturb property rights, the state could achieve the same realization of the housing right, then the principle of necessity

[160] Indeed, one of the criticisms of the test is that it is mirrors legislative practice: *see* Sadurski, "Reasonableness and Value Pluralism in Law and Politics," *supra* note 155.

[161] Alexy, *A Theory of Constitutional Rights*, *supra* note 134, 102.

[162] Kai Möller, "Balancing and the Structure of Constitutional Rights," 5 Int'l. J. Const. L. 453 (2007).

[163] *See* the constitutionality of the government's actions in *Minister of Pub. Works v. Kyalami Ridge Envtl. Ass'n.* 2001 (3) SA 1151 (CC).

would be infringed.[164] In our flood victim's example, the burden would be on the government to indicate that alternative housing is not available.[165] Thirdly, Alexy's principle of proportionality in the narrow sense requires comparing the weights of the competing principles in concrete cases, which requires the deliberation of norms. By balancing the two competing principles—for example, property and housing—one determines the limits of what is legally possible.

Alexy suggests that this structural protection advances rights far more than building a "firewall ex ante."[166] He is also committed to rights in hybrid form—as representing both rules and principles. Without rules, he suggests that written constitutions are not taken seriously enough. He is committed to the view that an interpretation must proceed from text, and only depart from it where this is warranted by special reasons. For Alexy, constitutional rights, such as economic and social rights, may constitute rules and principles. Principles require the optimization of the rights, to the greatest extent possible in law and fact. Rules, on the other hand, are fixed points in the field of the legally and factually possible: they are always either fulfilled or not.[167] Nonetheless, as rules, they may be subject to an exception that applies to a particular case, and which is based on a principle. The relatively greater weight of rules is established because of other formal principles, such as that rules are generally followed.

Hence, for example, a constitutional right to housing may be considered a principle, such as that housing should be optimized. Counter-principles may limit the right to housing, and it is within the discretion of the legislature, rather than the courts, to identify and choose which principles run counter to the limit. When legislation is passed which interferes with the right to housing in order to promote economic development, for example, whether this is justified depends on whether the principle of access to housing or the counter-principle of economic development takes precedence in the concrete case.[168] If a default on a mortgage has been brought about by the failure to repay a petty debt, then the limitation upon the right to housing is not justified.[169]

[164] *Compare President of the Republic of South Africa v. Modderklip Boerdery (Pity) Ltd* 2005 (5) SA 3 (CC); with *Modderklip Boerdery v. President Van Die RSA En Andere* 2003 (6) BCLR 638 (T).

[165] E.g., *Minister of Pub. Works v. Kyalami Ridge Envtl. Ass'n.* 2001 (3) SA 1151 (CC).

[166] *Cf. Jürgen Habermas, Between Facts and Norms* (trans. William Rehg, 1996).

[167] Alexy, *A Theory of Constitutional Rights*, *supra* note 134, 48. The contrast between rules and principles presented by Alexy differs from that presented by Dworkin, *Taking Rights Seriously*, supra note 116. We can compare the distinction drawn, too, between rules and standards in *supra* Chapter 3. Both standards and principles introduce more flexible, substantive considerations than rules, and, depending on how the term is used, principles are more general and cross-doctrinal than standards.

[168] E.g., *Residents of Joe Slovo Community Western Cape v. Thubelisha Homes*, 2010 (3) SA 454 (CC).

[169] E.g., *Jaftha v. Schoeman* 2005 (2) SA 140 (CC); *see also Maphango v. Aengus Lifestyle Properties (Pty Ltd)* Case CCT 57/11 [2012] ZACC 2 (March 13, 2012) (CC) (landlord investments versus rights of poor tenants).

Alexy's theory leaves room for a constitutional right to housing to operate as a rule. For example, the prohibition on forced evictions is a rule, enshrined in the Constitution, which may escape balancing. For Alexy, this is itself subject to a framework of principles: the principle that rules laid down by a legitimate authority must be followed carries weight.

Alexy's "maximizing" lens has been criticized as introducing an unduly consequentialist and utilitarian theory into constitutional rights. The latter moral theories, which seek to maximize utility, happiness, and so forth, may be entirely at ease with the optimization inquiry. Yet even deontologists can subscribe to optimization, as long as they recognize that conflicts between values may exist. Such a rationale does not lead to a "perversion" of rights, as some have suggested.[170] As long as the reasons justifying the infringement of rights have a special strength, then rights will be protected from policy considerations of general welfare.[171] Strength derives from either a perspective of substantive morality,[172] or, more practically, a perspective on the judicial role in a democracy.[173] If they are not sufficiently strong, then one does not have much by virtue of having an economic and social right.[174]

At base, the proportionality requirement is linked to the culture of justification. Like reasonableness review, which may be seen as a significant subset of proportionality analysis, proportionality brings transparency to a legislative or judicial assessment by revealing to the public all the ingredients of the decision-making calculus.[175] Proportionality is said to build consensus, by reducing the sense of defeat of the losing party within adjudication, because their asserted claim has been weighed during a process of deliberation.[176] Any challenge under rights is therefore not seen as a means to preclude democratic dialogue, but rather as a means of facilitating and structuring an inquiry into the justifiability of official conduct and the policy choices that are made through it.[177] Further, the content and meaning of the standards of justification alter with shifts in the social contexts, in the background political morality, as described in Part III, and in the accepted role of the judiciary, as detailed in Part II of this book. It is to these efforts we now turn.

[170] Stavros Tsakyrakis, "Proportionality: An Assault on Human Rights?," 7 Int'l. J. Const. L. 468 (2009).

[171] Kumm, "Political Liberalism and the Structures of Rights," *supra* note 159.

[172] Möller, "Balancing and the Structure of Constitutional Rights," *supra* note 162, 468.

[173] Michelman, "Foxy Freedom," *supra* note 118, 962.

[174] Kumm, "Political Liberalism and the Structures of Rights," *supra* note 159.

[175] Sadurski, "Reasonableness and Value Pluralism in Law and Politics," *supra* note 155.

[176] Ibid.

[177] Johan van der Walt and Henk Botha, "Democracy and Rights in South Africa," *supra* note 113, 342 (on Etienne Mureinik).

PART II

CONSTITUTING RIGHTS BY ENFORCEMENT

How rights are enforced goes to the very fact of their legal significance. Rights which are deemed merely "aspirational" attract a host of skeptical questions. How can they be taken seriously if they lack institutions to back them up? How can they bind legal decision-makers if they are not applied in courts? How do they work to change conflicting laws if they do not bind courts? These questions go to the foundations of how rights—as more than desirable, more than hortatory, more than commendable moral concepts—effect change in our public legal systems. They determine what is understood to be most fundamental in a society, and what commands the institutional support of the state—the violence of sanctions and of prohibitions—through the force of law. The enforcement of economic and social rights, like all rights, is constitutive of their significance and meaning.

Yet these questions run up against other challenges. With the evident ambiguity of meaning and a plurality of interpretive standpoints, how can courts do justice to enforcement? Without recourse to expertise or administrators, how can judges stipulate a minimum calorific content for food programs, or the requisite number of teachers per classroom? How can they decide when sufficient state resources are, or are not, available, for the satisfaction of a particular right? If they approximate an answer, how can claimants and others protest their reasons? Must litigation (and litigation's requisite requirements of money, expertise, and time) settle these questions? If so, will other democratic processes become redundant, and indeed will this settlement jeopardize the interests of those whom the rights purport to protect? These concerns reflect the intuition and popular belief that economic and social rights are not justiciable. Since the Universal Declaration of Human Rights of 1948, the question of enforceability can be summarized in the answer of nonjusticiability. Despite certain exceptions, economic and social rights were hands-off for courts, thus foreclosing this vital forum of contestation, interpretation, and application.

Yet in between these positions of merely aspirational statements and judicially controlled law lie a range of alternatives. Indeed, these have been around since the 1950s. Economic and social rights can be entrenched in law as "directive principles of state policy," requiring legislators, policy-makers, and officials to take them into account. Courts cognizant of this attention, required by law, are on notice to interpret legislation and policy in a similar way. Similarly, courts themselves, when exercising interpretive latitude, can use directive principles as a guide to other, enforceable, rights. Moreover, courts can adopt a variety of stances of judicial review towards expressly justiciable rights, utilizing more or less exacting postures of scrutiny, or ordering more or less interventionist remedies, to enforce particular rights. Leaving courts to one side, statutory bills of rights can establish scrutiny procedures to ensure draft legislation complies with rights or face political consequences if it does not. Human Rights Commissions, and other administrative bodies, can also investigate and advise on the state's compliance with rights. Economic and social rights are constituted through this variety of enforcement.

The chapters in this Part focus on the degree, and institutional variety, of enforcement. Chapter 5 sets out a typology of judicial review, which describes the different stances towards review and remedy assumed by different courts (or by the same court, in different cases). Chapter 6 describes the role conceptions of courts, which allow them to assume such different attitudes of enforcement. In introducing the model of the "catalytic court," it suggests that such variegated techniques, which I attribute to the South African Constitutional Court, can respond to the obstacles of intransigence, incompetence, or inattentiveness on the part of government, and prompt other actors to resolve these obstacles. Chapter 7 establishes a second typology, this time of role conceptions, which are observed in other constitutional systems. Apex courts in Colombia, India, and the United Kingdom are compared. The chapter also describes the constitutional backdrop of nonjudicial enforcement procedures. The presence of these procedures goes in part to explain the divergence between courts, and also suggests new, and different, public forums for constituting economic and social rights.

5

A Typology of Judicial Review

If economic and social rights are as indeterminate as other rights, approaches to the interpretation of rights and of their justifiable limitations respond to and (to some extent) address this indeterminacy. This interpretive task often falls to courts, and is often governed by jurisdictional rules. In enforcing the duty to respect, protect, or promote economic and social rights—indeed, in being a duty-holder themselves—courts may be called upon to decide on the nature of such rights, their scope, and the obligations that flow from them. Facing the complexity of the myriad institutions which impact upon the material terms of social life, they must discharge their role in enforcing the negative and positive arrangements that determine who does what in order to secure economic and social rights.

While there are additional philosophical dimensions to the question of the foundations of, and justification for, economic and social rights,[1] it is the institutional challenges of recognizing and enforcing economic and social rights that have been the most salient in arguments against their recognition in constitutional (or even legislative) terms. These questions are concentrated on the judiciary: the problem of "justiciability" still presents a central objection to the recognition of economic and social rights in national and international law.[2] The concerns of justiciability are based on opposing extremes: the problems of judicial usurpation on the one hand, and judicial abdication on the other.[3]

[1] These are canvassed in Chapters 1 and 2, *supra*.

[2] *See*, as traditionally expressed in US constitutional law, Robert H. Bork, Commentary, "The Impossibility of Finding Welfare Rights in the Constitution," Wash. U. L.Q. 695 (1979); *see also* Frank Cross, "The Error of Positive Rights," 48 UCLA L. Rev. 857 (2001); Michael J. Dennis and David P. Stewart, "Justiciability of Economic, Social, and Cultural Rights: Should There Be an International Complaints Mechanism to Adjudicate the Rights to Food, Water, Housing, and Health?," 98 Am. J. Int'l. L. 462 (2004) (applying a justiciability critique to the international level).

[3] Frank I. Michelman, "Socioeconomic Rights in Constitutional Law: Explaining America Away," 6 Int'l. J. Const. L. 663 (2008).

A. USURPATION VERSUS ABDICATION: THE TWO WRONGS OF ENFORCEMENT

Judicial usurpation occurs when the judiciary interprets and applies rights in such a manner that it assumes control of the political system, crowding out or crabbing the democratically elected branches.[4] Abdication occurs when the judiciary declines to protect constitutional rights, risking (it is said) debasement of all fundamental rights.[5] Of course, these two challenges, although perhaps exaggerated in the context of economic and social rights because of their more apparent resource implications, apply to the place of courts in upholding the rights required by constitutionalism in general.[6] Yet when economic and social rights raise positive obligations for governments to act, rather than negative obligations for governments to desist,[7] the traditional adjudicative role of courts is challenged to an exceptional degree. The concerns about usurpation and abdication have been most pronounced because of the emphasis on positive obligations that attach to economic and social rights.

The two concerns are not always mutually held. It is fair to say that US commentators are generally more worried about judicial usurpation, and South African commentators are generally more concerned with judicial abdication.[8] At base, both positions accept the terms of the debate within separation of powers concerns. These concerns are not simply derived from a merely formal respect for the doctrine of separation of powers, prevalent in constitutionalist systems since Montesquieu. The division of labor between roles is substantial. Since judges do not face the discipline of election or reelection, they are not subject to the same democratic safeguards as the elected branches. They lack access to information-building bureaucracies and competencies, apart from the resources marshaled by adversarial parties as relevant to their own disputes. They are incapable of dealing with the inevitable polycentricity of the outcomes of adjudication,

[4] Ran Hirschl, *Towards Juristocracy: The Origins and Consequences of the New Constitutionalism* (2004).

[5] Cass R. Sunstein, "Against Positive Rights," in Andras Sajo (ed.), *Western Rights? Post-Communist Application* (1996), but *see* Cass R. Sunstein, "Why Does the American Constitution Lack Social and Economic Guarantees?," 545 Syr. L. Rev. 1 (2005) (revising his earlier warning).

[6] Jeremy Waldron, "The Core of the Case against Judicial Review," 115 Yale L.J. 1346 (2006).

[7] For a discussion of this distinction, *see* Chapter 4.

[8] For the former, *see* Mark Tushnet, *Weak Courts, Strong Rights: Judicial Review and Social Welfare Rights in Comparative Constitutional Law* (2008); Cass R. Sunstein, *The Second Bill of Rights: FDR's Unfinished Revolution and Why We Need It More Than Ever* (2004). For the latter, Sandra Liebenberg, "Socio-Economic Rights: Revisiting the Reasonableness Review/Minimum Core Debate," in Stuart Woolman and Michael Bishop (eds.), *Constitutional Conversations* (2008) 305; *see also* David Bilchitz, *Poverty and Fundamental Rights: The Justification and Enforcement of Socio-Economic Rights* (2007) 198. For a directly comparative perspective, *see* Mark S. Kende, *Constitutional Rights in Two Worlds: South Africa and the United States* (2009).

whereby numerous (and absent) parties will be affected in dynamic, complex, and often unpredictable ways.[9] In addition, since judges may have limited expertise in ethics or political theory, they are arguably not able to provide a special forum of insight in moral or political principle. And even if they are right in reasoning, their decisions may nevertheless be futile or produce contrary results in the long run.[10]

Two prescriptions are currently offered to address this concern: the first counsels avoidance, the second, embrace. On the one hand, courts should stay out of the contestations around economic and social rights, which are better employed as moral "talk" in politics, or, at most, as unenforceable guides for legislative or administrative decision-making. Usurpation is managed, and abdication cannot come about if expectations of enforcement are not raised. Hence such concerns, suggests Frank Michelman, may provide "moral cover for a choice that moral ideal theory condemns"[11]—the continued exclusion of economic and social rights from constitutional law. The second argument, on the other hand, suggests that courts should acknowledge that they are adjudicating economic and social rights in their everyday application of private law. "Every constitutional court," claims Mark Tushnet, "enforces some vision of social or economic rights"[12] when they negotiate the terms of property, contract, or tort law. Usurpation, in particular, becomes a tendentious argument when one considers the existing power of courts.

The apparent opposition of these prescriptions loses force when balanced against the variety of ways in which constitutional courts actually respond to the complaints of economic and social rights infringements—a variety now seen as representative of "weak" courts. By "weak courts," Tushnet has demarcated processes of judicial review, especially those outside the United States, which allow courts to "assess legislation against constitutional norms, but do not [give them] the final word on whether statutes comply with those norms."[13] Once we give further detail to this variety of "strong" and "weak" courts, we can loosen the hold of an alternative, third, prescription: that courts should adjudicate by assuming the posture of "weak" review. This chapter provides this detail by engaging one court in context—the South African Constitutional Court's enforcement of economic and social rights.

[9] Lon Fuller, "The Forms and Limits of Adjudication," 82 Harv. L. Rev. 353 (1979).

[10] Cass R. Sunstein, *Radicals in Robes: Why Extreme Right-Wing Courts Are Wrong for America* (2005) 35–6.

[11] Michelman, "Explaining America Away," *supra* note 3, 683.

[12] Tushnet, *Weak Courts, Strong Rights*, *supra* note 8, 227.

[13] Ibid., ix.

B. DISAGGREGATING ENFORCEMENT

This book argues that the South African Constitution's commitment to economic and social rights is not unique in a survey of constitutional models around the world. Even in the United States, we find examples of "constitutive" societal commitments, from New Deal efforts onwards, that continue to command widespread support.[14] Hence, even in a jurisdiction where the ideology of social democracy faced many obstacles,[15] there is evidence of judicial support for economic and social rights, both in the presently abandoned Supreme Court equal protection and due process jurisprudence,[16] in the more inexplicit directions taken in other constitutional cases,[17] as well as in the more specific and explicitly entrenched examples from state constitutional law.[18] And of course, there are many other examples of judicial attention to economic and social rights, including from Canada, Colombia, Germany, India, and the United Kingdom.[19]

Despite its lack of singularity in constituting economic and social rights, South Africa clearly enjoys one of the most extensive and explicit constitutional permissions for judicial involvement. As a critical part of its "transformative" ambition, the South African Constitution of 1996 protects the rights of everyone to access housing, health care, food, water, social security, and education.[20] The government is obliged to take reasonable legislative and other measures to realize them. Such rights trigger both negative duties of noninterference with fundamental material interests, and positive duties to provide the goods and services necessary to secure them.[21] Each duty may give rise to complaints that are justiciable—an issue debated by drafters and subsequently confirmed explicitly by the Constitutional

[14] Franklin D. Roosevelt, Message to Congress on the State of the Union (11 January 1944), in Vol. 13, Samuel I. Rosenman (ed.), *The Public Papers and Addresses of Franklin D. Roosevelt* (1950) 40; Sunstein, *The Second Bill of Rights*, *supra* note 8.

[15] Seymour Martin Lipset and Gary Marks, *It Didn't Happen Here: Why Socialism Failed in the United States* (2001).

[16] Cass R. Sunstein, "Why Does the American Constitution Lack Social and Economic Guarantees?," *supra* note 5; *see further* Frank I. Michelman, "Foreword: On Protecting the Poor through the Fourteenth Amendment," 83 Harv. L. Rev. 7 (1969).

[17] Lawrence G. Sager, *Justice in Plainclothes: A Theory of American Constitutional Practice* (2004).

[18] Helen Hershkoff, "Positive Rights and State Constitutions: The Limits of Federal Rationality Review," 112 Harv. L. Rev. 1131 (1999).

[19] *See further* Chapter 7.

[20] S. Afr. Const. 1996 §§ 26 (housing), 27 (health care, food, water, and social security), 29 (education). *See also* § 28 (children's rights). For a lengthier discussion of these clauses, *see* Chapter 1 section B(1) and introduction to Part I; *see also* Appendix I.

[21] *Compare* S. Afr. Const. 1996 § 26(3) (prohibition of arbitrary evictions) with § 26(1) (rights of access to adequate housing); *See also* § 7(2) ('The state must respect, protect, promote and fulfil the rights in the Bill of Rights').

Court.[22] Courts are vested with a broad discretion to grant "just and equitable" remedies.[23] Hence, the structural terms of the Constitution, as well as the constitutional culture that was responsible for its entrenchment and that continues to agitate around it, litigate it, and hence legitimate it, are all part of this conferral of judicial power.

So far, the Constitutional Court has adjudicated primary claims to housing, health care, water, and social security rights, as well as secondary claims for electricity, sanitation and lighting, and access to education.[24] In each of these cases, the Constitutional Court has advanced distinctive techniques for dealing with the challenge of enforcing economic and social rights. First, the Constitutional Court has rigorously examined claims of institutional self-certainty, peering into the rationale of legislatures or of bureaucracies when they make decisions that obstruct, limit, or condition the delivery of social goods and services. As we have seen, this is achieved by inquiring into the "reasonableness" of government actions, assessed in context against the substantive promise of each right.[25] Second, the Constitutional Court has ordered diverse remedies to address detected unconstitutionality, attempting to bring about change at different levels in different sectors by declaring particular infringements and incompatibilities, by ordering engagement between the parties, by issuing timelines and other terms of delivery, by suspending its orders, or by reading-in "curing words" to legislation.

The variety that such measures represent can be attributed to three main elements of the process of judicial review: the judicial approach to interpretation; the degree of scrutiny of the government's action; and the remedy ordered. This analysis is helped by Tushnet's depiction of "strong" and "weak" courts and the forms of judicial review that accompany their enforcement of "strong" and "weak" rights.[26] Within this classification,

[22] *In re Certification of the Constitution of the Republic of South Africa ("Certification Judgment")* 1996 (10) BCLR 1253 (CC).

[23] S. Afr. Const. 1996, §§ 38, 172(1)(b).

[24] The primary cases are all discussed *infra*. These secondary claims are represented by *Nokotyana v. Ekurhuleni Metropolitan Municipality* [2009] ZACC 33, Case CCT 31/09 (rights to toilets and safety lighting as part of the right of access to adequate housing); *Joseph v. City of Johannesburg* [2009] ZACC 30, Case CCT 43/09, (provision of electricity was argued to belong to the housing right, although ultimately held to fall within the duty of municipalities to provide basic services: S. Afr. Const. 1996, §§ 152, 153); *Head of Department: Mpumalanga Department of Education v. Hoërskool Ermelo* [2009] ZACC 32 (head of a provincial education department may override school policy on language, on reasonable grounds, which include considerations of the rights of access to education: S. Afr. Const. 1996, § 29).

[25] For the implications of this standard of review, *see* Chapter 4. This chapter extends that analysis by attaching the consequences of reasonableness review against the different stances of judicial review that can be adopted, simultaneously, by a court.

[26] Tushnet, *Weak Courts, Strong Rights*, *supra* note 8.

"strong" courts tend towards rule-like interpretations of rights, heightened degrees of scrutiny, and muscular remedies. The assertive—and perhaps supremacist—practice of the US Supreme Court in interpreting and enforcing US constitutional law is a case in point.[27] Weak courts, on the other hand, issue contextualized standards for interpreting rights, relaxed scrutiny, and, if liability is still found, relatively tentative and/or declaratory forms of relief. The interpretations issued by weak courts are then open to revision by a legislature, in a much shorter time frame than that observed in systems with strong-form review.[28] Importantly, the distinction of strong/weak is not represented as a dichotomy, but a continuum. "Blended" systems may exist, with "strong-form review with respect to some constitutional issues, weak-form review with respect to others."[29] Moreover, strong rights can coexist with weak remedies, and vice versa. A quadrant of judicial stances is established, with a range of possible approaches that categorize different courts in different jurisdictions, or at least the different judgments in the different courts of different jurisdictions.

Tushnet's descriptive model is also prescriptive. "Strong" articulations of rights and remedies in the area of economic and social rights may bring courts into disrepute and instigate popular backlash in civil society against the very interests that rights purport to protect. Weak courts, on the other hand, may combine muted expressions of rights and a more relaxed insistence on remedies, to protect themselves and the broader, long-term, non-represented beneficiaries of constitutional rights. While weak courts may therefore fail to protect the immediate interests at hand, the dialogue that they engender can assist those in a similar position, by effecting change in laws and policies over the longer term. Nonetheless, a weak court has a tendency to become strong, after the precedents of prior cases have accumulated and the court has become invested in the results of its decisions. The rights-protective advantages of weak courts may therefore be short-lived.

This chapter advances the argument that the weak/strong classification, while useful to comparative constitutional law, is suspended from the subtleties that contextualized study can provide. Attention to the degrees of "strength" and "weakness" of courts may obscure the variety of interactions between courts and other institutions in resolving the challenges behind justiciable economic and social rights. "Weak" review may bear some parallels with the style of judicial deference, or of dialogue, explicitly adopted by many courts, but fails to cast light on the matrix of inter-branch

[27] Ibid., 21–2, *see*, e.g., *Cooper v. Aaron*, 358 U.S. 1, 18 (1958), and *City of Boerne v. Flores*, 521 U.S. 507 (1997).

[28] Tushnet, *Weak Courts, Strong Rights*, *supra* note 8, 24.

[29] Ibid., 36.

and extra-branch relations that are required to secure economic and social rights. "Strong" review bears similarities to a more heavy-handed approach to judicial review by supremacist apex courts, but may just as easily describe the very different managerial, hands-on, approach by lower courts. Departing mid-way between these approaches, which is neither "weak" nor "strong" (neither in Tushnet's terms, nor in more conventional understandings of judicial power) is the judicial promotion of party-driven experiments within the scaffolding of certain deliberative requirements.

Indeed, the overall variety of the types of review that I survey here eschews classification in terms of judicial power or normative finality. The following typology opens the scene of action beyond that of the courts and the elected branches, to situate the court within a web of relations involving litigants, beneficiaries of rights who are similarly situated to the litigants, other parties who will be harmed or helped by the judicial action, and the wider public. This typology demarcates these forms of review, and describes the relations between them: One type of review has often arisen in response to the perceived disadvantages of another. Often, these advantages and disadvantages are perceived as such by assessing their ability to address the broad aims of protecting fundamental material interests, in line with dignity, that are encapsulated by economic and social rights. By connecting them in this way, the typology is irreducibly normative in scope. Before turning to the typology, we must address an initial question: how to understand the impact of this enforcement.

C. EVALUATING ENFORCEMENT

The models of review that are discussed below have grown out of appraisals of the "success" of a long, and live, tradition of public law cases, combining those delivered in postapartheid South Africa, with those decided in the United States and elsewhere. My typology of judicial review, and of the conceptions of the judicial role that are described in Chapters 6 and 7, does not so much herald a "new" form of judicial review for economic and social rights, as affirm and organize developments tracked elsewhere in public law scholarship, which are renewed by comparative study.

Key within this appraisal, of course, is the evaluation of the "success" of rights adjudication. Such an assessment raises normative and positive questions that often go unexpressed. Here, we are not merely concerned with an immediate win/loss case result, but rather with the creation of greater rights-protective outcomes. Hence, we are concerned with how the processes of adjudication—the micro-processes of judicial review in this chapter, and the macro-processes of courts' interaction with the broader constitutional culture in the following two—assist in constituting economic and social rights. Recent studies of cultural "backlash" indicate that the winning of an in-court battle may nevertheless result in the loss of the rights war.[30] So, too, can the prominent loss of a case be counterintuitively successful over the longer term.[31] These insights form the tip of a very large iceberg in the measure of success.

The socio-legal study of public law cases often equates "success" with "impact" (or a narrowing of the "gap" between law-in-action and law-in-books[32]); human rights literature, on the other hand, equates "success" with compliance or implementation. Both literatures are beset by internal contestations of each measure, as well as the overarching challenge of tracing cause with effect in multi-causal scenarios. With the entry of comparative scholarship in these debates, the institutional and normative assumptions have become more explicit.[33]

For example, a long scholarly tradition in public law has questioned the effect, over time, of judicial decisions seeking to adjudicate and enforce rights in relation to landmark litigations—encompassing challenges to gender-inequitable workplaces,[34] racially segregated schools,[35] and overcrowded prisons.[36] Yet this empirical approach has been dictated by the prior question of measuring "impact." On the one hand, the realist school has measured "impact" by focusing on the direct and tangible effects of litigation. Using (apparently) strict causality tests, realists measure the impact of adjudication by cause-and-effect results.[37] Hence, adjudication is successful if it produces an observable and material change in the conduct or interests of those it is targeted to: the parties, as well as broader institutions

[30] Jack M. Balkin and Reva B. Siegel, "Principles, Practices and Social Movements," 154 U. Pa. L. Rev. 927 (2006).

[31] Peter Houtzager and Lucie E. White, "The Long Arc of Pragmatic Economic and Social Rights Advocacy," in Lucie E. White and Jeremy Perelman (eds.), *Stones of Hope: How African Activists Reclaim Human Rights to Challenge Global Poverty* (2011).

[32] The expression is credited to Roscoe Pound, "Law in Books and Law in Action," 44 American Law Review 12 (1910); *see further* David Nelkin, "The 'Gap Problem' in the Sociology of Law: A Theoretical Review" The Windsor Yearbook of Access to Justice 35 (1981).

[33] Cesar Rodriguez-Garavito, "Assessing the Impact and Promoting the Implementation of Structural Judgments: A Comparative Case Study of ESCR Rulings in Colombia" (University of the Andes and Dejusticia, Colombia) (*available at* <http://www.escr-net.org/usr_doc/Rodriguez_-_Colombia.pdf>).

[34] Michael W. McCann, *Rights at Work: Pay Equity Reform and the Politics of Legal Mobilization* (1994).

[35] On this highly scrutinized question, *compare*, e.g., Michael J. Klarman, *From Jim Crow to Civil Rights: The Supreme Court and the Struggle for Racial Equality* (2004) with Martha Minow, *In Brown's Wake: Legacies of America's Educational Landmark* (2010).

[36] Malcolm M. Feeley and Edward L. Rubin, *Judicial Policy Making and the Modern State: How the Courts Reformed America's Prisons* (1998).

[37] For discussion, *see* César Rodríguez-Garavito, "Beyond the Courtroom: The Impact of Judicial Activism on Socioeconomic Rights in Latin America" 89 Tex. L. Rev. 1669 (2011).

that are encompassed in the claim. Such measurements can have surprising results. In this literature, the United States Supreme Court's famous extension of equal protection to African American school students in *Brown v. Board of Education*[38] triggered, not the judicially led dismantling of racial segregation in schools, as in the popular narrative, but instead an overhyped faith in courts.[39] For such scholars, the real effect on race relations occurred in legislative and cultural forums: the courts were epiphenomenal.[40] Added to this challenging causal question is the multiplicity of modes by which welfare state regimes achieve a greater protection of economic and social rights.[41] For political scientists, the wisdom has been to "watch what they do, not what they say,"—that is, for welfare states, it is critical to judge "their *performance*, not their protestations, promises or professed priorities."[42] The intersection of measurements, standards, and indicators is, therefore, critical to this endeavor.

The constructivist school within public law scholarship directly challenges the realist findings. For these scholars, measurement of success in court requires an understanding of indirect effects: of subtle changes in the political discourse of rights, in legal consciousness, and in social relations, within and outside of the parties.[43] Indeed, these effects may be even more important that the direct effects of litigation, over the long term.[44] Because this measurement is more qualitative, it is also more expressly interpretive. Promising studies have pursued this measurement, sometimes resulting in reverse appraisals of litigation success. *Brown v. Board of Education*, for example, stimulated a sea change in race relations, enabled African Americans (and white Americans) to think differently about their place in the US constitutional polity, motivated new coalitions of social movements to mobilize around rights, and indeed helped to connect equality-based social movements transnationally.[45]

38 347 U.S. 483 (1954).

39 Gerald N. Rosenberg, *The Hollow Hope: Can Courts Bring about Social Change?* (2nd edn., 1998).

40 Klarman, *From Jim Crow to Civil Rights*, *supra* note 35.

41 Gøsta, Esping-Andersen, *The Three Worlds of Welfare Capitalism* (1998).

42 *See* Robert Goodin et al, "The Real Worlds of Welfare Capitalism" in Christopher Pierson and Francis G. Castles (eds.), *The Welfare State: A Reader* (2000) 170, 183.

43 *See* Jeremy Perelman and Katharine G. Young, "Freeing Mohammed Zakari: Rights as Footprints," in White and Perelman, *supra* note 31.

44 McCann, *Rights at Work*, *supra* note 34.

45 Mary Dudziak, "*Brown* as a Cold War Case," 91 *The Journal of American History* 32 (2004). As Minow reflects from her extensive study, *Brown* may have had "more influence on racial justice outside the context of schooling, more influence on schooling outside the context of racial integration, and more significance to law outside of both race and schooling": Minow, *supra* note 35, 170.

A similar division can be observed in the literature on compliance with human rights. Much of this literature focuses on the role of courts in interpreting and applying human rights treaties, whether self-executing or incorporated by legislation. The realists perceive the compliance effect to be low where tangible, direct, and quantitative changes are not observed. Their conclusion is similar to the "hollow hope": better not to waste progressive effort and faith in ratification of treaties or in international courts when measurable compliance is elusive.[46] On the other hand, the constructivists suggest that changes in discourse and in consciousness, resulting from new (and unenforceable) treaty commitments or adverse (but unenforceable) international judgments, are significant. The acculturation of new norms produced by such commitments, or the mobilization of new coalitions of civil society, are just as important as the directly tangible indicia of success.[47] In turning to the following typology, the more interpretive, qualitative appraisal of both material and symbolic effects of litigation are pursued.

D. A TYPOLOGY OF JUDICIAL REVIEW

The variety of adjudicative stances employed in economic and social rights adjudication may be considered and appraised as a typology. I introduce five major stances adopted by courts in economic and social rights adjudication. In adopting *deferential review*, the court assumes that the greater decision-making authority is placed on the elected branches in interpreting economic and social rights and in determining the obligations that arise. In *conversational review*, the court is instead reliant on the ability of an interbranch dialogue to resolve the determination of rights. A third type of review is *experimentalist review*, whereby the court seeks to involve the relevant stakeholders—government, parties, and other interested groups—in solving the problem which obstructs a provisional benchmark of the right. *Managerial review* occurs when the court assumes a direct responsibility for interpreting the substantive contours of the right and supervising its protection with strict timelines and detailed plans. Finally, *peremptory review* is involved when the court registers its superiority in interpreting the right, and in commanding and controlling an immediate response. The divisions are represented in Figure 5.1 on page 143.

Importantly, these types do not sit along a plane of "strength" and "weakness" of judicial review because the power that the court deploys—its ability to enforce a predetermined norm with approximate finality—is

[46] Oona Hathaway, "Do Human Rights Treaties Make a Difference?," 111 Yale L.J. 1935 (2002).

[47] Ryan Goodman and Derek Jinks, "Incomplete Internalization and Compliance with Human Rights Law," 19 Euro. J. Int'l. L. 725 (2008).

multidimensional. The mode of review is coextensive with a number of different institutional responses, and is specified by the interpretation of the right at hand, the evaluation of the government's actions, and the design of a remedy. This typology presents a heuristic for understanding the variety of stances towards judicial review adopted in economic and social rights cases.

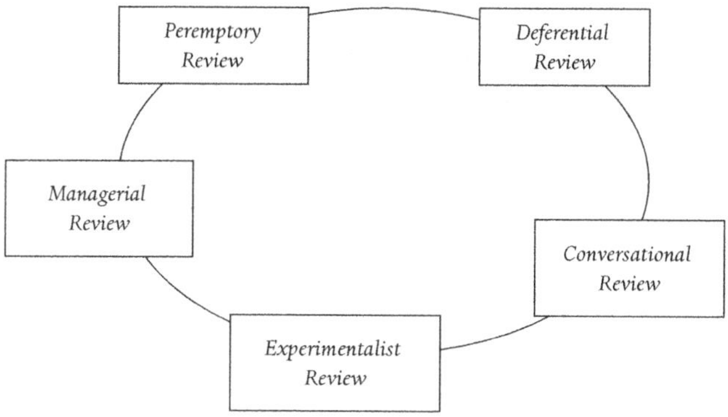

Figure 5.1
A typology of judicial review

(1) *Deferential review*

Deferential review is a model of review that is well established in the tradition of defending judicial review in democratic terms. In exercising deferential review, courts give credence to the democratic authority and epistemic superiority of, and textual conferral of tasks to, the legislative and executive branches. Indeed, arguments for deference can (but need not) parallel arguments for an obligation to obey the law.[48] While democratic authority is the best rationale for deference to the legislature, as the most electorally accountable and representative branch, epistemic authority is more fitting for the executive as the branch equipped with the most technical resources and information. Epistemic authority is also a good rationale for deference to legislatures, particularly in countries where the legislative branch maintains its own expert and technical staff and resources independent of the executive.

In deferring to the legal and epistemic authority of the elected branches, a court is able to address the double-pronged legitimacy and competency critiques applied to the adjudication of economic and social rights. By giving attention to the comparative competence of other institutions, deference

[48] Frederick Schauer, "Deferring," 103 Mich. L. Rev. 1567 (2005); *see generally* Joseph Raz, *The Authority of Law: Essays on Law and Morality* (2nd edn., 2009) 233–49.

suggests that the deferred-to decision-maker possesses important information, experience, and accountability that help in deciding relevant questions correctly, or at least in an abler fashion than the court could do. Deference therefore links up most closely to what is described as "non-judicial enforcement," by other governmental branches, in Chapter 7.[49] Deference, particularly epistemic deference on expertise grounds, therefore involves both a positive statement about the abilities of the executive or legislature as a decision-maker, and a negative statement about the weakness of the court as a decision-maker relative to these branches.[50] Although not usually given as a justification for deference, this relational feature can suggest a certain reciprocal obligation, on the deferred-to branch, to exercise the abilities that are attributed to it.[51]

On these grounds, a deferential court is slow to override or second-guess legislation or policy. Such is the constant mode of the United States Supreme Court in reviewing cases involving economic and social legislation.[52] In the most traditional formulation of deferential review, the court intervenes only when it detects a clear legislative mistake—one "so clear that it is not open to rational question."[53] Only thus, in Thayer's famous contribution to US constitutional theory, could courts reconcile the practice of constitutional democracy with the inevitable fallibility of courts and the distortions that their contributions present to the legislative process. While Thayer's demand for judicial restraint has not prevailed in cases involving the so-called fundamental values of political justice, there remains a "broad residual area of judicial passivity" in US constitutional law, in which economic and social rights may be included.[54] In these domains, deference is said to allow the three branches of government to assume their appropriate role responsibilities without impinging on each other.

Many of the South African Constitutional Court's earliest cases on economic and social rights have been characterized as deferential,[55] although the Court's postures were more engaged than is observable in the US Supreme Court (proving that degrees of deference are relative in

[49] *See* Chapter 7, section E. For the way in which this may assist the process of legitimately limiting rights, *see* Chapter 4, section A(6).

[50] Richard H. Fallon, Jr., "Judicially Manageable Standards and Constitutional Meaning," 119 Harv. L. Rev. 1274 (2006) 1291.

[51] Paul Horwitz, "Three Faces of Deference," 83 Notre Dame L. Rev. 1061 (2008).

[52] E.g., *Dandridge v. Williams*, 397 U.S. 471, 485 (1970).

[53] James Bradley Thayer, "The Origin and Scope of the American Doctrine of Constitutional Law," 7 Harv. L. Rev. 129 (1893) 138–52, 144.

[54] Sager, *Justice in Plainclothes*, *supra* note 17, 90.

[55] Dennis Davis, "Adjudicating the Socio-Economic Rights in the South African Constitution: Towards 'Deference Lite'?," 22 S. Afr. J. Hum. Rts. 301 (2006) 318.

comparative constitutional law). Deference can help us to understand the outcome of the first economic and social rights controversy heard in South Africa, in *Soobramoney v. Minister of Health*,[56] where the Constitutional Court held that no contravention of the right to access health care, to life or of the guarantee of emergency medical treatment occurred after the claimant was denied access to renal dialysis in a public hospital. In assessing the claim, the Constitutional Court deferred to both the hospital's guidelines for rationing treatment and the provincial authorities' allocations for the general health budget.[57] For the former, the Constitutional Court found no reason to gainsay the greater expertise of the hospital in making the agonizing choice of rationing life-prolonging health care. Expertise was found to exist in the medical practitioners' clinical experience and qualifications. Medical rationing, in the opinion of the majority, involved "areas where institutional incapacity and appropriate constitutional modesty require us to be especially cautious."[58] For the latter, the competency of political organs to set budgets was assumed.[59] In this respect, deference is consistent with a theory of democratic accountability.

Similarly, in *Grootboom*, where the Constitutional Court declared the government's housing policy to be inconsistent with the right of access to housing, the judicial stance was deferential. Refusing to articulate any self-standing dimension, or "minimum core," of the right to access housing, the Constitutional Court inquired only into the "reasonableness" of government policy.[60] The "minimum core" doctrine was rejected on grounds akin to those used to justify deference: the Constitutional Court felt it lacked the information, and capacity, to make such a determination.[61] The judicial posture nevertheless had some bite, since the Constitutional Court ultimately found that the housing policy did not meet the requirements of the

[56] *Soobramoney v. Minister of Health, Kwazulu-Natal* 1998 (1) SA 765 (CC) ("*Soobramoney*").

[57] Ibid.

[58] Ibid., [30] per majority; [58] per Sachs J. *See also* [45], per Madala J (noting the "clinical and incisive judgment of the [authorized medical] practitioner"). For another example of deference (to science, rather than government), *see* the terms of the order in *Minister of Health v. Treatment Action Campaign*, 2002 (5) SA 721 (CC), discussed *infra*.

[59] This position can be compared with the arguments in *Mahlangu v. Minister for Social Development* Case No. 025754/05 (North Gauteng High Court) in which the budgetary viability of a child support grant was explicitly argued: *see further* Debbie Budlender, Paula Proudlock, and Lucy Jamieson, "Developing social policy for children in the context of HIV/AIDS: A South African case study," A joint publication by the Children's Institute, University of Cape Town, and the Community Agency for Social Enquiry (2008) *available at* <http://www.ci.org.za/depts/ci/enews/April2009/pubs/casestudy.pdf>.

[60] *Government of the Republic of South Africa v. Grootboom* 2001 (1) SA 46, 66 (CC) (S. Afr.) ("*Grootboom*"). For analysis of the minimum core doctrine, and the alternative of reasonableness assessment, *see* Chapters 3 and 4.

[61] *Grootboom* 2001 (1) SA 46 (CC) 66; *Treatment Action Campaign*, 2002 (5) SA 721 (CC) 722; *Mazibuko v. The City of Johannesburg* 2010 (4) SA 1 (CC) [52]–[68].

right to access housing because it had failed to cater for the needs of the most vulnerable.[62] Yet even with this assessment, the Constitutional Court offered only declaratory relief, preferring to defer, in its remedial stance, to the Department of Housing's consideration of how best to meet the needs of vulnerable communities living in intolerable conditions or crisis situations. In the words of Justice Albie Sachs:

> [W]e left it open to the state to decide whether the programme for emergency shelter should operate nationally, provincially or locally, and how the programme should best be developed; whether the programme would involve only providing dry land on which people could erect shelters, or whether it would provide both land and houses, or whether it would be more efficacious for the state to provide sufficient financial assistance for the effected persons to make their own housing arrangements. Similarly, we left it to the state to decide where it was to get the money for the emergency programme; it could take it from defence, it could raise new taxes, it could take it from anywhere [where funds were not constitutionally protected].[63]

This open-ended and deferential remedy arguably lacked the hook required for monitoring and implementation to occur, leading to the charge of judicial abdication. Particularly in light of the positive obligations that flow from economic and social rights, and in the face of an intransigent or incompetent government actor, the subtle reciprocity that is expected to flow from deference may not ensure that rights are sufficiently protected by the elected branches.[64] Always troublesome, this problem is exacerbated in a constitutional system, such as South Africa's, in which the Constitutional Court has adopted the role of "guardian" of the present Constitution, and in which practices of deference are tainted by the apartheid past. Thayer's contemporary, A. V. Dicey, whose defense of parliamentary sovereignty had such a strong (if distorted) influence on the constitutional structure of apartheid South Africa, no longer enjoys the same appeal in that country. Parliamentary sovereignty in pre-1994 South Africa allowed apartheid to be institutionalized and upheld "through laws enacted to give them sanction and teeth by a Parliament elected only by a privileged minority."[65] Constitutionalism, and its enforcement by the Constitutional Court, has replaced it.

The problem of abdication is highlighted by the concrete lack of redress experienced by the claimants in the *Soobramoney* and *Grootboom* cases. Justice Albie Sachs, for example, described the reaction by the wider public to its decision in *Soobramoney* as one of anger with the Constitutional Court for

[62] *Grootboom* 2001 (1) SA 46 (CC) [44].

[63] Albie Sachs, *The Strange Alchemy of Life and Law* (2009) 178–9.

[64] Craig Scott and Philip Alston, "Adjudicating Constitutional Priorities in a Transnational Context: A Comment on *Soobramoney*'s Legacy and *Grootboom*'s Promise," 16 S. Afr. J. Hum. Rts. 206 (2000) 250.

[65] *AZAPO v. President of the Republic of South Africa* (4) SA 671 (CC), [1], per Mahomed DP.

failing to provide a more appropriate remedy when the stakes were so high.[66] Yet the apparent deference within the Court's judgment in *Grootboom* on declaratory relief was more complicated by the fact that it postdated a settlement agreement between the parties, which was made a court order, thereby narrowing the Court's attention to the state's housing program only.[67] Nonetheless, the apparent inattention of the Constitutional Court to the direct plight of the claimants in *Grootboom* registered dramatically when, eight years after the judgment, Irene Grootboom passed away, still without a home.[68] The shortcomings of deference, made clear in actual constitutional practice, open the way to a broader range of approaches.

(2) *Conversational review*

Where deferential review may rely on judicial passivity in order to spur a reciprocal protection of economic and social rights, or to concentrate political energy about perceived failings on the elected branches, conversational review actively creates this reciprocity by relying on the effect of interbranch dialogue. In conversational review, all three branches assume a shared interpretive role over the right at issue. By offering engaged scrutiny of government action that invites a response, and an order that opens the way for a range of options, the obligations that flow from economic and social rights are negotiated between courts and the elected branches over time.

Dialogue is perhaps the most resonant metaphor for describing the distance between strong US-style judicial review and other comparative constitutional examples.[69] In comparative accounts, dialogue describes a practice in which reason-giving courts are able to adjudicate rights, but elected and accountable legislatures are given the final word on the shape of the obligations that flow from them. At base is the expectation that both branches attempt to provide reasonable interpretations of constitutional provisions and come closer to an understanding that is "correct."[70] By allowing the legislature to disagree with the court, as long as this disagreement is reasonable and clearly expressed, both actors share the role in elaborating constitutional norms. Thus, these prescriptions have much in

[66] Albie Sachs, "Social and Economic Rights: Can They Be Made Justiciable?" 53 SMU L. Rev. 1381 (2000) 1386.

[67] Sandra Liebenberg, *Socio-Economic Rights: Adjudication under a Transformative Constitution* (2010) 400–5.

[68] Christopher Mbazira, "Non-implementation of Court Orders in Socio-Economic Rights Litigation in South Africa: Is the Cancer Here to Stay?," 9 ESR Review 2 (2008).

[69] Peter W. Hogg, Allison A. Bushell Thornton, and Wade K. Wright, "Charter Dialogue Revisited or 'Much Ado About Metaphors'," 45 Osgoode Hall L.J. 1 (2007). Of course, the metaphor is also part of a long-standing US analysis: Barry Friedman, "Dialogue and Judicial Review," 91 Mich. L. Rev. 577 (1993).

[70] Tushnet, *Weak Courts, Strong Rights*, *supra* note 8, 209.

common with the theory of deferential review by suggesting that courts should not control the contours of constitutional rights.[71] They give the court a greater role, however, in order that the court may contribute to the evolving interpretation of a right and of the obligations and remedies that flow from it.

So far, constitutional practice in Canada is the source of the most sustained study of dialogue between courts and legislatures. The limitations clause of Canada's Charter explicitly allows the legislature to provide a justification for limiting rights; the notwithstanding clause allows for an ex-post legislative override.[72] Courts may invite the legislature's interpretive participation by employing explicitly reasoned tests of proportionality. And a dialogic interaction may arise if the court issues a suspended declaration of invalidity.[73] This style appears apt for other systems that, like Canada (and South Africa), combine a historical commitment to parliamentary sovereignty with a present-day constitutionalism.[74] Notwithstanding this historical parallel, the effects of dialogue can also be observed in contexts that lack the institutional mechanisms that require and promote it. Hence, the use of dialogue has also been attributed to the US Supreme Court, both by local scholars and comparativists.[75]

The open communication between courts and legislatures in conversational review invites a different interpretation of the early South African experience with reasonableness review and declaratory remedies. On this account, *Grootboom* involves a deferential treatment to housing policy, but importantly contemplates the possibility of further "legislative sequels" to the judicial action.[76] The Constitutional Court's focus is not on resolving the immediate

[71] Christine Bateup, "The Dialogic Promise: Assessing the Normative Potential of Theories of Constitutional Dialogue" 71 Brook. L. Rev. 1109 (2006).

[72] Canada Act 1982 (UK) c. 11, sch. B pt. I ("Canadian Charter of Rights and Freedoms"), §§ 1, 33. *See further* Chapter 4.

[73] Hogg et al., "Charter Dialogue Revisited," *supra* note 69.

[74] *See*, e.g., Stephen Gardbaum, "The New Commonwealth Model of Constitutionalism," 49 Am. J. Comp. L. 707 (2001) 710 (noting that the constitutional and statutory bills of rights adopted in Canada, New Zealand, and the United Kingdom attempt to create "joint responsibility and deliberative dialogue between courts and legislatures"); *but see* Stephen Gardbaum, "Reassessing the New Commonwealth Model of Constitutionalism," 8 Int'l. J. Const. L. (2010) 14–15 (rejecting the "dialogue" concept as overinclusive and amorphous.)

[75] For the rigorous "descriptive" application to the United States, *see* Friedman, "Dialogue and Judicial Review," *supra* note 69. For a comparative assessment, *see* Kent Roach, "Sharpening the Dialogue Debate: The Next Decade of Scholarship," 45 Osgoode Hall L.J. 169 (2007) 187 (describing the effects of *Hamdi v. Rumsfeld* 542 U.S. 507 (2004) and *Rasul v. Bush* 524 U.S. 466 (2004) on the Detainee Treatment Act respectively, and *Hamdan v. Rumsfeld* 548 U.S. 557 (2006) on the Military Commissions Act, as well as the former on the rules for the tribunals determining enemy combatant status).

[76] Rosalind Dixon, "Creating Dialogue About Socio-Economic Rights: Strong-Form Versus Weak-Form Judicial Review Revisited," 5 Int'l. J. Const. L. 391; (2007) 393; *Grootboom* 2001 (1) SA 46 (CC), primarily

homelessness of the claimants, but instead on the effective change of housing policy over the longer term. Such interaction has paid off, according to some commentators. For example, four years after the decision, the Department of Housing adopted a new program, focused on assisting people in urban and rural areas with urgent housing needs as a result of natural disasters, evictions, demolitions, or imminent displacements.[77] In the interim, the decision helped in subsequent adjudication to alleviate red-tape impediments to government's acting to address the emergency housing needs of other vulnerable communities, which nearby property owners had commenced.[78]

When the Constitutional Court was required, two years after *Grootboom*, to adjudicate on the right to health care, it similarly deployed a conversational stance.[79] The *Treatment Action Campaign* case was a challenge to the government's decision to restrict the roll-out of antiretroviral drugs which could prevent the transmission of HIV from mother to child during childbirth. This time, while purporting to adopt a deferential stance, the Constitutional Court found the government's policy was unreasonable. It famously ordered the government to desist from preventing the roll-out of drugs and to meet other treatment and counseling expenses. The Court refused to endorse the structural interdict and injunction remedies that the High Court made at first instance, on the basis that "the government has always respected and executed orders of this Court."[80] Instead, the Constitutional Court made a mandatory order requiring the government to permit and to facilitate (in a minor respect) the public health sector use of the antiretroviral.

The Constitutional Court's decision in the *Treatment Action Campaign* case brought an end to a highly criticized aspect of the South African government's policy on HIV/AIDS, and set in motion many other changes to the government's general stance towards the disease. Yet the remedies were not immediately effective. In some provincial governments, compliance was not forthcoming. In one province, a further application to the High Court for a contempt order was required, which was not resolved until six months after the successful case.[81] With even minor delays, many lives were lost.

involved a court-executive, rather than court-legislative interaction; however these two interactions are clearly not mutually exclusive.

77 National Housing Code 2004, ch 12, 'Housing Assistance in Emergency Circumstances,' under authority of Housing Act No. 107 of 1999; *see further* Liebenberg, *Adjudication under a Transformative Constitution*, *supra* note 62, 401–7.

78 *Minister of Pub. Works v. Kyalami Ridge Envtl. Ass'n.* 2001 (3) SA 1151 (CC).

79 *Treatment Action Campaign* 2002 (5) SA 721 (CC).

80 *Treatment Action Campaign* 2002 (5) SA 721 (CC) [129].

81 *See Treatment Action Campaign v. MEC for Health, Mpumalanga & Minister of Health (Tranvsaal Provincial Division)* Case No. 35272/02.

The success of the remedies—in most of the provinces—was in large part due to the activities of the social movement that brought the case, rather than merely the interbranch conversation that was created by the Constitutional Court.[82] William Forbath has described the way in which the Treatment Action Campaign litigant worked to bring about the cultural transformation and institutional reforms required to secure the right to health care in this context; a strategy that was also indispensable to the success of the court order, and interdependent with the judicial stance adopted by the Constitutional Court.[83] This success points us to a further dimension of judicial review that the conversational model only indirectly highlights: the way in which a court facilitates the relationship between the government and the parties themselves,[84] especially as those parties connect with civil society.

(3) *Experimentalist review*

A third type of review is experimentalist in character. Experimentalist review describes a dynamic, systematic practice of adjudication. This posture puts further pressure on the conversational theme by directing the parties—including, but not only limited to government—to negotiate and devise their own solutions to the "problem" which diminishes the enjoyment of economic and social rights. This style of review is intended to confront the systemic, or structural, features of the lack of enjoyment of economic and social rights. In experimentalist review, a court is not deferential; rather, it is ready to engage in a vigorous assessment of the reasonableness of policy or legislation, involving a contextualized investigation against the commitments of the constitution. A court is further prepared to order remedies that may take on a limited structural form. This political project is achieved, not by prescribing the immediate steps toward a solution, but by "nudging," "linking," and "destabilizing" public institutions. These effects are borrowed from the observations of successful institutional interactions in the fields of behavioral law and economics, and from the

[82] Mark Heywood, "Current Developments: Preventing Mother-to-Child HIV Transmission in South Africa: Background, Strategies and Outcomes of the Treatment Action Campaign against the Minister of Health," 19 S. Afr. J. Hum. Rts. 278 (2003).

[83] William E. Forbath, "Realizing a Constitutional Social Right—Cultural Transformation, Deep Institutional Reform, and the Roles of Advocacy and Adjudication," in White and Perelman, *Stones of Hope*, *supra* note 31; *see also* Heywood, *supra* note 77. For a more extensive discussion of this feature, *see* analysis *infra*, Chapter 9.

[84] Christine Bateup, "Reassessing the Dialogic Possibilities of Weak-Form Bills of Rights," 32 Hastings Int'l. & Comp. L. Rev. 529 (2009); Michael A. Rebell and Robert L. Hughes, "Schools, Communities, and the Courts: A Dialogic Approach to Education Reform," 14 Yale L. & Pol'y Rev. 99 (1996) 114–36.

economic sociology underlying new governance.[85] These observations mark a departure from "national, top-down and sanctioned" law and government, in order to embrace a reflexive coordination between public and private actors, in which courts play a part.[86]

The capacity of such experiments to induce structural reform through litigation has been given prominence by scholars writing in the tradition of "new governance." These scholars see courts as one important (but not central) part of the project of "democratic experimentalism." Charles Sabel and William Simon, for example, suggest that the dynamic and reciprocal relationship between courts and other institutions of government and governance can spur structural change, while avoiding the problems of the traditional "command and control" courts.[87] This dynamic orientation is documented in adjudicatory processes in both the United States and Europe.

In the United States for example, experimentalist litigation has been described as "destabilization rights" enforcement, by which federal courts promote a direct form of democratic decision-making in relation to schools, mental health and housing programs. This is achieved because courts have been persuaded to disentrench the power of public institutions that have been otherwise immune from contestation.[88] The institutional implications of the obligations are then promoted within institutions, rather than dictated from above.[89] In the European Union, courts have acted as "catalysts" of the European Treaty values of participation, information, and principled decision-making by ensuring that substantively informed goals of representativeness and proportionality have been procedurally met.[90] Thus, superior courts promote democratic decision-making by providing an expansive interpretation of standing rules, a robust assessment of the adequacy of procedures for gathering scientific information for use in regulation, and a consideration of proportionality as informed by the commitment to transparency and accountability.

[85] Richard H. Thaler and Cass R. Sunstein, *Nudge: Improving Decisions about Health, Wealth, and Happiness* (2008); On Amir and Orly Lobel, "Stumble, Predict, Nudge: How Behavioral Economics Informs Law and Policy," 108 Colum. L. Rev. 2098 (2008); *See* analysis *infra*, Chapter 9.

[86] Orly Lobel, "The Renew Deal: The Fall of Regulation and the Rise of Governance in Contemporary Legal Thought," 89 Minn. L. Rev. 342 (2004).

[87] Charles F. Sabel and William H. Simon, "Destabilization Rights: How Public Law Litigation Succeeds," 117 Harv. L. Rev. 1016 (2004).

[88] Sabel and Simon, ibid.; *see also* Kathleen G. Noonan, Charles Sabel, and William H. Simon, "The Rule of Law in the Experimentalist Welfare State: Lessons from Child Welfare Reform," 34(3) Law & Social Inquiry 523 (2009).

[89] E.g., Sabel and Simon, "Destabilization Rights," *supra* note 87, 1078; *cf.* Colin S. Diver, "The Judge as Political Powerbroker: Superintending Structural Change in Public Institutions," 65 Va. L. Rev. 43 (1979).

[90] Joanne Scott and Susan Sturm, "Courts as Catalysts: Re-Thinking the Judicial Role in New Governance," 13 Colum. J. Eur. L. 565 (2006).

The case studies that have generated attention in new governance scholarship have generally not involved economic and social rights, neither as causes of action nor as otherwise juridical categories. There are exceptions, however, and experimentalist review has been suggested as the applicable model for the way in which US and Canadian courts have enforced "adequacy" standards in relation to US state constitutional rights in education and in Canadian provincial constitutional rights in health care.[91] There are institutional differences between the Constitutional Court of South Africa and the US and European courts emphasized in the new governance literature (as there are between these latter jurisdictions). Nonetheless, the Constitutional Court's approach to the judicial review of economic and social rights displays many similarities to the experimentalist tendencies observed in the United States and Europe.

First, there is general reluctance on the part of the Court in economic and social rights cases to prescribe a solution; but unlike deferential or conversational review, the Constitutional Court has sometimes delegated this task as a problem-solving activity to the parties themselves. Second, the Constitutional Court has affirmed that the judicial process should be used as a last, rather than first, resort. The Court continues to question the finality of its normative position taking. At the same time, it has issued explicit encouragement to parties to seek it out.

Third, while conversational review may allow for a more patient remedial result, as a court is content to signal its message to the legislature and wait for a response, experimentalist review is more provocative, insisting on a different prioritization of interests and the input of a new set of actors within the legislative scheme. Using various degrees of remedial intervention, it is more dynamic than the formal expectation that electoral politics will take its proper course. Moreover, experimentalist review goes further in forcing the active reconsideration of interests by the legislature. It is "linkage-forcing," seeking to link up the legislature's accommodation of minority interests,[92] by retesting the interests taken into account and rigorously resolving the balance of power if this test comes up short. This orientation has the potential to forestall the effect that economic and social rights tend to support only middle-class interests, because of the latter group's relative

[91] Noonan, Sabel, and Simon, "The Rule of Law," *supra* note 88; *see also* James S. Liebman and Charles F. Sabel, "A Public Laboratory Dewey Barely Imagined: The Emerging Model of School Governance and Legal Reform," 28 N.Y.U. Rev. L. & Soc. Change 183 (2003); Alana Klein, "Judging as Nudging: New Governance Approaches for the Enforcement of Constitutional Social and Economic Rights," 39 Colum. Hum. Rts. L. Rev. 351 (2008).

[92] For an example drawn from the US constitutional context, *see* V. F. Nourse and Sarah A. Maguire, "The Lost History of Governance and Equal Protection," 58 Duke L.J. 955 (2009).

ease of access in both legislative and judicial processes, as identified empirically in Eastern Europe, in Latin America, and in US poverty law.[93]

Experimentalist review has occurred in recent housing rights and eviction cases before the Constitutional Court, in which public municipalities sought to remove people from informal settlements, sometimes on grounds of safety and habitability of their dwellings; other times in an effort to upgrade the land and rezone it for other public housing purposes. In these cases, the Constitutional Court ordered a "meaningful engagement" between the parties, which, by decentering the judicial activity, introduces a process whereby the parties are able to express their interests from their own vantage point. The Constitutional Court is therefore able to oversee a process in which parties cast new light on their problem and deliberate over a solution; at the same time, public authorities previously immune from political scrutiny are placed in a position of justifying their strategies and goals.

Thus, in *Port Elizabeth Municipality v. Various Occupiers*,[94] the Constitutional Court refused to order the eviction of sixty-eight people from undeveloped public lands, holding that the municipality in question had not satisfied a constitutional duty to make reasonable efforts to provide alternative accommodation. In canvassing the circumstances that would be relevant to a "just and equitable" eviction, the Constitutional Court emphasized the need to consider the vulnerability of occupiers (in particular the elderly, children, disabled persons, and households headed by women[95]), the extent to which negotiations had taken place with the "equality of voice for all concerned," the reasonableness of offers made in connection to alternatives, the "time scales proposed relative to the degree of disruption involved," and the willingness of occupiers to respond.[96] Drawing on mediation and conciliation features of labor and family law, the Court saw considerable benefits to facilitating a "mutual give-and-take" between parties. This, held the Court, would challenge the stereotypes held about occupiers, on the part of those seeking eviction, and promote the agency and resourcefulness, on the part of those living on others' land.[97]

[93] András Sajó, "Social Rights as Middle-Class Entitlements in Hungary: The Role of the Constitutional Court," in Roberto Gargarella, Pilar Domingo, and Theunis Roux (eds.), *Courts and Social Transformation in New Democracies: An Institutional Voice for the Poor?* (2006) 83. *See*, e.g., Lucie E. White, "*Goldberg v. Kelly* on the Paradox of Lawyering for the Poor," 56 Brooklyn L. Rev. 861 (1990); Octavio Luiz Motta Ferraz, "Harming the Poor Through Social Rights Litigation: Lessons from Brazil," 89 Texas L. Rev. 1643 (2011); David Landau, "The Reality of Social Rights Enforcement," 53 Harv. Int'l. L.J. 189 (2012). For a tendency of "non-retrogression" standards to produce the same effect, *see* Chapter 4.

[94] 2005 (1) SA 217 (CC) ("*Port Elizabeth*").

[95] *Prevention of Illegal Eviction from and Unlawful Occupation of Land Act*, No. 19 of 1998 § 4(6) and (7). *See also* repeal of Prevention of Illegal Squatting Act, No. 52 of 1951.

[96] *Port Elizabeth*, 2005 (1) SA 217 (CC) [30].

[97] Ibid., [41]–[42]. *See further* Sachs, *The Strange Alchemy of Life and Law*, *supra* note 63, ch 3.

The Constitutional Court's interest in negotiation as a method for informing the standard of reasonableness, and for ensuring delivery of the result, continued and evolved in *Occupiers of 51 Olivia Road v. City of Johannesburg.*[98] In that case, the Court ordered that an eviction on housing safety and health grounds required first a "meaningful engagement" between public landholders and occupiers. It therefore suggested that the 400 occupiers of two buildings in inner city Johannesburg be allowed to engage first with the city, in order to establish whether the city could help in alleviating the consequences of eviction and whether the unsafe buildings could be improved for an interim period. The Constitutional Court's order required that negotiations include the question of when and how the city could fulfill the obligations to meet the housing rights of the occupiers.[99] Ultimately, the post-order negotiations between the City of Johannesburg and the occupiers focused on the question of whether alternative accommodation would be temporary or permanent, how much rent would be charged, and how the relocation would be conducted.[100] After negotiation and implementation, the occupiers have been left with a significantly beneficial, although impermanent, resolution.[101]

These cases have been described as portending "a hybrid dispute resolution mechanism that incorporates the flexibility of ADR [alternative dispute resolution] processes with the public norm creating capacity of traditional adjudication."[102] On this understanding, the Constitutional Court is attempting to generate values beyond the scope of the dispute, and yet spur the appropriate resolution in the particular case.[103] It is precisely this hybridity that undergirds a tension in the experimentalist position. First, the court's attempts to correct the power imbalances of the weaker party are fraught with complications, as is documented in Chapter 9. The very "immunity" rights that are relied on, in order to make participation meaningful and a destabilization of entrenched power effective, are the economic and social rights that are the subject of contestations.[104] It is not only access to the democratic process, but to a degree of social security underlying that access, that marks out the sensitivity of the

[98] 2008 (3) SA 208 (CC) ("*Olivia Road*").

[99] *Olivia Road*, 2008 (3) SA 208 (CC) [14].

[100] Stuart Wilson, "Planning for Inclusion in South Africa: The State's Duty to Prevent Homelessness and the Potential of 'Meaningful Engagement,'" 22 Urban Forum 265 (2011) (participant-observer presenting a case study of both negotiation and implementation phases).

[101] Ibid.

[102] Brian Ray, "Extending the Shadow of the Law: Using Hybrid Mechanisms to Develop Constitutional Norms in Socioeconomic Rights Cases," Utah L. Rev. 797 (2009).

[103] *Cf.* Susan P. Sturm, "A Normative Theory of Public Law Remedies," 79 Geo. L.J. 1355 (1991).

[104] *Compare* Sabel and Simon, "Destabilization Rights," *supra* note 87, with Roberto Mangabeira Unger, *False Necessity: Anti-Necessitarian Social Theory in the Service of Radical Democracy* (rev. sub. edn., 2004) 524–30.

court to democratic failures. Finally, engagement is difficult when there is a real hostility between the parties—a point made clear by the polarity of the positions between the social movement and the South African government (and the AIDS denialist tendencies that members of the government demonstrated at the time) in the *Treatment Action Campaign* case.[105] In that case, the Court was frustrated by the level of animosity between the parties, suggesting that its continuation would "bedevil future relations between government and non-government agencies that will perforce have to join in combating the common enemy [of AIDS]."[106] According to the new governance paradigm, effective deliberation may dislodge previous hostilities.[107] Yet this possibility may be elusive when the very position of unreasonableness—itself a precondition for a finding of an infringement of economic and social rights—is an obstacle to the formation of trust between parties, itself necessary for a negotiation between the parties to be effective. For a stronger remedial position, we turn to managerial review.

(4) *Managerial review*

Managerial review suggests a heightened review of government action and a structured and/or mandatory form of relief that requires a continuing, ground level, day-to-day control. In the first place, the alleged infringement of economic and social rights is closely scrutinized by the court, which may go so far as to prescribe the substantive content of the right in question. In the second place, detailed remedies are ordered and subject to ongoing supervision by the court. This can take place through varied stages, such as the court calling upon the state actor to present a plan for court approval, involving other parties in the scrutiny of the plan, and calling on the state to account for the implementation of the plan at later (assigned) dates and sometimes the expenditure of public funds. The court may also retain discretion to disapprove a plan and substitute its own, with the aid of interested parties and any court-appointed experts. This latter option was recommended for the South African Constitutional Court in the early days of its jurisprudence on economic and social rights.[108] Suspended declarations can be seen as belonging, on some occasions, to a managerial stance, requiring a supervision that goes beyond the reciprocal stance of conversational

[105] *Treatment Action Campaign* 2002 (5) SA 721 (CC).

[106] Ibid., [20].

[107] Sabel and Simon, "Destabilization Rights," *supra* note 87, 1073–7.

[108] Wim Trengove, *Judicial Remedies for Violations of Socio-Economic Rights*, Vol. 1, (4) ESR Review (1999).

review.[109] As well as structural or mandatory injunctions, judicial management can involve contempt proceedings against government officials.

The Constitutional Court purports to condone the "managerial role of the courts."[110] By embracing various remedial options, including the fashioning of new remedies, courts are able to—and in fact are textually required to[111]—ensure the protection and enforcement of constitutional rights. The "appropriate relief" mandated by the Constitution is said to depend upon the circumstances of each particular case, but the Court has stated that it may require:

> a declaration of rights, an interdict, a mandamus or such other relief as may be required to ensure that the rights enshrined in the Constitution are protected and enforced. If it is necessary to do so, the courts may even have to fashion new remedies to secure the protection and enforcement of these all-important rights.[112]

A resonant precursor to managerialism in the appellate court context—and noted by the South African Constitutional Court—is the judicial leadership shown by the US Supreme Court in both decisions in *Brown v. Board of Education*.[113] The finding that school segregation contravened equal protection broke heavily from previous interpretations and required a spectacular exercise of power by the US Supreme Court. Segregation was mandatory in seventeen states, and allowed in four. In ordering the elimination of segregation "root and branch,"[114] the Supreme Court had to contend with recalcitrant State governors and school boards. It later broached the deep structures of school segregation by upholding orders for compensatory education programs for African American students who had been segregated from majority schools,[115] and authorizing district courts to use quotas, redraw attendance zones, endorse optional school transfers for majority

[109] Kent Roach and Geoff Budlender, "Mandatory Relief and Supervisory Jurisdiction: When Is It Appropriate, Just and Equitable?," 122 S. Afr. L.J. 325 (2005); *cf.* Hogg et al., "Charter Dialogue Revisited," *supra* note 69.

[110] *Port Elizabeth* 2005 (1) SA 217 (CC) at [39] (endorsing "managerial role of the courts").

[111] S. Afr. Const., §§ 38 and 172(1)(b), which provides that the Constitutional Court may make any order which is just and equitable.

[112] *Fose v. Minister of Safety and Security* 1997 (3) SA 786 (CC) [19].

[113] *Brown v. Board of Education*, 347 U.S. 483 (1954); *Brown v. Board of Education*, 349 U.S. 249 (1955) ("*Brown II*") (suggesting that the federal courts engage in long-term supervision of the desegregation process).

[114] *Green v. County School Bd. of New Kent County, Va.*, 391 U.S. 430, 438 (1968) (noting, thirteen years after *Brown II* (349 U.S. 249 (1955)), that a freedom-of-choice plan in schooling would not be sufficient to discharge the affirmative duty on school boards to take "whatever steps might be necessary to convert to a unitary system in which racial discrimination would be eliminated root and branch").

[115] *See, e.g.*, *Milliken v. Bradley* ("*Milliken II*"), 433 U.S. 267 (1977) (affirming the district court's modified decree ordering compensatory education programs for victims of segregation).

students to minority schools, and order the busing of students to particular schools in order to advance desegregation.[116] The Civil Rights Act of 1964, for which *Brown* partially bears credit (although it should be noted that such credit is contested[117]), gave congressional and executive support to school desegregation. That is, when lower court judges refused to pressure Southern school systems to desegregate, Congress authorized Department of Justice school desegregation litigation through the Civil Rights Act and prohibited the dissemination of federal funds to schools that discriminated on the basis of race. Structural injunctions by federal—and state[118]—courts became more prominent in managing school desegregation. The judicial aftermath of *Brown* stands as an exemplary model of extraordinary managerialism, both for the normative steps taken (themselves extraordinary) and the remedial schemes that followed this commitment.[119]

In the United States, managerial judging went on to encompass new judicial activities in controlling the reform of prisons, school management, and mental health settings. Judith Resnik, in her early account of this development, focused on the trend of managerial judging in each sector, highlighting both pre-trial and remedial innovations.[120] In the latter respect, she found that "judges [had] become enmeshed in extended relations with institutions" and described a new intimacy between judges and the minutiae of administration of the institutions usually governed by other branches of government.[121]

In a study of US prison management, Malcolm Feeley and Edward Rubin emphasized the new articulations of prisoners' rights, and the interventionist remedies, that were playing a vital role in prison reform.[122] Linking the developments in prison reform causally to the success of the civil rights movement, Feeley and Rubin found new forms of judicial managerialism to be key. "Policy-making judges" challenged the previous model of judicial enforcement by adopting the same methods that guide agencies—indeed,

[116] *Swann v. Charlotte-Mecklenburg Bd. of Educ.*, 402 U.S. 1 (1971).

[117] The suggestion that the Court obstructed, rather than assisted, the enactment of the Civil Rights Act, has been made: Michael J. Klarman, *From Jim Crow to Civil Rights, supra* note 35. Klarman is highly critical of the violent backlash that resulted from the Court's judgment; and gives credit to African American achievements in the economic and educational spheres as an alternative cause.

[118] E.g., *Crawford v. Board of Education* 17 Cal. 3d 280, 296–7 (1976) (finding its substantive basis in the Californian as well as US Constitution).

[119] Theodore Eisenberg and Stephen C. Yeazell, "The Ordinary and the Extraordinary in Institutional Litigation," 93 Harv. L. Rev. 465 (1980).

[120] Judith Resnik, "Managerial Judges," 96 Harv. L. Rev. 374 (1982).

[121] Ibid., 410, *see also* 390.

[122] Malcolm M. Feeley and Edward L. Rubin, *Judicial Policy Making, supra* note 36 (suggesting "the basic relationship between the civil rights movement and prison reform is causal, not adventitious").

according to Feeley and Rubin, judicial and agency policy-making in modern government had become "indistinguishable."[123] Like administrators, judges could obtain information from multiple groups and courts (and should) "regularly [turn] to experts in the fields who [have] developed solutions through hands-on experience," and deal with problems of uncertainty "by proceeding incrementally."[124] They described the way in which judges appointed special masters and were able to draw up detailed injunctions to maintain control over lawsuits. Such developments produced their own legislative response. In 1996, a federal statute passed a restriction on injunctive orders, which were made to terminate after two years unless the court had made a new finding that the relief was still required to remedy current violations.[125]

Not everyone celebrated the managerial trend in the United States. Those skeptical of the desirability (and indeed, replicability) of the model to other areas of US law suggested that the institutional reform was achieved because judges could cherry-pick cases from multiple inmate petitions, covertly select counsel, and work in tandem with prison officials to "squeeze" money from the state.[126] Overall, these institutional coordinates do not match those characteristics of the economic and social rights cases heard by the South African Constitutional Court, although some may appear apt in prison cases.[127] For example, the Constitutional Court ordered the state to report on the progress it had made towards replacing prisoners' death sentences with another appropriate sentence in light of the Court's holding that the death penalty was incompatible with the Constitution.[128] In the housing, education, or health care cases now appearing before the court, it is unlikely that the flow of information from claimants would resemble the multitude of petitions that certain courts receive from prisoners. It is also unlikely that judges would collaborate with public housing agencies or health clinics to leverage greater finances from the state, because such institutional relationships require a long time to develop, although it is perhaps not implausible in the future.

[123] Feeley and Rubin, ibid., 322.

[124] Ibid., 343.

[125] Prison Litigation Reform Act of 1996 (PLRA) 18 U.S.C. § 3626(b)(1)(A)(i), (b)(3) (2000). *See further* Sabel and Simon, "Destabilization Rights," *supra* note 87.

[126] Neal Devins, "I Love You, Big Brother," 87 Cal. L. Rev. 1283 (1999) 1297. *See also* Feeley and Rubin, *Judicial Policy Making, supra* note 36, 81.

[127] *See August v. Electoral Commission* 1999 (3) SA 1 (CC); *Minister of Home Affairs v. Nat'l. Inst. for Crime Prevention and the Reintegration of Offenders (NICRO)* (S. Afr.) 2004 (5) BCLR 445 (CC).

[128] *Sibiya v. Dir of Public Prosecutions* 2005 (8) BCLR 812 (CC) at 9; *S. v. Makwanyane* 1995 (3) SA 391 (CC).

Even if presently absent from the Constitutional Court in its economic and social rights decisions, managerialism is evident in the lower court decisions in South Africa. When *Grootboom* was first considered by the trial court, Judge Dennis Davis found that the Constitution empowered the court "to issue an order which identifies the violation of a constitutional right and then defines the reform that must be implemented" while nevertheless "affording the responsible state agency the opportunity to choose the means of compliance."[129] Without being "prescriptive about the solutions," Judge Davis sought to "contain any future debate" by the provisional statement "that tents, portable latrines and a regular supply of water (albeit transported) would constitute the bare minimum."[130] The judge's order required shelter to be provided, as well as follow-up reports of implementation, within three months.[131] This stance was adopted pursuant to the categorical command of section 28 of the Constitution, which guarantees "[e]very child the right . . . to basic nutrition, shelter, basic health care services and social services,"[132] and does not incorporate the internal standard of "progressive realization" attached to the other general economic and social rights protected in the Constitution (although is responsive to a general limitations clause).[133]

Lower courts view managerial orders as an appropriate response to the problem of non-implementation of declaratory orders, which are said to leave litigants without redress.[134] In *Cape Town v. Rudolph*, for example, the High Court questioned whether "a declaration, standing on its own, will suffice." In criticizing the outcome of *Grootboom*, because the declaration did not induce the state to comply with its constitutional obligations, the High Court decided to issue structural relief:

> The circumstances, and in particular, the attitude of denial expressed by applicant in failing to recognise the plight of respondents [homeless evicted persons] . . . makes this an appropriate situation in which . . . a structural interdict, is "necessary," "appropriate" and "just and equitable."[135]

[129] *Grootboom v. Oostenberg Municipality* 2000 (3) BCLR 277 [25] per Davis J (Comrie J concurring).

[130] Ibid., [25] per Davis J.

[131] Ibid., [26]–[27] per Davis J.

[132] *Compare* S. Afr. Const., § 28 with §§ 26 and 27.

[133] For discussion of this distinction, *see supra*, Chapter 4.

[134] Mbazira, "Non-implementation of Court Orders," *supra* note 68.

[135] *Cape Town v. Rudolph* 2004 (5) SA 39 (C) (S. Afr.). *See also Strydom v. Minister of Corr. Servs.* 1999 (3) BCLR 342 (W); *Treatment Action Campaign v. Minister of Health* 2002 (4) BCLR 356 (T); *Rail Commuter Action Group v. Transnet Ltd* (1) 2003 (5) SA 518 (C); *Modderklip Boerdery v. President Van Die RSA En Andere* 2003 (6) BCLR 638 (T), affirmed, *President of the Republic of South Africa v. Modderklip Boerdery (Pity) Ltd* 2005 (5) SA 3 (CC).

By comparison with lower courts, the Constitutional Court has been less eager to adopt the managerial orientation. In *Grootboom*, it chose to set aside the lower court's order and substitute it with the more deferential declaration outlined above. There have been only limited departures from this trend.[136] More often, the detailed orders adopted by lower courts have been overturned, even when the substantive decision is affirmed.[137] This reluctance towards adopting a managerial orientation has been criticized by local commentators. According to Marius Pieterse, the Court's "pragmatic" hesitation to order structural injunctions and exercise its supervision has compromised the efficacy of previous court orders.[138]

One case in which the features of managerialism are observable is *Residents of Joe Slovo Community Western Cape v. Thubelisha Homes*.[139] In adjudicating the right to housing for those living on an informal settlement slated for upgrade, the Constitutional Court continued to underscore the necessity of meaningful engagement and the provision of alternative accommodation in the course of relocating 4,386 households (said to constitute 20,000 residents) in an informal settlement east of Cape Town.[140] Again, the Constitutional Court was not content to rule on the final contours of the right to housing, instead, finding only that the respondents had acted reasonably in seeking an eviction on the basis of redeveloping the land for formalized housing. Nonetheless, the decision was accompanied by an order requiring the respondents to ensure that 70 percent of the new homes built on the site would be allocated to the original informal residents, and not fewer than 1,500 houses.[141] The Constitutional Court also ordered that the temporary accommodation meet particular quality standards, including that each unit be:

> at least $24m^2$ in extent; . . . serviced with tarred roads; . . . individually numbered for purposes of identification; . . . have walls constructed with a [fireproof] substance called Nutec; . . . have a galvanised iron roof; . . . be supplied with electricity through a pre-paid electricity meter; . . . be situated within reasonable proximity of a communal ablution facility; . . . make reasonable provision (which may be communal) for toilet facilities with water-

[136] *See infra*, and *see further* Mitra Ebadolahi, "Note: Using Structural Interdicts and the South African Human Rights Commission to Achieve Judicial Enforcement of Economic and Social Rights in South Africa," 83 N.Y.U. L. Rev. 1565 (2008).

[137] Danielle Elyce Hirsch, "A Defense of Structural Injunctive Remedies in South African Law," 9 Or. Rev. Int'l. L. 1 (2007) 7–8.

[138] Marius Pieterse, "Coming to Terms with Judicial Enforcement of Socio-Economic Rights," 20 S. Afr. J. Hum. Rts. 383 (2004) 414–17.

[139] 2010 (3) SA 454 (CC) (*"Joe Slovo Community"*).

[140] Ibid. [141] Ibid., (18) [7].

> borne sewerage; and . . . make reasonable provision (which may be communal) for fresh water.[142]

These detailed substantive conditions were combined with an order that an ongoing process of engagement over the terms of the relocation would continue between residents and respondents.[143] The steps for vacating the land were set out in a timetable annexed to the judgment, revisable after engagement. These features were part of an overall judgment that was arguably highly permissive of government policy. Indeed, it can be seen that such permissiveness weakens the meaningfulness of the ensuing engagement: a weakness for which the case has been widely criticized.[144] The *Joe Slovo Community* case suggests perhaps the outer limit of the Constitutional Court's willingness to manage. The challenges of managerialism suggest its reasoning.

Despite its ability to address the immediate plight of litigants, managerial review may ultimately compromise judicial power by exacerbating the concerns about competency and legitimacy. There is an added reluctance, on the part of courts, to invest political and economic capital into each case. Judges are wary of tying the court's reputation to the career of the case after judgment. Second, motions of contempt against government officials inevitably draw publicity to the court, which, if portrayed as an expensive intervention, may be negative in character. Third, the budgetary consequences of managerialism are felt more directly by the court: managerialism may require the appointment of staff, masters, and other actors, which are both costly and divert time from the docket. And finally, managerialism cannot address the inevitable uncertainty of the regulatory consequences for all the interests affected, and of the responses of various affected actors. In this respect, Resnik's early work documented the unintended consequences of fine-tuned managerial judging in the United States: an order to add twelve officers to the correctional staff of one facility "altered the seniority rights of the prison's unionized personnel and reduced the staff resources available to other state prisons."[145] Such small decisions build up over time to promote unintended changes in institutions beyond the court's reach.[146] Such changes may not only be counterproductive to the objectives of the court order, but also result in backlashes for which the court will be held responsible.

[142] Ibid., (10) [7]. [143] Ibid., [7].

[144] *See* Liebenberg, *Adjudication under a Transformative Constitution*, *supra* note 67, 303–11.

[145] Resnik, "Managerial Judges," *supra* note 120.

[146] *See also* Margo Schlanger, "Beyond the Hero Judge: Institutional Reform Litigation as Litigation," 97 Mich. L. Rev. 1994 (1999).

These problems may be amplified in the economic and social rights context. For example, once the executive acts to implement a court order, and institutes a program involving the allocation or reallocation of goods or services protective of economic and social rights, it may be practically difficult for the executive to later withdraw or redesign such programs.[147] Moreover, a managerial approach to economic and social rights fuels the epithet of "queue-jumping" for successful litigants. Beyond the well-documented concern of a litigation explosion, and of setting public policy by judicial decree, lie effects on the wider pace and direction of transformation. In this way, managerialism can be seen as a precursor, rather than a response, to experimentalism.

(5) Peremptory review

A final stance offered by the Constitutional Court when adjudicating economic and social rights is described as peremptory. This type of review is closer to the conventional static model of judicial review that invites either the striking down of legislation or the upholding of it. Peremptory review involves the rigorous scrutiny of government legislation or policy. Once an infringement is found, the remedy may be for the Court to overturn the legislation or policy. Peremptory review also encompasses other remedies in order to enforce the positive obligations that flow from economic and social rights. Instead of overturning the legislation, the court may choose to uphold it with an amendment; instead of severing the impugned provision, it may read in new legislative words to "cure" it.

Peremptory review occurred in *Khosa v. Minister of Social Development*, when the Constitutional Court held that the exclusion of permanent residents from social benefits was contrary to the right of everyone to social security, and to equality.[148] The majority elected to take a "hard look" at the legislature's reasons for restricting benefits to South African citizens.[149] In doing so, the Court refused to exercise mere rationality review, noting that the search for reasonableness demanded more of the government than the search for rationality and nonarbitrariness; the latter standard, the Court conceded, would have been met by the legislation.[150] Instead, the Court's test for "reasonableness" was substantively based—and grounded in the

[147] Dixon, "Creating Dialogue About Socio-Economic Rights," *supra* note 76, 410.

[148] S. Afr. Const., §§ 9, 27.

[149] Liebenberg, *Adjudication under a Transformative Constitution*, *supra* note 67, 329.

[150] *Khosa v. Minister of Social Development* 2004 (6) SA 505 (CC) [67]. For a discussion of the Court's refusal to canvas the difference between the reasonableness standard within the internal limitation of §§ 26 and 27, and the limitations clause of § 36 of the S. Afr. Const, *see* at [84]; *see supra*, Chapter 4.

Constitution's guarantees. These relate to the values of dignity, equality, and freedom—and to the prohibition on unfair discrimination in section 9.[151]

The majority carefully assessed both the financial reasons for excluding noncitizens and the immigration policy's preference for creating self-sufficiency in permanent residents. It held that these were, though rational, insufficient justifications.[152] In South Africa, "[s]haring responsibility for the problems and consequences of poverty equally as a community represents the extent to which wealthier members of the community view the minimal well-being of the poor as connected with their personal well-being and the well-being of the community as a whole."[153] While the Court accepted a differentiation between permanent and temporary or illegal residents, it found the differentiation between permanent residents and citizens was incompatible with the Constitution's terms.[154] "Like citizens," the Court held, permanent residents "have made South Africa their home."[155] In this respect, the Court was willing to find morally irrelevant a difference that is ideologically laden in South Africa (as elsewhere).[156]

The remedy was to read in "curing words" in the legislation, thus making "citizens *and permanent residents*" eligible for grants.[157] This remedy had the virtue of ensuring that claimants would receive benefits immediately; and that the legislation would not be delayed for other people, in the position of the claimants, who would also be eligible for social benefits. This was a distinct remedy from previous economic and social rights cases, in which the Court ordered negotiation between the parties to settle the issue, as in the evictions decisions;[158] or ordered that the government desist from its actions (and provide some new services), as in the mother-to-child transmission of HIV/AIDS context in *Treatment Action Campaign*;[159] or evaluated and approved of the government's agonizing choices in relation to health care rationing, as in *Soobramoney*.[160] Instead, the Court instigated a new

[151] S. Afr. Const., §§ 9(3), 27. See also S. Afr. Const., preamble. For attention to socio-economic grounds as ground of prohibited discrimination, *see* Promotion of Equality and Prevention of Unfair Discrimination Act, No. 4 of 2000.

[152] *Khosa v. Minister of Social Development* 2004 (6) SA 505 (CC) [63]–[67]; *but see* [122]–[124] (Justice Ngcobo's dissent on this point).

[153] *Khosa* 2004 (6) SA 505 (CC) [74].

[154] The lower court had struck down the citizenship requirement, thereby implying that the state was responsible to provide assistance to both permanent and temporary residents experiencing indigence: *see* discussion in *Khosa* 2004 (6) SA 505 (CC) [9].

[155] *Khosa* 2004 (6) SA 505 (CC) [59].

[156] Siri Gloppen, "Courts and Social Transformation: An Analytical Framework," in Gargarella, Domingo, and Roux, *Courts and Social Transformation in New Democracies*, *supra* note 88, 35, 38 n. 10.

[157] *Khosa* 2004 (6) SA 505 (CC) [98].

[158] *Olivia Road*, 2008 (3) SA 208 (CC); *Joe Slovo Community*, 2010 (3) SA 454 (CC).

[159] *Treatment Action Campaign*, 2002 (5) SA 721 (CC).

[160] *Soobramoney* 1998 (1) SA 765 (CC).

legislative provision, without consultation, that was devised according to the infringement of exclusion that it found on the part of the government.

The Court's stance was peremptory in the following ways. First, it engaged in review that bordered on abstract review, agreeing to review the constitutionality of legislation that was not yet in force.[161] Second, it was quick to give substance to the reasonableness inquiry, linking this to the values of the Constitution, and insisting on their relevance to immigration and welfare policy. Third, it refused to ratify a settlement between the parties, since this would not address the legal uncertainty created by legislation impugned by the Court below, an uncertainty which would particularly impact the broader group of permanent residents as well as the applicants themselves.[162] In particular, it refused to resolve the immediate controversy, simply by extending the definition of citizen to a particular class of residents—Mozambican refugees.[163] A move to settle the case or minimally extend the definition of "citizens," at once decentralized and pragmatist, would not have resolved all of the affected interests in the dispute—which the Court conceived as the interests of other permanent residents. (This inclusive conceptualization nevertheless sidelined other, less privileged categories of noncitizens, such as temporary residents and undocumented immigrants,[164] which reveals the complexity of the consideration of "stakeholders" in any dispute.) Finally, its remedy was peremptory. Rather than agree to a suspended order of invalidity, as requested by the state, the Court insisted on a more interventionist remedy. The suspension would have given the South African legislature eighteen months to amend the legislation.[165] In earlier constitutional rights cases, the Constitutional Court had been prepared to suspend its order in order to avoid the adverse consequences of an immediate declaration of invalidity.[166] Yet in *Khosa*, the Court's reading in of the words "*or permanent resident*" to eligibility requirements took immediate effect.[167] In the result, the new Social Assistance Act 2004, which replaced the impugned legislation, did not incorporate the phrase "or permanent resident." Instead, the categories of

[161] *Khosa* 2004 (6) SA 505 (CC) [32] (particular legislation was not yet promulgated and thus not ready to enter into force: Welfare Laws Amendment Act, No. 106 of 1997, § 3).

[162] *Khosa* 2004 (6) SA 505 (CC) [35].

[163] This class had already been granted exemptions in the Aliens Control Act No. 96 of 1991.

[164] Lucy Williams, "Issues and Challenges in Addressing Poverty and Legal Rights: A Comparative United States/South African Perspective," 21 S. Afr. J. Hum. Rts. 436 (2005) 468.

[165] *Khosa* 2004 (6) SA 505 (CC) [33].

[166] *Cf. Fraser v. Children's Court, Pretoria North* 1997 (2) SA 261 (suspending enforcement of the court order striking down a portion of the state's adoption laws to permit Parliament to amend the law).

[167] *Khosa* 2004 (6) SA 505 (CC) [96].

permanent resident—and of refugees—were included as expressly eligible in new regulations.[168]

The technique of reading in "curing words" has been applied in other cases—some involving discrimination (such as in "curing" the unconstitutional provision of the immigration law by reading in, after the word "spouse," the words "or partner, in a permanent same-sex life partnership"),[169] and others involving economic and social rights. Thus in *Olivia Road*,[170] the Court read a proviso into building standards legislation imposing a criminal sanction upon a person who continued to occupy a potentially unsafe building after an administrative order to vacate.[171] The Court's created proviso reserved the application of a criminal sanction only upon a court order.[172] Finding that "[t]his is not a case in which there are a myriad ways in which the Legislature could cure this section,"[173] such an order was deemed entirely appropriate. Similarly, words were read in to the Magistrates' Court Act in *Jaftha v. Schoeman; Van Rooyen v. Stoltz*,[174] so that sales-in-execution against immovable property could only be authorized by a court "after consideration of all relevant circumstances." This relieved the burden on economic and social rights of mortgage holders who could not meet their payments because of petty debts.

For the Court, peremptory review offers substance over form, removing the prospect of further delay and providing instant relief, for both applicants and for others in a similar position.[175] Unlike the other positions in the typology, it allows the Court to act without assessing the likelihood of a favorable legislative or executive response. Yet it involves a striking arrogation of power to the courts. We have seen that the general problems of judicial power—unaccountability in electoral processes, inability to respond to polycentric effects—can be tailored and minimized in appropriate contexts. In peremptory review, however, we see their most exaggerated manifestations. Moreover, peremptory review invites the problem of "judicial overhang." That is, legislatures may be more likely to pass egregiously unconstitutional statutes if they know that an apex court is available to ensure that truly unconstitutional statutes never go into effect.[176] As

[168] *Social Assistance Act Regulations* (Government Gazette, 22 August 2008) (S. Afr.).

[169] *National Coalition for Gay and Lesbian Equality (NCGLE) v. Minister of Home Affairs* 2000 (2) SA 1 at [86].

[170] 2008 (3) SA 208 (CC).

[171] National Building Regulations and Building Standards Act, No. 103 1977.

[172] *Olivia Road*, 2008 (3) SA 208 (CC) [51].

[173] Ibid., [54].

[174] 2005 (2) SA 140 (CC) [63], [67].

[175] *Khosa* 2004 (6) SA 505 (CC) [88]–[89].

[176] Tushnet, *Weak Courts, Strong Rights*, *supra* note 8, 81.

Tushnet describes it, this effect can promote a legislative disregard of rights.[177] Of course, whether judicial overhang is created by peremptory review is an empirical question: otherwise the criticism works against every checks and balances procedure. The question as to whether there are models—and constitutional cultures—that confound this criticism is addressed below.

These forms of review—which have moved along a spectrum of deferential, conversational, experimentalist, managerial, and peremptory review—are all available in economic and social rights cases. Of course, the different forms of judicial review contain features that blend into one another. In the famous *Treatment Action Campaign* case, for example, the Court adopted a conversational posture to the problem of obstruction of HIV / AIDS drugs in the delivery of health care, but asserted a certain degree of managerialism in requiring the testing and counseling of expectant mothers with HIV / AIDS. The way in which the Court encouraged individual provinces to adopt their own arrangements has also been described in experimentalist terms.[178] Similarly, *Joe Slovo* can be read as deferential to government policy, and yet retains experimentalist and even managerial features. Despite this blending, I suggest that the archetypes of each approach help to demonstrate that different forms of review are being employed to perform distinct ends; and yet hint at an overarching function for the Constitutional Court. To understand this dimension, it is necessary to move the analysis outwards, to appreciate the various role conceptions of courts. This analysis is undertaken in Chapters 6 and 7.

177 Ibid.

178 Klein, *supra* note 91.

6

The Catalytic Court

The typology of specific forms of judicial review, provided in Chapter 5,[1] reveals important features about the adjudication of economic and social rights. The five forms collected—deferential, conversational, experimentalist, managerial, and peremptory—differ in terms of the mode of interpretation, scrutiny, and remedy deployed by the court. These diverse approaches have been adopted by a Constitutional Court which has demonstrated considerable unanimity since hearing its first economic and social rights complaint in 1998. These distinctive features do not turn, for now at least,[2] on an ascending or descending majority on the South African Constitutional Court.

These five distinctive forms are replicated—to greater or lesser degrees—in comparative constitutional law. The typology thus reveals the migration of distinctive approaches to interbranch and extra-branch interactions, as well as of constitutional doctrines and remedies.[3] In this migration, the South African Constitutional Court has been a prominent participant, encouraged by the terms of its Constitution, which behooves the Court to consider international law, and allows it to consider foreign law when interpreting the Bill of Rights,[4] and by the textual similarities between it and other constitutional and human rights. As depicted by the typology, the forms of review are akin to those that have been developed, employed, and described, in other constitutional systems, such as in Canada, Colombia, India, Germany, the UK, and the United States. Their influence has also extended to the supranational courts of Europe, as well as, to a lesser extent, the developing Inter-American, African and UN adjudicatory or quasi-adjudicatory systems. Moreover, these features are present in the cases,

[1] For depiction, *see* Figure 5.1, *supra* p. 143.

[2] *See below*, text accompanying section C(2), for a discussion of the changing composition of the Constitutional Court.

[3] For a study of migratory concepts, *see*, generally, Sujit Choudhry (ed.), *The Migration of Constitutional Ideas* (2006).

[4] S. Afr. Const., § 39(1).

controversies, and challenges that are outside of economic and social rights enforcement, and within the general realm of public law.

Each of the five institutional stances can be linked to a discrete theory of judicial review—of what courts should do under particular conditions. These theories of review can in turn be linked to broader theories of constitutional democracy and the counter-majoritarian role that courts inhabit. Indeed, I have shown that each of the stances may represent an answer to the problems of the others, and in turn create problems of their own. Thus, for example, experimentalist review increases the level of, and changes the site of, the deliberation that may occur from conversational review, in keeping with theories of direct democracy; managerial and peremptory review work to remove the representation challenges of experimentalist review, thereby seeking to move closer to a conception of representative democracy, and yet themselves fall short of democratic requirements. An illustration of this effect is seen in Figure 6.1 below

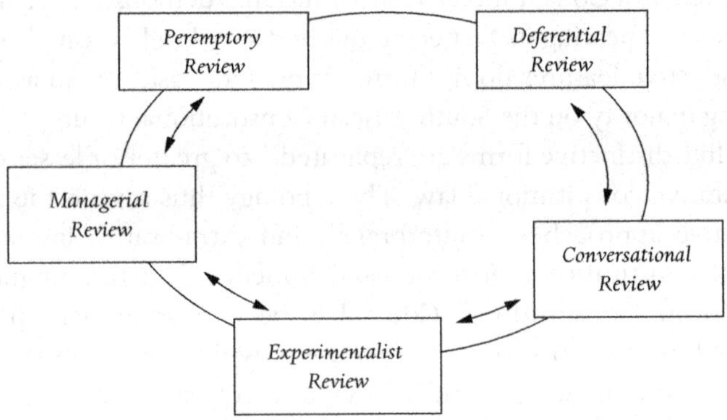

Figure 6.1
Interrelationships of judicial review

The variety expressed within this model suggests a question of its own. How do these distinct forms of review, drawing on different theories of constitutional democracy, coexist within a single court? Below, I suggest that the role conception of a court can explain how a court, overseeing a coherent practice of adjudication, can react eclectically in particular economic and social rights cases. Moreover, I describe how a catalytic role conception is a coherent depiction of this function.

A. THE ROLE OF THE COURT, AS UNDERSTOOD BY THE COURT

An understanding of the role of the judge is critical to understanding the enforcement of economic and social rights in a democracy. Much is written about the role of the judge, and of the special role that is attributed to an apex court in public law cases.[5] In such cases, judges move beyond the resolution and settlement of private disputes, and towards the reinforcement of the "public values" expressed in public law. The determination of such values, as well as the vastness of the reform that their reinforcement invites, is controversial.[6] The enforcement of constitutional rights, particularly economic and social rights, appears to increase this vastness. Public law adjudication thus must attract a form of democratic accountability—democratic, if not majoritarian[7]—that is different in degree and in scope from that held by the elected branches in a constitutional democracy.

Popular prescriptions given for the role of the court, that are apt in considering the enforcement of economic and social rights, range from the judicial minimalism advocated by Cass Sunstein,[8] to the representation-reinforcing role propounded by John Hart Ely,[9] the under-enforcement thesis of Lawrence Sager,[10] and to the proportionate decision-making theorized by Robert Alexy.[11] The first avoids ambitious theories of distributive justice and seeks only to resolve the case at hand, and yet may not, as Sunstein himself concedes, produce certainty and predictability in law, both highly desirable in economic and social rights cases.[12] The second molds the judicial role only to the protection of the rights of unrepresented minorities. Yet, whether an endorsement of representation counsels against poverty being considered a form of nonrepresentation is unclear, since Ely's process-focused account remains "radically indeterminate," relying on moral judgments that its author sought to avoid.[13] The third theory suggests a judicial cognizance of the distributive implications of enforced laws on minimum welfare that may be indirectly addressable, but never directly addressed by courts. The fourth advances an open calculus of balancing

[5] For seminal expression, *see* Abram Chayes, "The Role of the Judge in Public Law Litigation," 89 Harv. L. Rev. 1281 (1976).

[6] Owen M. Fiss, "The Supreme Court 1978 Term—Foreword: The Forms of Justice," 93 Harv. L. Rev. 1 (1979).

[7] For a pertinent difference of opinion on the relation between majoritarianism and democracy, *compare* Jeremy Waldron, *Law and Disagreement* (1999), with Ronald Dworkin, *A Bill of Rights for Britain* (1990).

[8] Cass R. Sunstein, *One Case at a Time: Judicial Minimalism on the Supreme Court* (1999). *See further, supra* Chapter 3.

[9] John Hart Ely, *Democracy and Distrust: A Theory of Judicial Review* (1980).

[10] Lawrence G. Sager, *Justice in Plainclothes: A Theory of American Constitutional Practice* (2004) 84–128.

[11] Robert Alexy, *A Theory of Constitutional Rights* (Julian Rivers trans., 2002) (1986).

[12] Cass R. Sunstein, "Beyond Judicial Minimalism," 43 Tulsa L. Rev. 825 (2008).

[13] Laurence H. Tribe, "The Puzzling Persistence of Process-Based Constitutional Theories," 89 Yale L. J. 1063 (1980).

which may allow for the consideration of material interests against other important social goals.[14]

Such prescriptions help to advance particular modes of judicial decision-making in economic and social rights, and suggest how they may be compatible with constitutional or democratic norms (and usually both). Some inform the accounts of judicial review expressed in the previous chapter. Notwithstanding the importance of such prescriptions, a "role conception" goes beyond the theoretical understanding of the role of the court, and looks to the understandings courts have of themselves. Courts must contend with their own forms of legitimacy, in order to maintain the justification for their ongoing democratic role, adherence to their opinions, and execution of their orders. This is contingent on the constitutional polity in which they find themselves. Their own understanding of their legitimacy, and the political capital needed to sustain it, forms the basis of my description of a "role conception." Substantive theories (or ideologies) of a democratically defensible distributive justice inhere in the constitutional polity itself.

In the following framework, a role conception is held, and upheld, by the court itself. Because it is critical to the court's continued legitimacy, a role conception is dependent on the background political history, legal tradition, and legal culture within the constitutional polity in which the court finds itself. The role conception is dependent on the common law or civil law decision-making conventions of the court, including those traditions' different models of judicial education and appointment.[15] It also depends on the tradition of local respect for law (summarized, but often obscured by rule of law models), and the persuasiveness and respect-worthiness of previous judicial opinions. This tradition is embodied in a constitutional culture, which is created not only by other judges, but also by members of the legislature and executive, the lawyers, litigants, political parties, journalists, and members of civil society (labor unions, employer organizations, interest groups, social movements, etc.) who participate in contestations around public law.[16]

This makes the judicial role conception quite distinct in different constitutions and political and constitutional cultures. It also makes a study of the judicial role conception ripe for comparative constitutional law. While everywhere one could generalize that courts must cultivate a political

[14] *See* discussion, *supra* Chapter 4 section B.

[15] *See, e.g.*, John H. Merryman, *The Civil Law Tradition: An Introduction to the Legal Systems of Europe and Latin America* (3rd edn., 2007); Mitchel de S.-O.-l'E. Lasser, *Judicial Deliberations: A Comparative Analysis of Judicial Transparency and Legitimacy* (2009).

[16] *See further*, *infra* Chapter 8.

capital that looks roughly the same, by making decisions according to the rule of law, for instance, or by exercising nonarbitrariness and procedural fairness,[17] the fact that these normative concepts are susceptible to some changes in local conditions means that the role conception will differ subtly between constitutional or apex courts. The fact that different understandings of distributive justice also inhere in the general political culture attenuates these differences.[18]

While a role conception is dependent on constitutional culture, it is also dependent on institutions. The ways in which rights are drafted and judicial power is conferred all alter the nature of the role conception. Standing rules, access to information sources such as *amicus curiae*, as well as the publication requirements for judgments,[19] also play a part in the development of a role conception. For those who attempt to articulate a philosophy of judging within democratic settings, institutional constraints are evident. Aharon Barak has defined this role in general, albeit institutionally responsive terms: endorsing "a judge who, within the bounds of the legitimate possibilities at his disposal, makes the law that, more than any other law he is authorized to make, best bridges the gap between law and society and best protects the constitution and its values."[20]

While the distinctiveness of role conceptions is made clear by comparative constitutional law, it is not the case that all judges on a single court hold the same role conception. It is likely that many of the sources of dissent lie, not with differences of opinion on substantive law, but with differences of opinion of role conception. There is no straightforward way to identify this difference, on the face of doctrine alone. Yet when judges describe the legacy or impact of their decisions (in sufficiently critical terms), their role conception—which may be more culturally and institutionally nuanced than their general theory of the constitution, or, in their minds, determined by the constitution—becomes evident.[21] Indeed, their own role conception may be more durable than the substantive theory of law they choose to

[17] E.g., Alec Stone Sweet, *Governing with Judges: Constitutional Politics in Europe* (2000).

[18] E.g., Seymoir Martin Lipset, and Gary Marks, *It Didn't Happen Here: Why Socialism Failed in the United States* (2001).

[19] *See*, e.g., S. Afr. Const., § 38. For the relevance of these particular features, *see* Robert Bennett, "Counter-Conversationalism and the Sense of Difficulty," 95 Nw. U. L. Rev. 845 (2001).

[20] Aharon Barak, *The Judge in a Democracy* (2006) 307.

[21] My own analysis of the South African Constitutional Court is based on interviews and substantive conservations with the following justices: Justice Arthur Chaskalson (in October 2008) (President of the Constitutional Court 1994–2001; Chief Justice 2001–2005); Justice Albie Sachs (in January 2010 and June 2011) (Justice 1994–2009); Justice Kate O'Regan (in June 2011) (Justice 1994–2009); Justice Laurie Ackermann (in June 2011) (Justice 1994–2004); Justice Richard Goldstone (in May 2007) (Justice 1994–2003) (all after retirement); and Justice Zak Yacoob (in June 2011) (appointed 1998).

adopt. The judiciary is a collection of individuals, and we have no guarantees that they will adhere to any prescribed interpretive standpoint.[22]

In political science terms, we might regard this disposition by courts as incorporating a self-perception of their own political capital. Despite the fact that the self-perception by judges of their own political capital may be criticized as a distraction from their main task of judging,[23] it is clear that effective courts have a certain perception of retaining the legitimacy of what they do. If the term "political capital" describes a form of political power that can be possessed, increased, or spent, we note that political capital may be converted into outcomes, and between different institutions. To capture the comparative point, we might say that the conversion of political capital into other forms of capital follows a different currency in different constitutional systems.

My theorization of role conceptions moves beyond the initial presentation of specific judgments and remedies. It does this by demonstrating how a court's adjudication of economic and social rights is linked to how the court perceives itself as an institution of governance and how this perception helps it to comprehend, and address, complaints. This is first demonstrated by one such role conception, which draws on every aspect of our typology of judicial review: the role conception of a catalytic court.

B. THE CATALYTIC COURT

The role conception of a catalytic court is one that sees itself in productive interaction with other political and legal actors. The metaphor of the catalyst suggests that the court acts to lower the political energy that is required to change the protection of economic and social rights, or at least the way in which the government responds to the protection of economic and social rights. In keeping with the metaphor of the catalyst, the court itself remains largely unchanged by the encounter (or is at least not the main focus of the change). The greater change occurs in the legislatures, bureaucracies, schools, hospitals, clinics, landlord and eviction companies, and the interest groups and/or social movements representing claimants, who are forced to interact together in ways that would otherwise require a greater expenditure of political energy, or, as we might call it, a great transfer of political capital.

[22] Adrian Vermeule, "The Judiciary Is A They, Not An It: Interpretive Theory and the Fallacy of Division," 14 J. of Contemp. Leg. Iss. 549 (2005) 553.

[23] *Cf.* Erwin Chemerinsky, *Constitutional Law: Principles and Policies* (2nd edn., 2002) 131–2 ("[T]he federal courts' legitimacy is quite robust . . . and, in any event, the courts' mission should be to uphold the Constitution and not worry about political capital."); Laurence Tribe, *American Constitutional Law* (2nd edn., 1988) viii ("The highest mission of the Supreme Court . . . is not to conserve judicial credibility.").

Lowering political energy is related to the idea of lowering the stakes of politics. For Adam Przeworski, this increases the stability of a constitution: "Constitutions that are observed and last for a long time are those that reduce the stakes of political battles."[24] For William Eskridge, a stakes-lowering constitution can support a stakes-lowering court, which dictates a particular role for judges. For Eskridge, building on Ely, judges facilitate democracy, especially pluralist democracy, "by countering or ameliorating some of the stakes-raising tendencies of the political process."[25] Features of stakes-lowering judicial review include enforcing neutral rules of political engagement, ameliorating culture wars, and reversing the burden of inertia against "weeding out" statutes made obsolete through shifts in normative commitments.[26] Here, there are two matters that are ripe for our understanding of a catalytic court. The first is the way in which it is able to weed out obsolete precedent and statute,[27] which impose unjustifiable burdens on economic and social rights. The second is the way in which it can channel political discourse away from prejudice and stereotypes: not only for the identity-based social movements focused on reforming law's prejudices in relation to sexual orientation, as in Eskridge's model, but also for the treatment of poor people or other groups seeking an openly redistributive politics.

The catalytic function of the court offers a principled, and yet nevertheless highly contextual, resolution to the challenges of adjudicating constitutional economic and social rights. The interactions are not normatively neutral. The catalyst is present to trigger and control certain changes, and not others. It is therefore a useful metaphor to represent the triggering of the positive obligations so integral to economic and social rights enjoyment. For instance, the metaphor has been used to capture the effect of US state courts on education policy. Courts acting as catalysts there contributed to an improvement in educational outcomes, by forcing changes in school finance policy in Texas, Kentucky, and North Dakota, changes which were blocked during normal political processes.[28]

[24] Adam Przeworski, *Democracy and the Market: Political and Economic Reforms in Eastern Europe and Latin America* (1991) 36–7.

[25] William N. Eskridge, Jr., "Pluralism and Distrust: How Courts Can Support Democracy by Lowering the Stakes of Politics," 114 Yale L.J. 1279 (2006).

[26] Ibid., 1310.

[27] Ibid., 1310, citing Guido Calabresi, *A Common Law for the Age of Statutes* (1982) (suggesting that courts should be empowered to overrule obsolescent statutes, in a similar way to overruling obsolescent precedents).

[28] Matthew H. Bosworth, *Courts as Catalysts: State Supreme Courts and Public School Finance Equity* (2001); *see* also James S. Liebman and Charles F. Sabel, "A Public Laboratory Dewey Barely Imagined: The Emerging Model of School Governance and Legal Reform," 28 N.Y.U. Rev. L. & Soc. Change 183 (2003).

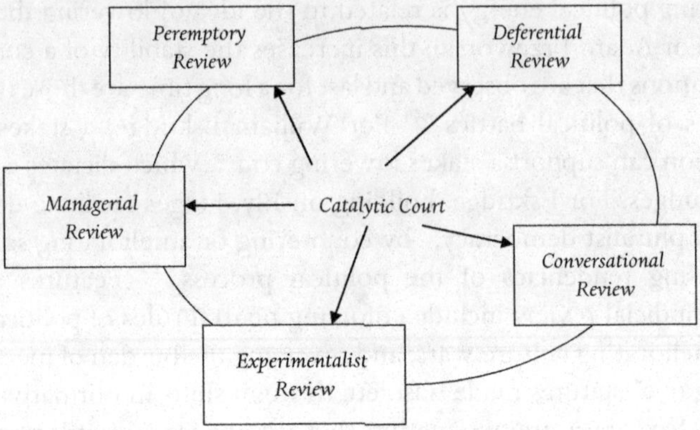

Figure 6.2
The catalytic court

The catalytic court captures the range of stances towards judicial review described in Chapter 5. Even deferential review, the least intrusive of all these stances, fits within the catalytic metaphor, due to the reciprocal role obligations that it can stimulate. An illustration is seen in Figure 6.2.

C. THE CATALYTIC COURT IN SOUTH AFRICA

The catalytic court depicts the eclectic modes of judicial review adopted by the South African Constitutional Court. Over fifteen years, the court has adjudicated economic and social rights with nuance and adeptness, combining principle with pragmatism in enforcing the postapartheid constitutional vision.[29] Of course, these two orientations—of principle and pragmatism—can be in tension. Yet the Constitutional Court appears to have shepherded its legitimacy through the very different coordinates dictated by governmental cooperation, public expectations, and adherence to principle. Local commentators have identified, in the Court's opinions, a continual moral consideration of the Constitution's values, in a distinctively lawyerly discourse and setting, which nevertheless invites a broader societal response.[30] By engaging in a catalytic function, the Constitutional Court opens up the relationship with the elected branches, continues a moral discourse of the

[29] Theunis Roux, "Principle and Pragmatism on the Constitutional Court of South Africa," 7 Int'l. J. Const. L. 106 (2008).

[30] Theunis Roux, "The Constitutional Value System and Social Values in South Africa," in András Sajó and Renata Uitz (eds.), *Constitutional Topology, Values and Constitutions* (2010) 205 (exploring how the judges, in "the process of constitutional adjudication, negotiate between the constitutional value system and other social value systems. This is not a philosophical question, but a matter of judicial practice that can be observed, interpreted, and more or less clearly understood") (at 206).

Constitution's values, and leaves it own arrangements undisturbed. In many cases, this catalyzes a rights-protective outcome.

The catalytic metaphor helps to demonstrate that the Constitutional Court of South Africa deploys the variety of stances of judicial review deliberately, and that certain criteria guide this deliberation. I suggest that the Court's choice of the form of review turns on the government action that has led to an alleged infringement of a right, and only indirectly on the content of the right itself. For example, the Constitutional Court's explicit reluctance to define the normative "content" of economic and social rights—to articulate, for example, the juridical implications of a dignity-based interpretation of the rights to housing or health care, or even to accept the very possibility of a judicial interpretation via a "minimum core" or otherwise "self-standing" right—is matched by an implicit reluctance to be held to a specific form of review in all economic and social rights cases. However, in some contradiction, it is worth nothing that where lack of access to a good or service that would secure an economic and social right is additionally affected by equality concerns, the Constitutional Court's stance is more likely to be interventionist in character, suggesting a liberal-egalitarian impulse (rather than, for example, communitarian or libertarian alternatives) in interpreting economic and social rights.

In broadly characterizing this catalytic role conception, I borrow partly from the writings of new governance scholars, who show how courts can catalyze various deliberative effects by elaborating and enforcing norms and by helping to "prompt and create occasions for normatively motivated and accountable inquiry and remediation by [other] actors."[31] In new governance scholarship, the primary action occurs outside the court: courts are decentered and secondary. Nonetheless, I suggest that the role conception that best approximates the Constitutional Court's efforts to navigate the challenges of economic and social rights is not, uniformly, a decentered one. As the presence of peremptory review in the typology makes clear, the Court's specific form of review may sometimes be cast as centralized and hierarchical.

The Constitutional Court's role is substantial and central, in part because of the postapartheid constitutional settlement and the role explicitly assigned to it. Despite the fact that the overthrow of apartheid was a victory over racial oppression and minority rule, in favor of majoritarian democracy and an end to the South African judiciary's association with oppression, the resulting settlement did not reject the centrality of courts. In fact, empowering a new Constitutional Court was a central outcome of the democratic

[31] Joanne Scott and Susan Sturm, "Courts as Catalysts: Re-Thinking the Judicial Role in New Governance," 13 Colum. J. Eur. L. 565 (2006).

transition.[32] The Court was given the powers to override legislation and policy, and its remedies were designed to be broad. In the postapartheid settlement, the Constitutional Court is required to confirm the declarations of invalidity issued by lower courts in order for them take effect, thus providing it with a critical supervisory, and centralized, role.[33]

The Constitutional Court is now responsible for catalyzing change in keeping with the Constitution's broad aspirations, entrenched rights, and overall commitment to transformation.[34] The Court perceives constitutional litigation to be vital to constitutional democracy, and has explicitly invited future litigation in order to air economic and social rights concerns.[35] For the Court, litigation around economic and social rights "fosters a form of participatory democracy that holds government accountable and requires it to account between elections over specific aspects of government policy."[36] A catalytic role conception is a response to the exhortation of transformation, perceived both by the Constitutional Court, and wider constitutional culture, of South Africa.[37] Yet the justifications for the catalytic function arguably run deeper than South Africa's own, and urgent, concerns.

In contrast to other constitutions under study, the requirement to transform South Africa is explicitly entrenched in its Constitution, which checks executive and judicial power at the same time as it issues a summons to all three branches of government to address the legacy of almost half a century of apartheid and its destructive imprint on the terms of social life.[38] The direction of change is itself the subject of constitutional pre-commitment: transformation is to be democratic, rights-protective, social-egalitarian, and focused on the burdens imposed by the period of officially sanctioned racial discrimination in employment, land-holding, schooling, and other critical determinants of prosperity and poverty.[39]

If transformation challenges the status quo, it is tempting to suggest that all constitutions—all of which contain an "is" and an "ought"—do so. Constitutions may be considered to have both preservative or transformative

[32] Heinz Klug, *Constituting Democracy: Law, Globalism and South Africa's Political Reconstruction* (2002).

[33] *See* S. Afr. Const., §§ 167(5), 172(2).

[34] *See further* Chapter 1 and Chapter 5, text accompanying text 20–24.

[35] *Mazibuko v. City of Johannesburg* 2010 (4) SA 1 (CC) (*"Mazibuko"*), [159]–[165], per O'Regan J.

[36] *Mazibuko* 2010 (4) SA 1 (CC) [160], per O'Regan J.

[37] *See further* Chapter 5.

[38] Dikgang Moseneke, "Transformative Adjudication, Fourth Bram Fischer Memorial Lecture" (25 April 2002), 18 S. Afr. J. Hum. Rts. 309 (2002).

[39] Karl E. Klare, "Legal Culture and Transformative Constitutionalism," 14 S. Afr. J. Hum. Rts. 146 (1998).

features, and perhaps a tilt towards one or the other. The US Constitution is famously preservative of the settlement reached after the gains of independence and the end of the civil war. Nonetheless, it contains its own transformative features, as originally expressed or as understood over time.[40] South Africa's transformative ambitions are explicitly drafted. Hence, South Africa's is a constitution that seeks to transform society from its authoritarian, racist traditions. At the very least, transformation refers "broadly to redressing the historical balance caused by past unfair discrimination," as confirmed by the Constitutional Court.[41] It remains for the exact contours of that redress to be defined; I suggest that the Court's catalytic role is nevertheless marked by this mandate. It may be deferential, conversational, experimentalist, managerial, or peremptory, in accordance with this requirement. Yet how does the court decide which form of judicial review to adopt, in keeping with transformation? Four explanations are available, which depict the mandate of transformation in various guises. I explore each of them, before suggesting a fifth. This explanation focuses on the responsiveness of the Court to the particular obstructive stance taken by the government, that underlies the complaint of an economic and social rights infringement. This explanation renders South Africa's role most generalizable to other constitutional systems.

(1) *Negative versus positive obligations*

The first explanation for the Court's choice of review is that it depends upon whether the complaint rests with a positive or a negative obligation with respect to the claimed economic and social right. This explanation relies on the truism that the enforcement of a negative obligation—an infringement of a duty to respect rights, because of active, and illegitimate, state interference—is less likely to threaten the traditional role of the court. The adjudication of negative obligations may require only a one-dimensional assessment of infringement, and, if found, conventional remedial intervention that merely orders the government to desist in its present actions. For the purposes of both judicial review and remedy, negative obligations are easier for a court to deal with.

In assessing rights infringements, negative obligations appear straightforward. Sandra Liebenberg suggests, for example, that the "reasonableness" inquiry is not applicable to the alleged infringement of negative obligations,

40 Theunis Roux, "Understanding Grootboom—A Response to Cass R. Sunstein," 12 Const. F. 41 (2002).

41 *Bato Star Fishing (Pty) Ltd v. Minister of Environmental Affairs* 2004 (4) SA 490 (CC), [71], n. 3 per Ngcobo J. E.g., Moseneke, "Transformative Adjudication," *supra* note 38; Klare, "Legal Culture and Transformative Constitutionalism," *supra* note 39; A. J. van der Walt, "The State's Duty to Protect Property Owners v. The State's Duty to Provide Housing: Thoughts on the *Modderklip* Case," 21 S. Afr. J. Hum. Rts. 144 (2005).

because the contextually sensitive standard underlying the duty of "progressive realization" is not invoked. The distinction, made at the level of obligations, is consistent with a rejection of the negative/positive rights distinction as categorizing different rights, but focusing on the obligations that correlate with them.[42] The infringement of a negative obligation, as opposed to a positive one, will only be justified by the (apparently) more stringent requirements of the general limitations clause.[43] Nonetheless, we have seen how negative duties—to respect rights—may also invoke a standard-based proportionality assessment.

As the *Treatment Action Campaign* case makes clear, even in remediating negative infringements on the part of the government, the Court may utilize the catalyzing features of conversational and managerial review. Despite the Court's later disavowal of the managerial aspects of this case, suggesting "all the Court did was to render the existing government policy available to all,"[44] the negative infringements that formed the basis of the dispute—the government's refusal to roll out a privately available and donated drug into the public hospital system—were met with different judicial techniques.

More fundamentally, the negative/positive distinction is complicated when we embrace a more comprehensive conception of state action, just as the South African Constitution, and the Constitutional Court, does. A clear lesson, from the American legal realists onwards,[45] is that the background vulnerabilities that make active government interference burdensome on rights are also the result of state action. We might say, for example, that an active eviction, which interferes with a negative obligation to respect an individual's right to housing, will not be an infringement if alternative accommodation is made available.[46] Or we might say that the enforcement of the common law rights of private property, in favor of property owners, does not exempt the state from its positive obligations of economic and social rights towards evictees.[47] Thus, in choosing to enforce one set of rights over the other, the state is at all times engaged in positive action. While this book does not explore the potentially far-reaching private

[42] Sandra Liebenberg, *Socio-Economic Rights: Adjudication under a Transformative Constitution* (2010) 54–9.

[43] Sandra Liebenberg, "Socio-Economic Rights: Revisiting the Reasonableness Review/Minimum Core Debate," in Stuart Woolman and Michael Bishop (eds.), *Constitutional Conversations* (2008) 305, 311.

[44] *Mazibuko* 2010 (4) SA 1 (CC) [64].

[45] Wesley Newcomb Hohfeld, "Some Fundamental Legal Conceptions As Applied in Judicial Reasoning," 23 Yale L.J. 16 (1913); Robert Hale, "Coercion and Distribution in a Supposedly Non-Coercive State," 38 *Pol. Sci. Q.* 470 (1923). *See further*, Duncan Kennedy and Frank Michelman, "Are Property and Contract Efficient?," 8 Hofstra L. Rev. 711 (1980).

[46] *Occupiers of 51 Olivia Road v. City of Johannesburg*, 2008 (3) SA 208 (CC).

[47] Van der Walt, "Thoughts on the *Modderklip* Case," *supra* note 41.

law dimensions of economic and social rights,[48] it suffices to note that a duty to consider the rights impacted upon by the current set of private rights may lead to a duty to develop the common law in a particular direction.

The recognition that the state acts whenever structures of private and public law are enforced indicates that constitutional or human rights, which are conventionally understood as protecting individuals from the actions of government, extend to private relationships between individuals. That is, the action of the state may be, at base, legally structuring the actions of private parties in ways that reveal its failure to comply with the duty to protect economic and social rights.[49] The recognition of the "horizontal effect" of constitutional rights, accepted in South Africa (and in other constitutional systems, most famously in Germany,[50]) reveals the continued instability of the negative/positive distinction of duties no less than rights.[51] This recognition marks the difference between a classical liberal constitution and a more affirmative constitution, which, some argue, separates the US Constitution from others around the world.[52]

Thus, in constitutional systems that recognize a form of horizontality, the traditional perception of negative and positive duties is less appropriate. While we can still give some credence to the action/omission distinction, we must do so while conceding that it can obscure the prior effect of law's creations—of privileges and immunities, as well as of rights and duties—on present arrangements.[53] It can obscure the way in which private contractual and interpersonal relations affect the enjoyment of economic and social rights.[54] Of course, courts are often comfortable to leave this obscurity in place, perhaps seeking to forestall charges of "activism" or "counter-majoritarianism." On this basis, the explanation that the court's choice of review is responsive to whether a positive or negative infringement is alleged can only be partly correct. For example, an infringement of a negative obligation may require more than an order to desist, and thus a court would appropriately engage in the variety of types of review, and expose the horizontality of rights more clearly.

[48] For an application to the US state constitutional context, *see* Helen Herschkoff, "'Just Words': Common Law and the Enforcement of State Constitutional Social and Economic Rights," 62 Stan. L. Rev. 1521 (2010).

[49] Van der Walt, "Thoughts on the *Modderklip* Case," *supra* note 41.

[50] *Lüth*, BVerfGE 7, 198 (1958) FCC. *See also* S. Afr. Const., § 8.

[51] E.g., Henry Shue, *Basic Rights: Subsistence, Affluence and U.S. Foreign Policy* (2nd edn., 1996).

[52] David P. Currie, "Positive and Negative Constitutional Rights," 53 U. Chi. L. Rev. 864 (1986) (interrogating the interpretation of the US Constitution as negative only).

[53] For a containment of Hohfeld's typology ("Some Fundamental Legal Conceptions," *supra* note 45), *see* Alan Gewirth, "Are All Rights Positive?," 30 *Phil. & Pub. Aff.* 321 (2002).

[54] For one view, *see* Marius Peiterse, "Relational Socio-Economic Rights," 25 S. Afr. J. Hum. Rts. 198 (2009) 216.

Nonetheless, while horizontality is conceptually linked to positive rights, and to duties of reforming private law, courts remain reluctant to catalyze change in this area. In South Africa at least, the Constitutional Court evidences a preference to adjudicate through public law, rather than reinterpret private property rights or other private law rights in the way that horizontality may invite.[55] In the *Modderklip* case, the Constitutional Court was required to adjudicate on the burden placed upon a large landowner's private property rights, after the large-scale squatting of the landowner's property by otherwise homeless people. The Court did not base its decision on the state's duty to protect property or housing rights,[56] nor on any tensions between them that would require the reinterpretation of the common law.[57] Instead, the court focused on the duty of the state, arising directly from the right of access to courts,[58] to provide suitable and effective enforcement procedures and to assist in implementing them when necessary. The Court emphasized the state's own duty to step in and assist the landowner in protecting property against unlawful occupation, especially in situations where the occupation was of such magnitude that the landowner would not be able to evict without state assistance.[59] Hence, the catalysis of the Court is projected onto the state's duty of enforcing present laws, rather than on the Court's duty to revisit and revise common law precedent.

The latest judgment of the Court on the right to housing confirms this emphasis. In *Maphango v. Aengus Lifestyle Properties (Pty Ltd)*,[60] the Court affirmed the rights of tenants to challenge a termination of their lease on the basis that it was unfair. The landlord had terminated the lease in order to oblige the tenants to leave or to enter a new lease at substantially increased rent. The Court insisted that both negative and positive obligations arising under the right to access housing impinge on private parties, in debt recovery or evictions proceedings.[61] Moreover, "[t]he second way in which the right of access to adequate housing ripples out to private rights

[55] *See President of the Republic of South Africa v. Modderklip Boerdery (Pity) Ltd.* 2005 (5) SA 3 (CC) ("*Modderklip*"). *See also* the careful treatment of common law in *Joe Slovo Community*, 2010 (3) SA 454 (CC). *cf.* S. Afr. Const., § 8(3).

[56] S. Afr. Const., §§ 25, 26.

[57] *See* also *Joe Slovo Community*, 2010 (3) SA 454 (CC).

[58] S. Afr. Const., § 34.

[59] *Modderklip*, 2005 (5) SA 3 (CC) [45], [48], *compare* with *Mkontwana v. Nelson Mandela Metropolitan Municipality* 2005 (1) SA 530 (CC) [59] (requiring owners of property to bear the primary responsibility to take reasonable steps to protect their property, including steps to have unlawful occupiers evicted). *See* van der Walt, "Thoughts on the *Modderklip* Case," *supra* note 41, 158.

[60] Case CCT 57/11 [2012] ZACC 2 (13 March 2012).

[61] Ibid., [32]–[33]. *See, e.g., Jaftha v. Shoeman* 2005 (3) SA 140 (CC); *City of Johannesburg Metropolitan Municipality v. Blue Moonlight Properties 39 (Pty Ltd)* 2012 (2) SA 104 (CC).

is when the state itself takes measures to fulfil the right. These may affect private relationships."[62] Hence, the Court concentrated its focus on the Rental Housing Act 1995, rather than on any contractual or common law arguments. It found that the constitutional right of access to adequate housing warranted a broad interpretation of the Act, passed to give it effect. The Act's unfair practice provisions, which regulated landlord–tenant conduct, therefore applied to the termination.[63]

(2) *Maturation of jurisprudence*

The second explanation that moves beyond a simple thesis of transformation is that the Court's stance towards review has changed as its jurisprudence matures. While the Court adopted deference as a key posture when developing an appropriate role in adjudicating economic and social rights, it became less appropriate as it grew in confidence. The Court developed more interventionist postures, such as managerial and peremptory review.[64]

This explanation has much in common with Tushnet's prediction of the strengthening of weak courts over time, supported by the polity (as well as the parallel prediction that weak remedies convert into strong).[65] Under this model, through investment in previous decisions, courts evolve into more insistent political actors, and arrogate a greater power to dictate the terms of rights and the necessary steps towards enforcement. Yet this explanation, while certainly plausible in describing the Court's tentative judgment in its first economic and social rights case in *Soobramoney*,[66] fails to account for its recent modes of review. Even now, we find a continuing willingness on the part of the Court to assume deferential or conversational review.[67] Perhaps Tushnet's less predictive reflection, that after their strengthening, and under certain conditions, courts may reconvert weak remedies back into more effective weak remedies, has better explanatory traction for the Constitutional Court.

This strong-weak dynamic is complicated by the changing composition of the South African Constitutional Court. In the Court's "first generation," its

[62] *Maphango*, Case CCT 57/11 [2012] ZACC 2, [34].

[63] Ibid., [57].

[64] Eric C. Christiansen, "Adjudicating Non-Justiciable Rights: Socio-Economic Rights and the South African Constitutional Court," 38 Colum. Hum. Rts. L. Rev. 321 (2007).

[65] Mark Tushnet, *Weak Courts, Strong Rights: Judicial Review and Social Welfare Rights in Comparative Constitutional Law* (2008) 249.

[66] *Soobramoney v. Minister of Health, Kwazulu-Natal* 1998 (1) SA 765 (CC). *See also* Craig Scott and Philip Alston, "Adjudicating Constitutional Priorities in a Transnational Context: A Comment on *Soobramoney*'s Legacy and *Grootboom*'s Promise," 16 S. Afr. J. Hum. Rts. 206 (2000).

[67] *Mazibuko* 2010 (4) SA 1 (CC) [56]; *Joe Slovo Community*, 2010 (3) SA 454 (CC).

judges served terms with compulsory twelve-year limits and delivered careful and often unanimous judgments in the building of an expected "homegrown" jurisprudence.[68] This first generation, led by its first President, Arthur Chaskalson, was appointed from a pool of lawyers, judges, and legal academics whose (often internationally renowned) reputations were associated with the struggle against apartheid.[69] This generation is held in high regard by the government and public, and even its unpopular decisions were readily followed and enforced.

The Constitutional Court is now heading into its "second generation." It now enjoys a significantly different character. A concern for racial and ethnic representation appears dominant in more recent appointments.[70] Six new judges have been appointed, five by current President Jacob Zuma, including the Chief Justice, Mogoeng Mogoeng. The new controversies facing the Court have involved contestations around the notions of judicial independence. These controversies have been very distant from those faced by the first generation,[71] revolving as they have around individual judges and the process of judicial appointments. A failure of government officials to implement court orders, particularly those requiring public officials to resolve systemic problems of public administration, especially in pension and social welfare grants, has been evident.[72] Conflict among government officials, and within the political parties (asymmetrically dominated by the ANC), has played out against the Court.

A maturing jurisprudence requires time, and yet time may be interrupted when a court's composition, and therefore its public character, changes relatively quickly. This is often the case for courts in legal systems with newer constitutions, whose judges are more likely to face term limits, or at the very least compulsory retirement ages, thus enjoying a more rapidly changing composition than the constitutional model of the US Supreme Court (where judicial independence is equated to life tenure). This suggests that a model of linear maturation, or even cyclical strengthening of courts, may be too simplistic. Nonetheless, it is equally simplistic to equate the strength of the court to the present judges serving on it. Heinz Klug has

[68] Justice Yvonne Mokgoro, *Creating a Home Grown Rights Jurisprudence for Emerging Democracies: The Case of South Africa* (2004).

[69] Lynn Berat, "The Constitutional Court of South Africa and Jurisdictional Questions: In the Interest of Justice?," 3 Int'l. J. Const. L. 39 (2005) 74.

[70] Heinz Klug, *The Constitution of South Africa: A Contextual Analysis* (2010), 234; *see also* S. Afr. Const., § 174(2).

[71] Klug, ibid., 236–7, 295–6. [72] Klug, ibid., 295.

described the Constitutional Court, as late as 2010, as "one of the most successful institutions to emerge in post-apartheid South Africa."[73]

A maturing jurisprudence tracks a maturing constitutional culture. Studies of transitional constitutions indicate that the constitutional, and particularly democratic, culture from which the Constitutional Court develops its role conception, does not itself stand still. Indeed, after authoritarian rule, the prospects for rapid democratization, and a brand new set of constitutional commitments, may develop. So much has at least been evident in some post-Communist transitions.[74] Yet the developing constitutional culture of South Africa—influenced by the apartheid legacy, which included the public memory of the anti-apartheid struggle, well-used forms of protest, and well-coordinated networks led by the ANC—followed its own pace of transition. The ANC had itself played a major role in creating the constitutional vision that was to unfold.[75]

The new Constitutional Court was not situating itself against a brand new world of democracy, with the space for a new constitutional vision, and a new multiparty democracy to develop of the kind described in other constitutional transitions.[76] Such a backdrop would dictate ever-more conversational stances in judicial review after peremptory beginnings.[77] Instead, the Constitutional Court has matured along with continued ANC dominance and, in much of South Africa, an increasing sense or urgency, and decreasing hopes, for a significant partisan counterweight. Maturation may explain the variety of choices of judicial review; however, its processes are too unsteady to predict or justify the choice of review taken by a catalytic court.

(3) Quantification of right

The third explanation is that the Court's choice of review differs on the basis of the judicial manageability of the economic and social right that is the subject of litigation. This explanation finds empirical support in the US experience. There, the Supreme Court was willing to differentiate between economic and social rights, suggesting that "[e]ducation, perhaps even more

[73] Klug, ibid., 243.

[74] Kim Lane Scheppele, "Democracy by Judiciary; Or, Why Courts Can be More Democratic than Parliaments," in Adam Czarnota et al. (eds.), *Rethinking the Rule of Law after Communism* (2005) 25, 33.

[75] Berat, "The Constitutional Court of South Africa and Jurisdictional Questions," *supra* note 69, 42–3, 56 (describing the ANC-dominated elections to both the constituent assembly that produced the interim constitution and the parliament that produced the final constitution).

[76] *Compare* with David Landau, "Political Institutions and Judicial Role in Comparative Constitutional Law," 51 Harv. Int'l. L.J. 319 (2010).

[77] Scheppele, "Democracy by Judiciary," *supra* note 74 (showing "courtocracy" became less over time).

than welfare assistance, presents a myriad of 'intractable economic, social and even philosophical problems.' ... [W]ithin the limits of rationality, 'the legislature's efforts to tackle the problems' should be entitled to respect."[78] To take another example, the right to health care is notoriously complex—its interpretation depends upon the availability and constraints of scientific and cultural knowledge, and its satisfaction (in an outcome sense) is partly contingent on genetics or luck.[79] Indeed, proponents of the right to health have suggested that an incompletely theorized meaning of the right to health, based on broad notions of human capability, may be the most we can do to secure it within a constitutional democracy.[80] The right to water, on the other hand, does not appear to share the conceptual quandaries of the rights to education or health. Water is apparently a readily measurable commodity that can link individual entitlements—by the liter—to consumption and sanitation needs.

If water is quantifiable, and education or health are not (a position disputed by certain neoliberal assumptions about the quantifiability and hence commodification of all basic services), the one would appear to be more judicially manageable than the other. This was the view adopted by the lower court in the South African case of *Mazibuko*.[81] This case was the first in South Africa to invoke the right to have access to water.[82] Residents of the Phiri neighborhood in Soweto challenged the amount of water they were provided with under the City of Johannesburg's program of free basic water supply given to all residents. The High Court and the Supreme Court of Appeal dealt with the case similarly. First, the High Court concluded that a free basic water policy of 25 liters per person per day was insufficient to meet the applicants' basic needs, to live in dignity, and to avoid threats to their lives and health. In so doing, the High Court judge determined that managerial review—including an approved minimum core (resting at 50 liters per day), and a detailed plan of response—would be most appropriate.[83] Hence, the High Court ordered the City of Johannesburg to supply 50

[78] *See, e.g.*, *San Antonio Indep. Sch. Dist. v. Rodriguez*, 411 U.S. 1, 42 (1973) (quoting *Dandridge v. Williams*, 397 U.S. 471, 487 (1970), and *Jefferson v. Hackney*, 406 U.S. 535, 546 (1972)).

[79] Katharine G. Young, "Securing Health through Rights," in Thomas Pogge, Matthew Rimmer, and Kim Rubenstein (eds.), *Incentives for Global Public Health: Patent Law and Access to Essential Medicines* (2010). *See* discussion, *supra* Chapter 3, text accompanying notes 63–69.

[80] Jennifer Prah Ruger, "Toward a Theory of a Right to Health: Capability and Incompletely Theorized Agreements," 18 Yale J. L. & Hum. 273 (2006) 306–11.

[81] 2010 (4) SA 1 (CC).

[82] S. Afr. Const., § 27.

[83] *Mazibuko v. City of Johannesburg* [2008] 4 All SA 471 (W); [2009] ZAGPHC 106 (18 April 2008); Case No. 06/13865, High Court of South Africa (Witswatersrand Local Division) (ordering the City to supply 50 liters of free water per person per day).

liters of free water per person per day. The right to access water appeared measurable and determinate, which the Supreme Court of Appeal affirmed. Nonetheless, the Supreme Court of Appeal, on the basis of different evidence, reduced the minimum entitlement to 42 liters per person per day.[84]

Both decisions were consistent with a quantification of the right to water. On further appeal, the Constitutional Court disagreed, refusing to engage in any statement of a quantified standard and deferring to the government's determination.[85] Managerial review was not considered appropriate, even for an apparently "manageable" right.

The *Mazibuko* case met with much criticism on the part of economic and social rights commentators. Parties to the case criticized the Court for failing to interrogate the neoliberal impulses guiding water policy in South Africa.[86] They suggested that the underlying payment methods, and hence the burden of risk—of either water cutoffs for consumers, or unpaid bills for the water corporation—was placed on to the poorest consumers for their failure to pay for water. This burden was of great moral significance to the case, with parties suggesting a new apartheid following economic lines to be the effect of neoliberalism in South Africa.[87] They also argued that the policy did not cater for the much larger households that were the norm in Soweto, with a greater likelihood of the allocations being too small.

Others suggested that the water authorities were doing the best they could to facilitate access to water efficiently and effectively. They pointed to a special program of additional allocations that people with HIV/AIDS or disabilities or other needs could join to avoid cut-offs: a proposal that evolved during the course of litigation, and that was commended by the Constitutional Court.[88] However, these allocations were only triggered if an account-holder (usually the head of a household or a number of adjacent households) first registered as indigent and agreed to the installation of a prepaid meter.

In the end, the Constitutional Court sided with the government. Clearly, it was reluctant to adopt modes of review—such as managerial review—that could have allowed it to begin to quantify the right to water, or to enforce some sort of minimum quantification. For present purposes, we can discard the explanation that the form of review depends upon the right under

[84] *City of Johannesburg v. Mazibuko* 2009 (3) SA 592 (SCA). The Water Services Act, No. 108 of 1997, had quantified a minimum of 25 liters per person, per day.

[85] *Mazibuko* 2010 (4) SA 1 (CC) [56].

[86] P. Bond and J. Dugard, "The Case of Johannesburg Water: What Really Happened at the Pre-paid 'Parish Pump'?," 12 Law, Democracy, and Development 1 (2008).

[87] Ibid.

[88] *Mazibuko*, 2010 (4) SA 1 (CC) [96]–[97].

dispute, and its ability to be quantified. But we may note the way the question of quantification is tied to the question of commodification—water, health care, and electricity provision are all basic services that may become both privatized and commodified, as they have been, through municipal services in South Africa. Courts have not changed their position in light of, say, the anti-commodification stance that is usually invoked in relation to economic and social rights.[89]

A comparison with the Federal Constitutional Court in Germany demonstrates the contingency of this judicial hesitation. In the case of *Hartz IV*,[90] unemployed individuals and their dependents challenged the constitutionality of legislation that reduced the level of basic subsistence grants. They claimed that the grants contravened the dignity clause of the German Basic Law,[91] because they fell below a subsistence minimum. While the Federal Constitutional Court agreed, it concluded that, consistently with separation of powers principles, the court itself could not quantify the basic level of subsistence amounts. In this respect, the position was superficially consistent with the stance taken by the South African Constitutional Court in *Mazibuko*. Yet the Court nevertheless engaged in a searching examination of the method of calculation relied on by the legislature in setting the grants.

In effect, the Federal Constitutional Court ("FCC") demanded justification for the legislature's quantification.[92] For justification to be satisfactory, the legislature's determination of benefits needed to be based on a sound empirical basis and coherent methods rather than random estimates. As the calculations did not meet this standard, the legislation was sent back to the legislature for a new quantification procedure. The Court's remedy was to order the legislature to implement a methodologically sound and constitutionally adequate procedure for determining realistic benefit amounts designed to ensure a subsistence minimum in line with human dignity, within a specified time. The provisions found unconstitutional were to remain in effect in the interim.[93] Moreover, the Court ordered the federal

[89] *See*, e.g., G. Esping-Anderson, *The Three Worlds of Welfare Capitalism* (1990) (finding decommodification and destratification as the central contributions made by economic and social rights).

[90] BVerfG, 1 BvL 1/09 vom 9.2.2010, Absatz-Nr. (1–220) ("*Hartz IV*").

[91] German Basic Law, arts. 1.1 and 20.1: *see* Appendix I; *see Hartz IV*, BVerfG, 1 BvL 1/09 vom 9.2.2010, Absatz-Nr. (1–220).

[92] *Hartz IV*, BVerfG, 1 BvL 1/09 vom 9.2.2010, Absatz-Nr. (1–220); *see supra*, Chapter 4, for a discussion of how limitations force justifications.

[93] *Hartz IV*, BVerfG, 1 BvL 1/09 vom 9.2.2010, Absatz-Nr. (1–220) paras. 204–7; *see also* Donald P. Kommers, *The Constitutional Jurisprudence of the Federal Republic of Germany* (2nd edn., 1997) 53 (describing the way in which the FCC utilizes two methods of softening the political impact of its decisions regarding unconstitutionality. The strategy used in *Hartz IV* is that of declaring a statute unconstitutional but not void, while providing general guidelines and a time frame within which the

government to cover the provision of special needs during the transition period.

The comparison between the South African case of *Mazibuko* and the German case of *Hartz IV* illuminates the question of quantification and review. The difference does not lie in separation of power concerns. Instead, it lies in the choice of judicial review—in the degree to which the courts probe the evidence supplied by the government to justify its policies, and their creativity in developing criteria and remedies. This comparison helps to answer the following question for economic and social rights: "when a social program designed to give effect to a constitutional entitlement to a social good—water, food, housing, and so on—turns on the amount—or minimum amount—of the good the government must provide in order to fulfill its constitutional obligations, to what extent, if any, may courts inquire into, demand explanation of, interrogate, and/or second-guess the government's data and calculation methods?"[94] The FCC went much further. I suggest that this difference is attributed to the role conception of each court, and of the modes of judicial review attached to that role conception. Peremptory review was available to the FCC in *Hartz IV*, and, despite the quantification question, it was not utilized by the South African Constitutional Court in *Mazibuko*. Again, we look elsewhere in predicting the mode of review adopted by the court.

(4) Consideration of budget

Fourth, is the explanation that a court chooses to engage in more vigorous review when the cost implications of its order are negligible. The peremptory stance adopted by the Constitutional Court in *Khosa* was sustained, for example, by the fact that the inclusion of indigent permanent residents in the social security regime would reflect "an increase of less than 2 percent on the present cost of social grants."[95] Similarly, the Court's experimentalist order in *Treatment Action Campaign* was assisted by the fact that the antiretroviral drugs were free: their donation by pharmaceutical companies was guaranteed for a period of five years.

Nonetheless, while this explanation tracks the cost-related objections to enforcing economic and social rights (which point to their tendency, to a greater extent than other rights, to require the reallocation of scarce resources

legislature is required to act. A second method is to sustain the challenged statute, but indicate to the legislature that the court will invalidate it in the future if the legislature does not take corrective action.).

[94] Lucy A. Williams, "The Role of Courts in the Quantitative-Implementation of Social and Economic Rights: A Comparative Study," 3 Constitutional Court Review 141 (2010) 182.

[95] *Khosa v. Minister of Social Development* 2004 (6) SA 505 (CC) ("*Khosa*") [62].

on the part of the state, prompted or dictated by the Court), it is insufficient to account for the Court's changing modes of review. In *Khosa*, the additional cost for the government to bear (ranging—in a speculative fashion—between R243 and R572 million) was demonstrably not negligible. Increased appropriations were clearly required by such orders, at least in the short term.

Understanding the Court's choice of review through the lens of the government's budget is problematic. The Court has acknowledged that the cost of economic and social rights is a legitimate government concern. Indeed, the obligation to provide access to particular economic and social rights is mediated by what is "reasonable . . . within its available resources, to achieve the progressive realisation of this right."[96] Nonetheless, the Court has also held that a raise in expenditure "may be a cost we have to pay for the constitutional commitment to developing a caring society."[97] More fundamentally, the Court does not engage in the task of assessing how its orders will increase or decrease expenses after their immediate defrayal: an extremely difficult conceptual and practical task. In acknowledging the difficulty of this task, for example, commentators have described the counterintuitive way in which judicial enforcement can reduce expenditure over the longer term by minimizing more expensive interventions, or by creating other value.[98] Courts are not designed to address this complexity. The modes of balancing discussed in Chapter 4 likewise do not involve monetary assessments. Courts are therefore reluctant to allow cost to dictate their style of review, although they may be attuned to such considerations at the remedial stage, making some impact likely then. If cost otherwise explains the government infringements of rights, it is more accurately portrayed as a capacity or competence issue, discussed below.

(5) Response to intransigence, incompetence, or inattentiveness

I suggest that, in partial contrast to these four explanations, the choice of review adopted by the Court is more immediately, if subtly, responsive to the government's actions. Thus, I argue that the choice of review responds to the government action: whether, for example, the government is deliberately obstructive and even hostile to economic and social rights, whether it is inadvertently overriding such rights, or whether it is genuinely unable

[96] S. Afr. Const., §§ 26(2), 27(2); *see also* ICESCR, art. 2(1) (obligating steps, to the "maximum of their resources" of each State Party).

[97] *Khosa* 2004 (6) SA 505 (CC), [65].

[98] Kathleen G. Noonan, Charles Sabel, and William H. Simon, "The Rule of Law in the Experimentalist Welfare State: Lessons from Child Welfare Reform," 34(3) Law & Social Inquiry 523 (2009).

to deliver them. To demonstrate this effect, it is useful to invoke Kent Roach and Geoff Budlender's characterization of government actions towards economic and social rights, which escalate in the gravity of the infringement at issue, by virtue of either intransigence, incompetence, or inattentiveness.[99]

In this model, an intransigent legislature or bureaucracy is one beset by inertia: immovable, through procedural practice or force of habit, to change policy. An incompetent government is technically unable to access or process the information, or is practically constrained by a lack of funds. Incompetence thus raises the challenge of the cost of remedying the perceived infringement (as suggested above), but places it within a contextualized assessment of options available to the government. An inattentive government, on the other hand, fails to comprehend the claims of the most materially vulnerable. This inattentiveness may be the product of the invisibility and exclusion of certain groups in public processes, due to the very fact of their material vulnerability, or because they are otherwise a politically vulnerable or unpopular minority.

This disaggregation of government action is a powerful way to understand the variety of modes of review employed by the Court, and the attempts it makes to catalyze various responses. While Roach and Budlender apply this model to suggest a range of appropriate remedies permitted by the Constitution,[100] it is also useful in understanding a range of modes of interpretation and evaluation of government's conduct, in South Africa no less than for other courts adjudicating economic and social rights.

For example, inattentiveness is best addressed by focusing political attention on the elected branches. Conversational review will be appropriate. However, if the inattentiveness is directed to a politically vulnerable class, which is unlikely to benefit from an increase in political attention, the Court is more likely to adopt peremptory review. This inattentiveness may be exacerbated by other deficiencies in the legislative process, such as single party dominance. Such systems may be highly competent, and yet also highly unrepresentative.[101] Incompetence is best addressed through adopting the problem-solving capacity of experimentalist review, or, if it results from a genuine lack of funds (that cannot be otherwise raised

[99] Kent Roach and Geoff Budlender, "Mandatory Relief and Supervisory Jurisdiction: When Is It Appropriate, Just and Equitable?," 122 S. Afr. L.J. 325 (2005) 345–50, borrowing from Chris Hansen, "Inattentive, Intransigent and Incompetent," in S. R. Humm (ed.), *Child, Parent and State* (1994) 224, 232. They also draw parallels to the principles of escalating regulatory responses in John Braithwaite, *Restorative Justice and Responsive Regulation* (2002).

[100] Ibid., S. Afr. Const., §§ 38 and 172(1)(b); *see also Fose v. Minister of Safety and Security* 1997 (3) SA 786 (CC) [19].

[101] *See*, e.g., Landau, "Political Institutions and Judicial Role in Comparative Constitutional Law," *supra* note 76, 330.

through experimentalist processes), deferential review. The creation of new channels of local knowledge may resolve such incapacity. Finally, intransigence is best dislodged by the dynamism of experimentalist review, or by the court's investment in managerial review. Under each model, intransigent positions and habits are destabilized, and new modes of policy are forged. These prescriptions are contingent on the robustness or weakness of political institutions and civil society, as we will see below.

This linking of review to the government's actions allows us to understand how the catalytic court is able to prompt a myriad of changes in order to secure the protection of economic and social rights. It also helps us to assess the choices made by the Constitutional Court, and to acknowledge that, in invoking certain types of judicial review in particular cases, the court may have miscalculated its catalytic function.[102] Moreover, the catalytic function of the South African Constitutional Court also assists in capturing the modes of judicial review of all constitutional rights, not just economic and social rights.

This explanation ties in with a normative account of how the catalytic function helps to increase the protection afforded to constitutional economic and social rights. The analysis of *Khosa* suggests that the Court seeks to make its intervention compatible with democracy, and that the Court's vision of democracy is attuned to political vulnerabilities and inequalities. The very assessment of the government's actions—whether classified as intransigent, for instance, or inattentive—relies on a normative understanding of the obligations which the right imposes. The Court is therefore not excused from engaging in prior interpretive work of the substance of economic and social rights when adopting the catalytic function.

We might say that the Constitutional Court is sounding out something like Ely's "representation-reinforcing" role as a justification for departing from deference, and from other forms of review.[103] Ely famously prescribed the limits that a counter-majoritarian institution should have on legislative action, when invalidating a statute on constitutional grounds. Borrowing from dicta of the US Supreme Court,[104] Ely suggested that review be restricted except in cases in which "discrete and insular minorities" had to be protected from the preferences and outcomes of the majoritarian electoral processes.

[102] For criticisms of *Mazibuko*, *see*, e.g., Liebenberg, *Adjudication under a Transformative Constitution*, *supra* note 42, 466–80.

[103] Ely, *Democracy and Distrust*, *supra* note 9; *see also* Eskridge, "Pluralism and Distrust," *supra* note 25.

[104] *US v. Carolene Products Co* 302 U.S. 144, 142 (Stone J.) (1938).

The catalytic function arguably allows the Court to address two elements that were underemphasized in Ely's account. First, the Constitutional Court arguably recognizes that procedural protections are reliant on substantive interpretations of constitutional democracy—a large part of which is the liberal-egalitarian protection of economic and social rights.[105] Secondly, we might attribute a certain degree of pragmatic self-knowledge to the Constitutional Court of the pitfalls of judicial overreach and public backlash.[106] The court's conception of its role allows it to exercise more interventionist measures only in exceptional cases. This justification returns us to the elusive goal that runs through this book: the means to secure economic and social rights within constitutional democracy.

[105] Frank I. Michelman, "The Constitution, Social Rights, and Liberal Political Justification," 1 Int'l. J. Const. L. 13 (2003).

[106] Roux, "Principle and Pragmatism," *supra* note 29.

7

A Comparative Typology of Courts

What lessons does the South African Constitutional Court hold for other courts called to respond to claims of economic and social rights? How generalizable is the experience of a catalytic court, interpreting a "transformative" constitution, for the adjudication of economic and social rights elsewhere? Does the typology of Chapter 5 help us to understand the contemporary response to economic and social rights in other judicially rights-protective jurisdictions, such as India, Colombia, Germany, and the United States? Does it recommend the adjudication of economic and social rights for courts that are not explicitly authorized to enforce many of the recognized economic and social rights in their own human rights jurisprudence, like Australia or New Zealand, and does it tilt the balance towards an implied authorization, leading to new interpretations of extant constitutional provisions? How does South Africa's catalytic stance help us to understand the legislative, rather than constitutional, incorporation of economic and social rights, such as occurs for the right to education in the United Kingdom? Or their sub-national, provincial, constitutional protection, such as in the diffused system of federal legislative authority in Canada, where authority over labor relations, social security, and health care rests with states?[1] Does the South African experience clarify and suggest a more extensive scope for the regional, and international, adjudication of economic and social rights?[2]

I suggest that it does. In viewing the judgments of other courts, and the attendant commentary, we find evidence of some of the stances of judicial review adopted by the South African Constitutional Court, on the part of other courts adjudicating economic and social rights. This assists us in depicting other role conceptions that bring about a different response to

[1] *See further* Patrick Macklem, "Social Rights in Canada," in Daphne Barak-Erez and Aeyal M. Gross (eds.), *Exploring Social Rights: Between Theory and Practice* (2007) 213, 215–25.

[2] For a recent endorsement of South Africa's model for international enforcement, *see* Beth A. Simmons, "Should States Ratify? Process and Consequences of the Optional Protocol to the ICESCR," 27 Nordic J. Hum. Rts. 64 (2009).

the challenge of economic and social rights. It will be seen that the catalytic function, described in Chapter 6, is not the only one available to courts in economic and social rights cases. Indeed, there are many others, which may be represented along a continuum.

The presentation of role conceptions is therefore a second typology of economic and social rights adjudication, that overlays the first. Such a theorization moves beyond the initial presentation of specific judgments and remedies, by showing how a court's adjudication of economic and social rights is linked to the way the court perceives itself as an institution of governance. Second, the demarcation of role conceptions indicates how a court's self-perception helps it to comprehend, and address, complaints. Third, it indicates how the typology of judicial review, initially drawn from South Africa, helps us to understand the role of other countries' courts in the adjudication of economic and social rights.

A. A TYPOLOGY OF ROLE CONCEPTIONS

Apart from the catalytic court, three other role conceptions respond to complaints of economic and social rights infringements by utilizing parts of the initial typology of judicial review. These three opposing role conceptions—which I label a detached court, an engaged court, and a supremacist court—all utilize certain features of judicial review. These role conceptions may openly reject many of the five stances discussed, but none of them reject them all, and most employ at least two. They resemble the diagram shown in Figure 7.1.

A detached appellate court evinces the features of deferential or, at most, conversational review. An engaged court displays the features of conversational and experimentalist review. A supremacist court acts in both managerial and peremptory directions. The tendency of a court to avail itself of one or other approach may be guided by the same justifications undergirding catalytic review: that is, to engage with, or demand, a suitable democratic response to the claimed-for economic and social right, as calibrated to the background constitutional culture and institutions. The court's choice will also be influenced by its own institutional design features, such as access to court and standing rules, reporting and reason-giving requirements, and the other legal encouragements or impediments described in Chapter 6. Indeed, the very laws entrenching economic and social rights may stipulate or limit their treatment by judiciaries.[3] The text of these laws, although possibly the result of borrowing, is nowhere the same.

[3] For a discussion of Directive Principles, and underenforcement, *see* Chapter 4, section A(6).

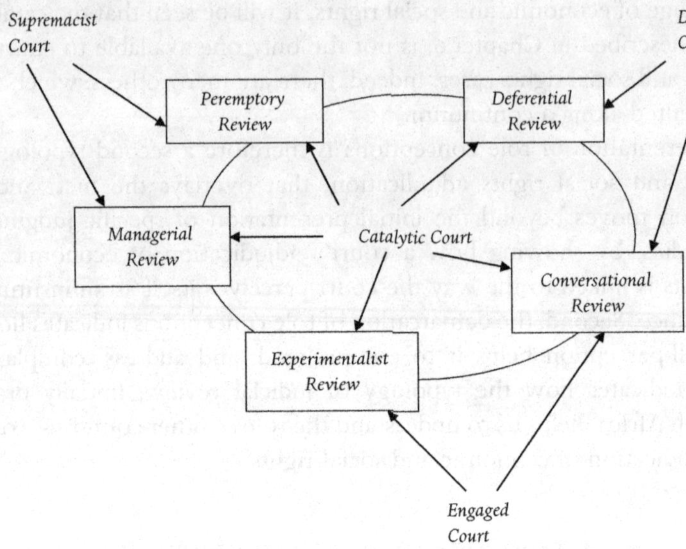

Figure 7.1

The typology of role conceptions

My depiction of different role conceptions helps to evaluate courts, not on the basis of their jurisdiction—at least, not as a primary matter—but on their likelihood to adopt one or another approach. The breadth of the typology frees up our current thinking about justiciable economic and social rights. First, it provides a different measure with which to evaluate, and usefully categorize, courts. This measure has the potential to depart from an ideology-bound classification. Our understanding may not be constrained, for example, by the ideology that we attribute to judges, or by their formalist or attitudinal bent. The cautions that such characterizations of the judiciary raise for economic and social rights—that is, of formalist judges being disoriented by the complexity of allocative decision-making, of conservative judges justifying their preference for deregulation on a theory of economic growth, and of liberal judges demanding greater public spending and producing a public backlash against the poor[4]—is managed (if not overcome) by the forms of review available.

Second, an examination of the general role conceptions of courts that exist within the corners of this typology allows us to resist a country-specific classification with respect to economic and social rights. We can see, for example, what the Indian Supreme Court and the South African Constitutional Court critically share, and why we may evince a reluctance to prescribe justiciable economic and social rights for a supremacist court in a

[4] Frank B. Cross, "The Error of Positive Rights," 48 UCLA L. Rev. 857 (2001) 901–23.

constitutional culture which does not share the democratic conceptions of distributive justice that are minimally required for the protection of economic and social rights.[5] Yet we can also recognize the situationally specific aspects of these features, which itself is an important breakthrough, and one of the best justifications for constitutional comparison that one can provide. The result is not the critiqued "South African obsession," caused by an exclusive emphasis on innovations occurring in that country,[6] but rather a deeper lens with which to view innovations and differences occurring elsewhere.

The characterizations of courts provided below delivers a broad depiction of how their approach to economic and social rights adjudication is akin to certain ideal types of this second typology. In focusing only on explicit economic and social rights cases, this is a necessarily selective enterprise. Whether the local character of the court is completely aligned with this depiction—in adjudication that indirectly enforces economic and social rights,[7] or in other forms of constitutional adjudication—is an empirical question, and one I do not answer here.

The function of a typology is familiar to comparative legal analysis. A typology can classify previously disjointed features, and present clusters of analysis that were previously kept apart. Nonetheless, in advancing new clusters, and the insights that they deliver, typologies create blind spots and contradictions, or can operate to rationalize the status quo. Hence, this typology, like the one presented in Chapter 5, is intended to provide a heuristic for understanding. In my analysis, the depiction of elements of catalysis in South Africa, supremacy in Colombia, engagement in India, and detachment in the United Kingdom, are reasonably cogent descriptors of current arrangements. There will be counterpart forms in each system—and indeed jurisdictions such as Canada, Germany, and Ghana resist such direct classification—but none will be wildly off this map. Moreover, the typology may be viewed, for comparative purposes, as attached to a local default norm. This explains why "deferential" may equate to a different stance in South Africa and the United States; and why "engagement" may appear different in Canada and India. The main point of the exercise is to show the

[5] Frank I. Michelman, "Socioeconomic Rights in Constitutional Law: Explaining America Away," 6 Int'l. J. Const. L. 663 (2008).

[6] *Cf* David Landau, "The Reality of Social Rights Enforcement," 53 Harv. Int'l. L.J. 189 (2012), rejecting the focus on South Africa, especially on the *Grootboom* case (*s.v. Grootboom* 2001 (1) SA 46 (CC)), as irrelevant to the "majority of trends occurring elsewhere," and suggesting that "neither approach seems to function well or to accurately describe the majority of social rights enforcement occurring around the world.")

[7] Lawrence G. Sager, *Justice in Plainclothes: A Theory of American Constitutional Practice* (2004). Sager's underenforcement is indirect and unexpressed. *Cf* the directive principles of state policy in India, which are indirect and expressed. *See further* Chapter 4.

ongoing variety of forms of review, and of judicial roles, in the project to enforce economic and social rights.

B. ELEMENTS OF SUPREMACY: COLOMBIA

If a supremacist court favours managerialist and peremptory review, the Colombian Constitutional Court's approach to economic and social rights adjudication makes it a good candidate. Since the adoption of the country's 1991 Constitution, this young, specialized Constitutional Court, whose nine justices serve nonrenewable eight-year terms,[8] has developed a robust role conception of supremacy against the elected branches. The conception contains both managerial and peremptory dimensions. The managerial orientation towards judicial review is evidenced in a range of economic and social rights cases, in which the Court has directed quotas for primary education, devised new tests for including treatment in state-supported health care, and overseen new housing financing arrangements. The Court has used the peremptory mode in striking down legislation and policies, such as overriding legislation that sought to implement national pension cuts.[9] In these cases, the Constitutional Court collected information, held large-scale and regular public hearings, dictated policy, and managed resources in judicial techniques that echo the supremacist role.

The Constitutional Court's engagement with rights has been wide and insistent. Working with a constitution that entrenches the vision of a "social state rule of law,"[10] it has devised new ways to protect the economic and social rights of Colombians. The two most striking examples occur in protecting and overseeing the fulfillment of the right to health, and in protecting the rights of internally displaced persons, often indigenous peoples rendered homeless and insecure by violent displacements occurring within Colombian society. In the former, the Constitutional Court has, through a series of judgments, acted to transform the structure of health financing in Colombia.[11] In the latter, the Constitutional Court initiated a new bureaucracy to deal with and end the "unconstitutional state of affairs"

[8] *See* Constitution of Colombia [1991] [Constitución de Colombia de 1991] ("Colombian Constitution"), art. 239. *See further* Appendix I.

[9] David Landau, "Political Institutions and Judicial Role in Comparative Constitutional Law", 51 Harv. Int'l. L.J. 319 (2010) 359.

[10] Colombian Constitution, art. 1; Rodrigo Uprimmy Yepes, "The Enforcement of Social Rights by the Colombian Constitutional Court: Cases and Debates," in Roberto Gargarella, Pilar Domingo, and Theunis Roux (eds.), *Courts and Social Transformation in New Democracies: An Institutional Voice for the Poor?* (2006) 127, 128–31.

[11] The presentation of such cases below draws on Katharine G. Young and Julieta Lemaitre, "Follow the Money, Follow the Courts: What We Can Learn from the Comparative Fortunes of the Right to Health," 26 Harvard Human Rights Journal (forthcoming, 2013).

of the thousands of internally displaced persons rendered homeless, destitute, and without recourse to the administration, as a result of both state and non-state action. Both lines of constitutional innovation have commanded much comparative attention.

Two design features complement this supremacist role conception. First, the Constitutional Court has reinterpreted its civil law traditions, retaining the information-gathering, inquisitorial independence, but dispensing with the bureaucratic, technocratic timidity associated with courts in civil law systems. The change in judicial training, appointments, and the new constitutional agenda arguably prompted this reinterpretation from 1991. Second, the Constitution invites wide standing and access through the *accion de tutela*, which is a petition procedure that allows any individual to seek protection of fundamental human rights in the courts. The *tutela* may be used by any citizen before any judge to seek an immediate judicial injunction against actions or omissions of any public authority that they claim violates their constitutional fundamental rights. Courts must hand down a ruling within ten days of receiving a petition. The trend in the use of the *tutela* is increasing—in 1992, a total of 8,060 *tutela* judicial decisions reached the Court for discretionary review, but by 2005 there were 221,348.[12] All *tutela* must be sent to the Constitutional Court for *certiorari* selection: since 1992, it has received about 1,400,000 *tutela* decisions (from a national population of 44 million.) Pension and health cases make up more than half of *tutelas*; most others impact indirectly on economic and social rights as well.[13]

As well as institutional features, the Constitutional Court's self-perception has guided the development of the supremacist role. The Constitutional Court sees its role, not in separation of powers terms, but in terms of a substantive constitutional vision. This conception is furthered by an "ideational belief," on the part of judges, on the normative importance of rights, and the special role of the new judicial order to make them realized.[14] This is a consequence of both positive and negative beliefs. On the positive side lies the perception that the history of violence and authoritarianism in Colombia behooves the Constitutional Court to act as a central

[12] Colombian Constitution, art. 86; Manuel Jose Cepeda-Espinosa, "How Far May Colombia's Constitutional Court Go to Protect IDP Rights?," *Forced Migration Review: Putting IDPs on the Map* 21 (Special Issue, December 2006) 22; *see* T-025/04 §§ III.6.2–6.3 [Colombian Constitutional Court] reprinted in Corte Constitucional: Sentencias-Tutelas 1992–2008 (DMS Ediciones e Investigaciones Ltda 2009). Article 2 of the Colombian Constitution holds that "guaranteeing the effectiveness of the principles, duties, and rights consecrated in the Constitution" is an "essential duty of the state": The Court held that this created a positive duty on the state to do something about the displaced persons problem, even if it did not bear primary responsibility for creating the problem. *See* ibid. § III.8.

[13] Young and Lemaitre, *supra* note 11.

[14] Rodrigo Nunes, "Ideational Origins of Progressive Judicial Activism: The Colombian Constitutional Court and the Right to Health," 52 *Latin American Politics and Society* 67 (2010).

rights-protecting institution. On the negative side stands the perception that the legislature and executive are not fulfilling their own constitutional function to respond to this history.

A sense of legislative and administrative dysfunction seems widespread. Manuel Jose Cepeda-Espinosa, Former Justice of the Colombian Constitutional Court, reported on the Court's collective view: "that we had such a bad Congress that we had no choice but to try and do something."[15] A sense of the inability of the legislature to act according to even minimalist majoritarian principles, and of the inability of the bureaucracy to administer the law, created the space for supremacist thinking and action. In the extensive health rights cases, for example, the Constitutional Court perceived itself, not as overseeing the bureaucracy, but as taking it over: "we were the bureaucracy."[16] The dysfunction of the Colombian Congress thus subdues the import of the traditional counter-majoritarian concern with supreme judicial review.[17]

Despite these justifications for strong judicial action, these managerial and peremptory decisions suffer from many of the shortcomings described in Chapter 5. Managerial review has required, first, a huge amount of judicial resources, and stretched the capacity of the Constitutional Court in its other decisions. Second, a perception of queue jumping has carried forward in public discourses about health and pensions financing, in light of the massive costs to the systems in addressing the orders.[18] Third, the unintended effects of the cases—effects to which the arm of managerialism cannot stretch—has included a counterresponse by the government, in the case of health financing, in the attempt to suspend the Constitution, retrench its health care commitments, in turn spurring a heated cycle of public protest. Whether the net result—with the election of a new government, and new reforms to the health care system—is a good or a bad outcome in health care (including in health care access and equity) is still open to evaluation.[19]

Peremptory review has also attracted the predicted disadvantages accompanying that model. In this respect, the Court has received criticism for

[15] Landau, "Political Institutions and Judicial Role in Comparative Constitutional Law," *supra* note 9, 348 (Interview with Justice Cepeda-Espinosa in Bogotà, Colombia, 2009).

[16] Cepeda-Espinosa cited in ibid.

[17] Landau, "Political Institutions and Judicial Role in Comparative Constitutional Law," *supra* note 9, 373, citing Sergio Clavijo, *Fallos y Fallas Economicas de la Corte Constitucional: El Caso de Colombia 1991–2000* (2001), 45 (*available at* <http://www.hacer.org/pdf/clavijo.pdf>).

[18] Alicia Ely Yamin, Oscar Parra-Vera, and Camila Gianella, "Judicial Protection of the Right to Health: An Elusive Promise?" in Alicia Ely Yamin and Siri Gloppen (eds.), *Litigating Health Rights: Can Courts Bring More Justice to Health?* (2011) 103 (documenting the growth of *tutela* actions).

[19] Ibid; Young and Lemaitre, *supra* note 11.

enforcing a middle-class bias in its economic and social rights jurisprudence. Because the court has protected the status quo against legislative and executive interventions—disallowing any "retrogression" of economic and social rights—commentators have criticized the tendency of these negative injunctions to omit consideration of presently marginalized and vulnerable groups.[20] Civil servants and the middle class have benefited from the judicial override of austerity measures and public cuts. While these protections may nevertheless support broader democratic goals, it is arguable that those most in need of economic and social rights are not the primary beneficiaries.

On the other hand, and somewhat counterintuitively, both managerial and peremptory review may have enlarged majoritarianism and decreased the opportunities for legislative disregard of rights in Colombia. A striking channel of communication has opened up between the court and civil society, with justices attracting media attention, and the terms reached in constitutional decisions becoming publicly debated and defended in street protests. The Constitutional Court has gained immense approval ratings—estimated at over 50 percent of Colombians in favor of its role—which is an unusually high figure for both the political branches and the courts in Latin America.[21] Despite the enhanced accountability and responsiveness that flows from public participation, this development itself creates problems. There is a perception of an increasing populism amongst members of the judiciary, and the Court's effective reach for the median voter has not been universally celebrated.[22] It is noteworthy that, post their eight-year service on the bench, many Constitutional Court judges have entertained political careers. Indeed, against conventional understanding of the separation of powers, some justices have begun campaigning immediately after their terms end.[23]

Elements of the supremacist role conception are not uncommon in other South American jurisdictions. In Argentina and Brazil, courts have also imposed at times far-reaching positive duties on the state to protect and advance access to economic and social rights.[24] These developments have followed new, economic and social rights-protective constitutions, highly resourced courts, and relatively undeveloped forms of representative,

[20] Landau, "The Reality of Social Rights Enforcement," *supra* note 6.

[21] *See*, e.g., Julio Faundez, "Democratization Through Law: Perspectives from Latin America," 12 *Democratization* 749 (2005) 758.

[22] Ibid.

[23] Landau, "The Reality of Social Rights Enforcement," *supra* note 6.

[24] *See*, e.g., Gargarella, Domingo, and Roux (eds.), *Courts and Social Transformation in New Democracies*, *supra* note 10, 268–9 (noting the creation of special jurisdiction, sources of evidence, and remedies in India, Colombia, and elsewhere); *see also* Barak-Erex and Gross (eds.), *Exploring Social Rights*, *supra* note 1.

election-based democracy. Managerial and peremptory features are especially apparent in cases holding the state responsible for infringements of economic and social rights towards indigenous communities, as carried out by both private and public actors. In other jurisdictions, supremacist role conceptions have been adopted during the timorous first days of constitutional democracy, only to be later supplanted by other role conceptions. The Hungarian Constitutional Court, for example, was described as a "courtocracy" in the commencing years of its jurisprudence; yet its famously peremptory decision-making (over pension cuts, for example, or austerity measures) was replaced over time by a more interactive role conception.[25] The Constitutional Court was later reengineered, after the adoption of a new Constitution, into a position of deference.[26]

In all of these instances, models of judicial review dependent on legislative responsiveness or dialogue have appeared inapt. Where party systems have been incoherent, or political institutions otherwise unresponsive, court interactions have been more proactive and coercive than the alternative models of engagement or detachment suggests they should be.[27] It is no surprise that this model has been repeatedly prescribed for courts in new democracies, particularly when those courts are charged with an institutional role for supporting the poor.[28] What these jurisdictions appear to have in common is an attenuated responsiveness to government intransigence, incompetence, and inattentiveness in institutional contexts in which taking control has been the only option. The problems of judicial usurpation have followed, and yet, as against other problems, it remains plausible to surmise that these may be worth the price.

C. ELEMENTS OF ENGAGEMENT: INDIA

Like the Colombian Constitutional Court, the Indian Supreme Court was established after a postcolonial revolution and new constitutional settlement. The Indian Constitution of 1950 explicitly entrenched economic and

[25] Hungary, for example, according to Kim Lane Scheppele, became a "courtocracy": through the mid-1990s, "the Constitutional Court was for all intents and purposes running the country": Kim Lane Scheppele, "Democracy by Judiciary; Or, Why Courts Can Be More Democratic than Parliaments," in Adam Czarnota (ed.), *Rethinking the Rule of Law after Communism* (2005) 25, 44; *see* Landau, "Political Institutions and Judicial Role in Comparative Constitutional Law," *supra* note 9, 367, and noting the present changes to this conception. This change is compared with maturing of South Africa's constitutional system, *supra* Chapter 6, section C(2).

[26] European Commission for Democracy through Law (Venice Commission), *Opinion on the New Constitution of Hungary*, Adopted by the Venice Commission at its 87th Plenary Session (Venice, 17–18 June 2011), Strasbourg, 20 June 2011, Opinion no. 618/2011, Doc No. CDL-AD(2011)016.

[27] Landau, "Political Institutions and Judicial Role in Comparative Constitutional Law," *supra* note 9.

[28] Gargarella, Domingo, and Roux, *Courts and Social Transformation in New Democracies*, *supra* note 10.

social rights, albeit as Directive Principles, in a spirit of social revolution that has been likened to the transformative spirit of South Africa's Constitution.[29] Since the 1980s, the Indian Supreme Court has developed a strong tradition of social rights jurisprudence, enforcing rights to free primary education, emergency medical treatment, aspects of shelter and livelihood, and of food delivery. Drawing on features of conversational and experimentalist review, I describe India as an "engaged court" in my typology of economic and social rights adjudication.

Three institutional features have been key to the development of this role conception by the Indian Supreme Court. First, the Constitution entrenches a series of economic and social rights as Directive Principles of State Policy. Civil and political rights, such as the right to life, the right to equality, and freedom of speech and expression are protected in Part III of the Indian Constitution as "Fundamental Rights." Economic and social rights, including the right to livelihood, to health, to free legal aid, a clean environment, and to a minimum wage for workers, are expressed as Directive Principles of State Policy in Part IV; the right to primary education was transformed, after a constitutional referendum, from a Directive Principle to a Fundamental Right. The inclusion of the Directive Principles is tied to the Constitution's postcolonial goal of establishing a new social order based on social, economic, and political justice.[30]

Second, the Directive Principles have directly guided the Supreme Court. Because of the way in which the Supreme Court has held that the interpretation of the fundamental rights are informed by Directive Principles, and has thus integrated notions of interdependence and indivisibility in its fundamental rights jurisprudence, aspects of the right to housing, health care, education, and food have all been enforced, particularly through an encompassing interpretation of the right to life.[31] Moreover, the principle of equality is seen as integral to the right to life, suggesting that people cannot live without a semblance of human dignity where structural inequality prevails, and where the state has failed to address such inequality and its causes.[32] The entrenchment of Directive Principles has therefore led to an ambitious program of economic and social rights adjudication.

[29] Jayna Kothari, "Social Rights Litigation in India: Developments of the Last Decade," in Barak-Erez and Gross (eds.), *Exploring Social Rights*, *supra* note 1, 171, 173–4.

[30] Kothari, ibid., 174–5, citing Mahavir Tyagi from the United Provinces, during the Constitutent Assembly Debates: "the directive principles accommodate all the revolutionary slogans in a particular form as it is social and economic justice that is demanded by the most radical of the radicals of the world": Constituent Assembly Debates Official Report, 19 November 1948, Vol. No. VII, Book No. 2 (1999).

[31] Constitution of India [1950], art. 21. For this, and other rights, *see* Appendix I.

[32] Kothari, "Social Rights Litigation in India," *supra* note 29, 182.

Third, the Public Interest Litigation ("PIL") tradition has created, and been itself created by, an engaged Supreme Court. Under this tradition, the Supreme Court sought to address the inequities of access to justice experienced by the poor and disadvantaged by departing from the inherited British traditions of what we might see as detached and distanced common law courts.[33] As early as 1981, the Supreme Court held that the enforcement of the rights of the poor would make it "necessary to depart from the adversarial procedure and to evolve a new procedure which will make it possible for the poor and the weak to bring the necessary material before the Court."[34] From that point, the Court developed a broader and more community-oriented conception of standing,[35] allowing any member of the public to approach the Court for relief on behalf of any person or group themselves unable to approach the Court. The Court also developed a capacity to appoint lawyers to act as amicus curiae in such cases, and to famously relax the formal writ procedure to allow cases to be brought by letter, postcard, or newspaper report.[36] In dealing with the evidentiary requirements that are normally understood, in common law systems, to be discharged by adversaries and their legal representatives, the Supreme Court has appointed Commissioners to investigate the facts, who have included district magistrates, district judges, professors of law, advocates, and even journalists.[37]

Together, these three features have transformed the economic and social rights jurisdiction in India, leading to a demanding PIL and fundamental rights practice, both in the Indian Supreme Court and in other High Courts.[38] The right to life has been expanded to include several related rights within its enforceable reach, such as the right to a clean environment,[39] clean working conditions,[40] emergency medical treatment,[41] free legal aid, and release from bonded labour.[42] In such cases, the Supreme

[33] *See infra*, section D.

[34] *SP Gupta v. Union of India* (1981) Supp SC 87 (Indian Supreme Court).

[35] Ibid., 210.

[36] Ashok H. Desai and S. Muralidhar, "Public Interest Litigation: Potential and Problems," in B. Kirpal (ed.), *Supreme But Not Infallible: Essays in Honor of the Supreme Court of India* (2000) 159.

[37] Sandra Fredman, *Human Rights Transformed: Positive Rights and Positive Duties* (2008) 127.

[38] Arghya Sengupta and Sanhita Ambast, "Judicial Enforcement of Socioeconomic Rights: Lessons from the Use of Continuing Mandamus by the Supreme Court of India," in *Courts and New Governance* (forthcoming, 2012) (outlining numbers).

[39] *Subhas Kumar v. Bhhar* (1991) 1 SCC 598; *AP Pollution Control Board v. MV Naydud* (1999) 2 SCC 549.

[40] *Consumer Education & Research Centre v. Union of India* (1995) 3 SCC 42.

[41] *Parmanand Katara v. Union of India* (1989) 4 SCC 248.

[42] *Bandhua Mukti Morcha v. Union of India* (1984) 3 SCC 161; *see* Kothari, "Social Rights Litigation in India," *supra* note 29, 175.

Court has evinced a judicial stance similar to the conversational review described in Chapter 5.[43]

An early case dealing with the right to housing provides a useful example of conversational review. In *Olga Tellis*, the Supreme Court interpreted the right to life in light of the economic and social rights of the Universal Declaration of Human Rights ("UDHR") and the International Covenant on Economic, Social and Cultural Rights ("ICESCR"), and held that a duty to provide housing rested on a municipal corporation, which included the rights of "pavement dwellers"—those living in self-constructed squat accommodation near busy roads—to maintain accommodation near their place of work. The Court directed the corporation to frame the scheme for providing alternative housing, but left open the possibility of eviction for the pavement dwellers, with due process, if the corporations' options were not satisfied.[44] Other housing cases follow similar stances: of the Court recognizing the fundamental importance of state protection of rights, particularly for the vulnerable and destitute, of identifying shortcomings on the government's part, and of inviting the government to devise an appropriate response. These cases have been celebrated for the judicial innovation in responding to the constitutional vision.

These positions raise the advantages and disadvantages of conversational review described above. The disadvantages are apparent. Often, litigant parties have not had their positions altered after gaining a decision in their favor; other political institutions have chosen to ignore the judicial prompts in the massively impoverished country. On the exceptional occasions of successful litigants receiving a direct benefit from Court remedies, a wider political response to similarly situated beneficiaries has been glaringly absent. Finally, the innovations credited to the Court may, especially in recent times, have stalled.[45]

At the same time, the Indian Supreme Court has also enjoyed the successes that are attributed to conversational review. The courts have engaged the government, and the wider public, in realizing the vision behind the constitutional recognition of economic and social rights, in both symbolic and more material terms. The best evidence of the advantages of the conversational position comes from the right to education jurisprudence that began in the Supreme Court in the 1990s. The popularity

[43] *See supra*, Chapter 5, section D(2).

[44] *Olga Tellis v. Bombay Mun. Corp.* (1985) 3 SCC 545 (SCI); *Ahmedabad Municipal Corporation v. Nawab Khan Gulub Khan* (1997) 11 SCC 121 (SCI).

[45] *Narmada Bachao Andolan v. Union of India* (2000) 10 SCC 664 ("*Narmada Dams* case"); (Indian Supreme Court permitting the raising of the height of the Sardar Sarovar Dam, despite mass displacement, in the face of earlier right to housing and shelter precedent); Kothari, "Social Rights Litigation in India," *supra* note 29, 186.

of that decision led to an escalated response from governmental institutions, resulting in a formal amendment to the Constitution itself. Ironically, the case also stands for the deficiencies of conversational review and economic and social rights.

It is worth setting out this action in some detail. In 1993, the Court was called on to adjudicate the right to primary education. In interpreting this right, the Court referred to both the UDHR and the ICESCR, and found primary education to be fundamental. It issued a declaratory order.[46] As a result, any child below the age of 14 could approach a court for a writ of mandamus directing the authorities to initiate measures to secure their schooling. The line of litigation that followed then prompted the Constitution's amendment, so as to convert the apparently nonjusticiable promise of free primary education into a justiciable "Fundamental Right."[47] In addition, several states passed laws making primary education compulsory. While this reform attests to the legitimacy of continued judicial action in this area, it has suffered the same problems—of non-execution—as the judicial orders. It therefore evidences both the best, and worst, that conversational review can deliver.

In other respects, the Supreme Court has moved to a more experimentalist stance.[48] The much-cited right to food litigation is a case in point. There, the Supreme Court has exercised a jurisdiction that is continual, dynamic, responsive, and supervisory in perhaps the clearest articulation of experimentalist review available.[49] The litigation began as a campaign, which was spurred by a series of deaths by starvation in the drought-stricken areas of three States. These terrible consequences of starvation had occurred despite the country's immense, and surplus, food stocks. On hearing the matter, the Court broadened the scope of the litigants' petition to include all Indian States and Union territories.[50] The Court recognized the right to food as part of the constitutional right to life in mid-2001. In an unprecedented interim order, the Court directed all state governments and the Union of India to enforce eight schemes to address the problem, including income support for the elderly, maternity benefits, family benefits, and food distribution.[51]

[46] *JP Unni Krishnan v. State of Andhra Pradesh* (1993) 1 SCC 645; *Shantistar Builders v. Narayan Khimlal Totame* (1990) 1 SCC 520.

[47] Kothari, "Social Rights Litigation in India," *supra* note 29, 172. *See* Eighty-Sixth Constitutional Amendment Act 2002 (India); Constitution of India, art. 21A; *see* Appendix I.

[48] For a description, *see* Chapter 5, section D(3).

[49] For an examination, *see* Sengupta and Ambast, "Judicial Enforcement of Socioeconomic Rights," *supra* note 38.

[50] Kothari, "Social Rights Litigation in India," *supra* note 29, 179.

[51] C. Gonsalves, P. R. Kumar, and A. K. Srivastava (eds.), *Right to Food* (2nd edn., 2005).

The most striking was the Mid-Day Meal Scheme, which required cooked meals for children in government schools by January 2002. Specifying the minimum content of calories and protein within these meals, and that dry rations had to become cooked meals within three months, the Court also extended this to other parts of India. Similarly, the court expanded a Targeted Public Distribution Scheme to 25 kilograms of grain per family, and also sought a response from States on the framing of wage employment schemes.[52]

Unlike the housing rights jurisprudence, in which the Indian Supreme Court merely directed the states to formulate appropriate remedial schemes, the Court directed the strict implementation of already formulated and modifiable schemes within fixed time frames. These orders were ambitious and experimentalist. One key characteristic was the intervention of court-appointed Commissioners, who monitored the implementation of the interim orders, and repeatedly identified recalcitrant states. The appointment of Commissioners reflects the appointment of masters and court officers, which we identified with respect to the early US versions of managerial review.[53] Nonetheless, these Commissioners created scope to increase the channels of political communication between campaigners and the public, and their role was broader than the mere management of remedy. In this respect, the orders were more akin to an engaged, rather than supremacist, court.

Another key to the success of the right-to-food litigation was the reliance on stakeholder coalitions. For the Mid-Day Meal Scheme remedy, not all orders were implemented by the various States, and the media, academics, and participating social movements proved critical. The right to food campaign, for example, assisted in conducting field surveys which indicated that meal quality, administrative impediments, and budgetary allocations were continuing obstacles.[54] Street demonstrations persisted.

Commentators now report that 100 million children in India get a cooked meal at school, with compounded success in increasing the enrolment of girls and in general school attendance levels. While implementation of the several schemes is still uneven, in states where the right to food campaign is active, reports one observer, "these schemes have been internalized quite quickly by all concerned—school teachers, village administrators, state governments and the communities."[55] Nonetheless, while studies indicate

[52] Lauren Birchfield and Jessica Corsi, "Between Starvation and Globalization: Realizing the Right to Food in India," 31 Mich. J. Int'l. L. 691 (2010) 700.

[53] *See supra*, Chapter 5, section D(4).

[54] Kothari, "Social Rights Litigation in India," *supra* note 29, 181.

[55] Ibid., 181.

productive alliances between campaigners and the court, it is not clear how responsive these orders have been to the beneficiaries themselves.

Shortcomings of the litigation map the predicted criticisms of experimentalist and conversational review. For example, the right to food litigation has, to some extent, bureaucratized the right to food campaign—leaving the beneficiaries passive, rather than active, in the articulation of a localized response to the precariousness of their access to food. Such outcomes repeat the criticism, expressed above,[56] of an inaccurate theorization of power relations within the experimentalist model, or of the complexity of translating needs and solutions across class. It is worth recalling that the recipients of food, who are prohibited from the market from accessing or from growing food for themselves, are highly impoverished, rural, and disconnected groups. Moreover, experimentalism has sometimes drifted into managerialism, with continuous mandamus remedies sometimes precipitating periodic rather than innovative review, and becoming ritualized rather than responsive. Finally, the conversational review has at times precipitated no widespread effect. Reliance on the effect of nudging other political institutions has been challenging in India's vast layers of governance, and the obstructions between these layers.[57]

D. ELEMENTS OF DETACHMENT: UNITED KINGDOM

It will be recalled that a detached court, in my typology, engages deferential or at most conversational review. Elements of detachment are clearly seen in relation to the UK courts' treatment of economic and social rights under the Human Rights Act 1998 (UK) ("HRA"). In the United Kingdom, the courts are detached observers, standing by as the government determines its education, housing, welfare, or health care policy; at most, reminding the government of how its human rights obligations may require a certain change in response. In this respect, for example, the courts have read the Housing Act as incorporating a protection of an individual's rights to privacy, the family, and the home, in order to mitigate the harsh effects of a notice to vacate.[58] Another example comes from the enforcement of the

[56] More detail of the shortcomings of the theorization of power in the experimentalist position is provided in Chapter 9.

[57] Nick Robinson, "Expanding Judiciaries: India and the Rise of the Good Governance Court," 8 Wash. U. Global Stud. L. Rev. 1 (2009).

[58] *Poplar Housing and Regeneration Community Association Ltd v. Donoghue* [2001] 3 WLR 183, 204. This case contains the famous direction, by Lord Woolf CJ, that "courts have to adjust their traditional role in relation to interpretation so as to give effect to the direction in section 3 [of the HRA]. It is as though legislation, which predates the HRA and conflicts with the Convention has to be treated as subsequently amended to incorporate the language of section 3" (at para 75). *See infra* section E(2).

reason-giving duties in public administrative law, sometimes combined with an analysis of the right to life or other human rights. Here, the courts have set boundaries on the withdrawal or otherwise rationing of health and welfare services to previously eligible individuals.[59]

Of course, the human rights safeguarding of such interests are now sourced in the HRA, which is not a constitutional instrument in the positivist sense. The HRA may plausibly be repealed by a simple parliamentary majority and hence lacks the procedural entrenchment of a constitutional instrument. Yet the HRA is nevertheless said to enjoy the force and status of a "constitutional statute," meaning that an amending or repealing statute would require unambiguous words to be effective.[60] Amendment would face additional hurdles, since the HRA incorporates, for the UK, the European constitutional norms that announce the fundamental values of human rights across Europe. In that sense, it has been described as a constitutional instrument that "contemplates the future shaping of UK governance in accordance with moral and social values enshrined in the [European Convention on Human Rights] ECHR."[61] It also creates, purportedly for the first time, an adjudicative process that reasons from the general proposition of a protected right to the particular case before it (in contrast to the former common law principle of judicial reasoning from the particular to the general), accompanied by an explicit moral discourse.[62] In this respect, the detached self-conception of the British judicial role has evolved, ever so slowly, from what had earlier been a reluctant or hostile position towards economic and social rights. This change in role conception has been effected by European law, as well as by the expansion of judicial review in administrative decisions.

The HRA itself does not provide explicit protection of economic and social rights, just as the ECHR does not, apart from the right to education,[63] and privacy rights in relation to the family and the home.[64] Nonetheless, the

[59] Ellie Palmer, *Judicial Review, Socio Economic Rights and the Human Rights Act* (2007) 207 ff. (comparing the decisions at first instance and the Court of Appeal in *R. v. Cambridge Health Authority, ex parte B* [1995] 1 FLR 1056, [1995] 1 WLR 898).

[60] *Thoburn v. Sunderland City Council* [2002] EWHC 195, [2003] QB 151, [63].

[61] *Matadeen v. Pointu and Minister of Education and Science* [1999] 1 AC 98 PC, 108, [7] per Lord Hoffman.

[62] Lord Browne-Wilkinson, "The Impact on Judicial Reasoning," in Basil S. Markesinis (ed.), *The Impact of the Human Rights Bill on English Law* (1998) 21, 23.

[63] HRA, § 1, incorporating the rights of the ECHR, including its First Protocol (Council of Europe, *Protocol 1 to the European Convention for the Protection of Human Rights and Fundamental Freedoms*, 20 March 1952, ETS 9 ("ECHR First Protocol")), art. 2 ("No person shall be denied the right to education. In the exercise of any functions which it assumes in relation to education and to teaching, the State shall respect the right of parents to ensure such education and teaching in conformity with their own religions and philosophical convictions.").

[64] ECHR, art. 8 (everyone has the right to respect for his private and family life, his home and his correspondence).

development of a European jurisprudence of positive obligations under the ECHR,[65] which the Human Rights Act incorporates, as well as the increasingly recognized indivisibility between the sets of rights, has resulted in judicial intervention in cases involving housing, health, and welfare services for vulnerable and disadvantaged groups.[66] In her survey of UK law, for example, Ellie Palmer has listed judicial reversals of health care allocation decisions on grounds of irrationality, legitimate expectations, or unfairness.[67] Courts have also acted to reverse administrative *failures* to act in accordance with certain positive obligations to prevent poverty and destitution, when present laws constrain the ability of individuals to meet their basic needs for food and shelter.[68] This indirect protection of economic and social rights has cast the higher UK courts (including the Supreme Court, the Judicial Committee of the Privy Council, and the High Courts or Courts of Appeal[69]) in a significant (if nevertheless detached) role, with respect to the enforcement of economic and social rights.

The HRA contains several features that have brought about this deferential and/or conversational detachment.[70] The most obvious is the requirement for courts to make a "declaration of incompatibility" if legislation cannot be reconciled with the ECHR.[71] This remedy has no greater force than a public announcement of noncompliance—the declaration does not affect the validity, operation, or enforcement of the offending provision, and nor is it binding on the parties to the proceedings.[72] This is conversational review par excellence, and its effectiveness lies in the dialogical interactions that it is designed to prompt. What is intended is a mere signal from court to the Parliament that it has failed to comply with the ECHR; a signal that leaves it to the Parliament to decide what to do about it.[73] Indeed, the lack of legal bite to this signal is emphasized by the fact that the Parliament is also free to issue a statement, prior to passing legislation, that it is unable to

[65] ECHR, particularly arts. 3, 6, 9, 14 (positive obligations in relation to freedoms from torture, a right to a fair trial, freedom of thought, conscience and religion, and nondiscrimination); *see also* ECHR, First Protocol, art. 1.

[66] Palmer, *Judicial Review*, *supra* note 59 (describing health and welfare cases); *see also* Fredman, *Human Rights Transformed*, *supra* note 37.

[67] Palmer, ibid.

[68] *R v. Secretary of State for the Home Department, ex parte Limbuela* [2005] UKHL 66, [2006] AC 396.

[69] HRA, § 4.

[70] Descriptions of these positions are detailed in Chapter 5 sections D(1) and D(2).

[71] HRA, § 4.

[72] HRA, §§ 4(3) and 4(4).

[73] Subordinate legislation may also be passed in response: HRA, § 10.

make a statement of compatibility.[74] The courts have used their declaration sparingly.[75]

More far-reaching is the establishment (or arguably codification) of a principle of interpretation, which requires all legislation to be interpreted, and to be given effect, in a way that is compatible with the ECHR.[76] This interpretive principle goes further than similarly placed statutory bills of rights, such as the New Zealand Bill of Rights Act 1990, but not as far as other dialogic human rights instruments, such as the Canadian Charter, which allows for judicial override mediated by a notwithstanding clause.[77] At first glance, the conferral of power to the courts to "read in" the meaning of legislation (which applies even where there is no ambiguity in the meaning of the words of the legislation), establishes a form of judicial power that is akin to the peremptory power of constitutional courts.[78] At its most extreme, this power appears to provide no less than an invitation to rewrite legislation, an appearance somewhat confirmed by the rhetoric, if not the substance, of the courts' decisions.[79] Nonetheless, the power is not unlike the normal presumption of statutory interpretation that the Parliament has not legislated to contravene its international obligations, unless it does so expressly. Due to an ongoing deferential position, the interpretive power has not resulted in any (in some quarters, predicted and feared[80]) judicial insurrection.[81]

Thirdly, the courts may scrutinize the decisions of public authorities for conformity with human rights. In this activity, the courts are given greater remedial powers.[82] The obligations of public authorities extend to those making decisions concerning the provision of welfare and education—hence

[74] HRA, § 19. For a discussion of this feature, *see infra*, section E(2).

[75] Between 2000 and July 2006, only fifteen declarations of incompatibility were made, one of which was remedied by a section 10 remedial order: Department for Constitutional Affairs, Review of the Implementation of the Human Rights Act (July 2006); *see* Gerhard Van der Schyff, *Judicial Review of Legislation: A Comparative Study of the United Kingdom, the Netherlands and South Africa* (2010).

[76] HRA, § 3 (so far as it is possible to do so, primary legislation and subordinate legislation must be read and given effect in a way which is compatible with the Convention rights).

[77] Canada Act 1982 (UK) c. 11, sch. B pt. I ("Canadian Charter of Rights and Freedoms").

[78] *Cf. Khosa* 2004 (6) SA 505 (CC); *Port Elizabeth Municipality v. Various Occupiers* 2005 (1) SA 217 (CC).

[79] *Ghaidan v. Mendoza* [2004] 2 AC 557 (HL); *see also* Claudia Geiringer, "It's Interpretation, Jim, But Not As We Know It: *Ghaidan v. Mendoza*, The House of Lords and Rights-Consistent Interpretation," in Paul Morris and Helen Greatrex (eds.), *Human Rights Research*, Victoria University of Wellington: Papers presented at the Symposium on Interdisciplinary Approaches to Human Rights held at Victoria University of Wellington on 25 August 2004 (Victoria Human Rights Programme, 2005).

[80] *See*, e.g., the warnings expressed "against judicial enforcement" by Gearty in Conor Gearty and Virginia Mantouvalou, *Debating Social Rights* (2011).

[81] Aileen Kavanagh, *Constitutional Review under the UK Human Rights Act* (2009).

[82] Palmer, *Judicial Review*, *supra* note 59, 111.

these decisions are of great significance to the protection of economic and social rights. Nonetheless, there is a distance between centralized government and local authorities' expenditure. Because courts are often sympathetic to the funding predicaments of local authorities, they have appeared less likely to enforce duties against them.[83] The duties on public authorities also extend to courts themselves. Therefore, the duty requires the courts to develop the common law in a rights-protective direction, analogous to South Africa's provision; and is similarly underworked in respect of common law development.[84]

If the detached role is a feature of design, it is also a reflection of judicial culture. Courts in the UK act against a background tradition of parliamentary sovereignty and the reputational esteem of the common law, which obtains in the unwritten constitution and has configured the discourse around rights in the UK.[85] Indeed, the passage of the UK into a human rights jurisdiction has been smoothed by a continued acknowledgment of deference. In decisions impacting upon socioeconomic interests in health care, housing, and social security, "the notion of deference has been used to justify the boundaries that have been set by courts around their powers of legislative scrutiny," and has provided "a pivotal conceptual tool for determining the limits of judicial intervention in public law disputes in which questions about the proportionality of executive or other public authority conduct has been at issue."[86]

Nonetheless, the indirect enforcement of economic and social rights tests the culture of deference, spurring either denial or resistance. On the one hand, some judges have denied that they are being deferential when negotiating the implications of legalized human rights: "when a court decides that a decision is within the proper competence of the legislature or the executive, it is not showing deference. It is deciding the law."[87] Instead, two legal principles would apply: the first confirming the need for judicial independence, the second suggesting "majority approval is necessary for a proper decision on policy or allocation of resources."[88] Both positions evince elements of the deferential position, in spirit if not in name.

[83] Palmer, *Judicial Review, supra* note 59, 229–30.

[84] HRA, § 6; *see also* Palmer, *Judicial Review, supra* note 59, 110. *Compare* with S. Afr. Const., § 7, discussed at Chapter 6, section C(1).

[85] Neil Walker, "Setting English Judges to Rights," Oxford J. Leg. S. 133 (1999) (for discussion of the discursive impact of this conception). *See also* Palmer, *Judicial Review, supra* note 59, 106.

[86] Palmer, ibid., 115.

[87] Jeffrey Jowell and Jonathan Cooper, *Delivering Rights: How the Human Rights Act Is Working* (2003).

[88] *R. v. BBC ex parte Prolife Alliance* [2003] UKHL 23, cited by Jowell and Cooper, ibid., 3.

Other judges are more active in applying human rights, while rejecting the hold of deferential positions. In rejecting the legal principle that judges must desist from ruling on resource allocation issues, Lord Steyn argued "In common law adjudication, it is an everyday occurrence for courts to consider, together with principled arguments, the balance sheet of policy advantages and disadvantages. It would be a matter of public disquiet if the courts did not do so."[89] He noted that such assessment, if perceived as unacceptable by the elected branches, could quickly be changed: "Parliament can act with great speed to reverse the effect of a decision."[90]

In this mode, courts have moved to allow for greater standing, and have invited nongovernmental organizations ("NGOs") to appear as third party interveners. Thus, despite the fact that the HRA is confined only to affected individuals,[91] social movements such as the Shelter and the Child Poverty Action Group have made arguments in court, especially in test cases concerning access to public services.[92]

The elements of detachment evident in the UK HRA practice indicate a subtle, yet nevertheless present, role of courts. Critically, it is a role dependent on the responsiveness of other political institutions for its effectiveness. Some have suggested that a more explicit protection of economic and social rights in the UK will efface both detachment, and its advantages.[93] Others have pointed out the regular occurrence of the protection of socio-economic interests through other rights.[94] So far, it appears that the stability and traditions of the nonjudicial branches have reacted effectively. Along with the role conceptions of other courts, the effectiveness of detachment is institutionally and culturally contingent, and cannot be discarded, out of hand, as the appropriate mode of adjudicating economic and social rights.

It remains to comment on the elements of detachment evident in courts of other countries, particularly those subscribing to the importance of dialogic review. It is clear that the phenomenon is most prevalent in the courts of the former British Commonwealth—those colonized according to Diceyan principles of parliamentary sovereignty and the rule of law. Some commentators have confined their analysis to the developed countries of the former Commonwealth—Canada, New Zealand, Australia, and the United Kingdom—finding in this club of nations a concordant wish for rights,

[89] Lord Steyn, "Deference: A Tangled Story," Public Law 351 (2005) 356–7.

[90] Ibid.

[91] HRA, §§ 7(1) and 7(3) (only a person who is or would be a victim of a violation can bring an action).

[92] Palmer, *Judicial Review*, *supra* note 59, 28.

[93] Gearty, *supra* note 80.

[94] Palmer, *Judicial Review*, *supra* note 59; Fredman, *Human Rights Transformed*, *supra* note 37.

without any wish to disturb the present judicial role.[95] It is clear that we can find parallels to detachment in the right to life and equality jurisprudence under the Canadian Charter, as it has impacted on fundamental socio-economic interests in health care and social security,[96] at the more conversational end of the spectrum. The Supreme Court of Canada also employs other stances towards judicial review, a possibility available due to the voluntary construction of the dialogue-enhancing notwithstanding clause. Courts in New Zealand and Australia, on the other hand, are more likely to evidence detachment because the Bill of Rights (NZ) and the Australian human rights statutes do not allow legislation to be struck down (and at the Australian federal level, does not even ground a cause of action).[97] Yet to concentrate on such a narrow band of constitutions (or quasi-constitutional statutes) misses the comparable forms that have issued from other countries formerly committed to parliamentary sovereignty. Other members of the Commonwealth—who engage selectively in practices of transnational judicial communication with each other[98]—also evidence detachment. The Commonwealth brings together fifty-three countries across the world, many sharing similar legal traditions;[99] hence a focus on the effectiveness of detachment in such different constitutional settings is important. This becomes a question, not only of inherited legal traditions, but also of the effectiveness of counterpart branches in giving effect to rights. In this respect, we will turn to the question of non-court centric enforcement.

E. COURTS IN THEIR INSTITUTIONAL CONTEXT

As we have seen, courts operate in a system in which their legitimacy depends upon the appropriate conception of their role within the constitutional culture. That culture may perceive other institutions as having responsibilities for applying and enforcing the terms of the constitution. The roles of the government may be described blandly: the legislature legislates, the executive executes, and the courts adjudicate. Yet this picture obscures the very real responsibilities of different institutions for interpreting and upholding and even enforcing the terms of the constitution. These

[95] Stephen Gardbaum, "The New Commonwealth Model of Constitutionalism," 49 Am. J. Comp. L. 707 (2001).

[96] Martha Jackman and Bruce Porter, "Socio-Economic Rights under the Canadian Charter," in Malcolm Langford (ed.), *Social Rights Jurisprudence: Emerging Trends in International and Comparative Law* (2008) 209.

[97] *See*, e.g., Human Rights Act 1998 (UK), Human Rights Act 1993 (NZ), Human Rights (Parliamentary Scrutiny) Act 2011 (Cth) (Australia); Charter of Human Rights and Responsibilities Act 2006 (Vic); and Human Rights Act 2004 (ACT).

[98] *See*, e.g., Bangalore Principles, *infra* Chapter 10.

[99] For a database that serves this dialogue, *see* <http://www.interights.org> (accessed June 2012). For a discussion of Ghana, *see* Chapter 8.

responsibilities are revealed by the study of non-court-based standards of evaluation of economic and social rights, and non-court-based modes of enforcement. The expansion of this lens of enforcement is consistent with the overarching framework for constituting rights, laid out in Chapter 1 of this book.

The responsibility of the extrajudicial branches in upholding the constitution is less theorized in legal scholarship, often remaining under the purview of the disciplines of political science or sociology. Procedures of parliament, conventions, the strength of political parties, particularly in opposition, the orientation and influence of civil servants, particularly in justice departments, the independence of the press, the robustness of civil society, and the susceptibility of all of them to rights pressure from transnational sources, are all critical for the realization of economic and social rights.[100] Comparative legal scholarship has been useful for identifying certain aspects of non-court-centric protection, revealing what is taken for granted, and what is perhaps overvalued, in this analysis. Three developments have brought this study to the fore.

First, comparative studies of economic and social rights have shown that the focus on "pragmatic" justiciability issues is a particularly North American one.[101] The observers of other constitutional systems have more readily accepted that aspirational principles can be realized without the direct protection of the judiciary, or without even the dim prospect of judicial review. If rights are constitutive of democracy, rather than individualistic burdens on majoritarian processes that can only be protected by courts, then legislators can indeed lead a role.[102] Nonetheless, the European approaches that prize aspirational principles often do so with the tools of formalism, which sees the passage or existence of any positive law as resulting in positive change. What is needed is a post-formalist conception of law that appraises the quality of its existence beyond court-centric or formalist approaches, and which understands the processes of implementing rights in broader terms.

Second, the attraction to a conception of "dialogue," which sees the interaction between courts and other institutions as intrinsic to the workings of an open democracy, has commanded attention across many jurisdictions. As we have seen in relation to processes developed in the UK and India described above, in this conception courts no longer command the central role of enforcing the terms of constitutional law, but share this role with the

[100] For further development, *see infra* Chapter 8.

[101] Cass R. Sunstein, *The Second Bill of Rights: FDR's Unfinished Revolution and Why We Need It More Than Ever* (2004).

[102] Jeremy Waldron, *Law and Disagreement* (1999).

elected branches and beyond. This theme has coexisted with the rise of statutory bills of rights, which can be amended under usual, or only slightly tweaked, legislative processes. Attention is then set on the cultural and institutional processes that can maximize enforcement outside of courts.

A third reason for a renewed attention of non-court-centric enforcement is that it may present a more fundamental solution to the judicial usurpation/abdication problem described in Chapter 5. While we have seen that the disaggregation of judicial review can alter the character of these problems, non-court-centric enforcement can resolve them head-on. The interplay of nonjudicial actors can resolve questions of enforcement, monitoring and implementation, and follow-up concerns with a more reflective interpretation of the content and scope of rights. In response to the shortcomings of courts in bringing about social change—whether through supremacist, engaged, detached, or catalytic positions—the spotlight continues to rest on the capacity of other institutions to exercise scrutiny, marshal evidence, and lead change towards greater rights protection.

At the same time, the politics around economic and social rights in developing countries has become decidedly more "court-centric" in recent years. As a result of the efforts to support the immense "rule of law" development projects in the 1990s, courts in such countries often have access to greater, and more targeted, resources than the elected branches. This has not come about through the juristocracy of expanded constitutions and of rights alone.[103] Rather, international investment in projects to increase judicial independence, compliance with court orders, and access to information networks has flowed from an acceptance of enforceable law as a precursor to economic development. Hence, the establishment of the rule of law, particularly via more independent courts, has been seen as necessary for increased foreign investment, market stability, and the boons of globalized trade. Ironically, courts have sometimes relied on entrenched economic and social rights to forestall the financial prescriptions that often accompany the rule of law projects.[104] Because of the representation problems attached to these international processes, as well as more general representation deficiencies of newly established legislatures, some suggest that courts, when other legal opportunity structures are present, are the most robust institutional voice for the poor in new democracies, as against the market dictates of their local executive and of international institutions.[105]

[103] *Cf.* Ran Hirschl, *Towards Juristocracy: The Origins and Consequences of the New Constitutionalism* (2004).

[104] Kim Lane Scheppele, "A Realpolitik Defense of Social Rights," 82 Tex. L. Rev. 1921 (2004).

[105] *See, e.g.*, Boaventura de Sousa Santos and César A. Rodriguez-Garavito, *Law and Globalization from Below* (2005); Gargarella, Domingo, and Roux, *Courts and Social Transformation in New Democracies*, *supra* note 10.

Nevertheless, by exploring the category of non-court-centric enforcement, we can examine the work of legislatures, executive officials, and non-state actors, such as corporations, social movements, and the global networks of which they are part. Below, we will briefly explore the legislative and executive techniques that have been utilized in the non-court-centric enforcement of economic and social rights. Other techniques include those exercised by private actors, such as those seeking to self-regulate according to the social responsibility norms of local and transnational business networks. In a parallel domain, we can also add the United Nations treaty scrutiny and monitoring systems, and the institutions falling under the United Nations Charter, including not only the international human rights treaty bodies such as the Committee on Economic, Social and Cultural Rights, but also the Special Rapporteurs which have been appointed to investigate issues of economic and social rights.[106] These are discussed further in Part III of this book.

(1) *Investigative and advisory "enforcement" in the administrative sphere*

In keeping with a focus outside of courts, one cannot help but note the growing collection of nonjudicial institutions, which enjoy an advisory and quasi-implementation role in comparative systems. Tribunals, ombudspersons, and legislated commissions all contribute to the enforcement of economic and social rights. National Human Rights Commissions, and commissions dealing with related areas, such as equal opportunity and disability rights, as well as privacy, information, anticorruption, and electoral concerns, are less constrained counterparts to courts.[107] Such commissions are designed to be independent institutions that may contribute to the realization of rights, not by adjudicating disputes, but by investigating government conduct (or the conduct of others, such as employers), or suggesting policy reforms. They also form relationships with business groups, NGOs, or social movements. While such commissions most often enjoy an advisory mandate, some also have specialized regulatory and administrative duties, as well as, at times, prosecutorial agendas.

National human rights commissions often accompany countries with newer constitutions and human rights commitments. When instituted with coercive powers of investigation, they can increase accountability for

[106] Special Rapporteurs investigate and report at the international level. *See*, e.g., appointments related to the rights of education (1998), food (2000), adequate housing (2000), and health (2002). Specific expertise has also been created, in this format, on the international issue of extreme poverty (1998), the right to development (1998), and structural adjustment policies and foreign debt (2000).

[107] Christopher S. Elmendorf, "Advisory Counterparts to Constitutional Courts," 56 Duke L.J. 953 (2007).

economic and social rights infringements.[108] Indeed, a set of international principles suggests any human rights commission be authorized to hear "any person and obtain any information and any documents necessary for assessing situations falling within its competence."[109] Sometimes, courts delegate their power to a human rights commission for investigative purposes.[110] On other occasions, courts task commissions to monitor the remedies that they award in economic and social rights adjudication. Their ability to do so has been mixed.[111] One could speculate that such activities are less influential, the closer the courts are to deferential or conversational judicial review (and on the irony that the courts are more justified in taking a deferential or conversational position when the commissions are sufficiently influential). An exploration of the techniques and successes of human rights commissions against various backdrops is a rich agenda for future comparative study.

Much also depends upon the funding and resources of nonjudicial implementation systems. There is as yet no instantiation of any separate branch to oversee the protection of economic and social rights. Under a proposal made by Bruce Ackerman in 2000, a "Distributive Justice Branch" could avoid the accountability and implementation problems of the judicial branch, and the representation challenges of the legislative and the executive in enforcing economic and social rights.[112] Specifically, Ackerman suggests that such an institution could work to enforce a minimum cash grant for all citizens,[113] rather than embark on more complex administrative exercises, such as minimum education or health care. Nonetheless, regardless of whether this proposal might work against egregious poverty, it is a modest proposal in light of the fuller economic and social rights

[108] Barbara von Tigerstrom, "Implementing Economic, Social, and Cultural Rights: The Role of National Human Rights Institutions," in Isfahan Merali and Valerie Oosterveld (eds.), *Giving Meaning to Economic, Social, and Cultural Rights* (2001) 139, 146–7 (describing El Salvador).

[109] Principles Relating to the Status of National Institutions, G.A. Res. 48/134, U.N. Doc. A/RES/48/134 (20 December 1993), *available at* <http://www2.ohchr.org/english/law/parisprinciples.htm>.

[110] *See infra*, section C (presenting engagement in India); *see also* Raj Kumar, "National Human Rights Institutions: Good Governance Perspectives on Institutionalization of Human Rights," 19 Am. U. Int'l. L. Rev. 259, 274–5 (2003) (celebrating the delegation to the National Human Rights Commission of India of the "powers of a civil court").

[111] *See*, e.g., the criticisms of the supervision of the *Grootboom* remedy. The South African Human Rights Commission has a mandate to promote access to information, but its other investigative and advisory functions are less specific; *cf.* Promotion of Access to Information Act 2000 (S. Afr.).

[112] Bruce Ackerman, "The New Separation of Powers,' 113 Harv. L. Rev. 663 (2000) 724–5.

[113] For justification of cash grants for post-industrial societies, *see* Bruce Ackerman and Anne Alstott, *The Stakeholder Society* (1999) 4–5, 8–12; Philippe Van Parijs, *Real Freedom for All: What (If Anything) Can Justify Capitalism?* (1995) 32–5.

commitments necessary to address health, education, and housing needs in the long term.[114]

(2) Investigative and advisory "enforcement" in the legislative sphere

Legislatures, too, can work with processes of scrutiny and justification, so that the legislation passed complies with economic and social rights. Supporting such nonjudicial institutional processes is the belief that legislatures act according to the preferences of constituents, and can be prompted to enhance rights protection in suitably rights-protective polities. As Mark Tushnet notes, "[a] legislator whose interest in reelection leads her to cater to constitution-oriented constituent preferences is (indirectly) orienting her legislative activity to the nation's constitutional traditions."[115] Moreover a legislator can "vote her conscience" on matters about which the constituency is indifferent.[116] Clearly, this support for the model falls short when a rights culture is absent, or when majorities are hostile to economic and social rights. Instead, the view that a culture of justification can be brought about through such legislative processes is the better grounding for legislative enforcement. If the legislature is forced to give reasons, there is a prophylactic pressure extended to rights. Even where rights are not realized, the pressure to limit them according to reasons may play an important role.[117]

We have already seen the ways in which economic and social rights, as Directive Principles, are designed to guide the path of policy-making and legislating towards economic and social rights.[118] Although these principles have become the subject of judicial interpretation, and have, in interpreting the expanse of other rights, led to the enforcement of fundamental economic and social interests in India, such Principles have not worked universally in this direction. These Directive Principles work to put their own limits on the legislature's overwhelming incentives to advance the interests of the majority at the expense of minority rights, or of the short-term (and vote-gaining) interests of the majority at the expense of the polity as a whole. Nonetheless, there is little conceptualization of this self-enforcement of Directive Principles by the legislature.

[114] *Compare* with Roberto Mangabeira Unger, *What Should Legal Analysis Become?* (1996) 30–3.

[115] Mark Tushnet, *Weak Courts, Strong Rights: Judicial Review and Social Welfare Rights in Comparative Constitutional Law* (2008) 88.

[116] Tushnet, ibid., 91 (identifying free conscience votes in Canada and Great Britain on issues relating to abortion, capital punishment, and research on embryos).

[117] Etienne Mureinik, "Beyond a Charter of Luxuries: Economic Rights in the Constitution," 8 S. Afr. J. Hum. Rts. 464 (1992); *compare* with Tushnet, *supra* note 115, 96, who suggests that there is no institutional duty on legislatures to give reasons. *See further* Chapter 4.

[118] *See supra*, Chapter 4, presenting the operation of such Principles in Ghana, Ireland, and India.

One innovation that lends substance to this process is the pre-legislative scrutiny of bills before their enactment as legislation. This process has proved popular in many of the so-called "Commonwealth" legal systems of the United Kingdom, New Zealand, and Australia, where human rights are protected by statute. This system could be equally utilized in common law or civil law, parliamentary or presidential systems. Indeed, its form, while originating in parliamentary systems, appears akin to the advisory opinion of a tribunal or council, or even of a constitutional council.[119]

Consider the UK example, where the parliament has utilized the committee system to enhance the protection of human rights. The Joint Committee on Human Rights ("JCHR"), established in 1999 after the passage of the HRA, is composed of members of both Houses of Parliament, and overseen by a fulltime legal adviser. This advisor reviews all Bills, once introduced, for compatibility with the ECHR rights as well as other human rights obligations of the UK, such as under the International Covenant on Civil and Political Rights ("ICCPR'), the ICESCR, or the Convention on the Rights of the Child ("CRC"). Where a statement of compatibility cannot be made, it is intended that "parliamentary scrutiny will be intense,"[120] thus attracting the attention of the public. Similar systems work in Canada, New Zealand, and in Australia.[121] Uninhibited from the constraints that judges must face, this legislative monitoring has provided for critical scrutiny in areas of health, housing, and asylum law. For example, JCHR Reports on the compatibility of mental health legislation with ECHR rights, homelessness legislation with international human rights treaties, including CRC, and a legislative proposal to withdraw basic living support from destitute asylum seekers, have all been influential.[122] The interactions that are established operate in the reverse direction of the forms of dialogue discussed above: rather than the courts' interpretations influencing the next steps from legislators, scrutiny committees and parliament can indeed influence the interpretive positions of the judiciary. In this sense, the reports of the JCHR

[119] Consider the *a priori* review exercised by the French Constitutional Council (Conseil Constitutionnel), which assesses legislation, after its enactment through the parliamentary process, for consistency with the Constitution and the ECHR.

[120] Hansard HL Official Report, 2nd Reading (5th series) vol. 582 col. 1233 (3 November 1997).

[121] Bill of Rights (NZ); Charter of Human Rights and Responsibilities Act 2006 (Vic); Human Rights Act 2004 (ACT); Human Rights (Parliamentary Scrutiny) Act 2011 (Cth). *See further* Janet L. Hiebert, "Parliamentary Bills of Rights: An Alternative Model?," 69(1) Mod. L. Rev. 7 (2006).

[122] *See* Mental Health Bill 2002; Homelessness Bill 2001; Immigration and Asylum Seekers Act 2001; e.g., JCHR, 23rd Report: Nationality Immigration and Asylum Bill: Further Report (2003–3) HL 176 HC 1255 (23 October 2002); Palmer, *Judicial Review*, *supra* note 59, 113–14, 257–70, including discussion in *R v. Secretary of State for the Home Department; ex parte Limbuela* [2005] UKHL 66 [2006] 1 AC 396. On this latter issue, *see further* Michelle Foster, *International Refugee Law and Socio-Economic Rights: Refuge from Deprivation* (2007).

can provide "democratic support for a strong judicial stance against legislation that appears to fly in the face of international treaty obligations."[123]

In conclusion, it is clear that there are far more institutions of enforcement than courts, conceived as acting alone, can muster. The option for nonjudicial enforcement can influence the role conception taken by the court itself. Of course, the central issue in evaluating these measures is that it is relative—sometimes such measures work better, sometimes worse, than courts.[124] Sometimes courts work best in interpreting and defining rights, but work badly in enforcing them. Yet sometimes other institutions can interpret, and enforce them, with more effective results.

In a system with judicial review, it is usually the court that provides the norms against which official behavior is available, and norms (or standards) are enforced. In systems without judicial review, or with detached courts, the norms to be enforced are not produced by courts. Such norms are sourced in the constitution;[125] and supplemented by legislative instruments, and international and comparative law. Of course, sourcing norms is only the beginning. We are required to travel through our interpretive standpoints, presented in Part I, and through the steps in which this meaning is translated from, and into, new cultural and institutional understandings, described in Part III. It is to these processes that we now turn.

[123] Palmer, *Judicial Review*, *supra* note 59, 113.

[124] Tushnet, *supra* note 115, 80. [125] Ibid., 85.

PART III

CONSTITUTING RIGHTS BY CONTESTATION

Parts I and II of this book provide a descriptive account of emerging practices of interpretation and enforcement, and an analysis of why those practices help to constitute economic and social rights. This Part reveals how such practices are ultimately dependent upon others. Indeed, I suggest that the contestations around economic and social rights, progressed by social movements and other private actors, are a vital part of the relevance of such rights to our legal and social institutions. In this Part, we shift from the analysis of rights to the analysis of rights talk; and from the demarcation of the roles of the separated branches of government, to the linkages with each other and to the market and civil society.

This analysis unsettles our theories of economic and social rights by assuming an interpretive position not usually taken by constitutionalist scholars—the position of private actors purporting to act in the public interest, rather than the public institutions themselves. We build on, and in some ways depart from, the conventional focus on courts, and from the less conventional focus on the institutions of the legislature or executive. This opens the way to a socio-legal understanding of how such rights are constituted, and their meaning forged, by the nebulous processes in which law is recognized more clearly in its relation to politics and governance. The legal realism that has guided our analysis of adjudication and enforcement also guides our assumptions about these other political actors. How social movements effect the cultural change necessary for the ideational, and ideological support of economic and social rights, and how private actors effect governance structures necessary for the practicable delivery of economic and social rights, are intrinsic to their operation and their meaning.

The ways in which social movements contribute to constitutional law has been the subject of historical and sociological scholarship, which competes against both originalist theories of constitutional meaning, and the court-centric understanding of constitutional development. Under the obdurate conditions that apply to the US Constitution, social movements utilizing constitutional arguments are often resolute in their vision of the state's obligations to them. In many cases, they work through formal amendment processes; more often (and when these processes fail), they apply this vision through offering revisionist interpretations of constitutional text. The observations about US-based social movements that are made in constitutional scholarship offer rich and textured prescriptions for social movements in other constitutional contexts. Non-US based associational collectivities focused on constitutional change agitate against a target that is less immovable, and less chronologically distant, from the US example. Yet their focus on cultural change is similar. Taking two non-amendment-seeking, non-court-centric case studies from Ghana and South Africa, Chapter 8 examines how movements constitute economic and social rights.

Equally, the structures of governance have attracted considerable scholarly attention, as governance, rather than government, offers a more accurate depiction of the sites in which law is contested, ignored, applied, and changed. In disparate contexts, a designed interchange between public and private actors has secured accountable, and sometimes more effective, responses to law. The emphasis on reflexive learning and information sharing made possible by this interchange expands into what has been termed a "new" governance, or "experimentalist," approach. For economic and social rights, new governance structures offer opportunities to reconceive state, market, and civil society coordinates. Experimentalist approaches offer the market as a counterintuitive model to deliver economic and social services in order to meet fundamental interests. Such approaches also prescribe the courts as an overseer of forms of problem-solving by interested parties, rather than a final adjudicator. Whether the features of governance depart from the precepts of constitutionalism, or complement it, is the question addressed in Chapter 9. Again, a case study from South Africa supplies the backdrop for understanding the potentials, and limits, of new governance.

Chapter 10 concludes the book with an overview of what we have observed from the processes and actors which constitute economic and social rights, as human rights or as constitutional rights, in today's constitutional democracies. It suggests directions for the extraterritorial application and for private law applications, of economic and social rights. It also summarizes the implications for public law that are germane to this study. This helps us to understand what might be gained or lost in the conditions for interpretation, enforcement, and contestation that such democracies will assemble in the future.

8

Social Movements and Economic and Social Rights

Social movements are galvanized by, and in turn galvanize, demands for economic and social rights. Such movements play an obvious role in effecting change in formal law: through litigation, petitioning, lobbying and protest. Less obvious, but no less important, is the impact that these movements have at the intersection of law and social fact: by reframing how people think about law's promises, and how they expect law's promises to deliver. Together, these actions bring law and legal consciousness closer together by effecting both law reform and cultural change. The legal meaning of the rights to food, water, health care, housing and education is thus not simply the product of the possibilities for keen reasoning or perceptive enforcement, documented in previous chapters. It is the product of social movements, formed as associational collectivities to contest, mobilize, agitate, articulate and insist upon the fundamental importance of material interests, and of their links with human dignity or other values. Indeed, that we have a discourse of economic and social rights at all is the result of at least two centuries' of contestations by individuals and groups who have insisted upon the responsibility of the state to organize its laws and institutions to ensure fundamental material protections for all: contestations first led at the domestic level, before entering both the international and transnational domains. How social movements create this large-scale legal change, on the basis of cultural shifts or institutional reforms, is a critical dimension of the framework of constituting rights, established in this book.

What are social movements? The definition is itself contested. One way of demarcating social movements from other forms of collective action (interest groups, political parties, or informal associations) is to examine the presence of three or more of the following criteria: "collective or joint action; change-oriented goals or claims; some extra- or non-institutional collective action; some degree of organization; and some degree of temporal continuity."[1] Sometimes, categorizations are drawn between associations propelled by "interests" and those motivated by "values"; however, this demarcation is unhelpful with respect to movements engaged in economic and social rights, which are motivated by material conditions and the values such conditions flout or uphold. In one seminal definition, the term applies to "collective challenges by people with common purposes and solidarity in sustained interaction with elites, opponents and authorities."[2] This inclusive definition may apply to the change-oriented claims pursued by nongovernmental organizations ("NGOs"), grassroots groups, community-based organizations, and unions.

There are many familiar examples of social movements organized around economic and social rights. Labor unions contest workplace remuneration and conditions; patient support groups and environmental justice organizations contest medicine pricing and the health impacts of pollution; welfare rights groups and food security groups contest nutritional services and food production conditions; parental associations and civil rights organizations contest the delivery of education; and antipoverty lawyers and legal aid lawyers contest the impact that poverty and inequality has on the aims of justice in the legal system. All of these movements contain internal divisions. I argue that when they adopt "rights-talk," along with tactics of persuasion and resistance,[3] they belong within our study of the contestations around economic and social rights. Sometimes, such interests are expressed as raising civil and political rights, such as the right to information which links farmers and health patients in contests around agricultural and medicinal intellectual property protections.[4] To reject their relevance to economic and social rights is to ignore the indivisibility of such rights and to maintain the problematic divisions that should be dispelled.

This chapter examines the effectiveness of social movements in constituting economic and social rights. It begins with a case study of a community in Ghana and its Legal Resources Centre, which together organized around, petitioned for, and litigated the right to health. Secondly, it parses this case study to demonstrate three common features of social movements—of jurisgenesis, of disturbing market and legal orthodoxies, and of the framing of injustice—which help to effect widespread change in social and legal

[1] D. A. Snow, S. Soule, and H. Kriesi (eds.), *The Blackwell Companion to Social Movements* (2004).

[2] Sidney Tarrow, *Power in Movement: Social Movements and Contentious Politics* (2nd edn., 1998) 206–7.

[3] Tactics of social disruption, protest, civil disobedience, and procedural irregularities, therefore belong within this study: *see*, e.g., Frances Fox Piven and Richard A. Cloward, *Poor People's Movements: Why They Succeed, How They Fail* (1979). Those tactics which disrespect the most basic features of rights protection, such as brute violence or terror, are outside of its scope. *See further* Tarrow, *supra* note 2, 94–6, 203–4.

[4] Amy Kapczynski, *The Access to Knowledge Mobilization and the New Politics of Intellectual Property*, 117 Yale L.J. 804 (2008).

understandings of economic and social rights. Thirdly, against otherwise complementary popular constitutionalist accounts, the chapter examines how countermovements and backlash oppose such movements, and how an undue focus on cultural change can impinge on institutional change. It concludes by examining other social movements from South Africa, particularly those formed in support of the right to housing and against evictions.

The focus on contestation introduces the book's broader focus on discourse. In part, economic and social rights provide a way of talking about poverty, inequality, and redistribution, that transcends the other attributes that they bring: of the ready insertion of rights talk in our legal institutions, or of the ready constituencies of human rights professionals to act on their behalf, or of their interdependence with the civil and political freedoms that both mobilize and safeguard their advocates. In short, economic and social rights provide a discourse which ensures that agency and participation are a vital part of the politics of a demanded-for legal order which recognizes that certain needs must always be met. Hence, when human needs are articulated as rights, a pathway of justice that is centered on the experience of the individual is opened. This language offers an important device for the expression of human agency in a constitutional democracy.[5]

Part of the aim of this chapter is to break the assumed link between rights talk and litigation or litigiousness. Of course, against certain background legal-cultural constraints, rights talk may combine inexorably with litigation, given the power and resources of the professional constituencies of lawyers and of courts.[6] As we have foreshadowed earlier, the background role conception of courts, for example, either prompts social movements to engage in litigation, or dissuades them from approaching courts.[7] What is less contingent is the fact that these movements contest their claims against the backdrop of law and the state. Our first case study, from Ghana, demonstrates this effect.

A. PROLOGUE: THE RIGHT TO HEALTH IN GHANA

In 2003, a new meaning and legal application of the right to health in Ghana was generated by the contestations of a small community and its legal center. Ghana belongs within our comparative study for several reasons. Inheriting many of its legal institutions from colonial Britain, its courts are

[5] Jeremy Waldron, "Rights and Needs: The Myth of Disjunction," in Austin Sarat and Thomas R. Kearns (eds.), *Legal Rights* (1996) 87.

[6] Mary Ann Glendon, *Rights Talk: The Impoverishment of Political Discourse* (1991).

[7] *See supra*, Part II.

detached in character, and deferential in application.[8] More importantly, Ghana's post-independence Constitution—now as its Fourth Republican Constitution of 1992—contains both civil and political, and economic and social rights protections.[9] The latter appear as "directive principles of state policy," much like those enumerated in the Indian or Irish Constitutions.[10] Among these is "the right to good health care,"[11] which is present to guide all the branches of government—including the legislature, executive, and judiciary—in constitutional interpretation and in policy formation and implementation. These principles do not give rise to causes of action or to direct enforcement. Neither do Ghana's international obligations, such as under the International Covenant on Economic, Social and Cultural Rights ("ICESCR"), which recognizes the right to "the highest attainable standard of physical and mental health,"[12] and imposes a duty to progressively realize the right,[13] or similar duties under the African Charter on Human and Peoples' Rights.[14] Up until 2003, the right to good health care had not been tested in court, although it had oriented a number of human rights campaigns.

One such campaign was run by the Legal Resources Centre of Ghana (the "LRC"), a community-based legal aid organization located in the impoverished Nima community of Accra. As part of a contingent of visiting interns, I was both an observer and a participant, an experience which I have co-documented elsewhere.[15] For several years, the LRC had used human rights

[8] *See* Chapter 5, section D(1), Chapter 7.1, section D; *see also* Figure 7.1, page 194.

[9] There is currently an official review of the Ghanaian Constitution: Constitution Review Commission of Inquiry Instrument, 2010. The Final Report of the Constitutional Review Commission called for the recognition of economic, social and cultural rights as "fully fledged rights": Speech of Prof. Albert Kodze Fiadjoe, Chairman of the Constitution Review Commission (CRC) during the presentation of its final report to President John Evans Atta Mills, 20 December 2011, *available at* <http://www.crc.gov.gh>.

[10] *Compare* the discussion of such directive principles in Chapter 4, section A(6) and in Chapter 7, section C.

[11] Constitution of the Republic of Ghana [1992], ("Ghana Const."), § 34:

(1) The Directive Principles of State Policy . . . shall guide all citizens, Parliament, the President, the Judiciary, the Council of State, the Cabinet, political parties and other bodies and persons in applying or interpreting this Constitution or any other law and in taking and implementing any policy decisions, for the establishment of a just and free society.

(2) The President shall report to Parliament at least once a year all the steps taken to ensure the realization of the policy objectives contained in this Chapter and, in particular, the realization of basic human rights, a healthy economy, the right to work, the right to good health care and the right to education.

[12] International Covenant on Economic, Social and Cultural Rights, 16 December 1966, 993 U.N.T.S. 3 (entered into force 3 January 1976), art. 12 ("ICESCR").

[13] ICESCR, art. 2(1).

[14] OAU Doc. CAB/LEG/67/3/rev. 5 (27 June 1981), reprinted in 21 I.L.M. 58 (1981) (entered into force 21 October 1986, arts. 1, 16 ("AfCHR").

[15] The details of this decade-long, community-based, campaign are described in Jeremy Perelman and Katharine G. Young, "Rights as Footprints," in Lucie White and Jeremy Perelman (eds.), *Stones of Hope: How African Activists Reclaim Human Rights to Challenge Global Poverty* (2011) 122.

education in relation to the right to health care, particularly to confront the regressive effects of Ghana's user fees system of health care. This system of financing and distributing health care had long harmed the human rights of Ghana's poor.[16]

User fees for public health services deliver health care to those who pay. They utilize a quintessential market mechanism, in order to reduce inefficiency, raise revenue, and improve public facilities. Since 1986, this system has been the predominant method of health financing in Africa.[17] UN agencies, such as the United Nations Children's Fund ("UNICEF") and the World Health Organization ("WHO"), were supportive of user fees during the 1980s. The World Bank and the International Monetary Fund began to recommend user-fee mechanisms for delivering social services, like health and education in 1987, and since then have conditioned loans to many countries on the basis of their implementation.[18] In 1998, for example, 75 percent of ongoing World Bank projects in sub-Saharan Africa included the establishment or expansion of user fees.[19]

As well as improving efficiency, user fees are said to foster equity by cross-subsidizing the increased revenues from richer users to those unable to afford the fees themselves. This benefit is achieved by exempting the poor from user fees, especially for essential interventions that will have the biggest impact on their (and others') health, such as immunizations.[20] Thus, the user fees and exemptions package purports to combine efficiency and equity in health care. In Ghana's case, the Hospital Fees Act 1971 exempts children, the elderly, and those "unable to pay . . . fees on the ground of poverty" from the payment of fees.[21] Exemptions are key to ensuring poor people are treated for health care.

Nonetheless, exemptions are rarely enforced. Clinics and hospitals demand payment from all. Hence, the LRC's campaign had adopted the language of the right to health care to challenge the non-enforcement of health care exemptions, and the terrible burdens on poor people that this

[16] For a general overview of the implications of health policies on the poor, and their relationship with "structural violence," *see* Paul Farmer, *Pathologies of Power: Health, Human Rights, and the New War on the Poor* (2003).

[17] The Bamako Initiative, coordinated between African Health Ministers and launched in 1987, was implemented by almost every country in sub-Saharan Africa: *see* WHO, *Guidelines for Implementing the Bamako Initiative* (1988).

[18] *See*, e.g., World Bank, *Financing Health Services in Developing Countries: An Agenda for Reform* (1987).

[19] Guy Hutton, "Charting the Path to the World Bank's 'No Blanket Policy on User Fees'" IDFID Health Systems Resource Centre (2004), 2.5.

[20] World Bank, *Agenda for Reform*, *supra* note 18.

[21] Hospital Fees Act, 1971 (Ghana), §§ 2(a), 4(2).

lack of enforcement had created.[22] Yet after many years of LRC staff and community volunteers seeking to educate patients about their rights to exemptions at clinics and hospitals, and health professionals about the law, little change had been made. In fact, no budget was available for the exemption on grounds of poverty to operate.

The action in 2003 was triggered after Mohammed Zakari, a subsistence farmer from Ghana's north, encountered the user fee health-care system. At 62, he was earning roughly 20 cents per day growing seasonal cassava and maize (or about US$ 70 per annum).[23] He therefore had little income to pay for health care. Moreover, as elderly, male, and rural, he belonged to the three cohorts least likely to trust in, and seek out, Western medicine.[24] Yet when he suffered sudden and acute abdominal pain in the afternoon of 1 November 2002, his relatives brought him to the public Ridge Hospital in Accra, where he was admitted for emergency hernia surgery, a relatively uncomplicated procedure with a high rate of success. Three weeks later, he had a second operation. After his recovery, he was discharged and handed a bill that included the costs of his dressing, injections, laboratory, theatre, sanitation, and accommodation. This bill totaled 2,396,000 cedis (about US$ 240).

Unable to pay an amount which represented more than three times his annual wage (and an almost incomprehensible multiplication of his savings), Mr. Zakari was informed by the social welfare officer at the hospital that he would not be released until he assembled the funds. His hospital bed and food were taken away, and he was prevented from leaving the hospital grounds. For the next six weeks, he was detained within the boundaries of the Ridge Hospital, a boundary guarded by private security and a high fence.[25] During this period of detention, he was only allowed outside the fence under the supervision of hospital staff, and in this case only to buy plantains to eat. He paid for these with donations from his family and the community of Nima, Accra's poorest district, where his brother resided. He slept on a bed in the porch of the hospital ward, for which he was charged a daily fee of 15,000 cedis (about US$ 1.50).[26]

[22] One US estimate from 2007 suggests that 28.5% of Ghanaians live below the poverty line: Central Intelligence Agency, *The World Factbook*, available at <https://www.cia.gov/library/publications/the-world-factbook/geos/gh.html>.

[23] According to the World Bank, 59% of food crop farmers live below Ghana's national poverty line. The average per capita income in northern Ghana was 2–4 times lower than that of the southern regions in the late 1990s: World Bank, "Bridging the North South Divide in Ghana?" in *Background Paper for the 2006 World Development Report* (2006).

[24] Randolph Quaye, *Underdevelopment and Health Care in Africa: The Ghanaian Experience* (1996).

[25] The Ridge Hospital is one of Ghana's oldest hospitals, established during the colonial period to cater for the health of the British. As such, it is located in an old and affluent residential area of Accra.

[26] This fee evokes the phenomena of prison systems charging for imprisonment: *see* Loic Wacquant, "The Penalization of Poverty and the Rise of Neo-liberalism," 9 Euro. J. on Crim. Pol. & Res. 401 (2001).

Mr. Zakari's plight came to the attention of the LRC at one of the community meetings held at its premises. In fact, this form of detention is a common consequence of the user fees system in Ghana and in other developing countries in Africa and elsewhere, and represents one aspect of the systems' severity on the poor.[27] Indeed, it has become a banal and routinized aspect of under-resourced public health-care services. Yet unlike the other burdens experienced by the poor with the health-care system—the harms caused by no treatment, self-treatment, or half-treatments—this aspect of the user fees system was actionable in the courts. The lawyers responded by assembling a habeas corpus action to release Mr. Zakari from his hospital detention, based on the long-standing constitutional protection of personal liberty from arbitrary incarceration at the hands of the state. This action would require the state to show due cause for Mr. Zakari's detention, and if none were forthcoming, literally release the body.

Yet the lawyers embarked on a broader challenge, claiming the protection of Mr. Zakari's body not only from detention, but also from the foreseeable effects of the user fees system as a system of financing health care. In so doing, they challenged the fact that the Ridge Hospital not only detained Mr. Zakari, but also failed to provide him an exemption from his hospital fees, given his indigent status. And in recognition that this failure extended far beyond the hospital's own discretion, they added the Ministry of Health and the Ministry of Finance to their statement of claim, challenging the state's failure to make regulations as to the criteria and procedures for defining at the time of initial registration whether a prospective patient is "unable to pay . . . fees on the ground of poverty,"[28] and the failure to allocate funds in the state budget towards making this exemption scheme operative.

The broader claim against these additional public departments was based on both the failure to implement the relevant statute and the failure to respect the constitutional protection of the right to health care. Given that the directive principles of state policy are understood to be unenforcable by the judiciary, there was no cause of action based on the right to health care. Habeas corpus, and the requirement to protect the body from unlawful

[27] The practice of "hospital detentions" has become disturbingly widespread, with reports of this practice in Burundi, Kenya, the Democratic Republic of Congo and Zimbabwe, as well as in Colombia, Haiti, Mexico, the Philippines and Venezuela: *see* Arachu Castro, "In and Out: User Fees and other Unfortunate Events during Hospital Admission and Discharge," 24 *Cadernos De Saude Publica* 1174 (2008) (collecting data from the United Nations Children's Fund, Médecins Sans Frontières, Human Rights Watch, Physicians for Human Rights, and the Pan American Health Organization); *see also* Juliane Kippenberg et al., "Detention of Insolvent Patients in Burundian Hospitals," *Health Policy & Planning* 14 (2008).

[28] Hospital Fees Act, 1971 (Ghana), §§ 2(a), 4(2).

incarceration, provided this cause of action, and allowed the health-care system to be put to constitutional scrutiny.[29] However, the simple remedy for habeas corpus—the literal "release of the body"—would do nothing to disturb the injustice of the present health care system.

Indeed, a habeas remedy could set a pernicious precedent: of ending hospital detentions but at the same time of removing the hospital's only means of treating impoverished patients. Thus, the suit sought to emphasize the right to health care in order to ground the broader remedies that were needed to solve the problem of user fees. The brief canvassed comparative constitutional arguments about the right to health care, from South Africa and India,[30] which established an obligation on the government to take reasonable measures to protect health care or to provide emergency treatment. The brief also drew attention to Ghana's international treaty obligations with respect to health care under the ICESCR and the African Charter on Human and Peoples' Rights ("AfCHR").[31]

The remedy sought the establishment of new regulations for the Hospital Fees Act, which would specify criteria as to who would be eligible for fees exemption on the basis of poverty and would earmark appropriate funds for implementation. Decisions as to both criteria and funding were to be reached by a negotiation between the two ministries, health system and finance experts, health-care providers, low-income health consumer groups, and community representatives. Such a remedy—experimentalist in character[32]—was unfamiliar to the local judiciary, and yet necessary to resolve the deep-seated problems in relation to health care.

At the same time, a petition was circulated in the local community of Nima, demanding Mohammed Zakari's release from hospital and the recognition of the entitlements of people in poverty to emergency health care and to exemptions. Due to be submitted to the Parliament of Ghana on the same day as the filing of the suit, it stated:

> We, the people of the Nima, Mamobi, and Newtown communities, believe that our right to health is being neglected. We know that paupers, pregnant women, the elderly over 70 years old, and children under 5 are legally exempt from medical fees. However, this exemption policy is not enforced. We often do not go to the hospital when sick or injured because we know that we will not be able to afford medical care there. In emergencies, we should always receive medical

[29] Ghana Const., § 14; *see also* AfCHR, art. 6; ICCPR, art. 9 (prohibition of arbitrary detention).

[30] *See Soobramoney v. Minister of Health, Kwazulu-Natal* 1998 (1) SA 765 (CC); *Minister of Health v. Treatment Action Campaign* 2002 (5) SA 721 (CC); *Pashim Bana Khet Mazdoor Samity v. State of West Bengal* (1996) 4 S.C.C. 37 (SCI).

[31] AfCHR, arts. 1, 16; ICCPR, arts. 2(1), 12.

[32] *See further* Chapter 5, section D(3).

care even before we are asked to pay. Finally, like Mohammed Zakari, we should never be detained in the hospital because we cannot pay.[33]

Things did not go entirely to plan. In the early hours of that morning, Mr. Zakari obtained his freedom. An anonymous benefactor settled his bill and informed his relatives that he was free. To this day, the identity of the benefactor remains unknown—most likely, certain officials recognized that trouble was brewing and sought to end it. The habeas claim was no longer actionable. Yet, not to be deflected from their challenge to the administration of the user fee system, Mr. Zakari's lawyers changed their cause of action from habeas corpus to wrongful imprisonment, and retained the additional requests for relief. Plans for the press conference were only slightly altered—Mohammed Zakari himself was asked to speak. Thus, on 22 January 2003, after one month of hospital treatment and almost two months of hospital detention, he stood before the community of Nima and local journalists, and recounted his experience at the Ridge Hospital.[34]

Was the campaign a success? After the political attention received during the press conference and lawsuit, the government promised to put aside 3 billion cedis (US$ 350,000) in the health-care system to pay for the exemptions scheme, so that hospitals would not detain people who genuinely could not pay their fees. Mr. Zakari walked free. And the lawyers from the LRC were invited to take part in negotiations towards a new system of health financing in Ghana, which would organize payments through a national health insurance scheme.[35] A positive assessment of success is (cautiously) due.

Such success cannot simply be attributed to the techniques of litigation, the unarguable logic behind the indivisibility of Mr. Zakari's civil and health rights, or the savvy of his lawyers in joining underenforced constitutional rights with their interpretation of Ghanaian statute and constitutional law. The success came from a long-term social movement engaged in cultural strategies towards economic and social rights. This movement, located in one of the poorest districts of Accra, warrants close attention.

The movement itself rested in the links between the LRC and the local community. An unconventional legal aid and human rights center, the LRC provided meeting space for local mothers' groups and youth groups, as well as legal advice. This center adopted its name, and critical elements of its practice, from the Legal Resources Centre (the LRC) of South Africa. It was established by two progressive lawyers, Mahama Ayariga and Raymond Atuguba, while still at the University of Ghana Legon, who both later

[33] Petition by the Nima Community, Presented to Parliament 23 January 2003.

[34] "Government Sued over Hospital Fees Act," *Ghanaian Times*, 23 January 2003, p. 1.

[35] *See now* National Health Insurance Act 2003; National Health Insurance Regulations 2004.

studied at Harvard Law School before their involvement in high levels of Ghanaian politics.[36] The LRC began to host student interns from the United States every year, coordinated by Harvard Law Professor Lucie White, whose antipoverty and human rights scholarship had long critiqued the power dynamics of conventional lawyering, and proposed alternative methods for involving members of communities in organizing strategies.[37] With these critical resources of knowledge and prestige, the LRC had already campaigned around other economic and social rights, such as the lack of street lighting in Nima, the pitfalls of the open drain which snaked its way between local homes, and the refusal of the public works to remove rubbish from Nima's streets.

The Zakari campaign introduced a new set of tactics. Before taking up Mr. Zakari's claim, the LRC's "right to health" campaign had engaged in educative strategies to inform Nima's residents about their entitlements to exemptions, and to encourage them to demand them at their point of care. However, these had reached a stalemate: local clinics and hospitals simply did not have the resources to grant exemptions. Mr. Zakari's litigation presented a new focal point for litigation and protest, and a new moment of shifting the community's consciousness about their economic and social rights. Knowing that a successful habeas corpus litigation could worsen the opportunities for health care for the poor by removing a cost-generating practice for cash-strapped hospitals and clinics, the LRC dovetailed the habeas corpus litigation with the community-supported protest about the right to health, using both to target the many different political actors involved in health-care distribution and financing. During the petition process, members of the youth group, together with the US student interns of the LRC, walked the streets of Nima and gathered 1,500 signatures, asking community residents a series of questions about their experience with user fees, and informing them about the detention of Mohammed Zakari and of the disjuncture between their legal rights and their everyday experience.

The story of Mr. Zakari's release in Nima portrays the role of social movements in contesting and securing economic and social rights. In many ways, the story is typical of social movement action: involving a community-based organization, a persistent mix of strategies, an unpredictable outcome, and an uncertain "cause and effect." Its contestations also presage the governance effects described in Chapter 9. Yet the anatomy of this social

[36] One, Mahama Ayariga, was afterwards elected to the Ghanaian Parliament, serving from 2004 until 2008. The other, Raymond Atuguba, now serves as the Executive Secretary to the Constitutional Review Commission.

[37] *See*, e.g., Lucie E. White, "Facing South: Lawyering for Poor Communities in the Twenty-First Century," 25 Fordham Urban L.J. 813 (1998); Peter Houtzager and Lucie E. White, "The Long Arc of Pragmatic Economic and Social Rights," in White and Perelman, *supra* note 15, 172.

movement is worthy of closer focus. Years later, Nihad Swallah, a community organizer with the LRC, described the case as "one of the biggest achievements of what legal aid has done in this community. And because everyone, almost all the community members were involved, it became like a footprint in everybody's mind; anybody you ask around knows the story."[38] How the LRC and Nima community were able to shift and create cultural change is a critical part of how economic and social rights change law itself. The next section provides a closer analysis of how social movements are currently constituting economic and social rights, and are constituting themselves in the process.

B. ANATOMY OF AN ECONOMIC AND SOCIAL RIGHTS SOCIAL MOVEMENT

If social movements create cultural meaning, successful movements move culture in order to create law. In constitutional contestation, their medium is "constitutional culture": a construct that alludes to the "network of understandings and practices that shape [the]... constitutional tradition."[39] Judges and other members of the legal profession are usually the prime agents in this activity; but the development of a constitutional culture can also occur within the community at large. Constitutional culture develops from "a web of interpretative norms, canons, and practices which most members of a particular community accept."[40] It is a malleable concept,[41] and provides a lens that, unlike strict legal positivism, avoids a "screening out" of the motivations of advocates in holding the positions they do in constitutional controversy.[42]

[38] Interview by Jeremy Perelman with Nihad Swallah, Community Organizer, Legal Resources Center, in Accra, Ghana on 13 January 2005, described in Perelman and Young, "Rights as Footprints", *supra* note 15.

[39] Robert C. Post, "The Supreme Court, 2002 Term—Foreword: Fashioning the Legal Constitution: Culture, Courts, and Law," 117 Harv. L. Rev. 4 (2003)

[40] John Ferejohn, Jack Rakove, and Jonathon Riley (eds.), "Editors' Introduction," *Constitutional Culture and Democratic Rule* (2001) 10.

[41] Post, "Fashioning the Legal Constitution," *supra* note 39, suggesting definitions of "constitutional culture," and "constitutional law" will always depend on why one is asking the question. *Compare* the robust practices of constitutional culture described in the United States with those elsewhere: i.e. H. W. O. Okoth-Ogendo, "Constitutions Without Constitutionalism: Reflections on an African Political Paradox," in Douglas Greenberg et al. (eds.), *Constitutionalism and Democracy: Transitions in the Contemporary World* (1993) 67 (examining the lack of constitutionalist commitments held by political elites in Africa); Miguel Schor, "Constitutionalism Through the Looking Glass of Latin America," 41 Tex. Int'l. L.J. 1 (2006) 5 (examining the lack of constitutionalist commitments held by political elites in Latin America).

[42] Reva B. Siegel, "Text in Context: Gender and the Constitution from a Social Movement Perspective," 150 U. Pa. L. Rev. 297 (2001) 317–18.

The cultural change that occurs through the discourse of economic and social rights provides strong support for the "democratic" credentials of such legal protections. As popular constitutionalist theories record, law is formed "on both sides of the courthouse door."[43] Drawing attention to developments in the popular beliefs that undergird constitutional arrangements helps us to understand how the authority of judges is modulated, and to answer the so-called "counter-majoritarian" objections to judicial review by displacing the focus on courts. Under this view, law creation is for everyone: not just elected officials or appointed judges; nor even just the elite (the bureaucracies, litigators, or lobbyists who make up the professional legal field). The constitution's meaning is open to the wider polity. An analysis of social movements helps us to parse this wider political field and the change in culture and beliefs that occur there. Three features help us to understand this effect, which are highlighted by the lessons of the LRC. First, the success of movements in shaping the emerging meaning of rights lies in their creation of a new constitutional vision—a vision that we might term "jurisgenerative" in character.[44] The politics is focused on an interpretive battle, waged primarily by the social movement, over what the public laws must mean, and what the state is responsible for. Secondly, the movement provides an alternative presentation of the present orthodoxies that preclude access to economic and social rights, challenging economic or institutional assumptions as inaccurate or irrelevant. Thirdly, the movement engages explicitly in framing the injustice of present-day arrangements. These features are given detail below.

(1) Jurisgenesis of rights

In Ghana, the LRC sought to reinterpret the Ghanaian Constitution's promise of the right to health care to require a different mode of health-care financing in Ghana. Members of the community, with the LRC, worked together to articulate a conception of justice in health, and to create the means through which this conception could be accepted elsewhere. The movement adopted the discourse of the right to health care, and performed this discourse through litigation, petitions, protests, and other forms of public action. It worked to shift the cultural understanding of rights by community members, as well as within official channels. It offered a

[43] Ibid., 314. For legislative-driven constitutional politics, *see* Robert C. Post and Reva B. Siegel, "Legislative Constitutionalism and Section Five Power: Policentric Interpretation of the Family and Medical Leave Act," 112 Yale L.J. 1943 (2003).

[44] For the rich presentation of "jurisgenesis," as a way to understand the creation of legal meaning, *see* Robert M. Cover, "The Supreme Court, 1982 Term—Foreword: Nomos and Narrative," 97 Harv. L. Rev. 4 (1982) 12–19.

redemptive reading on Ghana's laws in three ways: by seeking to make the directive principles of state policy on the right to health care judicially cognizable; by emphasizing the legal import of Ghana's obligations under international and regional human rights treaties, and the influential role of comparative human rights law; and by seeking to legitimize the Nima community's understanding and agitation around their rights. Together, these tactics created a shift in law—a jurisgenesis—of the right to health.

Jurisgenesis is law-creation. The concept of jurisgenesis was developed to capture the long-term impact of social movements in US constitutional law. In Robert Cover's terms, cultural worlds make legal meaning.[45] These cultural worlds exist collectively and socially. The ties of law-creating social movements are strong, celebratory, expressive, and performative. Such movements create normative universes, their own *nomos*. When their claims extend to the social world in which they inhabit, they engage in a transformative politics and a transformative vision of the law.[46]

Cover was interested in the ways in which social movements attempt to redeem the very laws that are responsible for their grievances. He described a form of redemptive constitutionalism, which sought to reinterpret the given legal framework in ways that redeem its implications for justice. Often, in economic and social rights claims, redemptive constitutionalism introduces or reintroduces ideologies of distributive justice, based on human rights or constitutional texts. These can be opposed to rejectionist strategies, which renounce constitutional and other legal texts in order to precipitate the dissolution of government.[47] This template between redemptive and rejectionist interpretations can be applied to today's social movements. Rights-based social movements often seek to transform the understanding of present-day legal arrangements—whether constitutional, legislative, or incorporated into law through international human rights treaties. They offer redemptive readings of the terms of each; for example, that the Equal Protection clause of the US Constitution provides for a minimum financial baseline for all in the United States,[48] or that the Due Process Clause calls for an affirmative requirement of government aid,[49] or that both should be interpreted in line with the Universal Declaration of Human Rights

[45] Ibid. [46] Ibid.

[47] Ibid., (distinguishing abolitionist movement leader, Frederick Douglass, with William Lloyd Garrison, who sought a perfectionist, insular renunciation of the pro-slavery Constitution). *See also* J. M. Balkin, "Agreements with Hell and Other Objects of Our Faith," 65 Fordham L. Rev. 1703 (1997) 1708–10.

[48] US Const., 14th Amt. *See*, e.g., Frank Michelman, "Welfare Rights in a Constitutional Democracy," 3 Wash. U. L. Q. 659 (1979).

[49] US Const., 14th Amt. *See*, e.g., David P. Currie, "Positive and Negative Constitutional Rights," 53 U. Chi. L. Rev. 861, 864 (1986).

("UDHR") (or the ICESCR) to achieve a similar effect.[50] Other movements contesting the terms of distribution or production may do so in the insular terms of renunciation of the present legal order. In Ghana, the LRC sought to reinterpret the import, and influence, of the Constitution's text.

This distinction can be applied to many other antipoverty or otherwise redistributive social movements. These movements might forge the agenda for a redemptive globalization or an antiglobalization; redemptive capitalism or anticapitalism.[51] Yet economic and social rights may accommodate both capitalism and globalization and many of its alternatives. It is the posture adopted by the movement towards the state, and towards law, that is more dispositive of the changes in public law, of which this book is concerned. Social movements may call for action to redeem the state or abandon it, and to redeem the law or to reject it, by turning to plural legalities, or self-sufficient social norms.

What is redemptive within movements oriented towards economic and social rights, and their posture towards the law and the state, is neither uniform nor united. As this book goes to press, the Occupy Wall Street movement, and its coordinated movements in city parks across the United States and in other parts of the world, have united opposition to the practices of capital flows in Wall Street, and yet have made no other unified demands.[52] Their call for a representation of "the 99 percent," as opposed to the "1 percent" who benefit from the global capitalist system, suggests a form of alliance with developing countries. Whether a human rights movement,[53] or a popular constitutionalist movement with a constitutional agenda (for example, to redeem the US Constitution from "the malefactors of great wealth" who benefit disproportionately from current arrangements),[54] the Occupy movement is transnationally linked, via its use of the Internet, the press, the occupation of public space, and by the mutual (if elusive) foe of the global banking system. It is too early to categorize this incipient movement, yet its relationship with economic and social rights will

[50] E.g., *Dandridge v. Williams*, 397 U.S. 471 (1970) per Marshall J. For the parallels between international human rights and constitutional rights, *see infra*, Chapter 10.

[51] Katharine G. Young, "Symposium on Framing Economic, Social and Cultural Rights for Advocacy and Mobilization: Redemptive and Rejectionist Frames," 4 Northeastern U. L.J. (2012, forthcoming).

[52] *See* the history of this movement, in the broadsheet <http://www.scribd.com/doc/67837516/Occupied-Wall-Street-Journal>.

[53] The discourse of both commentators and participants has varied. For example, philosopher Judith Butler noted that "If the right to shelter, food and employment are impossible demands than we demand the impossible": Judith Butler, Composite Remarks, Washington Square Park, 23 October 2011, via human microphone, *available at* <http://occupywriters.com/works/by-judith-butler>.

[54] Jack Balkin, "Occupy the Constitution," Wednesday, 19 October 2011, *available at* <http://balkin.blogspot.com/2011/10/occupy-constitution.html>.

undoubtedly develop, particularly against constitutional backdrops where the call for social justice in the language of economic and social rights has already begun.

Such backdrops are formed by the ongoing "rights revolutions" that are occurring in different parts of the world. Yet, so far, these documented shifts have privileged a focus on civil and political rights. In jurisdictions such as the United States, India, Britain, and Canada, lawyers have brought about new legal protections for civil and political rights; and indeed litigation support structures are argued to be the necessary preconditions for the "rights revolution" to occur.[55] Nonetheless, because jurisgenesis emphasizes the cultural processes that occur in dynamic effect, drawing attention away from litigation-focused structures, other forms of rights-based contestations and their transformation in law are included. Our case study from Ghana reveals the important shadow effect of litigation, but also the effectiveness of wider political strategies. Again, this is contingent across different constitutional and political cultures. For example, the rights culture in Australia is sustained in the absence of judicial and litigation-based support.[56] Although selective in the rights that are deemed worthy of protection, this culture has supported particular human rights with relative effectiveness, including labor and other economic and social rights,[57] in the absence of support from legal professionals, and indeed in the presence of that group's professional hostility. Lawyers are neither necessary nor sufficient for jurisgenesis, although they do have a role in helping or hindering its effectiveness.

Indeed, jurisgenesis seems to offer a mode of informal enforcement for the unenforced and underenforced in our constitutional commitments.[58] Individuals become the authors of contemporary constitutional meaning. The meaning of legal rights belongs to all, as long as their aspirations are legitimately expressed.[59] Within this "Catholic" understanding of constitutional authority, the social movement forms one part in a relatively nonhierarchical constitutionalist whole.[60] We do not require an official decision-maker, such as a court, to ratify the constitution's interpretation

[55] Charles Epp, *The Rights Revolution: Lawyers, Activists and Supreme Courts in Comparative Perspective* (1998).

[56] Brian Galligan and F. L. (Ted) Morton, "Australian Exceptionalism: Rights Protection Without a Bill of Rights," in Tom Campbell, Jeffrey Goldsworthy, and Adrienne Stone (eds.), *Protecting Rights Without a Bill of Rights* (2006) 17.

[57] Ibid.

[58] *See* Part II generally, and Chapter 4 section A(6).

[59] Hendrik Hartog, "The Constitution of Aspiration and 'The Rights That Belong to Us All'," 74 *J. Am. Hist.* 1013 (1987) 1014.

[60] *See* Sanford Levinson, *Constitutional Faith* (1988) (contrasting "Protestant" with "Catholic" tropes of constitutional self-understanding).

by a social movement for it to become legitimate. This can be contrasted with a more "Protestant" understanding of constitutions, which emphasizes the exclusivity of written scripture or text as the basis of doctrine,[61] and does not welcome plural interpretive sources. Jurisgenesis favours the former, more inclusive view, which both lowers the bar for, but also complicates, our measures of legal change.

(2) Disturbance of orthodoxies

As well as challenging the legal meaning of the Ghanaian Constitution's economic and social rights, the LRC and members of the Nima community also challenged the conventional acceptance of user fees as a legitimate form of financing health care. This challenge came at the same time as liberal economists were themselves questioning the wisdom of user fees in countries with poorly resourced economies. Legal heterodoxies allied with economic and development heterodoxies to oppose present arrangements. Hence, the LRC insisted on challenging the assumptions about the operation of the market, of the agency of the individuals living within the community, and of the capacity of courts to deal with such questions. These arguments were made in the language of economic and social rights.

A redemptive interpretation already disturbs previous orthodoxies about the law. As social movements contend with the challenge of transforming their unpopular or marginal views into popular and accepted ones, they must challenge present-day orthodoxies and present possible alternatives. As against other rights-based arguments, this is particularly apt in the area of economic and social rights (and particularly so for the United States), where the prevailing view of both the legal profession, and the legal academy, is to assume both the impossibility and inefficacy of their entrenchment and realization through law. For social movements working with economic and social rights, the nature of the orthodoxies (of the ideologies, beliefs, and assumptions that are dominant and rarely questioned) are culturally contingent. Nonetheless, the present day globalization of a certain form of capitalist orthodoxy (despite variations within it) offers a loosely categorizable target along the axes of market, individual, and juridical assumptions.

The critical target, in conditions of global capitalism, is the market. In summarized form, the general orthodoxy in relation to markets has been that states need to deregulate, privatize, and liberalize markets—and should regulate them only in case of demonstrated market failure. The role of law under the terms of the Washington consensus is to enforce property and contract rights, thus securing the conditions for market certainty. Within

[61] Ibid.

this field of thought, the decommodification of public goods and their guarantee through public law—such as via universal housing, health care, food, social security, or education protections—is seen as antithetical to both efficiency and welfare. Recognizing "rights" to access such goods would remove them from the market, thereby distorting present markets, slowing economic growth, and with it aggregate social welfare.[62]

Social movements contesting economic and social rights challenge the market orthodoxy. These movements propose unorthodox interpretations of the relations between the regulation, distribution, and production of particular goods and services, using the language of freedom, dignity and rights. In many cases, such movements avoid the language of class: a language that also offers a means of challenging such relations, but whose framework of historical inevitability sits uneasily with present-day developments. Claims for rights-based protection evidently disturb the distributional frames of market rightness. They appear odd and uninformed, against the apparent consensus on economic policy and growth. Yet this unorthodoxy can be seen as their virtue: such interpretations "dare to disturb the universe,"[63] move the inconceivable to the conceivable,[64] and transform fringe arguments to constitutional common sense.

Second, these movements challenge the role of the individual that accords them limited agency in securing their material needs. The present-day orthodoxies about individual agency are confronted in two directions. The first opposition is to the view that individuals should have no say in the economic decisions that affect them—instead, economic and social rights movements insist on the political nature of the economy, and their participation in it. In this respect, they share much with the "conservative" antigovernment movements of the right, such as the Tea Party movement in the United States, whose representatives seek to wrest control from what they see as too much government involvement in economic decision-making. Yet, unlike such movements, the second stance taken is to link their asserted agency with greater collective (government and non-government) involvement. In particular, this view rejects the narrative of personal responsibility, which has powerfully justified economic deprivation in individual terms, and which has had particular salience in certain political

[62] For an influential summary of this position, *see* Joseph E. Stiglitz, *Globalization and Its Discontents* (2002).

[63] Jack M. Balkin and Reva B. Siegel, "Principles, Practices and Social Movements," 154 U. Pa. L. Rev. 927 (2006) 946.

[64] William N. Eskridge, Jr., "Some Effects of Identity-Based Social Movements on Constitutional Law in the Twentieth Century," 100 Mich. L. Rev. 2062 (2002) 2217 (noting that the ideal of diversity "would have been inconceivable before the civil rights and women's rights movements reshaped American public norms").

cultures such as the United States. In these cultures, the phenomenon of poverty is often seen as a pathology of personal failing, rather than of structural effect.[65] Under this view, a guaranteed source of income defeats the incentives on individuals to pull themselves up by their bootstraps, and to contribute to the economy and to the community.[66] In challenging this orthodoxy, the economic and social rights movements contend instead that the state must be responsible, along with its regulation of other private actors, for creating the necessary minimum support for individuals, just as it is responsible when such support is systematically lacking. Hence, these movements seek to maximize a collective agency in politics, and a collective responsibility in the market, using the discourse of individual rights.

Finally, such movements challenge juridical-based orthodoxies, and in particular the role of courts in addressing questions of economic and social rights. One prominent commentator captured the gist of this orthodoxy well. For Kim Lane Scheppele, drawing attention to economic and social rights produced "the sort of polite dismissal that is reserved for particularly excited children who are not mature enough to understand the full practical consequences of the evidently charming things they say."[67] In the United States, constitutional economic and social rights appear "off-the-wall."[68] While the dismissal, as it relates to economic arguments, canvasses the debates described above, the dismissal on legal-institutional grounds is distinctive. This orthodox view accepts the link between justiciability and a denial of democracy to be inevitable—meaning that economic and social rights must always invite the usurpation by the judicial branch over the elected branches, or the abdication of their review function. Our typology of institutional models has already questioned the anti-justiciability, anti-court view. As described in Part II of this book, the justiciability concerns are countered by comparative evidence of the ability of—and indeed need for—courts to safeguard and support democracy, as well as to the variety of judicial review and judicial role conceptions available. Social movements can also serve as the vehicle for this challenge, through the discourse they adopt, as well as the litigation or other political tactics that they pursue.

[65] Peter B. Edelman, "Toward a Comprehensive Antipoverty Strategy: Getting Beyond the Silver Bullet," 81 Geo. L.J. 1697 (1993).

[66] *See* these arguments reviewed in Philippe Van Parijs, "Why Surfers Should be Fed: The Liberal Case for an Unconditional Basic Income," 20 *Phil. & Pub. Aff.* 101 (1991).

[67] Kim Lane Scheppele, "A Realpolitik Defense of Social Rights," 82 Tex. L. Rev. 1921 (2004) 1922.

[68] William Forbath, "Constitutional Welfare Rights: A History, Critique and Reconstruction," 69 Fordham L. Rev. 1821 (2001) 1824; *but see* Cass R. Sunstein, *The Second Bill of Rights: FDR's Unfinished Revolution and Why We Need It More Than Ever* (2004) (suggesting the commitments advanced by FDR remain constitutive).

(3) Framing of injustice

In Ghana, the LRC reframed the health situation to portray its inherent injustice and to mobilize around this portrayal. The consequences of user fees were given a context and a protagonist: the detention of Mohammed Zakari. The narrative was not of Mr. Zakari's unfortunate illness, of his brother's decision to take him to hospital, nor of his, or his family's, responsibility for their poverty. Rather, the narrative was directed to the political—economic decisions that instituted a user fees structure of payment for people without means of payment in Ghana, and to the decision-makers who became aware of its regressive effects and carried on despite this awareness.

The LRC and the community's work to change law and policy in relation to user fees also changed the movement participants themselves. In so doing, the movement gave a depth to the politics around the right to health, rooting it in the subjectivity of individual experience, and setting in motion a transformation there. For theorists of jurisgenerative change, a movement exists to "give people a sense of who they are and why they should be aggrieved by existing practices."[69] Their original aims may therefore be transformed after an encounter with law, and the movement's aims may be transformed after the encounter with individual members. A focus on the transformation in subjectivity helps to interrogate the way in which the institutionalization of rights may not end the trend of objectifying or humiliating the apparent beneficiaries of rights claims, and how these tendencies may be resisted.[70] Such a focus may also highlight how knowledge of rights can transform a beneficiary's everyday experience, outside of any apparent relation to the formal structures of law.[71]

The term "legal consciousness" describes the fact and forms of "participation in the process of constructing legality."[72] Such studies often bypass formal changes—amendments to legal text or doctrine—to locate the effectiveness of rights in bringing about change within social relations. Elsewhere, Jeremy Perelman and I have described the work of the LRC in Ghana as contributing to a new "rights footprint," which mobilized the community and other actors over a lengthy period of time.[73] The focus in

[69] Balkin and Siegel, "Principles, Practices and Social Movements," *supra* note 63, 948.

[70] E.g., Lucie White, "Subordination, Rhetorical Survival Skills and Sunday Shoes: Notes on the Hearing of Mrs G," 38 Buff. L. Rev. 1 (1990).

[71] David M. Engel and Frank W. Munger, *Rights of Inclusion: Law and Identity in the Life Stories of Americans with Disabilities* (2003).

[72] E.g., Patricia Ewick and Susan Silbey, *The Common Place of Law: Stories from Everyday Life* (1998) 45, 224–6.

[73] Perelman and Young, "Rights as Footprints", *supra* note 15.

this section is how a change in legal consciousness corresponds with a change in law.

The LRC story highlights the importance of framing for social movements. Sociologists devised the concept of framing as a way to convey the effects of the terms of a discourse on how social actors interpret, understand, and express their interests.[74] A frame creates an interpretive field, a way of parsing a problem that can attract support and discredit opposition. Applying the frame of rights to a condition such as hunger may help to foreground the social-structural causes of the problem (or, in normative terms, disclose an entrenched injustice), and suggest different objects of recourse or remedy.[75] Economic and social rights claims are vehicles by which social actors, agitating for the protection of their material interests, convey how their condition or treatment is unacceptably damaging to their dignity, why it is a wrong, why others must take notice, and which actors bear or share responsibility.

In framing their complaints, social movements create and communicate stories, and with these stories they help to form a collective memory of an injustice and a different rights consciousness. A coherent narrative forms the background for new interpretations of, and new support for, economic and social rights. Stories of injustice or grievance fuel heightened moments of politics, and may produce a shared memory that sustains long-term community support. When constitutional scholars discuss constitutional moments,[76] and legal mobilization scholars discuss focal points,[77] they are often describing the same frame-based jurisgenerative phenomena. Constitutional moments occur when deep understandings of norms of law undergo shifts, often sustaining constitutive commitments in legislation or formal constitutional change. Focal points occur when movements mobilize around a single issue or event, driving on renewed energy and resources. When contestations occur over constitutional rights, these movements can be understood as a part of these two phenomena.

In her work on *The Faces of Injustice*, Judith Shklar described the importance of the translation of a private misfortune into an injustice.[78] In Shklar's example, once the political roots of the Irish potato famine of the nineteenth century were uncovered, the understanding of starvation dramatically

[74] David A. Snow, "Framing Processes, Ideology, and Discursive Fields," in Snow et al. *supra* note 1, 380.

[75] *See* the steps of this argument, Chapter 2, section A(2). *See also* Katharine G. Young, "Freedom, Want and Economic and Social Rights: Frame and Law," 24 Maryland J. Int'l. L. 182 (2009).

[76] Bruce Ackerman, *We the People: Foundations* (1991) 266–7.

[77] Michael W. McCann, *Rights at Work: Pay Equity Reform and the Politics of Legal Mobilization* (1994).

[78] Judith N. Shklar, *The Faces of Injustice* (1990).

changed. The misfortunes wrought by drought were suddenly understood in light of the agricultural and political–economic decisions that preceded the famine, and the decision-makers who became aware of it and yet did not take steps to end it. Shklar's insights on the political causes of famine apply to more recent infringements of economic and social rights caused by undemocratic background conditions, such as in India.[79] As Jean Drèze has described, new democratic politics around the right to food may be sufficient to call attention to this injustice, and prevent famine from occurring, without any judicial enforcement. But it is Shklar's commentary on translation that bears significance for our present discussion. Economic and social rights provide a frame for a political narrative of responsibility and accountability.[80]

The success of the economic and social rights frame articulated from constitutional law, and international human rights law, is threefold.[81] First, it establishes a universalized language that differs from a particularist assertion of the satisfaction of the human needs specific to one or another individual or group. We might say that this universalism is postnational, because it signals the importance of common interests across different countries' arrangements and across the varied experiences of particular groups within them. Hence, the shared minimum of resources established by the implementation of economic and social rights extends to everyone. In this way, the frame of rights, rather than of religion, race, national origin, or class can unify the claims of a diverse group that may be grappling with a systemic problem from different perspectives.[82] Of course, during the recruitment of a movement around economic and social rights, there may be a degree of separation associated with the experience of socioeconomic marginalization and urgent economic need. Yet the language of claim-making invited by economic and social rights is open to all.

The universalism of rights claiming reflects—and confronts—an age-old problem of distributive politics: that political power usually corresponds with economic power, and that political disadvantage usually corresponds to economic disadvantage. This fact applies to both well-established democratic settings, where serious material deprivations may be confined to a minority, and to low-income (and often new) democracies, in which

[79] Amartya Sen, *Poverty and Famines* (1981).

[80] Ibid.; *see also* Jean Drèze, "Democracy and the Right to Food," in Philip Alston and Mary Robinson (eds.), *Human Rights and Development: Towards Mutual Reinforcement* (2005) 45, 57–8.

[81] These are enumerated in more detail in Young, "Freedom, Want and Economic and Social Rights," *supra* note 75.

[82] E.g., Jennifer Gordon, *Suburban Sweatshops: The Fight for Immigrant Rights* (2005) 162–6 (suggesting the ways in which rights worked to unite and motivate a Latino immigrant group more effectively than faith traditions or class solidarity).

deprivation may be experienced by a majority in an increasingly unresponsive state.[83] It has been demonstrated that by fashioning universalist programs, which only implicitly target particular groups, redistributive claims improve their prospects for success in the United States.[84] Directly distributive contestations attract stigma towards claimant groups—creating apathy at best, and backlash at worst, in those required to transfer resources. When the frame is drawn so that all are cast as equally worthy or entitled to resource minimums, political support is more likely to be maintained. Universalism within redistributive politics is an innovation of international human rights declarations and treaties, and of constitutional rights. This redistributive politics may be shared with other emancipatory agendas and codes, but is settled within the powerful discourse of rights.

Secondly, the frame of economic and social rights establishes a claimant–duty-holder relationship that is different from the frames provided by other distributive contestations, such as those calling for the satisfaction of "basic needs" or the urgent attainment of certain "development goals."[85] To concede a right to food, water, housing, education, or medical care is to affirm a duty or responsibility on someone's part—whether individuals or institutions—to work to secure it. Such an implication is absent from the vocabulary of needs, which offers a more passive and supplicant plea to meet certain material requirements without the (admittedly more difficult) prescription of how such needs must be addressed and by whom.[86]

Unlike needs claims, rights attribute agency to both claimant and duty-holder. Within international human rights law, the duty-holder is assumed to be the state, which is in charge of both agreeing to obligations and of using its legal system to direct private actors to respect such rights. Within constitutional law, the state's obligation is understood in much the same way: either as a direct provider of basic goods and services, or as a regulator of the private relations that may help or hinder access to those goods and services.

Thirdly, the frame of normativity provided by the rights to food, health, housing, or education is not extra-legal or legal-skeptic. Just as the claims of economic and social rights are addressed to the state, while maintaining a

[83] E.g., Peter P. Houtzager, "Introduction: From Polycentrism to the Polity," in Peter P. Houtzager and Mick Moore (eds.), *Changing Paths: International Development and the New Politics of Inclusion* (2003) 1.

[84] For an early example, *see* Theda Skocpol, *Protecting Soldiers and Mothers: The Political Origins of Social Policy in the United States* (1992) 44 (describing the dependence, before the New Deal, of "cross-class distributions rather than . . . class-oriented categorical measures"). Skocpol concedes the difference in the path to European social democracy and the United States: ibid. at 48.

[85] *See* United Nations Millennium Declaration, G.A. Res. 55/2, UN Doc. A/RES/55/2 (18 September 2000); *see also* UN Millennium Development Goals, *available at* <http://www.un.org/millenniumgoals> (last visited June 2012).

[86] Waldron, "Rights and Needs," *supra* note 5.

focus on other institutions, they also address law. This relationship is often overlooked, as commentators of economic marginalization have sought to prove their radicalism by advocating disengagement from the law, purporting to identify an alternative emancipatory possibility outside of current legal arrangements, and thus to create a politics immune from cooptation or domination.[87] The recommendation to maintain localized projects towards material security within civil society, and outside of the state, is a prime example.[88]

Too often, radicalism of this kind conflates the (sometimes) demobilizing effect of litigation with the effect of law itself.[89] In the current environment, such skepticism misfires. The widespread influence of neoliberal ideology, accompanied by projects of privatization and deregulation, has in many places diminished access to economic and social protections and the responsiveness of the state.[90] While the chastening of this agenda, and the recent global financial crisis, may have cooled the enthusiasm for these projects, it has not led to greater protections.[91] Under these conditions, an antistate, antilaw agenda provides no resources with which to counteract the further evisceration of the state. Indeed, the relegation of the aspiration to material security to an "extra-legal" space would do nothing to halt the diminishing access to certain goods and services and would probably accelerate it.[92]

Instead, the frame of economic and social rights continues to hold the state responsible for its delivery of entitlement or, conversely for the way in which it confers rights, privileges, and immunities on private actors. In administrative, educational, or even disruptive terms, the politics of economic and social rights inevitably involve law and cannot absolutely shun litigation. Rather, effective agents of change deploy economic and social rights in pragmatic and innovative ways.[93]

[87] For a response to the critique, *see* Orly Lobel, "The Paradox of Extralegal Activism: Critical Legal Consciousness and Transformative Politics," 120 Harv. L. Rev. 937 (2007) (refuting the cooptation critique as specifically cogent to legal strategies).

[88] Ibid., 962–6 (citing examples from the localized global movements of "glocalization" and civil society revivalism).

[89] For a diagnosis of this tendency that remains pertinent, *see* Alan Hunt, "Rights and Social Movements: Counter-Hegemonic Strategies," 17 J. L. & Soc'y 309 (1990).

[90] *See* Special Rapporteur on the Realization of Economic, Social and Cultural Rights, Danilo Türk, *The Realization of Economic, Social and Cultural Rights*, delivered to the UN Econ. & Soc. Council, UN Doc. E/CN.4/Sub.2/1992/16 (3 July 1992). *See also* World Bank, *The World Bank Group's Response to the Global Crisis: Update on an Ongoing IEG Evaluation (Evaluation Brief 8)*, Independent Evaluation Group (2009).

[91] E.g, "Concluding Observations on Spain by the Committee on Economic, Social and Cultural Rights," UN Doc. E/C.12/ESP/CO/5 (18 May 2012), *available at* <http://www2.ohchr.org/English/bodies/cescr/cescrs48.htm>.

[92] E.g., Frank I. Michelman, "W(h)ither the Constitution," 21 Cardozo L. Rev. 1062 (2000) 1081.

[93] For a collection of notable examples, *see* White and Perelman, *supra* note 15 (presenting examples from Ghana, Kenya, Nigeria, South Africa, and Tanzania).

C. BEYOND POPULAR CONSTITUTIONALISM

Jurisgenesis, as a theory of legal change that emphasizes social and cultural change, offers a powerful set of explanations for the role of social movements in constituting economic and social rights. Movements are temporary—their energy dissipates, and what can be achieved during their moment of mobilization is important. Yet movements do not enjoy a linear path to institutional success. Their cultural focus faces challenges in both institutional and counter-cultural terms.

The first is that movements are sometimes ill-equipped to address the institutional questions that arise, as soon as the enforcement or implementation of rights is required. Their emphasis on symbolism and cultural change can sometimes detract from the details and reforms required for institutional change. In similar terms, there is an inability, on the part of commentators, to accord an equivalence to a movement's quest for recognition, and its quest for redistribution.[94] Due to the historical sidelining of economic and social rights, as against civil and political rights, observers in the fields of constitutional law and international human rights law have pursued a research program which privileges the identity-based and/or anti-repressive goals of movements, and equates redistributive movements as merely interest groups. These challenges, of observation and perception, present considerable barriers to understanding social movement success for economic and social rights. Secondly, movements inevitably produce countermovements, which may challenge the principles and reforms using the same tactics, and sometimes even the same rights discourse. It is to these features that this section turns.

(1) *Cultural versus institutional change*

A "jurisgenerative" vision of economic and social rights appears to avoid the institutional problems of judge-centered rights and remedies, by locating a gradual cultural change that takes place during an intensive movement effort both inside and outside of courts. The promise of this theory is that it frees movements to persuade others of what constitutional terms mean, and whether their status-based or distributive claims are included. Yet in reaching for the heights of normative ambition, those who describe jurisgenesis may fail to give due respect to the institutional features that are at the center of the claims of economic and social rights.

[94] For a well-known presentation of this distinction, *see* Nancy Fraser and Axel Honneth, *Recognition or Redistribution? A Political-Philosophical Exchange* (2003).

Whether the protection of economic and social rights calls for poor relief, social security, publicly financed hospitals, schools, railways or roads, changes to the background structures of property and contract, ex post requirements for home mortgage contracts or ex ante regulation of their terms, or public access to preventive antiretrovirals, our social institutions are both the barriers and the vehicles.[95] As remedies or as programs, law-creation in the area of economic and social rights is about the hard work of institutional creation or reform. From this viewpoint, jurisgenesis has far too much faith in the constitutional imaginary, and far too little (institutional) realism.

Of course, the institutional omission is deliberate: movements, for jurisgenesis, are pre-institutional or extra-institutional; law itself seems to float free as a system of meanings rather than a system of institutions backed by sanctions.[96] But the focus on cultural change, rather than institutional change, has other explanations. Social movements are wary of cooption and dilution from the state. This is well documented, and recalls our redemptive and rejectionist frames discussed above. Moreover, the movements described within the literature on jurisgenesis are invariably identity-based in form, favoring tactics of recognition, rather than of redistribution. Wariness of, and a certain blindness to, the necessity of institutional change, risk sidelining the lessons of popular constitutionalism in the politics of economic and social rights.

The popular social movements of the West have favored an identity politics that fits more easily within present judicial and legislative constraints than a more openly distributive politics would allow. Again, US constitutional theory provides an example. The positive theories of those writing about "jurisgenesis" provide little space for the welfare rights movement,[97] which met with failures, both ideological and institutional, in the United States. Lawyers who had organized around a constitutional "right to welfare" suffered major setbacks in the 1970s, and the civil rights formula of spearheading litigation and civil disobedience did not prove successful.[98] Despite a clear connection between welfare rights and the Constitution—Jacobus

[95] E.g., John Rawls, *A Theory of Justice* (1971); *cf.* Liam Murphy, "Institutions and the Demands of Justice," 27 *Phil. & Pub. Aff.* (1999).

[96] Cover, "Nomos and Narrative," *supra* note 44; Siegel, "Text in Context," *supra* note 42, 317–18.

[97] For example, Reva Siegel does not, in her survey of US movements in constitutional law, discuss the welfare rights movement: Reva B. Siegel, "The Jurisgenerative Role of Social Movements in United States Constitutional Law," paper presented at Harvard Law School Public Law Workshop, (2004). William Eskridge includes a short discussion of the welfare movement and its demise: Eskridge, "Some Effects," *supra* note 64, 2261–2.

[98] *See* Martha F. Davis, *Brutal Need: Lawyers and the Welfare Rights Movement, 1960–1973* (1993); *See also* Forbath, "Constitutional Welfare Rights," *supra* note 68, 1838.

tenBroek, for example, had worked to mobilize around the constitutional requirement of a "right to live"[99]—the hostility of courts and other legal actors was not overcome. That is not to say that the welfare rights movement did not enjoy other successes: in uniting African American women to become the rank and file of a new social movement, and in introducing a new, citizenship-based reading of socioeconomic protections.[100]

Identity politics strives for recognition: if won, redistribution may follow. Of course, claims of recognition or status (symbolic capital) and economic wealth (economic capital) are fundamentally related.[101] Yet the hierarchy of these arguments ensures rights come before remedies; normative argument follows this hierarchy, and this hierarchy has proved successful in the courts.[102] Many constitutional scholars are committed to this approach, finding narrowly defined liberty interests are more resonant than other interests on strategic grounds.[103]

The rub is that recognition claims resemble symbolic claims, and recognition gains can be "purely" symbolic. There are long-standing criticisms of the harms that apparently beneficial symbols do to groups experiencing the material consequences of prejudice and inequality.[104] Status harms may be more intractable than the cure of recognition allows. In his famous study, *An American Dilemma*, economist Gunnar Myrdal suggested the "vicious circle" of poverty and inequality based on race in America, should be addressed by reversing the negative stereotypes that white Americans had applied to African Americans.[105] The study informed the arguments of the advocates and of the US Supreme Court in its ruling on the desegregation of schools, in *Brown*.[106] Nonetheless, this emphasis failed to address the more intractable forms of discrimination that contributed to material inequality.[107] *Brown's*

[99] Edward V. Sparer, *The Right to Welfare*, in Norman Dorsen (ed), *The Rights of Americans: What They Are—What They Should Be* (1971).

[100] Felicia Kornbluh, *The Battle for Welfare Rights: Politics and Poverty in Modern America* (2007).

[101] Pierre Bourdieu, *Distinction: A Social Critique of the Judgement of Taste* (Richard Nice trans., 1984) (1979).

[102] *See*, e.g., J. M. Balkin, "The Constitution of Status," 106 Yale L.J. 2313 (1997).

[103] Eskridge, "Some Effects," *supra* note 64.

[104] Derrick Bell, *And We Are Not Saved, The Elusive Quest For Racial Justice* (1989); Michael J. Klarman, *Brown v. Board of Education and the Civil Rights Movement* (2007) (study of movement); *see also* e.g., Michael J. Klarman, *From Jim Crow to Civil Rights: The Supreme Court and the Struggle for Racial Equality* (2004) (study of court).

[105] Gunnar Myrdal, *An American Dilemma: the Negro Problem and Modern Democracy* (1944).

[106] *Brown v. Board of Education*, 347 U.S. 483 (1954).

[107] *See* the criticism of Alan Freeman, "Antidiscrimination Law from 1954 to 1989: Uncertainty, Contradiction, Rationalization, Denial," in David Kairys (ed.), *The Politics of Law: A Progressive Critique* (3rd edn., 1998) 285, 306–7.

inability to disrupt the pronounced link between educational disadvantage and economic disadvantage, and ground more ambitious strategies for economic justice, has grown ever more evident over time.[108]

When legislative or judicial victories occur without additional remediation, the energy of a movement can quickly dissipate. Symbolic gains, whether through courts or through legislatures, can appear empty and fraudulent without institutional reform.[109] This leads to the inescapable irony of movement success: that active defeat may be energizing, whereas formal victory (and passive defeat) can destroy the spontaneous and ever-fragile energy of a movement.[110] An understanding of the intertwinement of both recognition and redistribution, and of cultural change and institutional change, is required before the aspects of failure and success in economic and social rights social movements can be adequately appreciated.

(2) *Countermovements and other forms of backlash*

As we have seen in Part I, rights may be Janus-faced: they are open to multiple interpretations that may support or resist the protection of fundamental material interests. Just as the abstract concept of rights sustains multiple meanings, contestations around rights can promote supportive or resistance movements that adopt a contesting rights discourse. The dynamics of backlash are well studied in social movement and constitutional theory.

Thus, it has been observed that when certain legal principles become "unstuck,"[111] other movements become invigorated to resettle them. This brings an unpredictable direction to the success of movements. Some scholars attribute success to the injection of greater democracy into the practice of constitutionalism, rather than the satisfaction of the movement's own demands.[112] Yet if we explore the results of contestation and "meaning making" in seeking the protection of fundamental material interests, and

[108] Martha Minow, *In Brown's Wake: Legacies of America's Educational Landmark* (2010) 81–3, 90–5; *see also San Antonio Indep. Sch. Dist. v. Rodriguez*, 411 U.S. 1 (1973) (USSC declining to find education a fundamental right).

[109] Lani Guinier, "The Triumph of Tokenism: The Voting Rights Act and the Theory of Black Electoral Success," 89 Mich. L. Rev. 1077 (1991) 1083.

[110] Stuart A. Scheingold, *The Politics of Rights: Lawyers, Public Policy, and Political Change* (1974) 6–7.

[111] Balkin and Siegel, "Principles, Practices and Social Movements," *supra* note 63, 929. *See also* J. M. Balkin, "Ideological Drift and the Struggle over Meaning," 25 Conn. L. Rev. 869 (1993) 870.

[112] Robert Post and Reva B. Siegel, "*Roe* Rage: Democratic Constitutionalism and Backlash," 42 Harv. C. R.-C.L. L. Rev. 373 (2007) (canvassing the potentially constructive features of backlash).

support a theory of democracy that protects basic minimums, this measure becomes a more controversial one.[113]

The backlash may come from a countermovement; conservative movements may mobilize against progressive interpretations of the constitution; pro-property groups may mobilize against pro-poor groups. Backlash may also come from the professional legal field, when judges or officials contend that a movement's gains have gone too far.[114] (In the latter case, the gains to democracy, both procedural and substantive, are more ambivalent.)

At a practical level, success in claiming economic and social rights in one area, such as health, can bring heated opposition to the "slippery slope" of other claims of social protection; or can energize different movements that may overburden the claims of economic and social rights. Clean air advocates may line up against workers in contesting air pollution laws: both may have a theory of the right to health behind them, through either the air they breathe or the food and medical care that they can afford through employment. School choice movements and integration movements may agitate for rights in education with vastly different agendas. Health rights groups might line up against housing rights groups, perceiving the constituency to be too different, or the reason for injustice too distant.

Moreover, backlash may come from official quarters. Underlying popular constitutionalism is a complex relation between (often minority) social movements, majority opinion, legislative opinion, and judicial opinion. This relation is never linear, although legislative and judicial opinion is never wildly out of step with majority opinion. The history of the rights of the South African Constitution demonstrates this nonlinearity. The text of the Constitution was informed by social movement activity, although the intensity or robustness of the debates was not itself determinative.[115] For example, of the major public issues at the time of the drafting of the Constitution—support for the death penalty, opposition to South Africa as a secular state, opposition to the legalization of abortion, opposition to including sexual orientation in the antidiscrimination clause, support for the protection of animal rights, and support for the right to firearms—only

[113] Consider discussion of "success," *supra* Chapter 5, section C. *Compare* the equality and school choice movements that coalesce around demands for educational opportunity in the US, and the very distinct implications for democracy in their demands, discussed in Minow, *supra* note 108, 116–37.

[114] Eskridge, "Some Effects," *supra* note 64, 2401 (describing judicial backlash in a model of law as equilibrium).

[115] Hassen Ebrahim, *The Soul of a Nation: Constitution-making in South Africa* (1998) (recounting the written or oral submissions, public meetings, Constitutional Assembly talk line, Internet, popularized newspaper (*Constitutional Talk*), with programs debated on public television and radio in the process of constitution-making in South Africa. The Constitutional Assembly received more than 2 million submissions, mostly as signatures of petitions.).

one was entrenched in the Constitution: that of including Afrikaans as an official language. The others were left for the legislature or the courts to decode and decide. In the end, the Constitutional Court decided some of the Constitution's public issues contrary to majority popular opinion.[116] In an important example of other social movement activity, for example, the Court addressed a series of strategic cases brought by organizations from the gay and lesbian movement and individuals challenging sexual orientation discrimination.[117] These outcomes were still considerably distant from majority public support, but were buttressed by the negotiated text of the Constitution, as well as a well-resourced and strategic social movement, backed by strong international networks. It is worthwhile to return to the economic and social rights jurisprudence in South Africa, presented in Chapters 5 and 6, using the social movement lens.

D. THE ROLE OF SOCIAL MOVEMENTS FOR ECONOMIC AND SOCIAL RIGHTS: SOUTH AFRICA

Chapters 5 and 6 of this book focused on the South African Constitutional Court's role in leading the enforcement of economic and social rights. Yet the contribution of social movements to the economic and social rights jurisprudence has also been key; indeed the success or failure of each case has often tracked the presence or absence of a social movement. In the first case involving the right to health care, Mr. Soobramoney represented his own interests in his appeal to the Constitutional Court, turning to (somewhat reluctant) lawyers after his financial resources for private care were exhausted.[118] He attracted no significant social or organizational support from dialysis patients in similar positions.[119] While the second case, *Grootboom*,[120] involving the right to housing, was noticeably distinct, a similar dynamic of absence in movement support was present. Indeed, the failure of

[116] *See, e.g.*, *S. v. Makwanyane* 1995 (3) SA 391 (CC) (overturning death penalty).

[117] *National Coalition for Gay and Lesbian Equality v. Minister of Justice* 1999 (1) SA 6 (CC) (Court holding criminalization of sodomy constituted unfair discrimination); e.g., *Satchwell v. President of the Republic of South Africa* 2003 (4) SA 266 (CC) (holding an unfair exclusion of same-sex couples from judges' pensions); *Du Toit v. Minister for Welfare and Population Development* 2003 (2) SA 198 (CC) (finding provisions which limited joint adoption to married people to the exclusion of same-sex couples unconstitutional); *Minister of Home Affairs v. Fourie* 2006 (1) SA 524 (CC) (requiring state to legislate for same-sex marriage); *see also* Civil Union Act, No. 17 of 2006 (S. Afr.).

[118] *Soobramoney v. Minister of Health, Kwazulu-Natal* 1998 (1) SA 765 (CC).

[119] This can be contrasted with the mobilization around the issue of renal dialysis (amongst veterans) in the United States, leading to successful legislative support. This provision of renal dialysis has for a long time varied widely among countries. Guido Calabresi and Philip Bobbitt, *Tragic Choices* (1978).

[120] *S. v. Grootboom* 2001 (1) SA 46 (CC).

the *Grootboom* case to provide a remedy directly to the claimants (despite its proclaimed success for other housing beneficiaries and indeed other economic and social rights claimants[121]) has been attributed to the lack of organization within and for Irene Grootboom's Wallacedene community.[122] Lawyers from the Community Law Centre of the University of the Western Cape, with the LRC in South Africa, acted for the community, free of charge, but they were appointed without social movement support. Once the Constitutional Court made its declaration in favor of the claimants, the Wallacedene community was left without means to exert pressure on those responsible to deliver or to monitor remedies. While the South African Human Rights Commission participated in the hearing and was given a monitoring responsibility in the remedy, the claimants were not able to see any change to their situation for many years after their court success.

Nonetheless, the *Grootboom* case did catalyze other social movements in approaching the Court, especially in relation to housing and health care contestations. The Treatment Action Campaign, for example, brought the next case, after *Grootboom*, after engaging with nonlegal strategies in progressing the right to health care: strategies described in Chapter 9. Other movements organized around the right to housing began in several urban areas in South Africa. A network of "radical poor people's movements" now employ some of the strategies of protest and claiming that are described above with respect to the Nima community in Ghana. In Cape Town, the Western Cape Anti-Eviction Campaign emerged in November 2000, claiming the right to housing, and an array of other demands.[123] In Durban, the Abahlali baseMjondolo shack dwellers' movement emerged in 2005 with a significant focus on the injustice presently experienced by the poor in South Africa.[124]

These movements draw their membership from many of the most desperately poor South Africans. Despite the lack of resources, organizers maintain active websites and e-mail list servers. With these and other electronic resources, they communicate with their members and broadcast their efforts.[125] The stories told, and notices posted, express grievances in the context of a coherent vision of the South African Constitution. For

[121] *See*, e.g., Sandra Liebenberg, *Socio-Economic Rights: Adjudication under a Transformative Constitution* (2010) 303ff.

[122] Claire Horton, "Interview with Geoff Budlender: Basic Needs: Enforcing Constitutional Rights," Naledi Policy Bulletin (November 2002) 6.

[123] *See* <http://antieviction.org.za/about-us/> (describing the group as "formed in November of 2000 with the aim of fighting evictions, water cut-offs and poor health services, obtaining free electricity, securing decent housing, and opposing police brutality").

[124] *See* Abahlali website, *available at* <http://www.abahlali.org/>.

[125] *See*, e.g., Anti-Eviction Campaign, *available at* <http://antieviction.org.za/about-us/>.

Abahlali baseMjondolo, for example, the movement is organized around the rights of shack dwellers—indeed, all city dwellers—to participate in the decisions which affect their lives. Litigation is a strategy, and, if the timing and rhetoric is a guide, the Constitutional Court has catalyzed the movement in its broader strategies as well.[126]

One example of this constitutional influence was the protest by the Abahlali movement against proposed provincial legislation that would have greatly expanded government powers to evict shack dwellers.[127] In 2007, Abahlali engaged in Town Hall meetings to critique the proposed Slums Act and to work out a campaign. In March, they sent a delegation to the provincial legislature on the public hearings on the Bill. By September, several thousand marched against the Bill. During these protests, the movement took legal advice from the LRC in South Africa and the Centre for Applied Legal Studies ("CALS"), a public interest law unit connected to the University of Witswatersrand.[128] Despite the constitutional experience of these organizations, the movement reported that it was the community, not the lawyers, that led the action. The website publicity noted that "[w]hen our lawyers step into court they will not only be carrying the hopes of thousands of people but they will also be guided by the thinking done in our communities."[129]

When KwaZulu-Natal, contrary to the protests, enacted the Slums Act, Abahlali lodged a High Court action to declare the legislation unconstitutional. At the same time, the movement called "for a Housing Summit at which all democratic shack dwellers' organizations can negotiate a new partnership and new Act with government."[130] When the arguments, which failed in the provincial High Court, reached the Constitutional Court, the movement organized a mass march, with other members of the poor people's alliance, "to see and to witness the will of the people being brought forward in front of the highest Court in the land."[131] One reporter described members of the group at the steps of the Constitutional Court, "singing, dancing and heralding the Constitution as their 'bible'."[132]

[126] Brian Ray, "Demosprudence in Comparative Perspective," 47 Stan. J. Int'l. L. 111 (2011).

[127] The KwaZulu-Natal Elimination and Prevention of Re-Emergence of Slums Bill 2006.

[128] CALS brought the anti-eviction litigation in *Olivia Road* and its lawyers had negotiated the first "meaningful engagement" remedy.

[129] <http://antieviction.org.za/about-us/>.

[130] Ibid.

[131] <http://www.abahlali.org/node/5959>.

[132] Niren Tolsi, "Shack Dwellers' Victory Bus," *Mail & Guardian*, 24 May 2009, *available at* <http://abahlali.org/node/5293>.

In delivering judgment, the Constitutional Court held that the Slums Act was unconstitutional, noting that "eviction can take place only after reasonable engagement." In applying *Olivia Road*,[133] the Court held that such engagement would require "taking into proper consideration the wishes of the people who are to be evicted; whether the areas where they live may be upgraded in situ; and whether there will be alternative accommodation."[134] The movement's leader, Sbu Zikode, declared that the decision validated the movement's "role as protector of the Constitution, and a champion of the rights of the ordinary people of South Africa."[135] In the face of what was described as an ANC-led backlash and violence, the movement held a celebration. Its intentions were pluralist and jurisgenerative: "[t]he reason we are having this rally of celebration is so that the judgment can be read, discussed, analyzed and provide a way forward."[136]

The members of Abahlali have argued that "[t]he modes, language, jargon, concerns, times and places of a genuinely democratic and democratizing politics must be those in which the poor are powerful and not those in which they are silenced as they are named and directed from without."[137] This language is forged in moral terms:

> Our struggle is for the moral questions, as compared to the political questions as such. It is more about justice, it is more about moral questions . . . is it good for the shack dwellers to live in the mud like pigs, as they are living? Why do I have to live in a cardboard house if there are people who are able to live in a decent house? So it's a moral question.[138]

The community's ownership of its discourse, the targeted use of constitutional litigation, and the many references to constitutional principles together demonstrate the constraints and promises of a social movement seeking to transform the meaning of economic and social rights. What one commentator has described as a form of democratization can also be seen as portraying the radical spirit of jurisgenesis, the disturbance of orthodoxies, and the framing of injustice. Discussion at meetings is necessary: "There is no other way to build and sustain popular consent for a risky political

[133] *Occupiers of 51 Olivia Road v. City of Johannesburg*, 2008 (3) SA 208 (CC).

[134] *Abahlali baseMjondolo Movement of South Africa and Another v. Premier of the Province of KwaZulu-Natal*, 2010 (2) BCLR 99 (CC) [114].

[135] Gerhard Kienast, "Abahlali baseMjondolo—how poor people's struggle for land and housing became a struggle for democracy," 19 June 2010, *available at* <http://suedafrika.habitants.de/?p=15>.

[136] <http://www.abahlali.org/node/5959>

[137] "Anti-Eviction Campaign: Rethinking Public Participation from Below," *available at* <http://antieviction.org.za/related-writing-and-resources/rethinking-public-participation-from-below/>.

[138] S'bu Zikode, cited in Xin Wei Ngiam, "Taking Poverty Seriously: What the Poor Are Saying and Why It Matters," *available at* <http://abahlali.org/node/27>.

project amongst a hugely diverse group of vulnerable people with profound experiences of marginalisation and exploitation in multiple spheres of life, including political projects waged in their name."[139]

Economic and social rights offers a powerful discourse for social movements, and this chapter has described the anatomy of such movements that help to constitute such rights. Such movements effect social change through the jurisgenerative effects of organizing and litigation, assisted by the universalizable frame and discipline of economic and social rights. Of course, we must not romanticize these movements, nor assume that they are uniform.[140] Internal dissent, political missteps, and backlash are present; and there is no unified formula for success. Other collectivities contesting economic and social rights appear very different from the community-based LRC of Ghana or the Abahlali movement of South Africa. The International Network for Economic, Social and Cultural Rights lists 183 organizations from 67 different countries within its membership, which includes NGOs, social movements, and indigenous and grassroots groups.[141] Some contest a broad spectrum of economic and social rights, like the LRC in Ghana (and the LRC in South Africa); others focus on one right in particular, such as housing, education, or health care. Transnational linkages often support their efforts. Moreover, US-based international human rights NGOs, traditionally focused on civil and political rights and unwelcoming to economic and social rights, have expanded the advocacy efforts to economic and social rights.[142] Amnesty International now seeks to contest rights to food, health care, housing, and education across its international constituencies.[143] Much depends on background legal institutions, and background ideologies and interests. For a more institutional explanation of the movement's success, we must turn to the theories of governance.

[139] "Shack Dwellers on the Move in Durban," 141 *Radical Philosophy* (2007), *available at* <http://abahlali.org/node/871>.

[140] Tshepo Madlingozi, "Post-Apartheid Social Movements and the Quest for the Elusive 'New' South Africa," 34 J. of Law & Soc. 77 (2007).

[141] <http://www.escr-net.org/members/> (accessed June 2012). The South African AIDS Law Project, for example, extended its commitment to all economic and social rights, rather than just health, and was incorporated into the new center, "SECTION27" in 2010.

[142] *Compare* the early reluctance: Kenneth Roth, "Defending Economic, Social and Cultural Rights: Practical Issues Faced by an International Human Rights Organization," 26 Hum. Rts. Q. 63 (2004); Leonard S. Rubenstein, "How International Human Rights Organizations Can Advance Economic, Social, and Cultural Rights: A Response to Kenneth Roth," 26 Hum. Rts. Q. 845 (2004).

[143] *See*, e.g., <http://www.amnestyusa.org/our-work/campaigns/demand-dignity> (accessed April 2012).

9

The Governance Function of Economic and Social Rights

Many actors outside of courts, outside of the elected branches of government, and outside of social movements, help to define and constitute economic and social rights. So far, our focus suggests that actors engage economic and social rights in separate sites of interpretation and contestation. In this chapter, I explore how the economic and social rights discourse links these different actors, and how these linkages create a governance regime for economic and social rights. In particular, I track the role of market actors in contesting the terms of economic and social rights, and suggest ways in which they may play a constructive role. We will begin with another case study, this time from South Africa and the right to health care.

A. PROLOGUE: THE RIGHT TO HEALTH IN SOUTH AFRICA

South Africa's constitutional guarantee of the right to have access to health care has been litigated on several occasions. In 2002, the South African Constitutional Court, in the case of *Minister of Health v. Treatment Action Campaign*,[1] held that one part of the South African government's policy on HIV/AIDS infringed the constitutional right to health care. The apparent success of the case, in producing a legal declaration from the Constitutional Court that children born to mothers with HIV/AIDS must be protected, as far as medically possible, from the transmission of the disease during childbirth, helps us to understand the role of courts in constituting economic and social rights. Like the other cases discussed in this book, *TAC* forces us to rethink our assumptions about a state's ability to deliver guaranteed social protection, in the form of rights, and does so in the challenging domain of

[1] 2002 (5) SA 721 (CC) ("*TAC*"). The case was brought by the social movement, the Treatment Action Campaign, also known as "TAC." This chapter uses the acronym to refer to the case, rather than the movement.

health care. It invites reflection on the involvement of courts in that guarantee, and in shaping its delivery. It shows how social movements contribute to the "creation" of economic and social rights, just as economic and social rights contribute to the "creation" of social movements, as we saw in Chapter 8. And it reveals how a myriad of public and private actors become involved in the contestation, and ultimate determination, of the meaning of economic and social rights.

Almost a decade later, *TAC* has become a familiar case in the comparative constitutional literature on economic and social rights. So far, it has been treated as paradigmatic of an unstable compromise in the judicial review of economic and social rights: the Constitutional Court delivered an apparently strong form of review in a deferential guise, and an apparently negative mode of remedy accompanied by positive decree. These features mark out the catalytic role conception, discussed in Chapter 6, and suggest both a conceptual and practical triumph for the judicial review of economic and social rights. Conceptually, the Court's favored mode of reasonableness review, and its multilayered and revisable order, was able to bridge powerful dichotomies in relation to the positive and negative obligations attached to economic and social rights. Practically, the Court also brought an end to the government's denialist position on HIV / AIDS. The effect was the saving of tens of thousands of lives.[2]

Yet the immense contribution made by the litigant social movement in the course of the *TAC* decision has largely gone unnoticed.[3] Properly understood, that contribution changes the parameters of the judicial review debate, as well as our overall understanding of the nature of the contestations behind economic and social rights. This chapter seeks to shift the gaze away from courts to the other actors who are involved in agitating for, litigating, and attempting to force compliance with economic and social rights. The *TAC* case underlines the importance of a focus on the social movement or movements that are mobilized for economic and social rights protection. This is a lesson that we learned in respect to the Ghanaian

[2] A Harvard study noted that 35,000 babies were born with HIV between 2000 and 2005 as a result of the South African government's decision not to implement a program to prevent mother-to-child transmission. Using modeling, the study estimated that against what was reasonably feasible in South Africa with ARV treatment or prophylaxis, at least 330,000 lives and a total of 3.8 million person-years were lost during that period: Pride Chigwedere et al., "Estimating the Lost Benefits of Antiretroviral Drug Use in South Africa," 49 *Aquir. Immune Defic. Syndr.* 410 (2008).

[3] There are exceptions. *See* William E. Forbath, "Realizing a Constitutional Social Right—Cultural Transformation, Deep Institutional Reform, and the Roles of Advocacy and Adjudication," in Jeremy Perelman and Lucie White (eds.), *Stones of Hope: How African Activists Reclaim Human Rights to Challenge Global Poverty* (2011); Mark Heywood, "Current Developments: Preventing Mother-to-Child HIV Transmission in South Africa: Background, Strategies and Outcomes of the Treatment Action Campaign Against the Minister of Health," 19 S. Afr. J. Hum. Rts. 278 (2003).

anti-user fees and the South African anti-eviction campaigns in Chapter 8.[4] But the *TAC* case also illuminates the links between networks of movements, different branches of government, experts, scientists, pharmaceutical companies, doctors, nurses, lawyers, organizers, churches, and provincial leaders. In this light, the transformation of the right to health care appears as a governance experiment.

The *TAC* case played out in the context of one of the most politicized issues facing postapartheid South Africa: the response to the HIV/AIDS crisis. A unanimous Court held that a feature of the government's program on HIV/AIDS, namely, a decision to restrict an early roll-out of the antiretrovirals ("ARVs") that would prevent mother-to-child transmission of HIV, was unreasonable and thus incompatible with the constitutional right to access health care. The case represented a success for the social movement that brought it—the Treatment Action Campaign—on behalf of the children who would be infected at birth by HIV without the ARVs. It gave critical support to a major overhaul of the African National Congress ("ANC") government's position on HIV and AIDS, and had wider radiating effects on the politics of health care, HIV/AIDS treatment, and the availability of medicines more generally.

The claims of the Treatment Action Campaign were opposed in the Constitutional Court by the Minister of Health and by equivalent representatives from South Africa's provinces. Although the case was viewed—by both the government and the Treatment Action Campaign—as a challenge to then-President Thabo Mbeki's AIDS policy,[5] it was not one in which the government represented a single actor. In fact, some of the executive councils responsible for health in nine provinces, which enjoy concurrent legislative competence in the provision of health services,[6] would later engage in their own attempts to provide the ARVs to pregnant women, thus detracting from the strength of the government's case.[7] A background position was that pharmaceutical companies, after an earlier campaign by the Treatment Action Campaign and other access-to-medicine activists, had agreed to donate five years' worth of ARVs to prevent mother-to-child transmission in South Africa.[8]

[4] The Treatment Action Campaign brought the suit with the Children's Rights Centre and a medical practitioner, Dr. Haroon Saloojee.

[5] Heywood, *supra* note 3, 299 (describing the attitude of both the government and the Treatment Action Campaign).

[6] Constitution of the Republic of South Africa Act 1996 (South Africa) ("S. Afr. Const."), ch. 3 (Cooperative Government); ch. 6 (Provinces), sch. 4.

[7] Heywood, *supra* note 3, 291, 303.

[8] Mark Heywood, "Can Campaigns to Prevent and Treat HIV and AIDS Revive and Strengthen Campaigns for the Right to Health, Access to Legal Services and Social Justice?" (manuscript, 2008), *available at* Treatment Action Campaign <http://www.tac.org.za/community>.

President Mbeki's position was, at the time, infamously accommodating of AIDS denialism. Sourced in a so-called "dissident's science," denialism emphasized social causes (including malnutrition and poverty) to explain the spread of AIDS in South Africa. This attitude, involving the denial of the medical link between HIV and AIDS, drew sharp criticism from medical and scientific communities.[9] And yet, for reasons that remain unclear, denialism influenced many high-level officials in the Mbeki administration.[10] In 2000, for example, President Mbeki issued a challenge to the science behind the etiology of the AIDS infection and the efficacy of its treatment through ARVs.[11] Nonetheless, when the case came before the Court, the government did not rely on denialism as part of its decision to restrict the ARVs to prevent mother-to-child transmission of HIV.[12] Instead, the government defended its position on the grounds that the effective provision of ARVs was unaffordable, that the efficacy and safety of the ARV at issue—Nevirapine—was not proven, and that its use would risk a negative impact on public health.[13]

Founded in 1998 by Zackie Achmat, an outspoken and charismatic campaigner in South Africa, the Treatment Action Campaign is well mobilized and politically astute. The movement operates through several hundred branches throughout South Africa, staffed by volunteers who include people living with HIV/AIDS and people supporting people living with HIV/AIDS.[14] With some 12,000 members, operating in 600 branches, the membership of Treatment Action Campaign is a fraction of the total number of the estimated 5 million people living with HIV and AIDS in South Africa. These "volunteers" are overwhelmingly black and poor: as its founder reports, its demographics "are 80 percent unemployed, 70 percent women ... 70 percent in the 14–24 age group and 90 percent African."[15]

[9] Jon Cohen, "AIDS Researchers Decry Mbeki's Views on HIV," 288 *Science* 590 (2000). The Mbeki administration took over from President Nelson Mandela upon his retirement in June 1999. It governed until September 2008.

[10] For a careful description of these politics, and an attempt at explanation, *see* Didier Fassin, *When Bodies Remember: Experiences and Politics of AIDS in South Africa* (2007).

[11] *See* Mbeki's letter to world leaders, 20 April 2000, BBC News, *available at* <http://news.bbc.co.uk/2/hi/africa/720448.stm> (excerpt of Mbeki's letter, which insisted that heterodox views on the science of HIV/AIDS could be important for understanding the course of the disease in Africa). The letter itself did not question the link between HIV and AIDS, although this position was held by the "dissidents" for whom Mbeki provided a forum: *see* Fassin, ibid., 8–9.

[12] Heywood, "Preventing Mother-to-Child HIV Transmission in South Africa," *supra* note 3, 282.

[13] *TAC*, 2002 (5) SA 721 (CC).

[14] The movement's "volunteers" usually live within the community represented by the branch. *See* Steven Friedman and Shauna Mottiar, *Rewarding Engagement?: The Treatment Action Campaign and the Politics of HIV/AIDS* (2004), A case study for the University of KwaZulu-Natal project, Globalisation, Marginalisation and New Social Movements in post-Apartheid South Africa, copy on file with author.

[15] Ibid, n. 59, citing Achmat.

Nevertheless, the Treatment Action Campaign also includes many white South Africans, often young and middle class, who are more likely to join because of moral concern, and who represent significant potential for cross-class alliances and tensions.[16] Nurses, doctors, and local councilors are encouraged to attend its meetings.

The Treatment Action Campaign's focus on the grassroots is combined with its collaboration with international human rights organizations, such as Doctors Without Borders/Médicins Sans Frontières. The movement was formed to "ensure access to affordable and quality treatment for people with HIV/AIDS," to "prevent and eliminate new HIV infections," and to "improve the affordability and quality of health-care access for all."[17] At its founding, the leadership of the Treatment Action Campaign expected that its work would be directed at the pharmaceutical industry, but it evolved, in Achmat's own words, to incorporate "a direct challenge to [President] Thabo Mbeki's outlandish views on the causes of AIDS and refusal to provide conventional treatment through the public health service despite South Africa having one of the highest HIV infection rates in the world."[18]

Litigation was not the first strategy considered by the Treatment Action Campaign in relation to the issue of preventing mother-to-child transmission of HIV: in fact, it was perceived by some within the movement as a disloyal and unpatriotic gesture.[19] The more typical methods for the Treatment Action Campaign include popular protest, Internet mobilization, pamphlets, meetings, letter writing, and advice to people undergoing treatment. Particular moments of the campaign have involved sit-ins, singing, dancing, and street protests. Some of these tactics descend from the repertoire of protest during apartheid rule: although members are now more likely to call for action by the state, rather than call on it to desist from a particular position,[20] both require a change in government policy or law.

A significant encounter with courtroom success occurred early in 2001, when the Treatment Action Campaign joined as amicus curiae in defending

[16] Ibid, n 52.

[17] *See* <http://www.tac.org.za>.

[18] Chris McGreal, "Zackie Achmat: Profile," *The Guardian* (UK), 12 September 2008, *available at* <http://www.guardian.co.uk/world/2008/sep/12/matthiasrath.aids>.

[19] Heywood, "Preventing Mother-to-Child HIV Transmission in South Africa," *supra* note 3, 300 (describing the public workshops that were conducted by the Treatment Action Campaign to justify the strategy).

[20] Jonathan Berger, "Litigation Strategies to Gain Access to Treatment for HIV/AIDS: The Case of South Africa's Treatment Action Campaign," 20 Wis. Int'l. L.J. 595 (2002) 599. ("While the distinguishing feature of public interest litigation in the apartheid era was the attempt to control the exercise of public power and thereby limit and reduce human rights violations, TAC's use of the law in securing access to treatment is to ensure—rather than prevent—state action.") This feature is complicated by the facts of government obstruction of the ARV in the *TAC* case.

the right to health care against a constitutional challenge to medicines regulation on the part of pharmaceutical companies.[21] Thirty-nine pharmaceutical corporations commenced litigation, asserting, inter alia, an infringement of their constitutional property rights. This litigation continued from 1998 to 2001, until it was withdrawn after significant protest within South Africa and in many other sites across the world.[22] Within months of the Treatment Action Campaign joining that case, the companies withdrew their suit. The success of the action spurred the Treatment Action Campaign to commence litigation of its own.[23]

During the *TAC* case, the Treatment Action Campaign founded a "Save Our Babies" campaign. It published interviews with many doctors who attested to their ethical dilemma in denying ARVs to mothers who sought treatment but could not afford them through the private health-care system. The court hearings, which were heavily publicized, provided an important focal point in this mobilization strategy. As well as its litigation in the Constitutional Court, the Treatment Action Campaign staged part of its protest against government policy at the United Nations, citing both international and constitutional protections of the right to health. Zackie Achmat delivered a speech to the United Nations Commission on Human Rights in 2002, decrying the situation in South Africa on the right to health and access to HIV/AIDS-related medication. The sensitivity of the government to international criticism made this an important locus of action.[24]

The role of the social movement in *TAC* thus forces us to revisit the categorization of the case as an instance in innovative judicial review or as movement-driven cultural change. Undoubtedly, the case enjoyed features of each. Yet the movement itself articulated a politics of access to medicines in which the state's responsibility was critical. Far from disregarding the state, it relied on it as a critical actor. The choice was not how to separate private from public actors, but rather how to combine their forces to make the roll-out of ARVs complete.

[21] *See* Mark Heywood, "Debunking 'Conglomo-talk': A Case Study of the Amicus Curiae as an Instrument for Advocacy, Investigation and Mobilisation," 6 Law, Democracy and Development 12 (2002).

[22] Katharine G. Young, "Securing Health through Rights," in Thomas Pogge, Matthew Rimmer, and Kim Rubenstein (eds.), *Incentives for Global Health* (2010).

[23] Heywood, "Preventing Mother-to-Child HIV Transmission in South Africa," *supra* note 3, 282.

[24] South Africa was elected as a non-Permanent Member of the United Nations Security Council for the period 2007–8. Its performance as a Member complicates a linear account of international accountability: *see*, e.g., Jimmy Mulla, "Modern South Africa, A Country with No Shame," Westlaw, *Sudan Tribune*, 11 August 2008 (noting the way in which South Africa suppressed resolutions condemning acts of violence and human rights violation elsewhere in Africa).

In 2002, the Court ordered the government to desist from preventing the roll-out, and to provide counseling and testing services in its public hospitals. But the campaign did not end with winning this order. After the *TAC* case, the Treatment Action Campaign's perseverance around HIV/AIDS and the right to health has progressed. Its rabble-raising, sloganed T-shirt-wearing activists continue to engender disruption, anguish, and protest: sometimes against the government, sometimes against others. To a significant degree, the Treatment Action Campaign continues to express complaints about the unevenness and ineffectiveness of the government's response to the Court's order.[25] But its energy has not dissipated. For a clearer understanding of this success, I suggest that new understandings of movement are required, beyond that of "law-creators," described in the popular constitutionalist model of Chapter 8. The movement understands the institutional obstacles to the ARV distribution and applies political pressure at those points, in order to create experiments with alternative forms of delivery. It utilizes the formal pressure of the Constitution against the government and the courts, and, afterwards, the formal pressure of the Court order in order to contest and create the right. It has forged alliances with political parties in a way that other social movements have found troubling.[26] We may explore how it acts as a stakeholder in the economic and social rights contestation, an analysis that takes place against the wider backdrop of governance.

B. FROM CONSTITUTIONALISM TO (NEW) GOVERNANCE

How do we understand the role of the Treatment Action Campaign in constituting economic and social rights? I argue that the constitutionalist model only goes part way towards supplying an answer. We need a new model to encompass the private actions and linkages established by the Treatment Action Campaign. A potential candidate is the model of governance. In the next sections, I present this model, by describing its approach to institutional design, inclusiveness, experimentation, and overall embrace of market actors. After introducing this model, I return to the Treatment Action Campaign case study. I also demonstrate how my conclusions in

[25] E.g., Jonathan Berger, "Litigating for Social Justice in Post-apartheid South Africa: A Focus on Health and Education," in Varun Gauri and Daniel M. Brinks (eds.), *Courting Social Justice: Judicial Enforcement of Social and Economic Rights in the Developing World* (2008); Carole Cooper, "Health Rights Litigation: Cautious Constitutionalism," in Alicia Ely Yamin and Siri Gloppen (eds.), *Litigating Health Rights: Can Courts Bring More Justice to Health?* (2011) (documenting several follow-up litigations and campaigns).

[26] Friedman and Mottiar, *Rewarding Engagement?*, *supra* note 14.

respect to this case study apply more broadly to contestations around economic and social rights.

The program of governance is sometimes seen as an alternative to constitutionalism. This is certainly the case if we see constitutionalism as a call for a system of limited government.[27] Nonetheless, if constitutionalism is understood as encompassing the formation and authorization of power, rather than its limitation, the program of governance appears more complementary than distinct. In this part, by demarcating the features of the governance program, I suggest the tendency of constitutionalism to anchor, rather than deflect, certain moral assumptions, and to theorize the operation of power, makes the two important partners in understanding processes of constituting economic and social rights.

The prominent (although not universal) institutions of constitutionalism are the separation of powers between branches of government (legislative, executive, judicial), an option of the additional division of power between geographical entities (federalism), and the entrenchment of individual rights. In this familiar view, accountability comes from the enforcement of the constraints on these institutions, usually by "hard" modes of judicial review according to "formal" constitutional text. The promise of constitutionalism is delivered on the basis of the stability of these constraints, and their obduracy to change. Civil society, as composed of interested associations who are grouped together by common interest, effects social change within the boundaries supported by this obdurate, constitutionalist structure. So, too, do market actors. At times of heightened politics, the basic constitutional structures may be exceptionally debated and changed; otherwise ordinary politics proceeds within these structures. The entrenchment of economic and social rights may put additional pressures on government to act positively to secure certain material conditions for all citizens; yet this pressure of positive performance is not new, given that civil and political rights also require positive state action.[28] Hence, regulation is a commonplace obligation on government, and rights affect both the limits of regulation and the duty to regulate.

This constitutionalist approach to institutional structure can be contrasted with the governance approach. The latter is concerned with the act of governing, rather than merely with the institution that is nominally elected to perform this function (the government). By necessity, governance encompasses nongovernmental actors, including the market and civil society. The separation of powers becomes, in this view, the orchestration of

[27] Jeremy Waldron, "Constitutionalism—a Skeptical View," *available at* <http://onlinelibrary.wiley.com/doi/10.1002/9781444310399.ch15/summary>.

[28] *See* discussion in Chapter 6, section C(1), and Chapter 10.

separated powers. The division of federal levels of government becomes here the coordination of federal innovations. Accountability comes, not from "hard" rights, but from soft law and performance standards. Stability comes, not from the obduracy of fundamental constraints, but from the flexibility of arrangements to deal with the pressures of complexity and change. The coordinated features of governance have been assigned to various aims of governing: good governance, for example, or global governance.

Approached from the governance, as opposed to the constitutionalist perspective, four institutional features appear to answer many of the obstacles of economic and social rights. First, governance emphasizes accountability in government while also enhancing the discretion and flexibility of government to coordinate solutions with the market and civil society. This becomes key in resolving the difficulties in service delivery or market access that are often seen as intractable, and a reason to deny the practical feasibility of economic and social rights. Second, the governance perspective simultaneously de-centers courts, while highlighting the capacity for judicial innovation in remediation and scrutiny. As we saw in Chapter 5, experimentalist review allows a court to deflect the justiciability criticism of economic and social rights.[29] Third, governance accepts that market actors can be an ally, rather than an obstacle, to the protection of rights, thus integrating economic and social rights with the precepts of liberal capitalist systems. And fourth, governance conceptualizes social movements as stakeholders, with an institutionalized role in the overall regime that impacts on the interests and values that these movements have emerged to defend.

As we will see below, these four elements open up the contestation around economic and social rights beyond a discussion of direct state provision of certain goods and services in housing, health care, education, or welfare towards a contestation of the appropriate extent of regulation, the locus of market failure, or the background common law rules that contribute to a lack of enjoyment of economic and social rights. Through decentralizing decision-making and problem solving, experimentalist governance engages the people within institutions in the efforts of their own reform, rather than having reform dictated abstractly from above. The perspective also incorporates other non-state actors (and importantly, market actors) who are influenced by the same processes of negotiation. Together, these processes generate a heightened political energy, and informational advantages, for democratic reform. After noting these features, we will consider their application to our case study of the Treatment Action Campaign.

[29] *See supra* Chapter 5, section D(3).

(1) *State, market, and civil society coordination*

"New" or "experimentalist" governance offers an intriguing diagnosis of the problems of the modern welfare state. As part of their vigorous institutional program, scholars who promote experimentalism question the wisdom that today's public institutions are failing because of too much state (for example problems of rent-seeking and command and control inefficiencies), or too much market (such as the problem of regulatory capture, or the expansion of private control), or civic deficits (such as the decline of trust in diverse societies).[30] Instead, experimentalists see the biggest problems lie in the boundaries that are set up between state, market, and civil society, which block effective strategies of problem solving, and cause coordination failures and democratic unresponsiveness.[31] In this view, the problem with today's regulatory and administrative structures is that they are never adequately tailored to constantly changing local circumstances to be effective, and involve a mismatch of means that are promoted at the same time, such as fines, incentives, and knowledge production. In this respect, review of public institutions is made more difficult because of the fact that institutions are not intentionally refusing to implement particular economic and social protections, but, rather, are simply unable to do so, through incompetence or through the institutional inattentiveness or intransigence that was described in Chapter 6.[32]

One answer to this diagnosis (the neoliberal answer) would be to dismantle public institutions to their thinnest conception and allow market actors to take over through a system of privatization and/or deregulation. This answer has been influential, and widely implemented. In South Africa, for example, the market-oriented strategy of the Growth, Employment, and Redistribution Policy ("GEAR"), adopted in 1996, was explicitly committed to privatization, fiscal restraint, widespread economic deregulation, and the promotion of foreign investment.[33]

Not so for experimentalists. While market actors are invited into the problem-solving process, so too are other stakeholders. The public institutions increase the coordination between the market and movement participants within civil society. Coordination reaches across movements mobilized against analogous problems, to transfer information about the alternatives expounded in similar situations.[34] An orchestration of knowledge-sharing and problem-solving is achieved across departmental, disciplinary, and institutional

[30] Joshua Cohen and Charles Sabel, "Directly Deliberative Polyarchy," 3 Euro. L.J. 313 (1997).

[31] Ibid.

[32] *See* specifically *supra* Chapter 6, section C(5).

[33] *See* Chapter 1, section C(1).

[34] Cohen, "Reflections on Habermas on Democracy," 12 Ratio Juris 385 (1999) 412.

divides. This can encompass the various individual and collective efforts that engage in the social provision of the goods and services that lie at the basis of economic and social rights, such as in health care, schools, income support, and subsidies for housing and food. Of course, these areas blend public and private, secular and religious, nonprofit and for-profit provision.[35]

In this view, coordination must occur across the political branches. Movements do not proceed in isolation from the state; nor do they rely on the sporadic bursts of energy that occur during perceived crises.[36] The tracks of constitutional democracy no longer run in separate grooves.[37] Movements are motivated continually, rather than episodically, by an appreciation of the problems of modern governance and the invitation to participate in the solution.[38] They proceed "inside," rather than "outside," the governance regime. This can occur through Governance Councils,[39] which are premised on the importance of coordinating participation, or through other information—and actor-aggregating—institutions.

This coordinated model of governance has been influential in Europe. In the European Union's Anti-Discrimination Regime, for example, social movements and other participants are included as part of the formal law-making and law-application process of states.[40] Particularly in the design of the open method of coordination ("OMC") within the European Union, experimentalist governance has been influential in addressing some of the criticisms of a democratic deficit in Europe.[41] The European application of experimentalism is relevant to this study, not only for its approach towards collaborating institutions across the "social" obligations undertaken within Europe, but for the way in which cross-national data and comparison has become integral to the experiment.[42]

Hence, legislatures "declare" areas of policy (like education, community safety, or environmental health) as open to local deliberation by public

[35] For a helpful division of "public" and "private" characteristics along different axes, *see* Martha Minow, "Public and Private Partnerships: Accounting for the New Religion," 116 Harv. L. Rev. 1229 (2003) 1229–31.

[36] Cohen, "Reflections on Habermas on Democracy," *supra* note 34, 410.

[37] Ibid., 410; *compare* with Jürgen Habermas, *Between Facts and Norms: Contributions to a Discourse Theory of Law and Democracy* (1998); Bruce Ackerman, *We the People* (1991).

[38] *See*, e.g., James S. Liebman and Charles F. Sabel, "The Fragile Promise of Provisionality," 28 N.Y.U. Rev. L. & Soc. Change 369 (2003) 370.

[39] Dorf and Sabel, "A Constitution of Democratic Experimentalism," 98 Colum. L. Rev. 267 (1998) 316–17.

[40] Grainne de Burca, "Stumbling into Experimentalism: the EU Anti-Discrimination Regime," in Charles F. Sabel and Jonathan Zeitlin (eds.), *Experimentalist Governance in the European Union* (2010).

[41] *See*, e.g., Grainne de Burca and Joanne Scott (eds.), *Law and New Governance in the EU and the US* (2006); Joanne Scott and David Trubek, "Mind the Gap: Law and New Approaches to Governance in the EU," 8 Euro L.J. 1 (2002).

[42] *See*, e.g., Grainne de Burca, "EU Race Discrimination Law: A Hybrid Model?," in de Burca and Scott, ibid., 97.

agencies, associations (including "citizen users"[43]), and market actors—all encompassed by the term "stakeholders." The legislature makes resources available to stakeholders and reviews the responsibilities taken on by them at regular intervals.[44] The normative floor of these deliberations is created by "benchmarks."[45] Benchmarking initiates a process of setting feasible standards, with ongoing peer review, where "laggards" are required to report back and are given technical assistance to improve their capacity to reach standards. This proposal goes beyond the legislative and administrative scrutiny and enforcement measures discussed in Chapter 7. This is because new linkages are actively forced between agencies and stakeholders, and information is shared with greater rigor. The meaning and responsibilities attached to economic and social rights are constantly contested, negotiated, and benchmarked.

Administrative agencies, in turn, provide the infrastructure for information exchange between and among these stakeholders, seeking to reduce the costs of information for different problem solvers. Administrative law extends beyond the provision of appeal avenues. These are usually supplied through social security administrations, employment or labor boards, workers' compensation boards, licensing agencies, equal opportunity commissions, and zoning boards, when certain individual benefits or aids have been terminated or limited. To be experimentalist, such agencies do more: they coordinate problem-solving to arrive at more collectively informed and locally responsive solutions. Effective and successful coordination has been reported in policy areas where actors are traditionally disjointed from each other, such as environmental protection,[46] occupational health and safety,[47] community policing,[48] labor standards,[49] housing,[50] and welfare.[51] These

[43] Dorf and Sabel, "A Constitution of Democratic Experimentalism," *supra* note 39, 328.

[44] Cohen, "Reflections on Habermas on Democracy," *supra* note 34, 413.

[45] Dorf and Sabel, "A Constitution of Democratic Experimentalism," *supra* note 39.

[46] Neil Gunningham and Darren Sinclair, "Regulatory Pluralism: Designing Policy Mixes for Environmental Protection," 21 Law and Policy 49 (1999); Bradley C. Karkkainen, "Information as Environmental Regulation: RTI and Performance Benchmarking, Precursor to a New Paradigm?" 89 Geo. L.J. 257 (2001).

[47] Cary Coglianese et al., "Performance Based Regulation: Prospects and Limitations in Health, Safety and Environmental Protection," 55 Admin L. Rev. 705 (2003).

[48] Archon Fung, *Empowered Participation: Reinventing Urban Democracy* (2004).

[49] Orly Lobel, "Orchestrated Experimentalism in the Regulation of Work," 101 Mich. L. Rev. 2146 (2003); Susan Sturm, "Second Generation Employment Discrimination: A Structural Approach," 101 Colum. L. Rev. 458 (2001).

[50] Charles F. Sabel. and William H. Simon, "Destabilization Rights: How Public Law Litigation Succeeds," 117 Harv. L. Rev. 1016 (2004); Lisa T. Alexander, "Stakeholder Participation in New Governance: Lessons from Chicago's Public Housing Reform Experiment," 16 Geo. J. Pov. L. & Pol. 117 (2009) 137–42.

[51] Kathleen Noonan, Charles F. Sabel, and William H. Simon, "Legal Accountability in the Service Based Welfare System," 34 Law & Soc. Inquiry 523 (2009).

successes suggest integrated responses to both the problem of a lack of enjoyment of economic and social rights, and a lack of consensus on their meaning.

New relationships between agencies, market actors, and movements are created, carefully disciplined by the process of benchmarking.[52] Sometimes these collaborations proceed without any court involvement—in community policing, for example, experimentalism creates the process for police and communities to actively and reciprocally consult about local security needs and goals. Far from impeding participation, experimentalists claim that this process may provoke entirely new mobilizations.[53]

For education rights in the United States, for example, experimentalist scholars describe the implementation of the core commitment to "universal" and "adequate" education. Decision-making is delegated to lower level institutions, districts, principals, teachers, and parent groups to work out what that commitment might mean on the ground.[54] Sometimes these collaborations occur outside of courts, between teachers and parents and students; in others, a court prompts such involvement. For instance, the Texas Supreme Court initiated a rigorous and effective degree of parental involvement in school affairs, after a suit was brought in relation to adequacy in education.[55]

The coordinating impulse of new governance would thus appear useful for resolving many of the obstacles of economic and social rights, both in establishing processes to clarify their meaning and to implement them. This includes a distinct, although not inevitable, role of courts. In the next section, we will see how courts may use their authority to "destabilize" rights.

(2) *Destabilization through courts*

Part II of this book describes a varied role for courts in enforcing economic and social rights, which includes a program of experimentalist review. In taking this stance, courts coordinate problem-solving processes between different actors, enhancing the accountability of government as well as the availability of an appropriately tailored remedy. Courts act to force new action and linkages to remove the institutional intransigence, incompetence, or inattentiveness that have led to the economic and social rights infringements. In

[52] Dorf and Sabel, "A Constitution of Democratic Experimentalism," *supra* note 39.

[53] James S. Liebman and Charles F. Sabel, "A Public Laboratory Dewey Barely Imagined: The Emerging Model of School Governance and Legal Reform," 28 N.Y.U. Rev. L. & Soc. Change 183 (2003) 233–4, 243–6; Sabel and Simon, "Destabilization Rights," *supra* note 50, 1027; Dorf and Sabel, "A Constitution of Democratic Experimentalism," *supra* note 39, 328.

[54] Liebman and Sabel, "A Public Laboratory Dewey Barely Imagined," *supra* note 53.

[55] Ibid.

Chapter 5, for example, we saw how a remedy requiring a "meaningful engagement" between the parties helped to resolve the infringement of the right to housing. Landlords and tenants were brought to negotiate towards a solution, whether it lay in alternative accommodation or other forms of assistance. I argued that this mode is one technique (used with others) in the overall program of a "catalytic court," where the court catalyzes other parties to reach a solution, rather than dictating one itself. In this chapter we see how experimentalist review is integrated within an overall experimentalist governance regime.

The experimentalist perspective prescribes neither court-centrism nor its anti-court opposite. Instead, the judicial program is described as one of "destabilization." "Destabilization rights" are those employed by claimants to disentrench the congealed power of public agencies, which may be otherwise immune from democratic challenge.[56] Through destabilization, the status quo is automatically challenged and settled interests are disrupted: a status quo which might otherwise be obstructing the appropriate delivery of housing services, or of welfare, or child protection. The courts put in motion processes of contestation, rather than diagnose the problem and prescribe solutions.

This revisability is counted as important, because of the recognition that bureaucracies can break down more regularly and more intractably than the courts can provide a remedy.[57] In the process, the political clout of social movements in contesting rights is strengthened: their minority disadvantage is addressed through a compulsory coordination process, such as a process of "meaningful engagement."[58] This process is also aimed at preventing the regulatory capture of government institutions by more powerful industries. The destabilization effect is also said to avoid the ineluctable prisoner's dilemma of which the movement and other stakeholders are a part, so that the court's coordination can ensure that perceived self-interest does not prevent overall best solutions.[59]

Within this model, courts do not set out to review arrangements on the basis of substantive rights, but promote decision-making elsewhere in a directly deliberative process, for example, by using the remedy to hand the decision back to "stakeholders."[60] Courts do not, therefore, define the

[56] Sabel, and Simon, "Destabilization Rights," *supra* note 50, 1029.

[57] This has been even more simply put by Gary L. Blasi, "Litigation Strategies for Addressing Bureaucratic Disentitlement," 366 PLI/Lit. 285 (1988) ("bureaucrats can break things faster than judges can fix them").

[58] *Occupiers of 51 Olivia Road v. City of Johannesburg*, 2008 (3) SA 208 (cc).

[59] Sabel and Simon, "Destabilization Rights," *supra* note 50, 1064–7.

[60] Susan P. Sturm, "A Normative Theory of Public Law Remedies," 79 Geo. L.J. 1355 (1991).

obligations that flow from rights: "the norms that define compliance . . . are the work not of the judiciary, but of the actors who live by them."[61] Conventional declaratory or structural remedies are put to one side: instead, experimentalists would have the court set forth a system of rolling or provisional rules under supervised negotiation and deliberation among parties and stakeholders.[62] This blueprint of cross-institutional negotiation would appear to offer significant lessons for making economic and social rights operative and meaningful, including the guarantee of health care, education, or housing.

The enforcement of mental health rights in the United States provides an example of an integrated, holistic, governance regime. Mental health is the least controversial of the examples of institutional reform litigation in the United States.[63] Indeed, given the effectiveness of litigation in holding mental heath institutions to account, the US Congress specifically authorized the Department of Justice to bring suits against mental health institutions in the Civil Rights for Institutionalized Persons Act of 1980. Rights for the mentally ill, to both treatment and to decent conditions, became actionable in the courts. For example, in *Wyatt v. Stickney*,[64] an Alabama decree required a diet meeting nutritional standards prescribed by the National Academy of Science, to which Alabama institutions were accountable in court. Yet litigation established the limit of a "command and control" remedy for an economic and social rights infringement. At the same time as this heightened protection occurred, a preference on the part of patients and professionals for community-based, rather than institutional, care emerged.[65] With a developing professional consensus about the therapeutic and monitoring advantages of noninstitutionalized care, a remedy that would dictate nutritional standards or minimum room temperatures proved redundant.[66] Thus, as the government moved from provider to guarantor of care, a parallel effect occurred for the courts.[67] Through negotiation processes, former adversaries came to agree on a remedial framework that would require ongoing cooperation.[68] The enforcement of mental health rights therefore stands for

[61] Sabel and Simon, "Destabilization Rights," *supra* note 50, 1020.

[62] *See further* Chapter 5, section D(3).

[63] Sabel and Simon, "Destabilization Rights," *supra* note 50.

[64] 344 F. Supp. 373 (M.D. Ala. 1972).

[65] Sabel and Simon, "Destabilization Rights," *supra* note 50, 1029.

[66] Ibid., 1039.

[67] Ibid. With respect to Medicaid protection of nursing homes, *compare* Jody Freeman, "The Private Role in Public Governance," 75 N.Y.U. L. Rev. 543 (2000).

[68] Sabel and Simon, "Destabilization Rights," *supra* note 50; *Wyatt v. Stickney*, 344 F. Supp. 373 (M.D. Ala. 1972).

the importance of ongoing, revisable, collaborative governance for the elaboration and implementation of fundamental rights. Courts were present, not to enforce pre-articulated rights, but to destabilize their current understanding, and set in place processes for deliberation and reform.

(3) Market as ally

A third feature of the new governance perspective, which is applicable to constituting economic and social rights, is the attention given to market actors. In governance models, markets are viewed as both a mechanism and an important locus of the solution. Markets create the information flows, and the incentives, to aggregate welfare efficiently. Rights become commodified and marketable, such as through housing or schooling vouchers, or through charging user fees for basic services, or through privatizing providers.[69] Hence, despite a traditional view, which suggests economic and social interests become rights only when they are decommodified—that is, protected from market risk and recognized as incommensurable with market value[70]—the governance approach views links with the market as efficient, supportive of individual choice, and more likely to solve the obstacles to goods and services delivery.

The market becomes an ally through careful design, based on individual rationality as well as the behavioral context in which individual choices are embedded.[71] Thus, for example, new default rules can be manipulated or the "choice architecture" of each model can be changed to ensure that markets work to the benefit of rights claimants. Hence, where people are prone to make bad choices, more information is provided, or beneficiaries are allowed to opt out of certain choices. These approaches provide an array of options for consideration of the state's duty to regulate, rather than the duty to simply provide, with respect to economic and social rights.

One such design option in socio-economic protection is privatization—that is, to transfer an industry or service (such as water, housing, health care, or education services) from public to private ownership and control. In so doing, efficiency gains are said to improve services, enhance consumer choice, and minimize waste. Another design option, which utilizes market principles, either separately or alongside privatization, is the user fee

[69] Varun Gauri, "Social Rights and Economics: Claims to Health Care and Education in Developing Countries," in Philip Alston and Mary Robinson (eds.), *Human Rights and Development: Towards Mutual Reinforcement* (2005) 78, 80.

[70] For the seminal statement of the traditional view, *see* T.H. Marshall, *Citizenship and Social Class* (1992).

[71] Richard H. Thaler and Cass R. Sunstein, *Nudge: Improving Decisions about Health, Wealth, and Happiness* (2008).

delivery model. Service meters for water or electricity ensure that beneficiaries pay for what they use, thereby reducing inefficiencies in supply; and providers themselves reduce inefficiencies in order to maximize their own profits. In theory, poorer users may be exempt from user fees, or given baseline quotas for minimum usage.[72] In practice, as we have seen, exemptions are often left unenforced, particularly for those without economic or political capital.

A third design option, compatible with market-based approaches, is vouchers. School or housing vouchers utilize the basic premise of maximizing efficiency through choice. In the education context, eligible voucher recipients are able to choose from among a range of providers (schools) certified as meeting basic standards. The voucher is exchanged with a chosen provider, who then collects a specified payment from the government. Private schools, oriented to attract students (by higher performance standards or other advantages), may flourish. In housing, recipients use certificates to induce landlords to rent to them. The tenant then pays a percentage of her or his income, and the government pays the difference between that amount and the officially determined "fair rental value" of the apartment. As with schooling, the theory behind the certificate is to give tenants a broader range of choice and more leverage than in traditional public housing models. Vouchers provide the "consumer" with the housing or schooling that she or he deems most valuable, and thus makes schools or landlords more directly accountable to those who use their services. If consumers are not satisfied, they go elsewhere and the providers lose the payments.[73]

Of course, these design options all require careful scrutiny. Vouchers, for example, are notorious for obstructing access to goods and services, by setting the wrong price, or by creating perverse incentives. In housing, for example, if the voucher price is too low, landlords will refuse to participate. If the price is too high, they get a windfall.[74] As far as incentives are concerned, there is a tendency to "cream" or "skim" the least costly consumer. Thus, instead of competing in the voucher market, providers can compete by better identifying and attracting the most rewarding applicants. Landlords, for example, will recruit the most stable families and ignore those most at need. Schools will seek out students with the most promising ability and obstruct those with more challenging behavioral

[72] *See* Chapter 8, section A; *see also Mazibuko v. City of Johannesburg* 2010 (4) SA 1 (CC).

[73] For a description, *see* Goodwin Liu, "Education, Equality, and National Citizenship," 116 Yale L.J. 330 (2006) 403.

[74] Charles F. Sabel and William H. Simon, "Minimalism and Experimentalism in the Administrative State," 100 Geo. L.J. 53 (2011).

traits, in turn leading to class stratification and racial segregation, to a degree that would be otherwise condemned.[75] Medical facilities will respond to the healthiest people, again leaving those most in need of services outside the system.[76] This should come as no surprise: market options have long been associated with harming the least well off within the overall less well off.[77]

Such perversities are clearly opposite to the values of economic and social rights. Yet with governance tools such as performance review, access to information, and coordination of local and center actors, the negative effects of the market mechanisms are said to be forestalled. The emphasis on accountability, participation, and experimentalism are predicted to make individualized services in health care, education, job training, mental health, and disability services more effective.[78] Communities are said to develop economically when both government agencies and private charities provide financial and technical assistance to community-based organizations, which implement locally devised plans for housing, job, and business development. Organizations that gain success against locally devised criteria receive priority in later rounds of funding.[79] Hence, with appropriate modifications, the market is seen as an important ally in an overall, effective, new governance regime.

(4) Movement as stakeholder

Finally, new governance relies on the continued participation of nonmarket stakeholders. We have seen how social movements can become a pivotal force in constituting economic and social rights. Yet in the experimentalist model, the movement plays a more targeted, localized, and flexible role. Social movements eschew the large symbolism of jurisgenesis because they are forced to integrate grand or abstract moral ideals into everyday experience. Such contextualism has its advantages for democracy: it is said to lessen the hold of "wedge" politics, and increase the likelihood of innovation.[80] The function of movements is therefore to inform and educate, to nudge and prompt, rather than to inspire.

[75] Martha Minow, *In Brown's Wake: America's Educational Landmark* (2010) 116–22.

[76] Sabel and Simon, "Minimalism and Experimentalism," *supra* note 74.

[77] Bruce Ackerman, "Regulating Slum Housing Markets on Behalf of the Poor: of Housing Codes, Housing Subsidies and Income Redistribution Policy," 80 Yale L.J. 1093 (1971).

[78] Noonan, Sabel, and Simon, "Legal Accountability in the Service Based Welfare System," *supra* note 51.

[79] William H. Simon, *The Community Economic Development Movement: Law, Business, and the New Social Policy* (2001); Fung, *Empowered Participation*, *supra* note 48.

[80] Dorf and Sabel, "A Constitution of Democratic Experimentalism," *supra* note 39, 344–5.

Stakeholders include all groups that are affected by a decision on economic and social rights, not just an active claimant. As "stakeholders," movements can be represented by organizations as diverse as registered charities, nongovernmental organizations ("NGOs"), community groups, faith-based organizations, professional associations, trade unions, self-help groups, informal associations, business associations, coalitions, and advocacy groups. When they are close to the ground, they can detect insincerity by others and the unintended consequences of past decisions.[81] The collective action may resemble more an "interest group" than a social movement, but the line between the two is blurred by a deliberate rejection of the "purity" of the social movement form.[82] The movement forms one unit of analysis in solving a definable public problem as a whole.[83]

This embrace of market and nonmarket actors in civil society creates new opportunities for collaboration and learning between them. This collaboration can also move beyond the nation state. Such a "movement" was arguably built through efforts to integrate human rights in the practices of transnational corporations. In this effort, the UN Secretary-General's Special Representative for Business and Human Rights, John Ruggie, was appointed to locate how businesses and industries integrate respect for human rights (including economic and social rights) in their practice. The UN Commission on Human Rights had requested his appointment, after two earlier efforts of regulation failed: the first, involving "voluntary" norms, were articulated as forms of self-regulation acceptable to the corporations themselves and yet were criticized by many as too lax to deal with the very real effect of corporate activities on the enjoyment of human rights; the second, a system of imposed international legal obligations, were devised by NGOs and lacked effectiveness. Instead, through a consultative process with all groups over a five-year period, the Special Representative issued a set of Guiding Principles which outline a "responsibility to protect" the economic and social rights of the Universal Declaration of Human Rights ("UDHR"), the International Covenant on Civil and Political Rights ("ICCPR"), the International Covenant on Economic, Social and Cultural Rights ("ICESCR"), as well as the principles concerning fundamental rights in the eight International Labour Organization ("ILO") core conventions as set out in the Declaration on Fundamental Principles and Rights at Work.

Ruggie's methodology was contextual and collaborative. He designed the Guiding Principles with the aim "not only to provide guidance that is

[81] Cohen, "Reflections on Habermas on Democracy," *supra* note 34.

[82] Mancur Olson, *The Logic of Collective Action* (1965); *cf.* Sidney Tarrow, *Power in Movement: Social Movements and Contentious Politics* (2nd edn., 1998) 206–7.

[83] Dorf and Sabel, "A Constitution of Democratic Experimentalism," *supra* note 39.

practical, but also guidance informed by actual practice."[84] His discussions, which involved "all stakeholder groups," included governments, business enterprises, and associations, as well as the "individuals and communities directly affected by the activities of enterprises in various parts of the world, civil society, and experts in the many areas of law and policy." His methodology was also provisional, as he sought "a common global platform for action, on which cumulative progress can be built, step-by-step, without foreclosing any other promising longer-term developments."[85] The resulting principles were intended to work as "benchmarks," against which other social actors assess the human rights impacts of business enterprises.[86]

Nonetheless, Ruggie also understood that the responsibility of business enterprises to respect human rights was distinct from their legal liability. In this respect, he relied on domestic enforcement.[87] Indeed, his emphasis on the additional duties on states to define and enforce human rights law, which is stipulated in the state's duty "to protect" human rights and "to remedy" their infringements, mark the largest part of the Ruggie framework.[88] Soft governance processes rely on a constitutional framework of harder constraints, which come about through the processes of interpretation and enforcement described elsewhere in this book.

We have seen that the governance framework introduces important features of collaboration between the state, the market, and civil society. In this respect, the approach emphasizes the efficiency gains, and indeed feasibility, of meeting fundamental interests for beneficiaries. We have also seen that such models also create problems, particularly for the least well off. The next section explores the precepts of experimentalism against our Treatment Action Campaign case study. Section D examines the shortcomings of the model that suggest that it can be only ever a partial solution to the elaboration and implementation of economic and social rights.

[84] Report of the Special Representative of the Secretary-General on the issue of human rights and transnational corporations and other business enterprises, John Ruggie, "Guiding Principles on Business and Human Rights: Implementing the United Nations 'Protect, Respect and Remedy' Framework," UN Doc. A/HRC/17/31, *available at* <http://www.business-humanrights.org/media/documents/ruggie/ruggie-guiding-principles-21-mar-2011.pdf> [11].

[85] Ibid., [13], *see also* [15] "While the Principles themselves are universally applicable, the means by which they are realized will reflect the fact that we live in a world of 192 United Nations Member States, 80,000 transnational enterprises, 10 times as many subsidiaries and countless millions of national firms, most of which are small and medium sized enterprises. When it comes to means for implementation, therefore, one size does not fit all."

[86] Ibid., Annex, Principle 12. [87] Ibid. [88] Ibid., [6].

C. EXPERIMENTALIST FEATURES OF THE TREATMENT ACTION CAMPAIGN

Our study of the Treatment Action Campaign is an example of an experimentalist stakeholder contesting the market and government's stance towards the rights of people living with HIV/AIDS. The Treatment Action Campaign was able to negotiate the complexity of meaning and enforceability of the right to health[89] through their vigorous mobilization and protest. By bringing about collaborations and linkages between the state, the market, and civil society, experimentalist governance may have assisted this process.

For example, the Treatment Action Campaign engaged in the widest possible targets of governance: its litigation, lobbying, and street protest put pressure on government, but also on different market and nonmarket actors. The campaign has forged critical relations with health providers. Indeed, seeking out the opinions of doctors, nurses, health clinics, hospitals, and scientists formed a key plank in gaining evidence and support for its law suit about the meaning of the constitutional right to access health care. The Treatment Action Campaign also became practiced in treatment literacy, with members assisting people living with HIV/AIDS and people living with people with HIV/AIDS to understand the complex regimens of treatment.[90]

The Treatment Action Campaign also engaged with pharmaceutical companies, seeking out ways in which corporate donations could alleviate the cost of antiretroviral ("ARV") medicine.[91] It did so while contesting the patenting of essential medicines and defending generic medicines, through litigation and lobbying. These private relationships were key in lowering the cost of medicines, and making the remedies sought in court feasible in the first place. The Treatment Action Campaign also created critical associations with other movements, enabling networks of protest to succeed transnationally. Hence, while the Treatment Action Campaign aims to contest the right to health care in South Africa, it understands its mission in the context of the right to health care experienced comparatively (with links forged to movements in Brazil, Thailand, and elsewhere) and internationally (with pressure put on the Agreement on Trade-Related

[89] The complexity of the right to health, in particular, is discussed in Chapters 3 (in terms of minimalism) and 4 (in terms of limits).

[90] Forbath, "Realizing a Constitutional Social Right," *supra* note 3.

[91] Heywood, "Campaigns," *supra* note 8; and for pitfalls of reliance on corporate social responsibility for essential medicines: Rajshree Chandra, "The Role of National Laws in Reconciling Constitutional Right to Health with TRIPS Obligations: An Examination of the Glivec Patent Case in India," in Thomas Pogge, Matthew Rimmer & Kim Rubenstein (eds.), *Incentives for Global Health* (2010).

Aspects of Intellectual Property Rights ("TRIPS Agreement") at the international level).

Did the movement help the Constitutional Court to be experimentalist in character? At first glance, the program appears complementary. First, the Court's remedy was directed at solving the problem: preventing mother-to-child transmission of HIV / AIDS, rather than at upholding a substantive and final content of the constitutional right of access to health care. Second, the remedy sought to disentrench the public monopoly involved in the administration of health, and engage other actors in negotiating the baselines for adequate health care. The benchmark of universal provision of the ARVs for all expectant mothers in public hospitals (usually lower income women) was set, although the key players in this process were not "leader" as opposed to "laggard" States (one province had agreed to an early roll-out, but this was late in the process), but rather the testimony of expert opinion. And third, the remedy provided for its ongoing revisability, in light of better information and improved developments in scientific and professional communities.

Yet on deeper analysis, the *TAC* case is not a textbook example of a court operating in the experimentalist framework. First, if the most effective negotiations occurred during the litigation, the Court did not oversee them. Indeed, the Court's own attempts to spur agreement proved unsuccessful. Although the Court adjourned the proceedings during the case, to allow time for the parties to discuss the terms of an agreement, none could be reached.[92] Instead, the parties pursued their negotiations privately, outside of the public spotlight, yet pressured by increasing public condemnation of the government's position. This public pressure was achieved through the Treatment Action Campaign's wider strategy: of protests, marches, and organizing, both within South Africa and transnationally. Before the Court had turned to the question of remedy, the government had changed its position on ARVs (which the Court itself commended). Yet with the degree of adversarial antagonism evident between the government and the Treatment Action Campaign, the Court was unwilling to put in motion a destabilization of the parties' entitlements in order for the predicted cognitive and psychological disruptions to occur.[93]

Secondly, the remedy did not call for further negotiations. The Constitutional Court ordered the government to desist from its restrictions of ARVs, and also ordered it to provide counseling and treatment to HIV-positive expectant women. This was a partial answer to the problem of

[92] E.g., Albie Sachs, "Enforcement of Social and Economic Rights," 22 Am. U. Int'l. L. Rev. 673 (2007).

[93] *Cf.* Sabel and Simon, "Destabilization Rights," *supra* note 50, 1073–82, 1099.

mother-to-child HIV transmission at childbirth. Indeed, patient counseling was a critical (and somewhat costly) aspect of the remedy that would help to make treatment effective. But other aspects of the problem were not addressed. The other social determinants of HIV transmission at childbirth—the proximity of the hospital or clinic to the patient, the ability of pregnant women to take command of their own care within their households, the cost of hospital or clinical care, the paternalist or negative assumptions made by professionals about their patients, and other major obstacles—were all relevant to the risk of mother-to-child transmission of HIV. Such aspects would have surfaced in any negotiation with other stakeholders, such as Nevirapine providers, doctors, nurses, clinics, and women's groups. A more targeted, informed, and institutionally complex solution might have resulted from participatory negotiation. Rather than take responsibility for this process, such governance levers were the responsibility of the Treatment Action Campaign.

Finally, in devising its own best-fit solution to the problem of mother-to-child transmission of HIV, the Court also remained within traditional approaches to implementation. The Court referred only obliquely to the ongoing importance of civil society, which it noted "should co-operate in the steps taken" to address the AIDS pandemic.[94] Clearly, the Court was not ignorant of the importance of the Treatment Action Campaign, not least because of the earlier gains of the Treatment Action Campaign in securing the corporate donation of free Nevirapine over five years.[95] Yet its reliance on the movement was an understated one: it did not explicitly incorporate the movement within its order.

The Treatment Action Campaign has reacted to this order proactively. It relies on its members and volunteers to engage directly with the institutions required to implement the remedy—the doctors, clinics, and hospitals—independently of the court order. Members of the various branches of the Treatment Action Campaign spend time visiting clinics, ensuring that medicines are present there; if medicines are not provided, they contact officials to remind them of the clinic's obligations. In so doing, they help to shore up the legitimacy of the Constitutional Court; they keep it to account. However, they do not assume this responsibility directly.[96] Importantly, the movement's own legitimacy is not tied to the success or failure of the court order or state policy. It remains free to promote its own ends: sometimes

[94] *TAC*, 2002 (5) SA 721 ¶ 126.

[95] Heywood, "Campaigns," *supra* note 8.

[96] Neither would experimentalists prescribe this: *see*, e.g., Cohen, "Reflections on Habermas on Democracy," *supra* note 34. But they part company from Habermas, for example, who would nominate the "momentous" role of movements during a perceived crisis: *see* Habermas, *supra* note 37.

with government, and sometimes against it. In this way, the Treatment Action Campaign retains an important distance from the remedial responsibility of the Court, as well as the remedial responsibility of the state. This distance did not obstruct the effectiveness of many of the orders, and much of the roll-out, of the ARVs. The next section explores whether certain shortcomings in the experimentalist model arise in relation to economic and social rights, suggesting that the model should be applied against a backdrop of constitutionalism.

D. A CONSTITUTIONALIST BACKDROP FOR EXPERIMENTALIST GOVERNANCE

Concerns about the usefulness of the full program of experimentalism lie in three standpoints that have grounded experimentalist theory: that participants, as "stakeholders," are interest-bearers; that deliberation may dislodge power imbalances; and that a political discourse should be shorn of values, lest ideological fights wedge or distract from solutions. These I call the stakeholder deficit, the power deficit, and the symbol deficit. Yet I suggest that the performance of "rights talk" has a particular capacity to remedy each defect; which reveals the appropriate place of governance within a constitutionalist approach.

(1) The stakeholder deficit

The first concerns lie in the question of the stakeholder. Due to the critical role of public and private actors in constituting economic and social rights, who counts as a stakeholder (and who, therefore, is included in the deliberative processes of the governance program) is a critical question. Experimentalist governance seeks to pluralize the exercise of normative authority,[97] decentralizing it from the confines of the state. It seeks to invite new modes of contestation and participation, on the basis of the view that "[p]eople disserved by the current system are sufficiently aggrieved by the resulting costs that it is worth their while to coalesce to disentrench established interests, provided that there is a minimally acceptable prospect of success and accountability."[98] Yet there remains an ambiguity in what is covered by the term "stakeholder."[99]

[97] For an examination, *see* Tara J. Melish, "Maximum Feasible Participation of the Poor: New Governance, New Accountability, and a 21st Century War on the Sources of Poverty," 13 Yale Hum. Rts. & Dev't. L.J. 1 (2010).

[98] Liebman and Sabel, "The Fragile Promise of Provisionality," *supra* note 38.

[99] Alexander, "Stakeholder Participation in New Governance," *supra* note 50.

First, those with an interest in the dispute are covered—whether the interest is as a professional, an expert, a consumer, or a "citizen-user." This appears an open-ended term. Moreover, accountability and peer review norms filter out the participation of certain groups. On the one hand, the filtering may be constructive. Antagonistic participants, such as the "quack" doctors who sell garlic or beetroot cures in response to HIV, or the "dissident" scientists who reject the connection between HIV and AIDS (and who were, to the outrage of many, invited by President Mbeki to many key conferences on HIV/AIDS in South Africa), might be precluded from negotiations on a solution to mother-to-child transmission of HIV. Moreover, the process of peer review might be instrumentally beneficial—it may unearth the reasons for the lay influence of some actors.

Yet other groups may actively withhold from negotiation for strategic reasons. The political field is about many things; but it is also a site of struggle, where political professionals compete for the "monopoly" of speaking and acting in the name of some, or of all, nonprofessionals.[100] To fold the movement into a stakeholder negotiation is to settle that competition, removing a key aspect of movement power and success. In our Treatment Action Campaign example, volunteers of the organization worked independently to participate in the project of health care, sometimes withholding participation and engaging in more adversarial, antagonistic approaches.

It is important to note that this position is not one of law and movement separation. The experimentalist acknowledgement of the importance of institutional alliances is a very important one, and one that may be too readily discounted in social movement studies. When the movement remains outside of the formality of the court order, it does not thereby become "extra-legal" or "extra-institutional" in its operation.[101] The movement remains engaged with both law and with remedies, yet an institutionalized coordinated process does not wholly dictate its responsibility.

Rather than work in permanent linkage with state institutions, a successful movement may take advantage of the fit between its interests and the points of leverage within political institutions.[102] Our example of health-care

[100] Pierre Bourdieu, *Language and Symbolic Power* (Gino Raymond and Matthew Adamson, trans., John B. Thompson, ed., 1991) 190.

[101] Orly Lobel, "The Paradox of Extra-Legal Activism: Critical Legal Consciousness and Transformative Politics," 120 Harv. L. Rev. 937 (2007) (refuting the cooptation critique as specifically cogent to legal strategies); *cf.* Tomiko Brown-Nagin, "Elites, Social Movements, and the Law: The Case of Affirmative Action," 105 Colum. L. Rev. 1436 (2005). *See* discussion, Chapter 8, section B(3).

[102] *See* Peter P. Houtzager, "Introduction: From Polycentrism to the Polity," in Peter P. Houtzager and Mick Moore (eds.), *Changing Paths: International Development and the New Politics of Inclusion* (2003) 1, 14 (deploying Theda Skocpol's polity approach to development analysis).

rights might be surprisingly more straightforward than other economic and social rights. Because health care attracts middle-class and professional support, coalitions may be formed that are not easily available to other groups, such as squatters who assert the right to housing, or the unemployed who assert the right to education.[103] The dictates of governance may write class out of the story.[104]

The promotion of movement activity within the de-structured structures of governance may lead to an enervation of its energy at the precise time when the movement needs it most: in confrontation with and perhaps resistance to powerful state and market actors. The fragile structure of movements, and the delicate balance of political energy, seems too unreliable in the staunch program of institutional experiment. The very uncertainty posited by experimentalism—of movements knowing their needs but unaware of the full solution, thus bringing into bear fruitful alliances with certain factions of the elite, or confusion in both—is an intuitive prescription for placing the disadvantages of instability on the weaker party. This leads us to the second challenge inevitably experienced in economic and social rights cases: the power deficit.

(2) *The power deficit*

Another concern lies, not in the identity of stakeholders, but in the unequal relations between them. Different stakeholders hold—and face—different stakes. This translates to a different set of resources in which to conduct negotiations and push for particular views. If an imbalance of power is an inevitable feature between negotiating parties, it is perhaps nowhere so obvious as in relation to economically disadvantaged segments of the population and their landlords, health providers, welfare officers, or school administrators. Not only does the stronger party appear to hold all the cards, they also have better access to information. Negotiations between the two are fraught. Indeed, the informal negotiation processes established under experimentalism appear to invite the same critiques levied at alternative dispute resolution and other informal processes decades ago.[105]

[103] Dennis Davis, "Adjudicating the Socio-Economic Rights in the South African Constitution: Towards 'Deference Lite'?" 22 S. Afr. J. Hum. Rts. 301 (2006) 326.

[104] For a parallel critique, see Risa L. Goluboff, " 'We Live's in a Free House Such as It Is': Class and the Creation of Modern Civil Rights," 151 U. Pa. L. Rev. 1977 (2003).

[105] For critiques of informal justice systems, *see* Richard L. Abel (ed.), *The Politics of Informal Justice* (vol. 1, 1982); *see also* Carrie Menkel-Meadow, "The Lawyer's Role(s) in Deliberative Democracy," 5 Nev. L.J. 347 (2004) 348; Amy J. Cohen, "Negotiation, Meet New Governance: Interests, Skills, Selves," 33(2) Law & Soc. Inq. 502 (2008).

Under careful conditions, negotiation may disrupt this effect. The experimentalist remedy of "meaningful engagement" is one in which the power of the Constitution's values—towards justice and equity—upends the power distribution between the parties themselves. If we recall the justification for this remedy in South Africa, it was presented as one that could shift the habits and assumptions of either side to a dispute. In the case of evictions, this encompasses the attitudes of both evictees and squatters. For the latter group:

> . . . those who find themselves compelled by poverty and landlessness to live in shacks on the land of others, should be discouraged from regarding themselves as helpless victims, lacking the possibilities of personal moral agency. The tenacity and ingenuity they show in making homes out of discarded material, in finding work and sending their children to school, are a tribute to their capacity for survival and adaptation. Justice and equity oblige them to rely on this same resourcefulness in seeking a solution to their plight and to explore all reasonable possibilities of securing suitable alternative accommodation or land.[106]

It is important to note that the constitutional obligations towards economic and social rights, and the role of a third party mediator, are seen as critical for this effect. For scholars of experimentalism more generally, negotiations can go some, if not all, the way to resolving power imbalances. As Michael Dorf and Charles Sabel have acknowledged, decentralized negotiation processes may not dislodge the most heavily entrenched power imbalances caused by economic deprivation. Yet for these observers, such imbalances may be so entrenched that no form of law can dislodge them. Hence, its adherents claim, experimentalism may be the most promising attempt.[107]

Nonetheless, the professional roles inscribed in other models of lawyering target such power imbalances more concretely, and perhaps more effectively.[108] In explaining this view, one commentator has objected to the misrecognition of lawyers within the experimentalist paradigm—of lawyers acting as litigators. For this critic, lawyers enjoy a discrete professional identity, and technical expertise and capacity, which distinguish them from other policy-based actors. Their professional expectations, self-interest, and career incentives might work against their acceptance of a negotiating side part in the overall system of governance. Nevertheless, the view of

[106] *Port Elizabeth Municipality v. Various Occupiers*, 2005 (1) SA 217 (CC) [41], *see further* Chapter 5, section D (3). One participant has commented that the engagement "reinforced the personhood of the occupiers," rather than the view that they were "a nuisance to be abated by eviction": Stuart Wilson, "Planning for Inclusion in South Africa: The State's Duty to Prevent Homelessness and the Potential of 'Meaningful Engagement'," 22 Urban Forum 265 (2011) 270.

[107] Dorf and Sabel, "A Constitution of Democratic Experimentalism," *supra* note 39, 409.

[108] Douglas NeJaime, "When New Governance Fails," 70 Ohio State L.J. 323 (2009).

lawyers in this critique is too narrowly cast. More pro-poor descriptions of lawyering, such as those offered by the "cause lawyering" paradigm, focus more carefully on the way in which the lawyer accepts the responsibilities for client and cause, and can rely on the law and on professional legal tools to address the imbalance of power.[109] The program of cause lawyers offers a highly detailed and power-sensitive set of precepts to upend the infringements of economic and social rights.

Rather than draw from lawyering models, the experimentalists approve of behaviors and trends in workplaces elsewhere. A key image in the experimentalist portrayal of negotiation and problem-solving is the Toyota firm, where production systems have learned to innovate and collaborate through destabilization rather than harmonization, and through continually adjusting social norms.[110] This image, deployed by William Simon, relies on innovations in economic sociology to support innovations in more public processes.[111] Nonetheless, the smooth functionary system of Toyota production is ensured by invisible sources of power—norms of the bottom line, efficiency, perhaps mimicry, and peer pressure, which are unrealistic in full-scale democratic settings and at the very least undesirable.

Within the public setting, and perhaps especially during contestations around economic and social rights, we can readily see the different power relations between differentially situated "stakeholders," who may agree on common goals but have very different concrete interests behind them. For example, patients in public health services, or teachers, parents, and students in public education, have starkly different resources of knowledge and even expectations of entitlement on which to draw. In schooling, some teachers, parents, and school advocates may lack the capacity to use the testing information in the ways envisaged: "to assess, monitor, and improve the schools."[112] Other sources of power imbalance, of poverty in the midst of poverty, for example, rather than poverty in the midst of plenty, as in the US setting, exacerbate the power differentials and make experimentalism even more troublesome in other sites of contestation.[113]

[109] Sandra R. Levitsky, "To Lead with Law: Reassessing the Influence of Legal Advocacy Organizations in Social Movements," in Austin Sarat and Stuart A. Scheingold (eds.), *Cause Lawyers and Social Movements* (2006) 145.

[110] William H. Simon, "Toyota Jurisprudence: Legal Theory and Rolling Rule Regimes," in Scott and de Burca (eds.), *Law and New Governance in the EU and the US*, *supra* note 41, 37.

[111] *See also* Dorf and Sabel, "A Constitution of Democratic Experimentalism," *supra* note 39, 286.

[112] Martha Minow, "School Reform Outside Laboratory Conditions," 28 N.Y.U. Rev. L. & Soc. Change 333 (2003) 336.

[113] Boaventura de Sousa Santos and Cesar A. Rodrigeuz-Garavito, "Law, Politics, and the Subaltern in Counter-Hegemonic Globalization," in de Sousa Santos and Rodrigeuz-Garavito (eds.) *Law and Globalization from Below: Towards a Cosmopolitan Legality* (2005) 1, 7.

In the words of one apprehensive critic, experimentalism seems to capitulate to the speed and the market priors of capitalism.[114] The problem flows from the way that the institutional reforms of experimentalism are directed to lessen the constraints on markets, without protecting nonmarketized interests and groups. Movements which purport to confront the inequalities that are invariably produced by liberal capitalism may be assisted by more, rather than less, constraint in politics: Within this view, their success requires a "slowing down" of markets, and the "enabling constraints" that are the heart of liberal constitutionalism. This position recognizes that not all social structures disenable freedom: "constraints imposed by one particular sphere of activity can expand freedom by creating whole new spheres of activity and by making possible greater flexibility in old ones."[115] The theory of constitutionalism is posited with these constraints front and center.

(3) The symbol deficit

The third concern relates to the content of negotiations prescribed by experimentalism. In experimentalism, negotiations are deliberately downgraded, low-to-the-ground affairs. They are rigorously evidential, and based on reason. The demands of the political arena bring together otherwise divergent "beliefs, preferences, self-understandings and habits of thought and action."[116] Through a pragmatist-inspired experiential learning, original habits and beliefs can be transformed, including habits of opinion, "the toughest of all habits" to break.[117] Destabilization occurs, not necessarily at the level of the hardened ideology of constitutional culture, but on the insulated routines of public agencies. Thus, where jurisgenesis offers grand, world-shifting discourse, experimentalism offers pragmatist problem-solving and incremental reform. Where jurisgenesis ends (at the institutional question), experimentalism begins.

The concern is that the rigorous institutional focus leaves the true source of social change wanting. Some have questioned whether experimentalist "networks can work well as motors for political community in the sense of identity-maintenance or the transmission of distinct cultures or the

[114] William E. Scheuerman, "Democratic Experimentalism or Capitalist Synchronization? Critical Reflections on Directly-Deliberative Polyarchy," 17 Can. J. L. & Jurisprudence 101 (2004).

[115] Bernard Yack, "Toward a Free Marketplace of Institutions: Roberto Unger's 'Super-Liberal' Theory of Emancipation," 101 Harv. L. Rev. 1961 (1988) 1967.

[116] Joshua Cohen and Joel Rogers, "Secondary Associations and Democratic Governance," in Joshua Cohen and Joel Rogers (eds.), *Associations and Democracy* (1995) 7.

[117] Dewey, *The Public and Its Problems* (1954) (1927).

protection of disadvantaged groups."[118] It is ironic that a program that relies on the energy of crisis—as advantageous to democracy[119]—in the absence of actual crisis, would deflect the major capacity of social movements to engineer it. The success of large-scale moral discourse and cultural change, discussed in Chapter 8, requires large-scale symbols.

How are these deficits resolved? I suggest that the program of governance offers partial, and complementary, insights for constituting economic and social rights. Combined with the anchoring premises of constitutionalism, it helps to break down governmental barriers to economic and social rights, harnessing market energy and rationality. Nonetheless, a strict application of the experimentalist program may expose the claimants of economic and social rights to power imbalances, and remove the potential of power from moral discourse and symbolism.

Of course, the model of constitutionalism that presents itself as a complementary power is one which itself constitutes and enables power, rather than simply limits it. It is therefore inaccurate to portray constitutionalism as a conservative institutional program, allowing for only the provision of cash grants and entitlements as the implementation of economic and social rights. Instead, it should be viewed as conceptualizing a theory of constraints (constraints which both require state action and limit it) on government. Thus, it has in common with experimentalism an active duty to explore the justice of arrangements beyond the status quo. However, unlike experimentalism, the government, courts, market actors, or civil society should not be "up for grabs" at the same time. Traditional constitutionalist theory settles certain questions to allow others to be contested and negotiated. It allows for certain contestations to proceed exceptionally. In this way, new modes of representation may be established, power imbalances may be confronted, and a language of injustice and of rights may proceed.

In closing, let us reconsider the actions of the Treatment Action Campaign. In seeking ARVs for expectant mothers, the Treatment Action Campaign employs a rights discourse that does not "paper over distributional policy," in the sense that rights claims are usually thought to suggest.[120] Instead, it claims that the government's distributive decisions are flawed with respect to this dimension of its health policy, by pointing to the government's obligations with respect to health care. It does so with

[118] Helen Hershkoff and Benedict Kingsbury, "Crisis, Community and Courts in Network Governance: A Response to Liebman and Sabel's Approach to Reform of Public Education," 28 N.Y.U. Rev. L. & Soc. Change 319 (2003) 323.

[119] Roberto Mangabeira Unger, *Democracy Realized: The Progressive Alternative* (1998).

[120] James Gray Pope, "Labor's Constitution of Freedom," 106 Yale L.J. 941 (1997). For a description of the way in which class was written out of the civil rights struggle, *see* Goluboff, "Class and the Creation of Modern Civil Rights," *supra* note 104.

heightened attention to the institutions that obstruct health care, and those that may play a part in the solution.

Yet this institutional literacy does not proceed at the cost of morally laden argument. Consider the movement's treatment literacy campaign. By instructing its members and other people living with HIV/AIDS about the discipline of their HIV/AIDS drugs regime, and by constantly reinforcing their right of access to medicine, the movement changes the self-understanding of their members about their condition. By encouraging its members to divulge their HIV status (and wear T-shirts pronouncing this effect), the movement authors the sense of rightness within the members themselves.[121] This is an important precursor to the movement's interaction with the Constitutional Court in claiming a right to access health care.

Zackie Achmat, the charismatic leader of the Treatment Action Campaign, performed this morality when he refused ARVs in denunciation of their prohibitive cost to fellow South Africans.[122] In Achmat's own view, the fact that this refusal threatened at one point to take his life is an example of tension between morality and strategy, rather than a conflation of the two.[123] The movement pursues both tangible interests and moral values, putting to one side a categorical separation that has played a prominent role in social movement description, which are labeled either as interest-based vehicles or as primarily intended as mediums for the expression of values.

In the words of its activists, the Treatment Action Campaign "approaches HIV differently. It talks and teaches positive living, that this illness is not a sin—life is not wasted or less valuable, it must go on."[124] Yet this is not identity politics as commonly understood: Although members are encouraged to accept the status of HIV and press past its stigma and negative associations, the movement is eclectic about the religious, political, and social identities that its members are associated with. The interest in treatment, or an empathy with those who need it, is the more pertinent spur to action.

121 For a bystander's description of the literacy campaign of the Treatment Action Campaign and its effect on social norms, and especially on social stigma, *see* Jonny Steinberg, *Sizwe's Test: A Young Man's Journey through Africa's AIDS Epidemic* (2008).

122 Conference interview with Zackie Achmat by Stones of Hope team members, Bellagio Center, December 2006; *see also* Edwin Cameron, First Jonathan Mann Memorial Lecture: "The Deafening Silence of AIDS," XIIIth International Aids Conference, Durban, 9–14 July 2000.

123 Achmat, cited in Friedman and Mottiar, *Rewarding Engagement?*, *supra* note 14, n. 225.

124 Freidman and Mottiar, *Rewarding Engagement?*, *supra* note 14, n. 54 (citing activists from Durban, 28 January 2004).

In this chapter, I have argued that experimentalist governance offers a highly productive set of features for constituting economic and social rights, by coordinating the state, market, and civil society. If pursued as a partial technique, in practice alongside the safeguards of constitutionalism, rather than its alternative, it suggests new and constructive ways to open up public practices to contestation around economic and social rights.

10

Conclusion: Economic and Social Rights as Human Rights and Constitutional Rights

Our modern legal systems have developed with both wealth and poverty in their midst. Theories of economic development have assumed that that state's responsibility for poverty can be chiefly addressed by the private law protections of contract and property, secured by police and courts. Theories of law have correspondingly assumed that the public laws applicable to legislatures, governments, officials, and courts have a lesser role to play in addressing the individual's lack of enjoyment of basic goods and services, such as food, water, health, housing, or education. At the same time, the breadth and scale of the current experiences of poverty and maldistribution are impossible to ignore. In high income countries, unemployment, discrimination, austerity measures, and other economic hazards have continued to create a large minority of individuals experiencing poverty or other forms of inability to access the goods and services that they need to participate—or simply to live with dignity—in the liberal market order. In the developing countries, even more staggering numbers of mass poverty, unemployment, and a dearth of medical and social services tell a story of hardship and suffering of a terrible magnitude. The data on extreme poverty, where individuals experience such chronic and prolonged economic insecurity that their lives may be permanently affected, is even more troubling. In all these cases, human dignity, and the capacity for freedom and human development, is severely undermined. Under these conditions, economic and social rights appear to promise the impossible: guaranteed rights to access food, water, health care, housing, and education, according to the resources available to each state (with assistance from other states and the international order). How such rights can move from promise to actuality, through the very legal systems that have contributed to this state of affairs, has been the theme of this book.

The book began with an analytical construction. To make sense of the actuality of economic and social rights, it is necessary to depart from the study of purely formal law, in spite of how entrenched and accepted many of its terms appear to be. The framework of "constituting" rights is a construction that allows us to recognize the practical importance of law, reason, and social fact in bringing rights into reality. Legal artifacts, including constitutions, statutes, human rights treaties, and judicial decisions, purport to give economic and social rights the authority of formal law. Reason, through providing the means to answer questions of social significance, universal reciprocity, and feasibility of the satisfaction of fundamental material interests, is required to sustain arguments that such interests amount to fundamental rights. The fact of acceptance and consensus of those living under law, and of the recognition of its validity, completes the book's central analytical edifice.

Under this construction, we are invited to explore the contours of interpretation, enforcement, and contestation that constitute economic and social rights, within the three Parts of the book. First, the methods of interpreting economic and social rights are described, through a combination of philosophical and comparative legal analysis. Interpretive positions, which draw on rationalist, or alternatively consensualist, approaches, are evidenced in both national constitutional regimes and international human rights regimes. Examples which draw on the paradigm value of human dignity, or of life, or alternatively on a consensus between participating parties, are depicted in South Africa, India, Germany, and Canada, and in the United Nations, and regional, human rights bodies.[1] In addition to these normative trends, the structural pressures of minimalism and of rights limitation result in greater practicability, and perhaps lowered ambitions, for the interpretation of economic and social rights. The internationally established "minimum core," created by the United Nations Committee on Economic, Social and Cultural Rights, set the agenda for national constitutional systems, as they turned to newly justiciable economic and social rights. Some domestic courts, such as the South African Constitutional Court, ultimately declined to internalize a minimum, justiciable core, while others, such as the Colombian Constitutional Court, chose to accept it.[2] Similarly, the important structural aspects of "limiting" rights, an exercise which I expand to include progressive realization standards, limitation clauses, suspensions, derogations, overrides, reservations, amendments, underenforcement, proportionality standards, or other balancing principles, simultaneously promises to strengthen and to undermine (depending upon one's perspective) the respect and protection given to rights in constitutional and international human rights law. From Germany, Canada, and

[1] Chapter 2. [2] Chapter 3.

South Africa (as prominent examples), to Europe and the United Nations bodies, and back, the cross-fertilization of the ideas of limiting and balancing rights has become almost untraceable.

The second dimension of constituting rights is the processes of enforcement that accompany economic and social rights, and which are described in Part II of this book. Evidence is supplied by the enforcement regimes of South Africa, Colombia, India, and the United Kingdom. These examples defy a presentation of economic and social rights adjudication as an inflexible, uniform, or unresponsive exercise. The adjudication of economic and social rights by the South African Constitutional Court, over fifteen years of case law, is conceptualized as a five-part typology of judicial review. Cases involving the right to health care, housing, social security, water, education, and electricity and sanitation services elicit features of deferential, conversational, experimentalist, managerial, and peremptory decision-making and remedies. These, I claim, help to enhance the democratic credentials of economic and social rights, and the feasibility of their implementation. At its most successful, I suggest the Court draws on these approaches in order to catalyze the actions of other actors, and increase the responsiveness and accountability of an otherwise intransigent, incompetent, or inattentive government.

The enforcement modes supplied by South Africa are relevant to constitutional democracies elsewhere. What exactly can be concluded from the South African experience is managed by two observations. Once the South African experience is attributed to the role conception enjoyed by the South African Constitutional Court, other apex or constitutional courts are appropriately differentiated. And once these systems are explored against the more concrete institutional features of their own constitutional systems, such as the responsibility taken for rights investigations and for rights-based advice by legislatures, governments, tribunals, and commissions, such role conceptions are adequately explained. Hence, I suggest that a supremacist court in Colombia, an engaged court in India, and a detached court in the United Kingdom undertake the enforcement of economic and social rights. These three examples draw on features of the original typology of judicial review, to demarcate the distinctive judicial and nonjudicial arrangements that themselves contribute to constituting economic and social rights.

Whether such lessons apply to the supranational tribunals and international human rights committees that are responsible for enforcing economic and social rights is beyond the scope of the present study. Such enforcement bodies draw on different operating procedures. Participating states and claimants present information differently, adjudicators or committee members use different decision-making processes, and the expectations of enforcement, or of otherwise gaining compliance with the orders made, are on very different scales. While international procedures often borrow from national courts and tribunals, they do so selectively and opportunistically, often merging different common law and civil law traditions of adjudication, and drawing on highly distinct models for securing compliance and for technically assisting states with their commitments. Nonetheless, there is a relevance of such domestic systems for a supranational or international body charged with deciding liability and delivering remedies in accordance with the treaty or customary obligations of economic and social rights.[3] Indeed, I suggest that my typologies may apply to a supranational or international body charged with enforcing economic and social rights, or at least can point to the useful questions that should be asked of supranational and international tribunals, and that also distinguish them from each other.[4] The adoption of a catalytic or engaged role, in particular, may resolve many of the challenges that international bodies face, with often vaguely stated communications, intransigent or incompetent States Parties, and highly motivated nongovernmental organizations ("NGOs").

The third and final dimension of constituting rights is observed through the contestations of social movements and other private actors. First, social movements adopt strategies of jurisgenesis, the disturbance of orthodoxies, and the framing of injustice to counter the current obstacles to economic and social rights present in law. They provide new narratives about rights, or about constitutions, treaties, and their influence on market arrangements: narratives which help to bridge the gap between the formal recognition of rights and their protection in everyday arrangements. While the concept of culture is a difficult one for constitutional theory, I suggest that it supplies a lens through which to understand how such movements can restructure constitutional meaning, the role conceptions of institutions, and the very theory of the state. The community-based Legal Resources Centre in Ghana gives evidence to these effects, effectively challenging the user fees system of health care, so punitive on the poor, by petition, protest, litigation, and negotiation, using the language of rights. The course of economic and social rights litigation in South Africa is re-analyzed using the framework of social movements, giving further context to the long-term failures and successes of the jurisprudence of the book's primary comparison.

[3] This will become more urgent as the Committee on Economic, Social and Cultural Rights hears complaints: *see* Optional Protocol to the International Covenant of Economic, Social and Cultural Rights, G.A. Res. 63/117, UN Doc. A/RES/63/117 (10 December 2008). Yet other international and regional bodies are also responsible for determining economic and social rights. *Compare*, i.e., the International Court of Justice with the Inter-American Court of Human Rights, the European Court of Human Rights, and the African Commission on Human Rights (and African Court on Human and People's Rights).

[4] Ibid. Of course, while characteristic differences often stem from institutional design, the analysis of role conceptions may highlight other features.

The same features of contestation apply to the South African Treatment Action Campaign. Yet this case study can be understood to offer additional insights into the linkages realized by private actors in a right to health campaign. The inclusion of nurses, doctors, hospitals, other medical experts, multinational pharmaceutical companies, people with HIV, and people living with people with HIV, in both urban and rural settings, provincial governments, and transnational social movements, reveals a multilayered solution to the polycentric problems that usually accompany economic and social rights (in that case, preventing mother-to-child transmission of HIV). These layers of governance appear to transcend the formal institutions and boundaries of constitutionalism. From the perspective of new governance, such linkages can create additional opportunities for learning, problem solving, and accountability. I suggest that the Treatment Action Campaign both confirms and diminishes the significance of this perspective. As a critical partner to constitutionalism, new governance prescribes new resources with which to coordinate the state, market, and civil society, to destabilize presently obstructive public arrangements, and to make use of the efficiency of the market. Yet because of representation problems, located in the stakeholders, power dynamics, and discourse of new governance, which are amplified in the context of a lack of formal economic and social rights or a cultural commitment to them, I suggest that this perspective is a complementary instantiation to the broader, and more anchored, precepts of constitutionalism.

There are three limits to this analysis. The first should be obvious. In each section of this book, I have treated human rights and constitutional rights as interchangeable, transposable, and compatible. This perspective is enabled by my post-interpretive examination of texts, institutions, and political formations, as well as by present-day realities. First, I draw from the normative resources of theories of universal rights and of human dignity that regard their institutional level of protection as largely beside the point. In each domain, the determinacy of language and of consensus may be just as elusive. Second, I emphasize the features common to both human rights and constitutional rights that focus on the responsibilities of the state towards the individual. I examine the "constitutional" texts of human rights law—primarily the Universal Declaration of Human Rights ("UDHR") and the International Covenant on Economic, Social and Cultural Rights ("ICESCR"), which, along with the International Covenant on Civil and Political Rights ("ICCPR") represent the international bill of rights—which have reflected, and shaped, the text of many domestic constitutions, as well as the cultural constitutional commitments of those living under them. Indeed, I suggest that the fashioning of legitimacy through the methodological focus on the individual (whether the worst off individual, or the average individual, or the abstract individual) is a key point of similarity between national constitutional law and international human rights law. Third, I utilize the cross-fertilization of ideas that occurs, to an increasing extent, across the public institutions of constitutional democracies. The transnational judicial dialogue established between courts, offers a central resource for understanding the merging relations between international and comparative law, and for reflecting on what is shared and what is distinct. Judicial reasoning techniques of minimalism or limitations, common to international human rights and constitutional rights, are doctrinally intertwined. Such cross-fertilization also occurs with respect to governmental and parliamentary branches, which is represented briefly in this book by the so-called "Commonwealth" parliamentary scrutiny procedures and the expected rights-protecting pressures of parliamentary debate. Provincial and local governments, too, incorporate treaties, and rely on international and comparative sources to guide the meaning and operation of local laws.[5] Finally, I acknowledge the transnational dimensions of social movements and NGOs agitating for economic and social rights, and of the globalized market order that often structures their claims. Even grassroots advocates, traditionally viewed as bound wholly within their local, and at the very least national, legal systems, are linked to movements elsewhere.[6] These claims often transcend the domestic borders of constitutional regimes, where the extraterritorial application of human rights responsibilities, or the internal application of human rights to noncitizens, explodes the framework of purely national constitutional democracy.[7] Hence, the boundaries of each constitutive community are porous—exactly how porous is not simply a question of constitutional text or of the genealogy of that text, but is determined by the strength of transnational alliances, the outward-looking nature of the constitutional culture, and the resonance of rights talk within it. For these reasons, I treat economic and social rights as, in all accuracy, integrated and transposable as international human rights and constitutional rights.

Nonetheless, there are evident differences between the two, which caution against their conflation. The further one departs from the suprapositive perspective of human dignity, and from the universal standpoint of what an individual can demand from the state, the less relevant appear

[5] Judith Resnik, "Law's Migration: American Exceptionalism, Silent Dialogues, and Federalism's Multiple Ports of Entry," 115 Yale L.J. 1564 (2006).

[6] Beth A. Simmons, *Mobilizing for Human Rights: International Law in Domestic Politics* (2009); *see also* Margaret E. Keck and Kathryn Sikkink, *Activists Beyond Borders: Advocacy Networks In International Politics* (1998).

[7] Gerald L. Neuman, "Understanding Global Due Process," 23 Geo. Immigr. L.J. 365 (2009): 382–91.

the connections between them. Constitutional rights are those that a political community might be said to have given to itself. Like all rights, they appear to be self-sufficient within that political community: concepts of self-government appear to demand that this be so. Human rights go beyond those contained within discrete political communities, purporting to hold every state to account while transcending all of them. As positive law, they are only as old as the UDHR: or younger, still.[8]

Moreover, there is evidence of both norm divergence and of conflicting claims of authority between the regimes of domestic and international human rights. When international economic and social rights conflict with their national expressions, or with each other, abstract theories of monism or dualism, or hierarchies of norms are unable to resolve the conflict. Such dissonances may be partially met, according to Gerard Neuman, by giving constitutional status to human rights treaties, or else a mandatory interpretive direction of the kind we have seen in South Africa, or permission for voluntary consideration of international (and comparative) law by national courts.[9] These go part way to confirming their interrelationship, and are the primary justification for their combined treatment throughout this book.

Such directions need not be explicit in constitutional text. In becoming an accepted judicial practice for many constitutions, judicial borrowing from international and comparative sources is explained by the increasingly linked networks of judges, the ease of reading international and comparative opinions, and the norms of professional reciprocity and respect that have formed between judges from different constitutional backgrounds.[10] More specifically, the emergence of the instruments and institutions of human rights lends force to a distinctively constitutionalist mode of reasoning about rights and justice.[11] For Jeremy Waldron, this reasoning can be considered analogous to scientific inquiry.[12] Judges relying on international law are engaging the problem-solving component of law. Together, they check results, duplicate experiments, credential useful findings, and forge ahead with knowledge about the difficult issues of human organization that are mediated by law—how we should live together, what we should owe to each other, and the like. Such principles may give rise to constitutionalist

[8] For an account which privileges the "human rights" that were called for in the decade after 1968 as the "truer" history, *see* Samuel Moyn, *The Last Utopia: Human Rights in History* (2010). Yet Moyn's account applies primarily to the civil and political rights embraced by the US human rights movement.

[9] Gerald L. Neuman, "Human Rights and Constitutional Rights: Harmony and Dissonance," 55 Stanford L. Rev. 1863 (2003).

[10] Anne-Marie Slaughter, *A New World Order* (2004).

[11] Katharine G. Young, "The World, through the Judge's Eye," 28 Aust. Y.B. Int'l. L. 27 (2009).

[12] Jeremy Waldron, "Foreign Law and the Modern *Ius Gentium*," 119 Harv. L. Rev. 129 (2005) 134.

ideas that fall outside of present-day, domestic interpretations of local constitutions. On this view, the reasoned persuasiveness of international, comparative, as well as past, unorthodox, and challenging interpretations of a constitution allows judges to retain their fidelity to that constitution, even when departing from the current official interpretations of text.

Despite controversy in certain quarters, many judges openly approve of this transnational judicial dialogue, and of the recourse, within it, to international law.[13] Perhaps with the attempt to codify this convention, diverse judicial representatives agreed, in 1988, that:

> (1) Fundamental human rights and freedoms are inherent in all humankind and find expression in constitutions and legal systems throughout the world and in the international human rights instruments. (2) These international human rights instruments provide important guidance in cases concerning fundamental human rights and freedoms.[14]

Moreover:

> . . . (5) In most countries whose legal systems are based upon the common law, international conventions are not directly enforceable in national courts unless their provisions have been incorporated by legislation into domestic law. However, there is a growing tendency for national courts to have regard to these international norms for the purpose of deciding cases where the domestic law—whether constitutional, statute or common law—is uncertain or incomplete . . .[15]

Judges have also provided the dialogue with a normative theory: the practice is welcomed "because it respects the universality of fundamental human rights and freedoms and the vital role of an independent judiciary in reconciling the competing claims of individuals and groups of persons with the general interests of the community."[16] For international law scholars, this practice suggests an ever-closer connection between international and domestic law, bringing to fruition a long-hoped-for source of enforcement for a notoriously underenforced body of law.[17]

[13] The Bangalore Principles were released as a summary of issues discussed at a Judicial Colloquium on "The Domestic Application of International Human Rights Norms," held in Bangalore, India from 24–26 February 1988. Reprinted in Commonwealth Secretariat, *Developing Human Rights Jurisprudence: The Domestic Application of International Human Rights Norms*, vol. 1, (1998) ix–x and in (1989) 1 African Journal of International and Comparative Law/Revue Africaine de Droit International et Comparé 345.

[14] Ibid.

[15] Ibid.

[16] Michael Kirby, "The Role of the Judge in Advancing Human Rights by Reference to International Human Rights Norms," 62 Aust. L.J. 514 (1988) 531. For commentary, *see* Young, "The World through the Judge's Eye, *supra* note 11.

[17] E.g., H. Hongju Koh, "International Law as Part of Our Law," 98 Am. J. Int'l. L. 43 (2004) 56 (celebrating a "transnational legal process" through which "interlinked rules of domestic and

This practice has been more often pursued with respect to civil and political rights than economic and social rights, since justiciability concerns have acted as an independent brake on the opportunities for the latter's judicial consideration. Yet as early as 1970, Justice Marshall of the United States Supreme Court referred to the economic and social rights of the UDHR in support of the application of the Fourteenth Amendment to welfare rights.[18] (The ICESCR had not, at that time, entered into force; nor has it yet been ratified by the United States.) I have elsewhere argued that Justice Marshall's recourse to the UDHR was unremarkable, due to the homegrown commitment to a "second bill" of rights in the United States.[19] This proposal, protective of the rights to a job, to trade, to "adequate medical care and the opportunity to achieve and enjoy good health," to a good education, and to "adequate protection from the economic fears of old age, sickness, accident, and unemployment"[20] was proclaimed by Franklin Delano Roosevelt, and the overarching "freedom from want" was adopted in the Preamble to the UDHR, as well as subsequent human rights instruments.[21] Members of the current Supreme Court continue to justify the relevance (but not the authority) of international and comparative sources, in spite of the controversy.[22] As Justice Breyer of the US Supreme Court has observed, because "foreign nations have become democratic; to an ever greater extent, they have sought to protect basic human rights; to an ever greater extent they have embodied that protection in legal documents enforced through judicial decision making."[23] When those democratic and rights-protective features become more accepted as applicable to economic and social rights, such recourse may occur again in the United States, as it has elsewhere.

Of course, the paradox in all this is that international norms represent a threat to, rather than an elaboration of, the supra-positive norms of

international law develop, and . . . interlinked processes of domestic and international compliance come about").

[18] *Dandrige v. Williams*, 397 U.S. 471, 521 n. 14 (1970).

[19] Katharine G. Young, "Freedom, Want and Economic and Social Rights: Frame and Law," 24 Maryland J. Int'l. L. 182 (2009).

[20] Franklin D. Roosevelt, "Message to Congress on the State of the Union (11 January 1944)," in Samuel I. Rosenman (ed.), *The Public Papers and Addresses of Franklin D. Roosevelt* (1950) 13, 40. *See* discussion, *supra*, Chapter 2, text accompanying notes 116–20.

[21] *See* ICESCR, 16 December 1966, pmbl., 993 U.N.T.S. 3; ICCPR, 16 December 1966, pmbl., 999 U.N.T.S. 171.

[22] E.g., Vicki Jackson, "Constitutional Comparisons: Convergence, Resistance, Engagement," 119 Harv. L. Rev. 109 (2005); *Roper v. Simmons*, 543 U.S. 551, 578 (2005); *Lawrence v. Texas* 539 U.S. 558, 572–3, 576–7 (2003).

[23] "The Relevance of Foreign Legal Materials in US Constitutional Cases: A Conversation between Justice Antonin Scalia and Justice Stephen Breyer," 3 Int'l. J. Const. L. 519 (2005).

constitutional law and democracy. This is due to the important norms of self-government that exist within national systems of constitutional law and within normative principles of constitutionalism. The age-old tension between constitutionalism and democracy is recast as one of international human rights obligations versus national democracy. This is particularly the case in certain constitutions, like the United States, which has tended to prize a procedural, majoritarian, democracy over more substantive considerations.[24] International law is said to intrude, and dominate, over national constitutional democracies.

Yet on at least two understandings of democracy, it may be the opposite. The first, presented by Eyal Benvenisti, is the idea that judges can bolster their own government's ability to resist the influence of more powerful international participants by strategically selecting what sources of international law to rely on, and by choosing the substantive legal principles that enhance national democratic processes.[25] In this justification, it is the forging of a "united judicial front" amongst courts, in regard to issues over which their own government's ability to represent their people may be restricted, which supports democracy. There is evidence that judges have applied independent review to their national government's responses to issues such as counterterrorism and the status of asylum seekers: policies and laws whose content has been influenced heavily by other governments, rather than by local actors.[26] The enforcement of economic and social rights, as against internationally determined austerity measures, structural adjustment, or development conditionality, would be a case in point.[27] The second, more ambitious, approach to understanding the transnational judicial dialogue in democratic terms is the idea that a new, global *demos* has challenged the territorial boundaries in which the basic unit of democracy can be understood.[28] From this cosmopolitan justification it would follow that seeking new opinions is democratically legitimate, if the judges are sufficiently attuned to the measures of political participation at the international level. Nonetheless, while the implications of a new, cosmopolitan, political order are highly relevant to the work of domestic judges, especially

[24] Jed Rubenfeld, "Unilateralism and Constitutionalism," 79 N.Y.U. L. Rev. 1971 (2004).

[25] Eyal Benvenisti, "Reclaiming Democracy: The Strategic Uses of Foreign and International Law by National Courts," 102 Am. J. Int'l. L. 241 (2008) 259–62. *See* discussion in Young, "The World through the Judge's Eye," *supra* note 11.

[26] Benvenisti, ibid., (providing examples of the judicial review of (coordinated) governmental responses in respect of counterterrorism measures, environmental protection in developing countries, and the status of asylum seekers in destination countries).

[27] Kim Lane Scheppele, "A Realpolitik Defense of Social Rights," 82 Tex. L. Rev. 1921 (2004).

[28] J. Habermas, *The Postnational Constellation* (M. Pensky trans., 2001) [trans. of: *Die postnationale Konstellation* (1998)].

in national systems belonging to a regional system (most fittingly, Europe), many constitutional judges do not experience anything comparable to European integration. For the purposes of this study, it is more straightforward to emphasize the continuity between international law and comparative law.[29] Economic and social rights belong to both domains, and each may provide guidance and inspiration on the development of national constitutional law.

The second limit to the analysis presented in this book is the focus on public, rather than private, law. This is despite the clear links between interpretations of property rights, and of other rights such as contract, to the respect and protect given to economic and social rights. Modern constitutions increasingly embrace the "horizontal effect" of their provisions, which allows (and requires) constitutional rights to radiate into private law settings, and to ensure the rights-protective relations between individuals. Even in legal systems where the "horizontal effect" of constitutional law is resisted, it is not entirely clear that the obligation on all organs of states—including judges—to respect, protect, and fulfill constitutional rights can allow them to enforce rights-infringing private laws without developing them in line with constitutional rights. Particularly for common law judges, a duty to develop the common law, which includes, in many places, a duty to develop the common law in line with international human rights law, makes an examination of their potential effect on private law compelling. Equally pressing is that the recognition of the negative and positive obligations that attach to all rights means that the US state action doctrine, which precludes the effect of the constitution on private relations (and yet occludes the state's prior effect on these relations), can only be preserved with significant damage to logic.[30] The full effect of economic and social rights on property rights and other private rights is worthy of substantial analysis, but is beyond the scope of this book.

After the provisional description of the boundaries of the constitutive community, and the relative neglect of private law, the third limit to the analysis is the selectivity of its constitutional examples. In choosing to analyze the economic and social rights that have been interpreted, enforced, and contested in South Africa, as well as in Colombia, Ghana, India, the

[29] The comparative turn in international law is explained well by K. Knop, "Here and There: International Law in Domestic Courts," 32 N.Y.U. J. Int'l. L. & Pol. 501 (2000); L. Amede Obiora, "Toward an Auspicious Reconciliation of International and Comparative Analyses," 46 Am. J. Comp. L. 669 (1998). For the international turn in constitutional law, *see*, e.g., B. Bryde, "International Democratic Constitutionalism?," in R. S. J. Macdonald and D. M. Johnston (eds.), *Towards World Constitutionalism* (2005) 103–25; Jeffrey Dunoff (ed.), *Ruling The World?: Constitutionalism, International Law, and Global Governance* (2009).

[30] *See* discussion, *supra*, Chapter 6, section C(1).

United Kingdom, and at the United Nations level, I have drawn on successful examples of changes in public law and in social institutions. There are, of course, just as many examples of failure. Nonetheless, the book's intention has been to describe the processes of constituting economic and social rights, including the conditions of possibility in law and culture. A country-specific, region-specific, legal family-specific, or level-of-development-specific analysis would reveal other dimensions to the enterprise, just as these would perhaps obscure the more general points that my comparative study has been able to uncover.

Rights to food, water, health care, housing, and education give us an opportunity to change the way we use the legal system, in order to unsettle the current experiences of maldistribution and poverty. By understanding how a legal framework can provide sufficient certainty, determinacy, and responsiveness to economic and social rights, we can use our public laws to protect people from the harms of poverty and to allow them to participate in the design of that protection. No less is required for the fulfillment of human dignity, freedom, and the end of gross inequality in our constitutional democracies. Constituting economic and social rights depends upon action in the legislatures, the courts, the bureaucracies, the markets, the hospitals, the schools, the streets, the Internet, and, most importantly, in our minds.

Appendix I

Excerpts from Various Constitutions

PRIMARY JURISDICTION—CONSTITUTION OF SOUTH AFRICA 1996

7. *Rights*

1. This Bill of Rights is a cornerstone of democracy in South Africa. It enshrines the rights of all people in our country and affirms the democratic values of human dignity, equality and freedom.
2. The state must respect, protect, promote and fulfil the rights in the Bill of Rights.
3. The rights in the Bill of Rights are subject to the limitations contained or referred to in section 36, or elsewhere in the Bill.

8. *Application*

1. The Bill of Rights applies to all law, and binds the legislature, the executive, the judiciary and all organs of state.
2. A provision of the Bill of Rights binds a natural or a juristic person if, and to the extent that, it is applicable, taking into account the nature of the right and the nature of any duty imposed by the right.
3. When applying a provision of the Bill of Rights to a natural or juristic person in terms of subsection (2), a court
   a. in order to give effect to a right in the Bill, must apply, or if necessary develop, the common law to the extent that legislation does not give effect to that right; and
   b. may develop rules of the common law to limit the right, provided that the limitation is in accordance with section 36(1).

9. *Equality*

1. Everyone is equal before the law and has the right to equal protection and benefit of the law.

2. Equality includes the full and equal enjoyment of all rights and freedoms. To promote the achievement of equality, legislative and other measures designed to protect or advance persons, or categories of persons, disadvantaged by unfair discrimination may be taken.
3. The state may not unfairly discriminate directly or indirectly against anyone on one or more grounds, including race, gender, sex, pregnancy, marital status, ethnic or social origin, colour, sexual orientation, age, disability, religion, conscience, belief, culture, language and birth.
4. No person may unfairly discriminate directly or indirectly against anyone on one or more grounds in terms of subsection (3). National legislation must be enacted to prevent or prohibit unfair discrimination.
5. Discrimination on one or more of the grounds listed in subsection (3) is unfair unless it is established that the discrimination is fair.

10. *Human dignity*

Everyone has inherent dignity and the right to have their dignity respected and protected.

26. *Housing*

1. Everyone has the right to have access to adequate housing.
2. The state must take reasonable legislative and other measures, within its available resources, to achieve the progressive realisation of this right.
3. No one may be evicted from their home, or have their home demolished, without an order of court made after considering all the relevant circumstances. No legislation may permit arbitrary evictions.

27. *Health care, food, water and social security*

1. Everyone has the right to have access to
   a. health care services, including reproductive health care;
   b. sufficient food and water; and
   c. social security, including, if they are unable to support themselves and their dependants, appropriate social assistance.
2. The state must take reasonable legislative and other measures, within its available resources, to achieve the progressive realisation of each of these rights.
3. No one may be refused emergency medical treatment.

28. Children

1. Every child has the right
   a. to a name and a nationality from birth;
   b. to family care or parental care, or to appropriate alternative care when removed from the family environment;
   c. to basic nutrition, shelter, basic health care services and social services;
   d. to be protected from maltreatment, neglect, abuse or degradation;
   e. to be protected from exploitative labour practices;
   f. not to be required or permitted to perform work or provide services that
      i. are inappropriate for a person of that child's age; or
      ii place at risk the child's well-being, education, physical or mental health or spiritual, moral or social development; . . .

29. Education

1. Everyone has the right
   a. to a basic education, including adult basic education; and
   b. to further education, which the state, through reasonable measures, must make progressively available and accessible.
2. Everyone has the right to receive education in the official language or languages of their choice in public educational institutions where that education is reasonably practicable. In order to ensure the effective access to, and implementation of, this right, the state must consider all reasonable educational alternatives, including single medium institutions, taking into account
   a. equity;
   b. practicability; and
   c. the need to redress the results of past racially discriminatory laws and practices.
3. Everyone has the right to establish and maintain, at their own expense, independent educational institutions that
   a. do not discriminate on the basis of race;
   b. are registered with the state; and
   c. maintain standards that are not inferior to standards at comparable public educational institutions.
4. Subsection (3) does not preclude state subsidies for independent educational institutions.

36. Limitation of rights

1. The rights in the Bill of Rights may be limited only in terms of law of general application to the extent that the limitation is reasonable and justifiable in an open and democratic society based on human dignity, equality and freedom, taking into account all relevant factors, including
   a. the nature of the right;
   b. the importance of the purpose of the limitation;
   c. the nature and extent of the limitation;
   d. the relation between the limitation and its purpose; and
   e. less restrictive means to achieve the purpose.
2. Except as provided in subsection (1) or in any other provision of the Constitution, no law may limit any right entrenched in the Bill of Rights.

39. Interpretation of Bill of Rights

1. When interpreting the Bill of Rights, a court, tribunal or forum
   a. must promote the values that underlie an open and democratic society based on human dignity, equality and freedom;
   b. must consider international law; and
   c. may consider foreign law.
2. When interpreting any legislation, and when developing the common law or customary law, every court, tribunal or forum must promote the spirit, purport and objects of the Bill of Rights.
3. The Bill of Rights does not deny the existence of any other rights or freedoms that are recognised or conferred by common law, customary law or legislation, to the extent that they are consistent with the Bill.

CONSTITUTION OF COLOMBIA 1991

Article 1

Colombia is a social State of law [Estado social de derecho] organized in the form of a unitary Republic, decentralized, with the autonomy of its territorial units, democratic, participatory, and pluralistic, based on the respect for human dignity, on the work and the solidarity of the persons who compose it, and the prevalence of the general interest.

Article 2

The essential goals [duties] of the State are to serve the community, promote the general prosperity, and guarentee the effectiveness of the principles, rights and duties consecrated in the Constitution . . .

Chapter 2 of the Social, Economic, and Cultural Rights

Article 44

Basic rights of children are: life, physical integrity, health and social security, a balanced diet, their name and nationality, to have a family and not be separated from it, care and love, instruction and culture, recreation, and the free expression of their opinions. They shall be protected against any form of abandonment, physical or moral violence, sequestration, sale, sexual abuse, labor or economic exploitation, and dangerous work. They will also enjoy the other rights consecrated in the Constitution, the laws, and the international treaties ratified by Colombia.

Article 48 [Amended by Legislative Act No. I of 2005]

Social Security is a public service of obligatory character which will be provided under the direction, coordination and control of the State, subject to the principles of efficiency, universality, and solidarity, in the terms established by the law. The irrenounceable right to Social Security is guaranteed to all inhabitants. The State, with the participation of individuals, shall progressively extend the coverage of Social Security which shall include the provision of services in the form determined by the law. Social Security may be provided by public or private entities, in conformity with the law. The resources of the institutions of Social Security may not be allocated or utilized for purposes different from it. The law shall define the means by which the resources designated for pensions maintain their constant purchasing power. The State will guarantee the rights, [and] the financial sustainability of the Pension System, shall respect the rights acquired with regard to the law and shall assume the payment of the pension debt that in accordance with the law is [of] its responsibility. The laws in pension matters that are adopted subsequent to the entry into force of this Legislative Act, shall assure the financial sustainability of that established in it. Without prejudice to the discounts, deductions and attachments [embargos] to pensions ordered in accordance with the law, for no reason may it [the State] no longer pay, or freeze or reduce the value of the allowance of the pensions recognized in accordance with the law.

Article 49 [Amended by Legislative Act No. 2 of 2009]

Attention to health and environmental sanitation are public services [of the] responsibility of the State. The access to services of promotion, protection and recovery of health are guaranteed to all persons. It corresponds to the State to organize, direct and regulate the provision of health services to the inhabitants and of [services of] environmental sanitation in accordance with the principles of efficiency, universality and solidarity. Also, to establish policies for the provision of health services by private entities, and to exercise supervision and control [over them]. Likewise, to establish the competences of the Nation, the territorial entities and individuals and to determine the contributions of [their] responsibility in the terms and conditions specified in the law. Health services shall be organized in a decentralized manner, by level of care [atencion] and with participation of the community. The law shall specify the terms under which basic care for all inhabitants will be gratuitous and obligatory. Every person has the duty to provide for [procurar] comprehensive attention to their health and to [that] of their community.

Article 51

All Colombians have the right to decent [digna] housing. The State shall specify the conditions necessary to make this right effective and shall promote housing plans of social interest, appropriate systems of long-term financing, and associative forms of execution of these housing programs.

Article 86

Every person has [recourse to] the action of protection [accion de tutela] to claim before the judges, at any time or place, through a preferential and summary proceeding, for themselves or by whoever acts in their name, the immediate protection of their fundamental constitutional rights whenever these [are] consequently damaged or threatened by the action or omission of any public authority. The protection [proteccion] will consist of an order so that [the party] from whom the protection [tutela] is solicited, acts or refrains from it. The decision, which must be of immediate compliance, may be challenged before the competent judge, and in any case, the latter may return it to the Constitutional Court for its subsequent [eventual] revision. This action will proceed only when the affected [party] does not dispose of another means of judicial defense, except when the former is used as a transitory mechanism to avoid an irreversible harm. In no case may more than ten days elapse between the request for protection [tutela] and its resolution. The law shall establish the cases in which the action of protection [tutela] proceeds against individuals entrusted with the provision of a public service or whose conduct affects seriously and directly the collective interest, or in respect of whom the applicant finds himself in a state of subordination or defenselessness.

Article 93 [Amended by Legislative Act No. 2 of 2001]

International treaties and agreements ratified by the Congress that recognize human rights and that prohibit their limitation in the states of emergency, have prevalence in the internal order. The rights and duties consecrated in this Charter will be interpreted in conformity with international treaties on human rights ratified by Colombia.

BASIC LAW OF GERMANY 1949

Article 1

(1) Human dignity shall be inviolable. To respect and protect it shall be the duty of all state authority.

Article 3

(1) All persons shall be equal before the law. (2) Men and women shall have equal rights. The state shall promote the actual implementation of equal rights for women and men and take steps to eliminate disadvantages that now exist. (3) No person shall be favoured or disfavoured because of sex, parentage, race, language, homeland and origin, faith, or religious or political opinions. No person shall be disfavoured because of disability.

Article 19

(1) Insofar as, under this Basic Law, a basic right may be restricted by or pursuant to a law, such law must apply generally and not merely to a single case. In addition, the law must specify the basic right affected and the Article in which it appears. (2) In no case may the essence of a basic right be affected. (3) The basic rights shall also apply to domestic artificial persons to the extent that the nature of such rights permits. (4) Should any person's rights be violated by public authority, he may have recourse to the courts. If no other jurisdiction has been established, recourse shall be to the ordinary courts.

Article 20

1) The Federal Republic of Germany is a democratic and social federal state.

CONSTITUTION OF GHANA 1992

Chapter Six The Directive Principles of State Policy

Article 34

(1) The Directive Principles of State Policy contained in this Chapter shall guide all citizens, Parliament, the President, the Judiciary, the Council of State, the Cabinet, political parties, and other bodies and persons in applying or interpreting this Constitution or any other law and in taking and implementing any policy decisions, for the establishment of a just and free society. (2) The President shall report to Parliament at least once a year all the steps taken to

ensure the realization of the policy objectives contained in this Chapter; and, in particular, the realization of basic human rights, a healthy economy, the right to work, the right to good health care and the right to education.

CONSTITUTION OF INDIA 1950

Part III Fundamental Rights

Article 21

No person shall be deprived of his life or personal liberty except according to procedure established by law.

Article 21A

The State shall provide free and compulsory education to all children of the age of six to fourteen years in such manner as the State may, by law, determine.

Part IV Directive Principles Of State Policy

Article 37

The provisions contained in this Part shall not be enforceable by any court, but the principles therein laid down are nevertheless fundamental in the governance of the country and it shall be the duty of the State to apply these principles in making laws.

Article 38

(1) The State shall strive to promote the welfare of the people by securing and protecting as effectively as it may a social order in which justice, social, economic and political, shall inform all the institutions of the national life.

(2) The State shall, in particular, strive to minimise the inequalities in income, and endeavour to eliminate inequalities in status, facilities and opportunities, not only amongst individuals but also amongst groups of people residing in different areas or engaged in different vocations.

Article 39

The State shall, in particular, direct its policy towards securing - (a) that the citizens, men and women equally, have the right to an adequate means of livelihood; (b) that the ownership and control of the material resources of the community are so distributed as best to subserve the common good; (c) that the operation of the economic system does not result in the concentration of wealth and means of production to the common detriment; (d) that there is equal pay for equal work for both men and women; (e) that the health and strength of workers, men and women, and the tender age of children are not abused and that citizens are not forced by economic necessity to enter avocations unsuited to their age or strength; (f) that children are given opportunities and facilities to develop in a healthy manner and in conditions of freedom and dignity and that childhood and youth are protected against exploitation and against moral and material abandonment.

Article 39A

The State shall secure that the operation of the legal system promotes justice, on a basis of equal opportunity, and shall, in particular, provide free legal aid, by suitable legislation or schemes or in any other way, to ensure that opportunities for securing justice are not denied to any citizen by reason of economic or other disabilities.

Article 41

The State shall, within the limits of its economic capacity and development, make effective provision for securing the right to work, to education and to public assistance in cases of unemployment, old age, sickness and disablement, and in other cases of undeserved want.

Article 45

The State shall endeavour to provide early childhood care and education for all children until they complete the age of six years.

Article 47

The State shall regard the raising of the level of nutrition and the standard of living of its people and the improvement of public health as among its primary duties and, in particular, the State shall endeavour to bring about prohibition of the consumption except for medicinal purposes of intoxicating drinks and of drugs which are injurious to health.

CONSTITUTION OF THE UNITED STATES 1789

Amendment XIV

No State shall make or enforce any law which shall abridge the privileges or immunities of citizens of the United States; nor shall any State deprive any person of life, liberty, or property, without due process of law; nor deny to any person within its jurisdiction the equal protection of the laws.

HUMAN RIGHTS ACT 1998 OF THE UNITED KINGDOM

Section 3

(1) So far as it is possible to do so, primary legislation and subordinate legislation must be read and given effect in a way which is compatible with the Convention rights.

Section 4

(1) Subsection (2) applies in any proceedings in which a court determines whether a provision of primary legislation is compatible with a Convention right. (2) If the court is satisfied that the provision is incompatible with a Convention right, it may make a declaration of that incompatibility. . . .
(6) A declaration under this section ("a declaration of incompatibility")– (a) does not affect the validity, continuing operation or enforcement of the provision in respect of which it is given; and (b) is not binding on the parties to the proceedings in which it is made.

Section 19

(1) A Minister of the Crown in charge of a Bill in either House of Parliament must, before Second Reading of the Bill- (a) make a statement to the effect that in his view the provisions of the Bill are compatible with the Convention rights ("a statement of compatibility"); or (b) make a statement to the effect that although he is unable to make a statement of compatibility the government nevertheless wishes the House to proceed with the Bill. (2) The statement must be in writing and be published in such manner as the Minister making it considers appropriate.

Appendix II

Excerpts from International Human Rights Instruments

UNIVERSAL DECLARATION OF HUMAN RIGHTS

Article 1

All human beings are born free and equal in dignity and rights.

Article 22

Everyone, as a member of society, has the right to social security and is entitled to realization, through national effort and international co-operation and in accordance with the organization and resources of each State, of the economic, social and cultural rights indispensable for his dignity and the free development of his personality.

Article 23

(1) Everyone has the right to work, to free choice of employment, to just and favourable conditions of work and to protection against unemployment.
(2) Everyone, without any discrimination, has the right to equal pay for equal work.
(3) Everyone who works has the right to just and favourable remuneration ensuring for himself and his family an existence worthy of human dignity, and supplemented, if necessary, by other means of social protection.
(4) Everyone has the right to form and to join trade unions for the protection of his interests.

Article 24

Everyone has the right to rest and leisure, including reasonable limitation of working hours and periodic holidays with pay.

Article 25

(1) Everyone has the right to a standard of living adequate for the health and well-being of himself and of his family, including food, clothing, housing and medical care and necessary social services, and the right to security

in the event of unemployment, sickness, disability, widowhood, old age or other lack of livelihood in circumstances beyond his control.

(2) Motherhood and childhood are entitled to special care and assistance. All children, whether born in or out of wedlock, shall enjoy the same social protection.

Article 26

(1) Everyone has the right to education. Education shall be free, at least in the elementary and fundamental stages. Elementary education shall be compulsory. Technical and professional education shall be made generally available and higher education shall be equally accessible to all on the basis of merit.

(2) Education shall be directed to the full development of the human personality and to the strengthening of respect for human rights and fundamental freedoms. It shall promote understanding, tolerance and friendship among all nations, racial or religious groups, and shall further the activities of the United Nations for the maintenance of peace.

(3) Parents have a prior right to choose the kind of education that shall be given to their children.

Article 28

Everyone is entitled to a social and international order in which the rights and freedoms set forth in this Declaration can be fully realized.

Article 29

(1) Everyone has duties to the community in which alone the free and full development of his personality is possible.

(2) In the exercise of his rights and freedoms, everyone shall be subject only to such limitations as are determined by law solely for the purpose of securing due recognition and respect for the rights and freedoms of others and of meeting the just requirements of morality, public order and the general welfare in a democratic society.

INTERNATIONAL COVENANT ON ECONOMIC, SOCIAL AND CULTURAL RIGHTS

Article 2

1. Each State Party to the present Covenant undertakes to take steps, individually and through international assistance and co-operation, especially economic and technical, to the maximum of its available resources, with a view to achieving progressively the full realization of the rights

recognized in the present Covenant by all appropriate means, including particularly the adoption of legislative measures.

2. The States Parties to the present Covenant undertake to guarantee that the rights enunciated in the present Covenant will be exercised without discrimination of any kind as to race, colour, sex, language, religion, political or other opinion, national or social origin, property, birth or other status.

Article 3

The States Parties to the present Covenant undertake to ensure the equal right of men and women to the enjoyment of all economic, social and cultural rights set forth in the present Covenant.

Article 4

The States Parties to the present Covenant recognize that, in the enjoyment of those rights provided by the State in conformity with the present Covenant, the State may subject such rights only to such limitations as are determined by law only in so far as this may be compatible with the nature of these rights and solely for the purpose of promoting the general welfare in a democratic society.

Article 5

1. Nothing in the present Covenant may be interpreted as implying for any State, group or person any right to engage in any activity or to perform any act aimed at the destruction of any of the rights or freedoms recognized herein, or at their limitation to a greater extent than is provided for in the present Covenant.
2. No restriction upon or derogation from any of the fundamental human rights recognized or existing in any country in virtue of law, conventions, regulations or custom shall be admitted on the pretext that the present Covenant does not recognize such rights or that it recognizes them to a lesser extent.

Article 6

1. The States Parties to the present Covenant recognize the right to work, which includes the right of everyone to the opportunity to gain his living by work which he freely chooses or accepts, and will take appropriate steps to safeguard this right.
2. The steps to be taken by a State Party to the present Covenant to achieve the full realization of this right shall include technical and vocational guidance and training programmes, policies and techniques to achieve steady economic, social and cultural development and full and

productive employment under conditions safeguarding fundamental political and economic freedoms to the individual.

Article 7

The States Parties to the present Covenant recognize the right of everyone to the enjoyment of just and favourable conditions of work which ensure, in particular:

(a) Remuneration which provides all workers, as a minimum, with:
  (i) Fair wages and equal remuneration for work of equal value without distinction of any kind, in particular women being guaranteed conditions of work not inferior to those enjoyed by men, with equal pay for equal work;
  (ii) A decent living for themselves and their families in accordance with the provisions of the present Covenant;
(b) Safe and healthy working conditions;
(c) Equal opportunity for everyone to be promoted in his employment to an appropriate higher level, subject to no considerations other than those of seniority and competence;
(d) Rest, leisure and reasonable limitation of working hours and periodic holidays with pay, as well as remuneration for public holidays.

Article 8

1. The States Parties to the present Covenant undertake to ensure:
  (a) The right of everyone to form trade unions and join the trade union of his choice, subject only to the rules of the organization concerned, for the promotion and protection of his economic and social interests. No restrictions may be placed on the exercise of this right other than those prescribed by law and which are necessary in a democratic society in the interests of national security or public order or for the protection of the rights and freedoms of others.

Article 9

The States Parties to the present Covenant recognize the right of everyone to social security, including social insurance.

Article 11

1. The States Parties to the present Covenant recognize the right of everyone to an adequate standard of living for himself and his family, including adequate food, clothing and housing, and to the continuous improvement of living conditions. The States Parties will take appropriate steps to

ensure the realization of this right, recognizing to this effect the essential importance of international co-operation based on free consent.

2. The States Parties to the present Covenant, recognizing the fundamental right of everyone to be free from hunger, shall take, individually and through international co-operation, the measures, including specific programmes, which are needed:
   (a) To improve methods of production, conservation and distribution of food by making full use of technical and scientific knowledge, by disseminating knowledge of the principles of nutrition and by developing or reforming agrarian systems in such a way as to achieve the most efficient development and utilization of natural resources;
   (b) Taking into account the problems of both food-importing and food-exporting countries, to ensure an equitable distribution of world food supplies in relation to need.

Article 12

1. The States Parties to the present Covenant recognize the right of everyone to the enjoyment of the highest attainable standard of physical and mental health.
2. The steps to be taken by the States Parties to the present Covenant to achieve the full realization of this right shall include those necessary for:
   (a) The provision for the reduction of the stillbirth-rate and of infant mortality and for the healthy development of the child;
   (b) The improvement of all aspects of environmental and industrial hygiene;
   (c) The prevention, treatment and control of epidemic, endemic, occupational and other diseases;
   (d) The creation of conditions which would assure to all medical service and medical attention in the event of sickness.

Article 13

1. The States Parties to the present Covenant recognize the right of everyone to education. They agree that education shall be directed to the full development of the human personality and the sense of its dignity, and shall strengthen the respect for human rights and fundamental freedoms. They further agree that education shall enable all persons to participate effectively in a free society, promote understanding, tolerance and friendship among all nations and all racial, ethnic or religious groups, and further the activities of the United Nations for the maintenance of peace.
2. The States Parties to the present Covenant recognize that, with a view to achieving the full realization of this right:
   (a) Primary education shall be compulsory and available free to all;

(b) Secondary education in its different forms, including technical and vocational secondary education, shall be made generally available and accessible to all by every appropriate means, and in particular by the progressive introduction of free education;
(c) Higher education shall be made equally accessible to all, on the basis of capacity, by every appropriate means, and in particular by the progressive introduction of free education;
(d) Fundamental education shall be encouraged or intensified as far as possible for those persons who have not received or completed the whole period of their primary education;
(e) The development of a system of schools at all levels shall be actively pursued, an adequate fellowship system shall be established, and the material conditions of teaching staff shall be continuously improved.

Article 16

1. The States Parties to the present Covenant undertake to submit in conformity with this part of the Covenant reports on the measures which they have adopted and the progress made in achieving the observance of the rights recognized herein.

OPTIONAL PROTOCOL TO THE INTERNATIONAL COVENANT ON ECONOMIC, SOCIAL AND CULTURAL RIGHTS

Article 2 Communications

Communications may be submitted by or on behalf of individuals or groups of individuals, under the jurisdiction of a State Party, claiming to be victims of a violation of any of the economic, social and cultural rights set forth in the Covenant by that State Party.

Article 8 Examination of communications

3. When examining a communication under the present Protocol, the Committee may consult, as appropriate, relevant documentation emanating from other United Nations bodies, specialized agencies, funds, programmes and mechanisms, and other international organizations, including from regional human rights systems, and any observations or comments by the State Party concerned.
4. When examining communications under the present Protocol, the Committee shall consider the reasonableness of the steps taken by the State Party in accordance with part II of the Covenant. In doing so, the Committee shall bear in mind that the State Party may adopt a range of possible policy measures for the implementation of the rights set forth in the Covenant.

Article 9 Follow-up to the views of the Committee

1. After examining a communication, the Committee shall transmit its views on the communication, together with its recommendations, if any, to the parties concerned.
2. The State Party shall give due consideration to the views of the Committee, together with its recommendations, if any, and shall submit to the Committee, within six months, a written response, including information on any action taken in the light of the views and recommendations of the Committee.

Selective Bibliography

Ackerman, Bruce, "Regulating Slum Housing Markets On Behalf of the Poor: Of Housing Codes, Housing Subsidies and Income Redistribution Policy," 80 Yale L.J. 1093 (1971)

—— "The Living Constitution," 120 Harv. L. Rev. 1737 (2007)

—— Anne Alstott, and Philippe Van Parijs, *Redesigning Distribution: Basic Income and Stakeholder Grants as Alternative Cornerstones for a more Egalitarian Capitalism* (Erik Olin Wright, ed., 2006)

Adler, Matthew D. and Michael C. Dorf, "Constitutional Existence Conditions and Judicial Review," 89 Va. L. Rev. 1105 (2003)

Aleinikoff, T. Alexander, "Constitutional Law in the Age of Balancing," 96 Yale L.J. 943 (1987)

Alexander, Gregory S., *The Global Debate Over Constitutional Property: Lessons For American Takings Jurisprudence* (2006)

Alexander, Lisa T., "Stakeholder Participation in New Governance: Lessons from Chicago's Public Housing Reform Experiment," 16 Geo. J. Pov. L. & Pol. 117 (2009)

Alexy, Robert, *A Theory of Constitutional Rights* (Julian Rivers trans., 2002) (1986)

Alston, Philip, "Human Rights and Basic Needs: A Critical Assessment," 12 Hum. Rts, J./Revue des droits de l'homme 19 (1979)

—— "The Committee on Economic, Social and Cultural Rights," in Philip Alston (ed.), *The United Nations and Human Rights: A Critical Appraisal* (1992)

—— "Ships Passing in the Night: The Current State of the Human Rights and Development Debate Seen through the Lens of the Millennium Development Goals," 27 Hum. Rts. Q. 755 (2005)

—— and Gerard Quinn, "The Nature and Scope of States Parties' Obligations under the International Covenant on Economic, Social and Cultural Rights," 9 Hum. Rts. Q. 156 (1987)

Alvarez, José E., "International Organizations: Then and Now," 100 Am. J. Int'l. L. 324 (2006)

Amir, On and Orly Lobel, "Stumble, Predict, Nudge: How Behavioral Economics Informs Law and Policy," 108 Colum. L. Rev. 2098 (2008)

An-Na'im, Abdullahi Ahmed (ed.), *Human Rights in Cross-Cultural Perspectives: A Quest for Consensus* (1991)

Arango, Rodolfo, "Basic Social Rights, Constitutional Justice, and Democracy," 16 Ratio Juris 141 (2003)

Baar, Carl, "Social Action Litigation in India: The Operation and Limits of the World's Most Active Judiciary," in Donald Jackson and C Neal Tate (eds.), *Comparative Judicial Review and Public Policy* (1992) 77

Balkin, J. M., "Ideological Drift and the Struggle over Meaning," 25 Conn. L. Rev. 869 (1993)

—— "The Constitution of Status," 106 Yale L.J. 2313 (1997)

—— "How Social Movements Change (or Fail to Change) the Constitution: the Case of the New Departure," 39 Suffolk L. Rev. 27 (2002)

—— "What Brown Teaches Us about Constitutional Theory," 90 Va. L. Rev. 1537 (2004)

——and Reva B. Siegel, "Principles, Practices and Social Movements," 154 U. Pa. L. Rev. 927 (2006)

Barak-Erez, Daphne and Aeyal M. Gross (eds.), *Exploring Social Rights: Between Theory and Practice* (2007)

Barnett, Jonathan M., "Rights, Costs, and the Incommensurability Problem," 86 Va. L. Rev. 1303 (2000)

Bateup, Christine, "The Dialogic Promise: Assessing the Normative Potential of Theories of Constitutional Dialogue," 71 Brook. L. Rev. 1109 (2006)

—— "Reassessing the Dialogic Possibilities of Weak-Form Bills of Rights," 32 Hastings Int'l. & Comp. L. Rev. 529 (2009)

Beatty, David, *The Ultimate Rule of Law* (2004)

Bennett, Robert, "Counter-Conversationalism and the Sense of Difficulty," 95 Nw. U. L. Rev. 845 (2001)

Benvenisti, Eyal, "Margin of Appreciation, Consensus, and Universal Standards," 31 N.Y.U. J. Int'l L. & Pol. 843 (1999)

Berat, Lynn, "The Constitutional Court of South Africa and Jurisdictional Questions: In the Interest of Justice?" 3 Int'l. J. Const. L. 39 (2005)

Berger, Jonathan, "Litigating for Social Justice in Post-apartheid South Africa: A Focus on Health and Education," in Varun Gauri and Daniel M. Brinks (eds.), *Courting Social Justice: Judicial Enforcement of Social and Economic Rights in the Developing World* (2008)

Bickel, Alexander M., *The Least Dangerous Branch: The Supreme Court at the Bar of Politics* (2nd edn., 1986)

Bilchitz, David, *Poverty and Fundamental Rights: The Justification and Enforcement of Socio-Economic Rights* (2007)

Birchfield, Lauren and Corsi, Jessica, "Between Starvation and Globalization: Realizing the Right to Food in India," 31 Mich. J. Int'l. L. 691 (2010)

Blasi, Gary L., "Litigation Strategies for Addressing Bureaucratic Disentitlement," 366 PLI/Lit. 285 (1988)

Bobinski, Mary Anne, "Health Disparities and the Law: Wrongs in Search of a Right," 29 Am. J. L. & Med. 363 (2003)

Bond, P. and Dugard, J., "The Case of Johannesburg Water: What Really Happened at the Pre-paid 'Parish pump'?," 12 Law, Democracy, and Development 1 (2008)

Borgwardt, Elizabeth, "FDR's Four Freedoms and Wartime Transformations in America's Discourse of Rights," in Cynthia Soohoo et al. (eds.), *Bringing Human Rights Home: A History of Human Rights in the United States* (2008).

Bork, Robert H., "Commentary, The Impossibility of Finding Welfare Rights in the Constitution," Wash. U. L.Q. 695 (1979)

Bourdieu, Pierre, *Language and Symbolic Power* (trans. Gino Raymond and Matthew Adamson, John B. Thompson, ed., 1991)

—— and Loïc J.D. Wacquant, *An Invitation to Reflexive Sociology* (1992)

—— *The Social Structures of the Economy* (Chris Turner trans., 2005)

Bradley, Curtis A., Jack L. Goldsmith, and David H. Moore, Sosa, "Customary International Law, and the Continuing Relevance of *Erie*," 120 Harv. L. Rev. 869 (2007)

Braithwaite, John, *Restorative Justice and Responsive Regulation* (2002)

Brand, Danie, "The Minimum Core Content of the Right to Food in Context: A Response to Rolf Künneman," in Danie Brand and Sage Russell (eds.), *Exploring the Core Content of Economic and Social Rights: South African and International Perspectives* (2002)

Brown-Nagin, Tomiko, "Elites, Social Movements, and the Law: The Case of Affirmative Action," 105 Colum. L. Rev. 1436 (2005)

Browne-Wilkinson, Lord, "The Impact on Judicial Reasoning," in Basil S. Markesinis (ed.), *The Impact of the Human Rights Bill on English Law* (1998)

Burkhalter, Holly, "Advocacy Strategies for Affording the Right to Health," in Chris Beyrer and H. F. Pizer (eds.), *Public Health and Human Rights: Evidence-Based Approaches* (2007)

Byrnes, Andrew, "Toward More Effective Enforcement of Women's Human Rights through the Use of International Human Rights Law and Procedures" in Rebecca J. Cook (ed.), *Human Rights of Women: National and International Perspectives* (1994)

Calabresi, Guido and Philip Bobbitt, *Tragic Choices* (1978)

Cavallaro, James L. and Emily Schaffer, "Less As More: Rethinking Supranational Litigation of Economic and Social Rights in the Americas," 56 Hastings L.J. 217 (2004)

Cepeda-Espinosa, Manuel Jose, "How Far May Colombia's Constitutional Court Go to Protect IDP Rights?," (Special Issue, December 2006) *Forced Migration Review: Putting IDPs on the Map* 21

Chandra, Rajshree, "The Role of National Laws in Reconciling Constitutional Right to Health with TRIPS Obligations: An Examination of the Glivec Patent Case in India," in Thomas Pogge, Matthew Rimmer, and Kim Rubenstein (eds.), *Incentives for Global Public Health* (2010) 381

Chapman, Audrey R. and Sage Russell (eds.), *Core Obligations: Building a Framework for Economic, Social and Cultural Rights* (2002)

Chaskalson, Arthur, "Human Dignity as a Foundational Value for Our Constitutional Order" 16 S. Afr. J. Hum. Rts. 193 (2000)

Chayes, Abram, "The Role of the Judge in Public Law Litigation," 89 Harv. L. Rev. 1281 (1976)
Chenwi, Lilian, "Putting Flesh on the Skeleton: South African Judicial Enforcement of the Right to Adequate Housing of Those Subject to Evictions," 8 Hum. Rts. L. Rev. 105 (2008)
Choudhry, Sujit, "Globalization in Search of Justification: Toward a Theory of Comparative Constitutional Interpretation," 74 Ind. L.J. 819 (1999)
—— "The *Lochner* Era and Comparative Constitutionalism," 2 Int'l. J. Const. L. 1 (2004)
—— "Migration as a New Metaphor in Comparative Constitutional Law," in Sujit Choudhry (ed.), *The Migration of Constitutional Ideas* (2006)
Chua, Amy, "Markets, Democracy, and Ethnicity: Toward A New Paradigm for Law and Development," 108 Yale L.J. 1 (1998)
Cohen, Amy J., "Negotiation Meet New Governance: Interests, Skills, Selves," 33(2) Law & Soc. Inq. 502 (2008)
Cohen, Joshua, "Minimalism about Human Rights: The Most We Can Hope For?," 12 J. Pol. Phil. 190 (2004)
—— "*Extra Rempublicam Nulla Justitia*?," 34 *Phil. & Pub. Aff.* 147 (2006)
—— and Charles Sabel, "Directly Deliberative Polyarchy," 3 Euro. L.J. 313 (1997)
Coomans, Fons (ed.), *Justiciability of Economic and Social Rights: Experiences from Domestic Systems* (2006)
Cover, Robert, "Violence and the Word," 95 Yale L.J. 1601 (1986)
—— "The Supreme Court, 1982 Term—Foreword: Nomos and Narrative," 97 Harv. L. Rev. 4 (1982)
Cranston, Maurice, "Are There Any Human Rights?," 112 *Daedalus* 12 (1983)
Craven, Matthew, *The International Covenant on Economic, Social, and Cultural Rights: A Perspective on its Development* (1995)
Crenshaw, Kimberle, "Were the Critics Right about Rights? Reassessing the American Debate about Rights in the Post-reform Era," in Mahmood Mamdani (ed)., *Beyond Rights Talk and Culture Talk: Comparative Essays on the Politics of Rights and Culture* (2000)
Cross, Frank B., "The Error of Positive Rights," 48 UCLA L. Rev. 857 (2001)
Currie, David P., "Positive and Negative Constitutional Rights," 53 U. Chi. L. Rev. 864 (1986)
—— *The Constitution of the Federal Republic of Germany* (1994)
Currie, Iain and Johan de Waal, *The Bill of Rights Handbook* (5th edn., 2005)
Cypher, James M. and James L. Dietz, *The Process of Economic Development* (2nd edn., 2004)
Daintith, Terence, "The Constitutional Protection of Economic Rights," 2 Int'l. J. Const. L. 56 (2004)
Daniels, Norman, *Just Health: Meeting Health Needs Fairly* (2008)
Davis, Dennis M., "The Case Against Inclusion of Socio-Economic Rights in a Bill of Rights Except as Directive Principles," 8 S. Afr. J. Hum. Rts. 475 (1992)
—— "Equality: The Majesty of Legoland Jurisprudence," 116 S. Afr. L.J. 398 (1999)

—— "Socioeconomic Rights: Do They Deliver the Goods?," 6 Int'l. J. Const. L. 687 (2008)

Davis, Martha F., *Brutal Need: Lawyers and the Welfare Rights Movement, 1960–1973* (1993)

—— "The Spirit of Our Times: State Constitutions and International Human Rights," 30 N.Y.U. Rev. L. & Soc. Change 359 (2006)

de Búrca, Gráinne and Scott, Joanne (eds.), *Law and New Governance in the EU and the US* (2006)

de Sousa Santos, Boaventura and Cesar A. Rodrigeuz-Garavito (eds.), *Law and Globalization from Below: Towards a Cosmopolitan Legality* (2005) 1

de Vos, Pierre, "Substantive Equality after Grootboom: The Emergence of Social and Economic Context as a Guiding Value in Equality Jurisprudence," Acta Juridica 52 (2001)

de Wet, Erika, *The Constitutional Enforceability of Economic and Social Rights* (1996)

Debeljak, Julie, "Balancing Rights in Democracy: The Problems with Limitations and Overrides of Rights under the Victorian Charter of Human Rights and Responsibilities Act 2006," 32(1) Melbourne U. L. Rev. 455 (2008)

Dennis, Michael J. and David P. Stewart, "Justiciability of Economic, Social, and Cultural Rights: Should There Be an International Complaints Mechanism to Adjudicate the Rights to Food, Water, Housing, and Health?," 98 Am. J. Int'l. L. 462 (2004)

Desai, Ashok H. and S. Muralidhar, "Public Interest Litigation: Potential and Problems" in B. Kirpal (ed.), *Supreme But Not Infallible: Essays in Honor of the Supreme Court of India* (2000)

Devins, Neal, "I Love You, Big Brother," 87 Cal. L. Rev. 1283 (1999)

Dewey, John, *Democracy and Education: An Introduction to the Philosophy of Education* (1916)

—— *The Public and Its Problems* (1954) (1927)

—— *Liberalism and Social Action* (2000) (1935)

Dezalay, Yves and Bryant G. Garth, *The Internationalization of Palace Wars: Lawyers, Economists, and the Contest to Transform Latin American States* (2002)

Dicey, A. V., *An Introduction to the Study of the Constitution* (10th edn., 1959)

Diver, Colin S., "The Judge as Political Powerbroker: Superintending Structural Change in Public Institutions," 65 Va. L. Rev. 43 (1979)

Dixon, Rosalind, "Creating Dialogue about Socio-Economic Rights: Strong-Form Versus Weak-Form Judicial Review Revisited," 5 Int'l. J. Const. L. 391 (2007)

Dorf, Michael C., "Legal Indeterminacy and Institutional Design," 78 N.Y.U. L. Rev. 875 (2003)

—— and Charles F. Sabel, "A Constitution of Democratic Experimentalism," 98 Colum. L. Rev. 267 (1998)

—— —— "Drug Treatment Courts and Emergent Experimentalist Government," 53 Vand. L. Rev. 831 (2000)

Dorsen, Norman, Michel Rosenfeld, András Sajó, and Susanne Baer (eds.), *Comparative Constitutionalism* (2002)

Drèze, Jean, "Democracy and the Right to Food," in Philip Alston and Mary Robinson (eds.), *Human Rights and Development: Towards Mutual Reinforcement* (2005) du Plessis, Lourens, "Interpretation," in Stuart Woolman, Michael Bishop, and Theunis Roux (eds.), *Constitutional law of South Africa* (2nd edn., 2006)

Dudziak, Mary L., *Cold War Civil Rights: Race and the Image of American Democracy* (2000)

Dugard, Jackie, and Theunis Roux, "The Record of the South African Constitutional Court in Providing an Institutional Voice for the Poor: 1995–2004," in Roberto Gargarella, Pilar Domingo, and Theunis Roux (eds.), *Courts and Social Transformation in New Democracies: An Institutional Voice for the Poor?* (2006)

Dworkin, Ronald, *Taking Rights Seriously* (1977)

—— *Freedom's Law: The Moral Reading of the American Constitution* (1996)

—— *Sovereign Virtue: The Theory and Practice of Equality* (2000)

—— *Justice for Hedgehogs* (2011)

Ebadolahi, Mitra, "Note: Using Structural Interdicts and the South African Human Rights Commission to Achieve Judicial Enforcement of Economic and Social Rights in South Africa," 83 N.Y.U. L. Rev. 1565 (2008)

Ebrahim, Hassen, *The Soul of a Nation: Constitution-Making in South Africa* (1998)

Eide, Asbjørn, "Economic, Social and Cultural Rights as Human Rights," in Asbjørn Eide, Catarina Krause, and Allen Rosas (eds.), *Economic, Social and Cultural Rights: A Textbook* (2nd edn., 2001)

Elhauge, Einer, "Allocating Health Care Morally," 82 Cal. L. Rev. 1449 (1994)

Ellickson, Robert C., *Order without Law: How Neighbors Settle Disputes* (1991)

Elster, Jon and Rune Slagstad (eds.), *Constitutionalism and Democracy: Studies in Rationality and Social Change* (1988)

Ely, John Hart, *Democracy and Distrust: A Theory of Judicial Review* (1980)

Engel, David M. and Frank W. Munger, *Rights of Inclusion: Law and Identity in the Life Stories of Americans with Disabilities* (2003)

Epp, Charles, *The Rights Revolution: Lawyers, Activists and Supreme Courts in Comparative Perspective* (1998)

Eskridge, William N., Jr., "Channeling: Identity-Based Social Movements and Public Law," 150 U. Pa. L. Rev. 419 (2001)

—— "Some Effects of Identity-Based Social Movements on Constitutional Law in the Twentieth Century," 100 Mich. L. Rev. 2062 (2002)

—— "Pluralism and Distrust: How Courts Can Support Democracy by Lowering the Stakes of Politics," 114 Yale L.J. 1279 (2006)

Esping-Anderson, Gøsta, *The Three Worlds of Welfare Capitalism* (1998)

Fabre, Cecile, *Social Rights under the Constitution: Government and the Decent Life* (2000)

Fallon, Richard H., Jr., "Judicially Manageable Standards and Constitutional Meaning," 119 Harv. L. Rev. 1274 (2006)

—— "The Linkage between Justiciability and Remedies—And Their Connections to Substantive Rights," 92 Va. L. Rev. 633 (2006)

Farber, Daniel A. and Philip P. Frickey, *Law and Public Choice: A Critical Introduction* (1991)

Farmer, Paul, *Pathologies of Power: Health, Human Rights and the New War on the Poor* (2003)

Fassin, Didier, *When Bodies Remember: Experiences and Politics of AIDS in South Africa* (2007)

Feeley, Malcolm M. and Edward L. Rubin, *Judicial Policy Making and the Modern State: How the Courts Reformed America's Prisons* (1998)

Ferejohn, John, Jack N. Rakove, and Jonathan Riley (eds.), *Constitutional Culture and Democratic Rule* (2001)

Fiss, Owen M., "The Supreme Court 1978 Term, Foreword: The Forms of Justice," 93 Harv. L. Rev. 1 (1979)

Fitzpatrick, Joan, *Human Rights in Crisis* (1994)

Forbath, William E., *Law and the Shaping of the American Labor Movement* (1991)

—— "Constitutional Welfare Rights: A History, Critique and Reconstruction," 69 Fordham L. Rev. 1821 (2001)

—— "Realizing a Constitutional Social Right—Cultural Transformation, Deep Institutional Reform, and the Roles of Advocacy and Adjudication," in Lucie E. White and Jeremy Perelman (eds.), *Stones of Hope: How African Activists Reclaim Human Rights To Challenge Global Poverty* (2011)

Forsythe, David P. and Eric A. Heinze, "On the Margins of the Human Rights Discourse: Foreign Policy and International Welfare Rights," in Rhoda E. Howard-Hassman and Claude E. Welch, Jr. (eds.), *Economic Rights in Canada and the United States* (2006)

Franck, Thomas M., *Fairness in International Law and Institutions* (1995)

Frankenburg, Gunter, "Why Care: The Trouble with Social Rights?" 17 Cardozo L. Rev. 1365 (1996)

Fraser, Nancy, *Scales of Justice: Reimagining Political Space in a Globalizing World* (2009)

—— and Axel Honneth, *Recognition or Redistribution? A Political–Philosophical Exchange* (2003)

—— and Linda Gordon, "A Genealogy of Dependency: Tracing a Keyword of the U.S. Welfare State," 19 *Signs* 309 (1994)

Fredman, Sandra, *Human Rights Transformed: Positive Rights and Positive Duties* (2008)

Freeman, Alan, "Antidiscrimination Law from 1954 to 1989: Uncertainty, Contradiction, Rationalization, Denial," in David Kairys (ed.), *The Politics of Law: A Progressive Critique* (3rd edn., 1998)

Freeman, Jody, "The Private Role in Public Governance," 75 N.Y.U. L. Rev. 543 (2000)

Friedman, Barry, "The History of the Countermajoritarian Difficulty, Part One: The Road to Judicial Supremacy," 73 N.Y.U. L. Rev. 333 (1998)

——"Mediated Popular Constitutionalism," 101 Mich. L. Rev. 2596 (2006)

Fuller, Lon, "The Forms and Limits of Adjudication" 82 Harv. L. Rev. 353 (1979)

Fung, Archon, *Empowered Participation: Reinventing Urban Democracy* (2004)

Gardbaum, Stephen, "The New Commonwealth Model of Constitutionalism," 49 Am. J. Comp. L. 707 (2001)
—— "The 'Horizontal Effect' of Constitutional Rights," 102 Mich. L. Rev. 387 (2003)
—— "Reassessing the New Commonwealth Model of Constitutionalism," 8 Int'l. J. Const. L. 167 (2010)
Gargarella, Roberto, Pilar Domingo and Theunis Roux (eds.), *Courts and Social Transformation in New Democracies: An Institutional Voice for the Poor?* (2006)
Gauri, Varun, "Social Rights and Economics: Claims to Health Care and Education in Developing Countries," in Philip Alston and Mary Robinson (eds.), *Human Rights and Development: Towards Mutual Reinforcement* (2005)
Gewirth, Alan, "Are All Rights Positive?," 30 *Phil. & Pub. Aff.* 321 (2002)
Gilman, Michele Estrin, "Poverty and Communitarianism: Toward a Community-Based Welfare System," 66 U. Pitt. L. Rev. 721 (2005)
Ginsburg, Tom, *Judicial Review in New Democracies: Constitutional Courts in Asian Cases* (2003)
Glendon, Mary Ann, *Rights Talk: The Impoverishment of Political Discourse* (1991)
—— *A World Made New: Eleanor Roosevelt and the Universal Declaration of Human Rights* (2001)
Gloppen, Siri, "Courts and Social Transformation: An Analytical Framework," in Roberto Gargarella, Pilar Domingo, and Theunis Roux (eds.), *Courts and Social Transformation in New Democracies: An Institutional Voice for the Poor?* (2006)
Goldsworthy, Jeffrey (ed.), *Interpreting Constitutions: A Comparative Study* (2006)
Goluboff, Risa L., "'We Live's in a Free House Such as It Is': Class and the Creation of Modern Civil Rights," 151 U. Pa. L. Rev. 1977 (2003)
Gonsalves, C., P. R. Kumar, and A. K. Srivastava (eds.), *Right to Food* (2nd edn., 2005)
Goodman, Ryan, "Human Rights Treaties, Invalid Reservations, and State Consent," 96 Am. J. Int'l. L. 531 (2002)
—— and Derek Jinks, "How to Influence States: Socialization and International Human Rights Law," 54 Duke L.J. 621 (2004)
Gordon, Jennifer, *Suburban Sweatshops: The Fight for Immigrant Rights* (2005)
Gordon, Linda, *Pitied But Not Entitled: Single Mothers and the History of Welfare 1890–1935* (1994)
Greenberg, Douglas, Stanley N. Katz, Melanie Beth Oliviero, and Steven C. Wheatley, (eds.), *Constitutionalism and Democracy: Transitions in the Contemporary World* (1993)
Grey, Thomas C., "Property and Need: The Welfare State and Theories of Distributive Justice," 28 Stan. L. Rev. 877 (1976)
Guinier, Lani, "The Triumph of Tokenism: The Voting Rights Act and the Theory of Black Electoral Success," 89 Mich. L. Rev. 1077 (1991)
—— "The Supreme Court, 2007 Term—Foreword: Demosprudence Through Dissent," 122 Harv. L. Rev. 4 (2008)
Gunningham, Neil and Darren Sinclair, "Regulatory Pluralism: Designing Policy Mixes for Environmental Protection," 21 Law and Policy 49 (1999)
Gutmann, Amy and Dennis Thompson, *Democracy and Disagreement* (1996)

Habermas, Jürgen, *The Theory of Communicative Action: Vol 2—Lifeworld and System: A Critique of Functionalist Reason* (trans. Thomas McCarthy, 1987) (1981)

—— *Between Facts and Norms* (trans. William Rehg, 1996)

Handler, Joel F., "Constructing the Political Spectacle: The Interpretation of Entitlements, Legalization, and Obligations in Social Welfare History," 56 Brooklyn L. Rev. 899 (1990)

Hart, H. L. A., *The Concept of Law* (2nd edn., 1994)

Hastrup, Kirsten, "Representing the Common Good: The Limits of Legal Language," in Richard Ashby Wilson and Jon P. Mitchell (eds.), *Human Rights in Global Perspective: Anthropological Studies of Rights, Claims and Entitlements* (2003)

Hathaway, Oona, "Do Human Rights Treaties Make a Difference?," 111 Yale L.J. 1935 (2002)

Haysom, Nicholas, "Constitutionalism, Majoritarianism, and Socio-Economic Rights," 8 S. Afr. J. Hum. Rts. 451 (1992)

Henkin, Louis and Albert J. Rosenthal (eds.), *Constitutionalism and Rights: The Influence of the United States Constitution Abroad* (1990)

Hershkoff, Helen, "Positive Rights and State Constitutions: The Limits of Federal Rationality Review," 112 Harv. L. Rev. 1131 (1999)

Hertel, Shareen, "Human Rights and the Global Economy: Bringing Labor Rights Back In," 24 Md. J. Int'l. L. 240 (2009)

Heywood, Mark, "Debunking 'Conglomo-talk': A Case Study of the Amicus Curiae as an Instrument for Advocacy, Investigation and Mobilisation," in 6 Law, Democracy and Development 12 (2002)

—— "Current Developments: Preventing Mother-to-Child HIV Transmission in South Africa: Background, Strategies and Outcomes of the Treatment Action Campaign Against the Minister of Health," 19 S. Afr. J. Hum. Rts. 278 (2003)

Hirsch, Danielle Elyce, "A Defense Of Structural Injunctive Remedies In South African Law," 9 Or. Rev. Int'l. L. 1 (2007)

Hirschl, Ran, *Towards Juristocracy: The Origins and Consequences of the New Constitutionalism* (2004)

—— "The Question of Case Selection in Comparative Constitutional Law," 53 Am. J. Comp. L. 125 (2005)

Hogg, Peter W., Allison A. Bushell Thornton and Wade K. Wright, "Charter Dialogue Revisited—Or 'Much Ado About Metaphors'" 45 Osgoode Hall L.J. 1 (2007)

Holmes, Stephen, "Precommitment and the Paradox of Democracy," in Jon Elster and Rune Slagstad (eds.), *Constitutionalism and Democracy* (1988)

—— and Cass R. Sunstein, *The Cost of Rights: Why Liberty Depends on Taxes* (1999)

Horwitz, Paul, "Three Faces of Deference," 83 Notre Dame L. Rev. 1061 (2008)

Houtzager, Peter P., "Introduction: From Polycentrism to the Polity," in Peter P. Houtzager and Mick Moore (eds)., *Changing Paths: International Development and the New Politics of Inclusion* (2003)

Humphrey, John P., *Human Rights and the United Nations* (1984)

Hunt, Alan, "Rights and Social Movements: Counter-Hegemonic Strategies," 17 J. L. & Soc'y 309 (1990)

Ignatieff, Michael, "Human Rights as Ideology," in Amy Gutmann (ed.), *Human Rights as Politics and Idolatry* (2001)
Iles, Kevin, "Limiting Socio-Economic Rights: Beyond the Internal Limitations Clause," 20 S. Afr. J. Hum. Rts. 448 (2004)
Ishay, Micheline R. (ed.), *The Human Rights Reader: Major Political Essays, Speeches, and Documents from Ancient Times to the Present* (2nd edn., 2007)
Jackson, Vicki C., "Constitutional Dialogue and Human Dignity: States and Transnational Constitutional Discourse," 65 Mont. L. Rev. 15 (2004)
—— "The Supreme Court, 2004 Term-Comment: Constitutional Comparisons: Convergence, Resistance, Engagement," 119 Harv. L. Rev. 109 (2005)
—— and Mark Tushnet (eds.), *Defining the Field of Comparative Constitutional Law* (2002)
Jolls, Christine, "Accommodation Mandates," 53 Stan. L. Rev. 223 (2001)
Judt, Tony, *Ill Fares the Land* (2010)
Kavanagh, Aileen, *Constitutional Review under the UK Human Rights Act* (2009)
Keck, Margaret E. and Kathryn Sikkink, *Activists Beyond Borders: Advocacy Networks in International Politics* (1998)
Kelman, Mark, "Health Care Rights: Distinct Claims, Distinct Justifications," 3 Stan. L. & Pol'y Rev. 97 (1991)
Kende, Mark S., *Constitutional Rights in Two Worlds: South Africa and the United States* (2009)
Kennedy, David, *The Dark Sides of Virtue: Reassessing International Humanitarianism* (2004)
Kennedy, Duncan, "The Stakes of Law, or Hale and Foucault!" in *Sexy Dressing Etc.* (1993)
—— *A Critique of Adjudication: fin de siècle* (1997)
—— and Frank Michelman, "Are Property and Contract Efficient?," 8 Hofstra L. Rev. 711 (1980)
Kingsbury, Benedict, Nico Krisch, and Richard Stewart, "The Emergence of Global Administrative Law," 68 Law & Contemp. Probs. 15 (2005)
Klare, Karl E., "Legal Culture and Transformative Constitutionalism," 14 S. Afr. J. Hum. Rts. 146 (1998)
Klarman, Michael J., *From Jim Crow to Civil Rights: The Supreme Court and the Struggle for Racial Equality* (2004)
—— *Brown v. Board of Education and the Civil Rights Movement* (2007)
Klein, Alana, "Judging as Nudging: New Governance Approaches for the Enforcement of Constitutional Social and Economic Rights," 39 Colum. Hum. Rts. L. Rev. 351 (2008)
Klug, Heinz, *Constituting Democracy: Law, Globalism and South Africa's Political Reconstruction* (2000)
—— *The Constitution of South Africa: A Contextual Analysis* (2010)
Koh, Harold Hongju, "Review Essay: Why Do Nations Obey International Law?," 106 Yale L.J. 2599 (1997)
Kommers, Donald P., *The Constitutional Jurisprudence of the Federal Republic of Germany* (2nd edn., 1997)

Kornbluh, Felicia, *The Battle for Welfare Rights: Politics and Poverty in Modern America* (2007)

Kothari, Jayna, "Social Rights Litigation in India: Developments of the Last Decade," in Daphne Barak-Erez and Aeyal M. Gross (eds.), *Exploring Social Rights: Between Theory and Practice* (2007)

Kramer, Larry D., *The People Themselves: Popular Constitutionalism and Judicial Review* (2004)

Kumm, Mattias, "Political Liberalism and the Structures of Rights: On the Place and Limits of the Proportionality Requirement," in S. Paulson, G. Pavlakos (eds.), *Law, Rights, Discourse: Themes of the Work of Robert Alexy* (2007)

Landau, David, "Political Institutions and Judicial Role in Comparative Constitutional Law," 51 Harv. Int'l L.J. 319 (2010)

—— "The Reality of Social Rights Enforcement," 53 Harv. Int. L.J. 189 (2012)

Langille, Brian, "Fair Trade is Free Trade's Destiny," in Jagdish Bhagwati and Robert Hudec (eds.), *Free Trade and Harmonization*, vol. 2 (1996)

Leckie, Scott, "The Human Right to Adequate Housing," in Asbjørn Eide, Catarina Krause and Allen Rosas (eds.), *Economic, Social and Cultural Rights: A Textbook* (2nd edn., 2001)

Legrand, Pierre and Roderick Munday (eds.), *Comparative Legal Studies: Traditions and Transitions* (2003)

Lehmann, Karin, "In Defense of the Constitutional Court: Litigating Economic and Social Rights and the Myth of the Minimum Core," 22 Am. U. Int'l. L. Rev. 163 (2006)

Lessig, Lawrence, *Fidelity in Translation*, 71 Texas L. Rev. 1165 (1993)

Levinson, Daryl J., *Rights Essentialism and Remedial Equilibration*, 99 Colum. L. Rev. 857 (1999)

Levinson, Sanford, *Constitutional Faith* (1988)

Liebenberg, Sandra, "The Value of Human Dignity in Interpreting Socio-Economic Rights," 21 S. Afr. J. Hum. Rts. 1 (2005)

—— "Socio-Economic Rights: Revisiting the Reasonableness Review/Minimum Core Debate," in Stu Woolman and Michael Bishop (eds.), *Constitutional Conversations* (2008)

—— *Socio-Economic Rights: Adjudication under a Transformative Constitution* (2010)

Liebman, James S. and Charles F. Sabel, "The Fragile Promise of Provisionality," 28 N.Y.U. Rev. L. & Soc. Change 369 (2003)

—— —— "A Public Laboratory Dewey Barely Imagined: The Emerging Model of School Governance and Legal Reform," 28 N.Y.U Rev. L. & Soc. Change 183 (2003)

Lipset, Seymour Martin and Gary Marks, *It Didn't Happen Here: Why Socialism Failed in the United States* (2001)

Liu, Goodwin, "Rethinking Constitutional Welfare Rights," 61 Stanford L. Rev. 203 (2008)

Lobel, Orly, "The Renew Deal: The Fall of Regulation and the Rise of Governance in Contemporary Legal Thought," 89 Minn. L. Rev. 342 (2004)

Lobel, Orly, "The Paradox of Extra-Legal Activism: Critical Legal Consciousness and Transformative Politics," 120 Harv. L. Rev. 937 (2007)

Mann, Jonathan, et al. (eds.), *Health and Human Rights* (1999)

Marcus, David, "The Normative Development of Socioeconomic Rights Through Supranational Adjudication," 42 Stan. J. Int'l. L. 53 (2006)

Marks, Susan and Andrew Clapham, *International Human Rights Lexicon* (2005)

Marx, Karl, "On the Jewish Question," in Robert C. Tucker (ed.), *The Marx-Engels Reader* (1972)

Mashaw, Jerry, "The Economics of Politics and the Understanding of Public Law," 65 Chi.-Kent L. Rev. 123 (1989)

McAdam, Doug, Sidney Tarrow, and Charles Tilly, *Dynamics of Contention* (2001)

McCann, Michael W., *Rights at Work: Pay Equity Reform and the Politics of Legal Mobilization* (1994)

McCrudden, Christopher, "A Common Law of Human Rights?: Transnational Judicial Conversations on Constitutional Rights," 20 Oxford J. Leg. Stud. 499 (2000)

Meier, Benjamin Mason, "Employing Health Rights for Global Justice: The Promise of Public Health in Response to the Insalubrious Ramifications of Globalization," 39 Cornell Int'l. L.J. 711 (2006)

Melish, Tara, "Rethinking the 'Less as More' Thesis: Supranational Litigation of the Economic, Social, and Cultural Rights in the Americas," 39 N.Y.U. J. Int'l. L. & Pol. 171 (2006)

—— "Maximum Feasible Participation of the Poor: New Governance, New Accountability, and a 21st Century War on the Sources of Poverty," 13 Yale Hum. Rts. & Dev't. L.J. 1 (2010)

Michaels, Jon D., "Note: To Promote The General Welfare: The Republican Imperative To Enhance Citizenship Welfare Rights," 111 Yale L.J. 1457 (2002)

Michelman, Frank, *Brennan and Democracy* (1999)

Michelman, Frank I., "Foreword: On Protecting the Poor through the Fourteenth Amendment," 83 Harv. L. Rev. 7 (1969)

—— "In Pursuit of Constitutional Welfare Rights: One View of Rawls' Theory of Justice," 121 U. Pa. L. Rev. 962 (1973)

—— "The Constitution, Social Rights and Reason: A Tribute to Etienne Mureinik," 14 S. Afr. J. Hum. Rts. 299 (1998)

—— "W(h)ither the Constitution," 21 Cardozo L. Rev. 1063 (2000)

—— "Constitutional Authorship," in Larry Alexander (ed.), *Constitutionalism: Philosophical Foundations* 64 (2001)

—— "The Constitution, Social Rights, and Liberal Political Justification," 1 Int'l. J. Const. L. 13 (2003)

—— "Reasonable Umbrage: Race and Constitutional Antidiscrimination Law in the United States and South Africa," 117 Harv. L. Rev. 1378 (2004)

—— "Socioeconomic Rights in Constitutional Law: Explaining America Away," 6 Int'l. J. Const. L. 663 (2008)

Minow, Martha, "Defining the Right to Adequate Health," in Jonathan Mann and Henry Steiner (eds.), *Social Rights and the Right to Health: An Interdiscplinary Discussion Held at Harvard Law School in September, 1993* (1995)

—— "Public and Private Partnerships: Accounting for the New Religion," 116 Harv. L. Rev. 1229 (2003)

—— *In Brown's Wake: Legacies of America's Educational Landmark* (2010)

—— Michael Ryan, and Austin Sarat (eds.), *Narrative, Violence and the Law: The Essays of Robert Cover* (1995)

Möller, Kai, "Balancing and the Structure of Constitutional Rights," 5 Int'l. J. Const. L. 453 (2007)

Moller Okin, Susan, "Is Multiculturalism Bad for Women?," in Joshua Cohen, Matthew Howard, and Martha Nussbaum (eds.), *Is Multiculturalism Bad for Women* (1999)

Moseneke, Dikgang, "Transformative Adjudication, Fourth Bram Fischer Memorial Lecture" (25 April 2002), 18 S. Afr. J. Hum. Rts. 309 (2002)

Moyn, Samuel, *The Last Utopia: Human Rights in History* (2010)

Müller, Amrei, "Limitations to and Derogations from Economic, Social and Cultural Rights," 9 Hum. Rts. L. Rev. 557 (2009)

Muralidhar, S., "Judicial Enforcement of Economic and Social Rights: The Indian Scenario," in Fons Coomans (ed.), *Justiciability of Economic and Social Rights: Experiences from Domestic Systems* (2006)

Mureinik, Etienne, "Beyond a Charter of Luxuries: Economic Rights in the Constitution," 8 S. Afr. J. Hum. Rts. 464 (1992)

Murphy, Liam, "Institutions and the Demands of Justice," 27 *Phil. & Pub. Aff.* 251 (1999)

Mutua, Makau W., "Hope and Despair for a New South Africa: The Limits of Rights Discourse," 10 Harv. Hum. Rts. J. 63 (1997)

Nagel, Thomas, "The Problem of Global Justice," 33 *Phil. & Pub. Aff.* 113 (2005)

Narula, Smita, "The Right to Food: Holding Global Actors Accountable under International Law," 44 Colum. J. Transnat'l. L. 691 (2006)

Neuborne, Burt, "Foreword: State Constitutions and the Evolution of Positive Rights," 20 Rutgers L.J. 881 (1989)

Neuman, Gerald L., "Human Dignity in United States Constitutional Law," in Dieter Simon and Manfred Weiss (eds.), *Zur Autonomie des Individuums [For Individual Autonomy]* (2000)

—— "Human Rights and Constitutional Rights: Harmony and Dissonance," 55 Stan. L. Rev. 1863 (2003)

Noonan, Kathleen G., Charles Sabel, and William H. Simon, "The Rule of Law in the Experimentalist Welfare State: Lessons from Child Welfare Reform," 34(3) Law & Social Inquiry 523 (2009)

North, Douglass C., *Institutions, Institutional Change and Economic Performance* (1990)

Nussbaum, Martha C., *Women and Human Development* (2000)

Okoth-Ogendo, H.W.O., "Constitutions Without Constitutionalism: Reflections on an African Political Paradox," in Douglas Greenberg et al. (eds.), *Constitutionalism and Democracy: Transitions in the Contemporary World* (1993)

Olson, Mancur, *The Logic of Collective Action* (1965)

Örücü, Esin, "The Core of Rights and Freedoms: The Limits of Limits," in Tom Campbell et al. (eds.), *Human Rights: From Rhetoric to Reality* (1986)

Perelman, Jeremy, "The Way Ahead? Access-to-Justice, Public Interest Lawyering and the Right to Legal Aid in South Africa: The *Nkuzi* Case," 41 Stan. J. Int'l L. 357 (2005)

—— and Katharine G. Young, "Freeing Mohammed Zakari: Rights as Footprints," in Lucie White and Jeremy Perelman (eds.), *Stones of Hope: How African Activists Reclaim Human Rights to Challenge Global Poverty* (2011)

Perju, Vlad, "Comparative Constitutionalism and the Making of a New World Order," 12 *Constellations* 464 (2005)

—— "Reason and Authority in the European Court of Justice," 49 Va J. Int'l L. 307 (2009)

Pieterse, Marius, "Coming to Terms with Judicial Enforcement of Socio-Economic Rights," 20 S. Afr. J. Hum. Rts 383 (2004)

Pildes, Richard H., and Elizabeth S. Anderson, "Slinging Arrows at Democracy: Social Choice Theory, Value Pluralism, and Democratic Politics," 90 Colum. L. Rev. 2121 (1990)

Piven, Frances Fox and Richard A. Cloward, *Poor People's Movements: Why They Succeed, How They Fail* (1979)

Pogge, Thomas, *World Poverty and Human Rights: Cosmopolitan Responsibilities and Reforms* (2nd edn., 2008)

Post, Robert C., "Foreword: Fashioning the Legal Constitution: Culture, Courts, and Law," 117 Harv. L. Rev. 4 (2003)

—— and Reva B. Siegel, "Legislative Constitutionalism and Section Five Power: Policentric Interpretation of the Family and Medical Leave Act," 112 Yale L.J. 1943 (2003)

—— —— "Popular Constitutionalism, Departmentalism, and Judicial Supremacy," 92 Cal. L. Rev. 1027 (2004)

Quinot, Geo and Sandra Liebenberg, "Narrowing the Band: Reasonableness Review in Administrative Justice and Socio-Economic Rights Jurisprudence in South Africa," 22 Stell. L.R. 639 (2011).

Rajagopal, Balakrishnan, *International Law from Below: Development, Social Movements and Third World Resistance* (2003)

Rawls, John, *A Theory of Justice* (1971)

—— *Political Liberalism* (1996)

—— *The Law of Peoples* (1999)

Ray, Brian, "Extending the Shadow of the Law: Using Hybrid Mechanisms to Establish Constitutional Norms in Socioeconomic Rights Cases," Utah L. Rev. 797 (2009)

—— "Policentrism, Political Mobilization and the Promise of Socioeconomic Rights," 45 Stan. J. Int'l. L. 151 (2009)

Raz, Joseph, The Authority of Law: Essays on Law and Morality (2nd edn., 2009)

Resnik, Judith, "Managerial Judges," 96 Harv. L. Rev. 374 (1982)

—— "Law's Migration: American Exceptionalism, Silent Dialogues, and Federalism's Multiple Ports of Entry," 115 Yale L.J. 1564 (2006)

Rittich, Kerry, "The Future of Law and Development: Second Generation Reforms and the Incorporation of the Social," 26 Mich. J. Int'l. L. 199 (2004)

Roach, Kent, "Dialogic Judicial Review and Its Critics," 23 Sup. Ct. L. Rev. 49 (2004)

—— and Geoff Budlender, "Mandatory Relief and Supervisory Jurisdiction: When Is It Appropriate, Just and Equitable?," 122 S. Afr. L.J. 325 (2005)

Robinson, Nick, "Expanding Judiciaries: India and the Rise of the Good Governance Court," 8 Wash. U. Global Stud. L. Rev. 1 (2009)

Rodrik, Dani, *One Economics, Many Recipes: Globalization, Institutions, and Economic Growth* (2007)

Roosevelt, Franklin D., "Message to Congress on the State of the Union," (11 January 1944), in Samuel I. Rosenman (ed.), *The Public Papers and Addresses of Franklin D. Roosevelt* (1950)

Rosenberg, Gerald N., *The Hollow Hope: Can Courts Bring about Social Change?* (2nd edn., 2008)

Rosenfeld, Michel (ed.), *Constitutionalism, Identity, Difference and Legitimacy: Theoretical Perspectives* (1994)

Roux, Theunis, "Continuity and Change in a Transforming Legal Order: The Impact of Section 26(3) of the Constitution on South African Law," 121 S. Afr. L.J. 266 (2004)

—— "Principle and Pragmatism on the Constitutional Court of South Africa," 7 Int'l. J. Const. L. 106 (2008)

—— "The Constitutional Value System and Social Values in South Africa," in András Sajó and Renata Uitz (eds.), *Constitutional Topology, Values and Constitutions* (2010)

Rubenfeld, Jed, "Unilateralism and Constitutionalism," 79 N.Y.U. L. Rev. 1971 (2004)

Ruger, Jennifer Prah, "Toward a Theory of a Right to Health: Capability and Incompletely Theorized Agreements," 18 Yale J. L. & Humanites 273 (2006)

Sabel, Charles F. and William H. Simon, "Destabilization Rights: How Public Law Litigation Succeeds," 117 Harv. L. Rev. 1016 (2004).

—— "Minimalism and Experimentalism in the Administrative State," 100 Geo. L.J. 53 (2011)

Sachs, Albie, *The Strange Alchemy of Life and Law* (2009)

Sachs, Jeffrey D., *The End of Poverty: Economic Possibilities for Our Time* (2005)

Sager, Lawrence G., *Justice in Plainclothes: A Theory of American Constitutional Practice* (2004)

Sajó, András, "Social Rights as Middle-Class Entitlements in Hungary: The Role of the Constitutional Court," in Roberto Gargarella, Pilar Domingo, and Theunis Roux (eds.), *Courts and Social Transformation in New Democracies: An Institutional Voice for the Poor?* (2006)

Sarat, Austin, and Thomas R. Kearns (eds.), *Legal Rights* (1996)

Schauer, Frederick, "Commensurability and its Constitutional Consequences," 45 Hastings L.J. 785 (1994)

—— "Deferring," 103 Mich. L. Rev. 1567 (2005)

Scheingold, Stuart A. and Austin Sarat, *Something to Believe in: Politics, Professionalism, and Cause Lawyering* (2004)

Scheppele, Kim Lane, "Aspirational and Aversive Constitutionalism: The Case for Studying Cross-Constitutional Influence through Negative Models," 1 Int'l. J. Const. L. 296 (2003)
—— "A Realpolitik Defense of Social Rights," 82 Tex. L. Rev. 1921 (2004)
Scheuerman, William E., "Democratic Experimentalism or Capitalist Synchronization? Critical Reflections on Directly-Deliberative Polyarchy," 17 Can. J. L. & Jurisprudence 101 (2004)
Scott, Craig and Philip Alston, "Adjudicating Constitutional Priorities in a Transnational Context: A Comment on *Soobramoney*'s Legacy and *Grootboom*'s Promise," 16 S. Afr. J. Hum. Rts. 206 (2000)
Scott, Joanne and Susan Sturm, "Courts as Catalysts: Re-Thinking the Judicial Role in New Governance," 13 Colum. J. Eur. L. 565 (2006)
Sen, Amartya, *Poverty and Famines: An Essay on Entitlement and Deprivation* (1982)
—— *Development as Freedom* (1999)
—— "Elements of a Theory of Human Rights," 32 *Phil. & Pub. Aff.* 315 (2004)
Sepúlveda, M. Magdalena, *The Nature of the Obligations under the International Covenant on Economic, Social and Cultural Rights* (2003)
Shany, Yuval, "Toward a General Margin of Appreciation Doctrine in International Law?," 16(5) Euro. J. Int'l. L. 907 (November 2005)
Shelton, Dinah, "Normative Hierarchy in International Law," 100 Am. J. Int'l. L. 291 (2006)
Shklar, Judith N., *The Faces of Injustice* (1990)
Shue, Henry, *Basic Rights: Subsistence, Affluence and U.S. Foreign Policy* (2nd edn., 1996)
Siegel, Reva B., "Text in Context: Gender and the Constitution from a Social Movement Perspective," 150 U. Pa. L. Rev. 297 (2001)
—— "The Jurisgenerative Role of Social Movements in United States Constitutional Law," paper presented at Harvard Law School Public Law Workshop (2004)
—— "Constitutional Culture, Social Movement Conflict and Constitutional Change: The Case of the De Facto Era," 94 Cal. L. Rev. 1323 (2006)
Simma, Bruno, "Consent: Strains in the Treaty System," in R. St. J. Macdonald and Douglas M. Johnston (eds.), *The Structure and Process of International Law* (1983)
Simmons, Beth A., "Should States Ratify? Process and Consequences of the Optional Protocol to the ICESCR," 27 Nordic J. Hum. Rts 64 (2009)
Simon, William H., "Toyota Jurisprudence: Legal Theory and Rolling Rule Regimes," in Grainne de Burca and Joanne Scott (eds.), *Law and New Governance in the EU and the US* (2006)
Skocpol, Theda, "Targeting with Universalism: Politically Viable Policies to Combat Poverty in the United States," in Christopher Jencks and Paul E. Peterson (eds.), *The Urban Underclass* (1991)
—— *Protecting Soldiers and Mothers: The Political Origins of Social Policy in the United States* (1992)
Slaughter, Anne-Marie, *A New World Order* (2004)
Smith, Adam, *An Inquiry into the Nature and Causes of The Wealth of Nations* (1975) (1776)

Snow, David A., "Framing Processes, Ideology, and Discursive Fields," in David A. Snow et al. (eds.), *The Blackwell Companion to Social Movements* (2004)

Stark, Barbara, "Economic Rights in the United States and International Human Rights Law: Toward an 'Entirely New Strategy'," 44 Hastings L.J. 79 (1992)

—— "Theories of Poverty/The Poverty of Theory," B.Y.U. L. Rev. 381 (2009)

Steinberg, Carol, "Can Reasonableness Protect the Poor? A Review of South Africa's Socio-Economic Rights Jurisprudence," 123 S. Afr. L.J. 264 (2006)

Steiner, Henry J., Philip Alston, and Ryan Goodman, *International Human Rights in Context: Law, Politics, Morals* (3rd edn., 2008)

Stiglitz, Joseph E., *Globalization and Its Discontents* (2002)

Sturm, Susan P., "A Normative Theory of Public Law Remedies," 79 Geo. L.J. 1355 (1991)

Sullivan, Kathleen, "Post-Liberal Judging: The Roles of Categorization and Balancing," 63 U. Colo. L. Rev. 293 (1992)

Sunstein, Cass R., "Against Positive Rights," in András Sajó (ed.), *Western Rights? Post-Communist Application* (1996)

—— *Designing Democracy: What Constitutions Do* (2001)

—— *The Second Bill of Rights: FDR's Unfinished Revolution and Why We Need it More Than Ever* (2004)

—— "Why Does the American Constitution Lack Social and Economic Guarantees?," 545 Syr. L. Rev. 1 (2005)

—— *Radicals in Robes: Why Extreme Right-wing Courts Are Wrong for America* (2006)

—— "Beyond Judicial Minimalism," 43 Tulsa L. Rev. 825 (2008)

't Hoen, Ellen, "TRIPS, Pharmaceutical Patents, and Access to Essential Medicines: A Long Way from Seattle to Doha," 3 Chic. J. Int'l. L. 27 (2002)

Tamanaha, Brian Z., *A General Jurisprudence of Law and Society* (2001)

Tarrow, Sidney, *Power in Movement: Social Movements and Contentious Politics* (2nd edn., 1998)

Tate, C. Neal, and Torbjörn Vallinder (eds.), *The Global Expansion of Judicial Power* (1995)

Thaler Richard H., and Cass R. Sunstein, *Nudge: Improving Decisions About Health, Wealth, and Happiness* (2008)

"The Relevance of Foreign Legal Materials in U.S. Constitutional Cases: A Conversation Between Justice Antonin Scalia and Justice Stephen Breyer," 3 Int'l. J. Const. L. 519 (2005)

Tribe, Laurence H., "The Puzzling Persistence of Process-Based Constitutional Theories," 89 Yale L.J. 1063 (1980)

Trubek, David M., and Alvaro Santos (eds.), *The New Law and Economic Development: A Critical Appraisal* (2006).

Tushnet, Mark, "The Possibilities of Comparative Constitutional Law," 108 Yale L.J. 1225 (1999)

—— *Taking the Constitution Away from the Courts* (1999)

—— "Some Reflections on Method in Comparative Constitutional Law," in Sujit Choudhry (ed.), *The Migration of Constitutional Ideas* (2006)

Tushnet, Mark, *Weak Courts, Strong Rights: Judicial Review and Social Welfare Rights in Comparative Constitutional Law* (2008)

Unger, Roberto Mangabeira, *What Should Legal Analysis Become?* (1996)

—— *Democracy Realized: The Progressive Alternative* (1998)

Uvin, Peter, *Human Rights and Development* (2004)

van der Walt, A.J., "Modernity, Normality, and Meaning: The Struggle Between Progress and Stability and the Politics of Interpretation: Part 1," 11 Stellenbosch L. Rev. 21 (2000)

—— "The State's Duty to Protect Property Owners v. The State's Duty to Provide Housing: Thoughts on the *Modderklip* Case," 21 S. Afr. J. Hum. Rts. 144 (2005)

Vermeule, Adrian "Foreword: System Effects and the Constitution," 123 Harv. L. Rev. 4 (2009)

Wai, Robert, "Countering, Branding, Dealing: Using Social Rights in and around the International Trade Regime," 14 Euro. J. Int'l L. 35 (2003)

Waldron, Jeremy, *Liberal Rights: Collected Papers 1981–1991* (1993)

—— *Law and Disagreement* (1999)

—— "The Core of the Case against Judicial Review," 115 Yale L.J. 1346 (2006)

—— "Foreign Law and the Modern *Ius Gentium*," 119 Harv. L. Rev. 128 (2006)

—— "Socioeconomic Rights and Theories of Justice," New York University Public Law and Legal Theory Working Papers. Paper 245 (2010)

Walzer, Michael, *Spheres of Justice: A Defense of Pluralism and Equality* (1983)

West, Robin, *Progressive Constitutionalism: Reconstructing The Fourteenth Amendment* (1994)

—— "Is Progressive Constitutionalism Possible?," 4 Widener L. Symp. J. 1 (1999)

Whelan, Daniel J. and Jack Donnelly, "The West, Economic and Social Rights, and the Global Human Rights Regime: Setting the Record Straight," 29 Hum. Rts. Q. 908 (2007)

White, Lucie E., "*Goldberg v. Kelly* on the Paradox of Lawyering for the Poor," 56 Brooklyn L. Rev. 861 (1990)

—— "Democracy in Development Practice: Essays on a Fugitive Theme," 64 Tennessee L. Rev. 1073 (1997)

—— "'If You Don't Pay, You Die': Death and Desire in the Postcolony," in Daphne Barak-Erez and Aeyal M. Gross (eds.), *Exploring Social Rights: Between Theory and Practice* (2007)

—— and Jeremy Perelman (eds.), *Stones of Hope: How African Activists Reclaim Human Rights To Challenge Global Poverty* (2011)

Wiles, Ellen, "Aspirational Principles or Enforceable Rights? The Future for Socio-Economic Rights in National Law," 22 Am. U. Int'l. L. Rev. 35 (2006)

Williams, Lucy A., "The Role of Courts in the Quantitative-Implementation of Social and Economic Rights: A Comparative Study," 3 Constitutional Court Review 141 (2010)

Wilson, Stuart, "Planning for Inclusion in South Africa: The State's Duty to Prevent Homelessness and the Potential of 'Meaningful Engagement'," 22 *Urban Forum* 265 (2011)

Winter, Ralph K., Jr., "Poverty, Economic Equality, and the Equal Protection Clause," Sup. Ct. Rev. 41 (1972)

Woods, Jeanne M., "Justiciable Social Rights as a Critique of the Liberal Paradigm" 38 Tex. Int'l. L.J. 763 (2003)

World Bank, *The World Bank Group's Response to the Global Crisis: Update on an Ongoing IEG Evaluation (Evaluation Brief 8)*, Independent Evaluation Group (2009)

Yamin, Alicia Ely and Siri Gloppen (eds), *Litigating Health Rights: Can Courts Bring More Justice to Health?* (2011)

Yepes, Rodrigo Uprimmy, "The Enforcement of Social Rights by the Colombian Constitutional Court: Cases and Debates," in Roberto Gargarella, Pilar Domingo, and Theunis Roux (eds.), *Courts and Social Transformation in New Democracies: An Institutional Voice for the Poor?* (2006)

Young, Ernest A., "Foreign Law and the Denominator Problem," 119 Harv. L. Rev. 148 (2005)

Young, Katharine G., "The Minimum Core of Economic and Social Rights: A Concept in Search of Content," 33 Yale J. Int'l. L. 113 (2008)

—— "Freedom, Want and Economic and Social Rights: Frame and Law," 24 Maryland J. Int'l. L. 182 (2009)

—— "The World, through the Judge's Eye," 28 Australian Y.B. Int'l. L. 27 (2009)

—— "Securing Health through Rights," in Thomas Pogge, Matthew Rimmer, and Kim Rubenstein (eds.), *Incentives for Global Public Health: Patent Law and Access to Essential Medicines* (2010)

Index

Made in the USA
Monee, IL
13 September 2026

62978025R00208